S.C.Clough

A CONJECTURAL DRAWING OF THE 1704 BOSTON LATIN SCHOOLHOUSE

This drawing, by Mr. Samuel C. Clough, an accepted authority on land titles in Boston, is based upon a study of the original records and deeds. According to Mr. Clough, the first schoolhouse was built on the north side of the present School Street, in the southeast corner of the first burial ground, possibly as early as 1645 or earlier. The date of construction is not recorded. The "town skoole house" is not mentioned in the *Boston Town Records* until March 29, 1652. The first King's Chapel, shown in the drawing, was built in 1688. This first schoolhouse and the 1704 schoolhouse stood on the site now occupied by the rear of the present stone King's Chapel, built in 1749, and a few feet adjacent to the east but not at the rear of the site now occupied by King's Chapel, as some historians have asserted. King's Chapel to-day covers more than one half of the land originally covered by the old schoolhouse

A TERCENTENARY HISTORY

OF

THE BOSTON PUBLIC LATIN SCHOOL

1635-1935

PAULINE HOLMES, M.A.

GREENWOOD PRESS, PUBLISHERS
WESTPORT, CONNECTICUT

FOREWORD

This book is the fruit of several years of study and research upon an institution whose history is unique.

The Boston Latin School has been a living witness not only to our whole national history but to the entire life of our people in this land. It has given three hundred years of unbroken service to the city, state, and nation, and its list of alumni reads like a compendium of American history.

The founding of the School on April 13, 1635 [Julian calendar], was the planting of the seed from which has grown the great structure of universal public education, the bulwark of democracy, the chief defense of the nation against ignorance and subversive doctrines.

The School adheres to the classical tradition in education. Not only does it offer its boys the logical training of the Latin and the Greek but it opens their minds and their imaginations to the treasures of a rich past, the sources of our artistic and intellectual heritage.

Profoundly convinced that the salvation of our civilization depends not upon our facility in making and operating machines but rather upon our ability to think straight and our willingness to work for the common good, the School devotes itself, not to vocational or utilitarian aims, but to the formation of right habits of study and the cultivation of high ideals of citizenship.

Saint Paul was addressing not merely the Corinthians when he wrote: "For the things which are seen are temporal; but the things which are unseen are eternal."

—JOSEPH LAWRENCE POWERS
Head Master of the Public Latin School
Boston, Massachusetts

PREFACE

This study of the Boston Public Latin School from 1635 to 1935 has been made almost entirely from the original sources, either in manuscript or in printed form. These are as follows: the *Town Records* and the *Selectmen's Minutes;* the *Records of the Governor and Company of the Massachusetts Bay in New England; Massachusetts Acts and Laws, Passed by the Great and General Court or Assembly of the Massachusetts-Bay, in New England, from 1692 to 1719;* the *Suffolk Deeds* and the *Suffolk County Probate Records;* the *Hutchinson Papers* and the *Usurpation Papers* in the Massachusetts State Archives Division; the Boston School Committee documents and records; the *Town Directories* from 1789 through 1822; Colonial textbooks; Boston booksellers' lists from 1684 to 1700; the diaries of Peter Edes, John Hull, Cotton Mather, Samuel Sewall, and John Tileston; the manuscript account book of Benjamin Wadsworth; the letter-book of Samuel Sewall; Governor John Winthrop's *Journal;* the *Autobiography* of Benjamin Franklin; the *Autobiography* of James Freeman Clarke; old Boston newspapers; old pamphlets; the *Annual Catalogues of the Boston Public Latin School;* and programs of declamation exercises. A study has also been made of rewards of merit; report cards; the Franklin Medals; pictures and portraits; old maps; plans of School Street drawn by Mr. Samuel C. Clough; and tombstones.

The work included two main phases: first, the collection and chronological arrangement of over 1400 documents, which the writer presented to the faculty of Wellesley College in 1923, in partial fulfillment of the requirements for the degree of Master of Arts; and second, the condensation and organization into chapters of the facts revealed by the documents.

ORIGINAL SOURCES

The first task was to make a complete compilation of all references to the Boston Latin School, found in the *Town Records* and in the *Selectmen's Minutes*, which have been printed in thirty-nine volumes by the Record Commissioners. The original manuscript volumes, which are now in the vaults of the City Hall on School Street, were also consulted. It is to be noted here that the Commissioners, in printing the records, made numerous changes in spelling and punctuation and failed to copy all of the marginal additions of the original. There is a possibility, therefore, that some references to the School have thus been omitted. The writer has not attempted to read page by page all of the original manuscript records. Such a task would have necessitated time far out of proportion to the value of any possible additions. Since the indices proved unreliable in the printed volumes, it was necessary to read each volume page by page.

The problem of chronology has been somewhat difficult. In 1582 Pope Gregory XIII corrected the error in the old Julian calendar by dropping ten days. It was not until 1752 that England and her colonies introduced the use of the Gregorian calendar, at which time it was necessary to drop eleven days from the calendar. March 25 had been adopted for New Year's day in the sixth century as being the day of Annunciation. England, in the seventh century, adopted Christmas day as New Year's day; it was not until the twelfth century that March 25, the day of Annunciation, began to prevail. In 1752 the beginning of the legal year was changed in England from March 25 to January 1. The Boston Latin School was established on "The 13th of the 2d moneth, 1635." This date was April 13 [The second month was April.], according to the Old Style calendar, and is April 23, according to the Gregorian intercalation of ten days.

In order to avoid confusion both systems of dating were sometimes used, as March 5, 1750/51, which means the year 1750 under the old system and 1751 under the new and present system of chronology. The *Boston Town Records* have been inconsistent, however. It has been necessary in many cases to study the documents very carefully in order to determine the real date. In cases of doubt it has been necessary to ·compare the printed reports of the Record Commissioners with the original manuscript volumes. The writer found that, in several cases, mistakes had been made in copying the original dates, and she has, as far as possible, corrected these dates.

The second step in the study of the original sources was an examination of the Boston School Committee documents. All of these documents are the original manuscripts and for this reason are interesting and extremely valuable. Professor Arthur Orlo Norton and the writer have rearranged them chronologically through 1822, giving a descriptive title to each. Here again the problem of chronology was encountered. The dates of some documents are still uncertain; these the writer has dated with a question mark. This list of documents relating to the Boston Latin School is in Appendix XII. There are also some School Committee records in the *Secretary's Book* beginning in 1792. The writer has examined these, but she did not find any additional material for this history.

Another original source is a collection of textbooks actually used in the Boston Latin School and now in the possession of the Harvard College Library, the Boston Latin School Library, the Boston Public Library, and the Massachusetts Historical Society. The Latin School textbooks in the Harvard College Library were identified in 1921 by Dr. E. R. Mosher, a student of Professor Arthur Orlo Norton in the Harvard Graduate School of Education.

SECONDARY WORKS

The secondary works are classified in the bibliography. These include the publications of various historical societies, histories of the Boston Public Latin School, general histories of Boston schools, histories of Massachusetts and Boston, general works on education, encyclopaedias and dictionaries of biography.

Among these a significant work which represents a study of the original sources and a long and painstaking collection of materials is Henry F. Jenks's *Catalogue of the Boston Public Latin School, established in 1635, with an Historical Sketch,* published in 1886 by the Boston Latin School Association. The sixteenth report of the Boston Record Commissioners was published in that same year. Since that time twenty-three more reports have been published, making a total of thirty-nine volumes. Later investigations concerning the Boston Public Latin School have added a good deal of material, all of which is incorporated in this history. The writer has found many additional references, in the *Town Records* and *Selectmen's Minutes,* which have enabled her to revise the list of Masters and Ushers of the Boston Latin School, with their respective dates in office.

Professor Kenneth B. Murdock, Dean of Harvard University, has in his possession the manuscript curriculum of the Boston Latin School in 1712, written by Mr. Nathaniel Williams, the Master of the School. With Professor Murdock's kind permission a facsimile is included in this work.

The writer wishes to acknowledge here the assistance rendered her by the staffs of the Wellesley College Library, the Harvard College Library, the Boston Latin School Library, the Boston Public Library, the Watertown Public Library, the Massachusetts State House Library, the Archives Division of the Secretary of Massachusetts, and the Boston Athenæum. She is also indebted to several societies for their help and kindness, namely, the Bostonian Society, the Colonial Society of Massachusetts, the Massachusetts Historical Society, the Society for the Preservation of New England Antiquities, the New England Historic and Genealogical Society, and the American Antiquarian Society, Worcester.

She wishes to thank Mr. Patrick Thomas Campbell, Superintendent of the Boston Schools, for his coöperation and encouragement and especially for his courtesy in allowing her to photostat some of the valuable manuscript documents in the possession of the Boston School Committee.

She thanks Mr. Joseph Lawrence Powers, Head Master of the Public Latin School, for his coöperation and for his permission to study the valuable original manuscripts in the possession of the Boston Latin School Library.

She is greatly indebted to Mr. Lee Joseph Dunn, the Librarian of the School, for his assistance in securing information concerning the lives of the recent Masters, in preparing the list of famous students, and in compiling the list of teachers from 1917 to date.

She is grateful to Mr. T. Franklin Currier, Assistant Librarian of the Harvard College Library, for valuable information, concerning the history of the School and colonial textbooks, based upon many years of research and study.

She is also grateful to Mr. Samuel C. Clough, an accepted authority on land titles in Colonial Boston, for maps and drawings and information concerning the location of the schoolhouses and of the Masters' homes.

She wishes to express her gratitude for the letter received from the late Chief Justice Oliver Wendell Holmes, in reply to a communication concerning the history of the Boston Latin School under the mastership of Epes Sargent Dixwell, whose daughter, Miss Fanny Dixwell, was Justice Holmes's wife. She also thanks Mr. Edward Jackson Holmes, nephew of Justice Holmes, for information concerning the Dixwell family. Mary Dixwell Wigglesworth (Mrs. George Wigglesworth), the youngest daughter of Epes Sargent Dixwell, has kindly allowed the writer to quote from her father's unpublished sketch of his life, which he wrote for his children.

She thanks Charles Gates Dawes, former Vice-President of the United States, for his communication concerning his ancestors who were students at the Boston Latin School.

She is greatly indebted to Miss Helen Parker Smith, former Head of the English Department of The Brimmer School, Boston, for valuable suggestions and criticisms.

Most of all she acknowledges her indebtedness to Professor Arthur Orlo Norton, Professor of the History and Principles of Education in Wellesley College and sometime Lecturer in the Harvard Graduate School of Education, for his untiring assistance and guidance, over a period of ten years, without which this book could never have been written.

What she owes to her mother she can never express.

—PAULINE HOLMES

Watertown, Massachusetts
January 1, 1935

CONTENTS

ILLUSTRATIONS AND MAPS

CHAPTER I

THREE CENTURIES OF PUBLIC EDUCATION IN BOSTON, 1635-1935

A GENERAL SURVEY

"To have existed for three hundred years, as things go, is re- markable; much more remarkable to have been constant, through those three hundred years, to one purpose and function. There may be older schools in other countries; but almost always they have suffered a complete change of spirit and have endured only by ceasing to be themselves. Even the neighboring Harvard College, one year younger than the Latin School, has undergone radical trans- formations, losing its original directive mission, and becoming a com- plex mirror of the complex society which it serves. But the Latin School, in its simpler sphere, has remained faithfully Latin. In spite of all revolutions and all the pressure of business and all the powerful influences inclining America to live in contemptuous ignor- ance of the rest of the world, and especially of the past, the Latin School, supported by the people of Boston, has kept the embers of traditional learning alive, at which the humblest rush-light might be lighted; has kept the highway clear for every boy to the pro- fessions of theology, law, medicine, and teaching, and a window open to his mind from these times to all other times and from this place to all other places.

"This fidelity to tradition, I am confident, has and will have its reward. The oldest forms of life, barring accidents, have the longest future. New ideas in their violence and new needs in their urgency pass like a storm; and then the old earth, scarred and enriched by those trials, finds itself still under the same sky, unscarred and pure as before. The Latin language and the study of classic antiquity are the chief bond for western nations with the humanities, with the normalities of human nature; and this not merely by transporting us, as in a vision, to some detached civilization—as Greek studies might do if taken alone—but by bringing us down step by step through all the vicissitudes of Christendom to our own age, and giving us a sound sense for the moral forces and the moral issues that now concern us. The merely modern man never knows what he is about. A Latin education, far from alienating us from our own world, teaches us to discern the amiable traits in it, and the genuine achievements; helping us, amid so many distracting problems, to preserve a certain balance and dignity of mind, together with a sane confidence in the future."

—GEORGE SANTAYANA (Boston Latin School, 1882; Harvard, 1886)

THE Boston Public Latin School, which celebrated its three hundredth anniversary on April 23, 1935, has the distinction and fame of being the oldest "free," public, non-endowed,[1] non-sectarian,[2] secondary school with continuous existence[3] in the United States.   The School has a most illustrious heritage, having had as pupils many famous personages, such as Cotton Mather, James Bowdoin, Charles Bulfinch, Ralph Waldo Emerson, Charles Francis Adams, Charles Sumner, Wendell Phillips, John Lothrop Motley, Henry Ward Beecher,

---

[1] See Philip Alexander Bruce, *Institutional History of Virginia in the Seventeenth Century*, Vol. I, pp. 350-356, for the history of the Symmes and Eaton endowed free schools of Virginia. See also Sadie Bell, *The Church, The State, and Education in Virginia*, pp. 123 and 656. See also Cornelius J. Heatwole, *A History of Education in Virginia*, pp. 44-48. The Boston Latin School agrees with the statement that Benjamin Symmes's bequest, according to his will dated February 12, 1634/35, is the earliest provision for a foundation for education made in English America, antedating John Harvard's famous bequest. There is no documentary proof, however, that the Symmes endowed school was in operation before April 13, 1635. In March, 1642/43, the General Assembly considered it necessary to pass a special act confirming the will. According to Mr. Bruce, the Symmes Free School by the end of 1647 "seems to have been resting on a firm foundation, and was in active operation." The Symmes and the Eaton Schools existed until 1805, when they were incorporated in one as the Hampton Academy.

[2] The Collegiate School of New York City, founded by the Dutch Reformed Church, celebrated its three hundredth anniversary in 1933. Professor William H. Kilpatrick of Teachers College, Columbia University, counts that the school is not warranted in claiming 1633 as the date of its origin, since there is "no evidence earlier than 1638 but there is considerable presumptive evidence to the contrary." For a detailed discussion see William H. Kilpatrick, *Dutch Schools of New Netherland and Colonial New York*, published in 1912 by the United States Bureau of Education. See also Professor Kilpatrick's letter to the *New York Times* which appeared on March 20, 1933.

[3] The Boston Latin School was temporarily suspended from April 19, 1775, until June 5, 1776.

Edward Everett Hale, Samuel Pierpont Langley, Phillips Brooks, and many others. It is worthy of note that five of the fifty-six signers of the Declaration of Independence had been Boston Latin School pupils, namely, John Hancock, Samuel Adams, Benjamin Franklin, Robert Treat Paine, and William Hooper. The School has given to Harvard University many of its most distinguished professors and four presidents—John Leverett, Samuel Langdon, Edward Everett, and Charles William Eliot.

When, on April 13, 1635 [O.S.], the citizens of Boston "Att a Generall meeting upon publique notice" agreed "y^t o^r brother Mr Philemon Pormort shalbe intreated to become scholemaster for the teaching & nourtering of children wth us,"[4] they not only established the free Latin Grammar School for boys, now named the Public Latin School, but they founded the public school system of America.[5] For this reason, a study of this famous school is indispensable for an appreciative understanding of the development of American education.

Who were these first citizens and what were their qualifications for leadership? The early settlers of Boston, which was founded in 1630, were the Puritans. Their leaders were well-educated English country squires and yeomen. They came of thrifty and well-to-do stock; all had had educational advantages and many had been students or graduates of Cam-

---

[4] See page 7 for facsimile of manuscript record. There is no record as to whether or not Philemon Pormort accepted, but there is indirect evidence that he did accept. On August 12, 1636, at a "general meeting of the richer inhabitants," forty-five persons subscribed between forty and fifty pounds "towards the maintenance of a free school master . . . M^r. Danyel Maud being now also chosen thereunto." The word "also" may possibly indicate that Mr. Pormort was continued in the School or it may connote that the richer inhabitants not only voted to support the School but also voted to appoint the Master.

[5] For the claims of Charlestown, Dedham, and other New England towns see Marcus Wilson Jernegan, *Laboring and Dependent Classes in Colonial America, 1607-1783*, pp. 69-83.

bridge and Oxford Universities. It has been asserted that probably never since has the proportion of college men in the community been so large.[6] Boston, as the chief settlement, became the center of the intellectual life of the Massachusetts Bay Colony.

With faith in education and desire for its persistence, such men as John Winthrop, Henry Vane, and the Reverend John Cotton were ideal founders of a commonwealth; they brought with them the spirit of English culture and were naturally anxious to perpetuate the tradition of scholarship which had been their heritage. We note the English influences in American Colonial education, not only in the development of the curriculum but also in the methods of teaching.

Religious freedom for themselves was the dominant motive of the Puritans who came from England to establish a colony in Massachusetts, and religion was the rock on which the State was founded. Their philosophy of education was fashioned not only by their conviction that learning was the foundation of Church and State but also by their experience in the schools and universities of the England of their time. It was quite natural that they sought to establish in New England educational opportunities such as they themselves had known in Old England. Since substantially every voter belonged to the established Congregational Church, the question of sectarian instruction did not arise.

The Massachusetts Bay Company adopted and maintained the principle that it is the right and duty of the government to provide for the instruction of the young. In 1642 the General Court[7] passed an act requiring the elementary education of all

[6] For a full discussion of English university men who emigrated to New England before 1646 see Samuel Eliot Morison, *The Founding of Harvard College*, pp. 359-410.

[7] King Charles I of England, in 1628/29, granted the first charter to "The Governor and Company of Massachusetts Bay in New England," empowering the Company to make laws at their quarterly meetings, to be called the "four great and general courts."

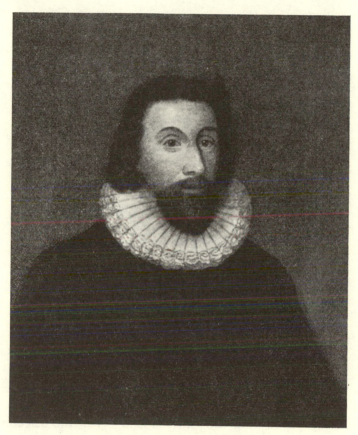

JOHN WINTHROP
From Samuel G. Drake's *The History and Antiquities of Boston.*

HENRY VANE
From Samuel G. Drake's *The History and Antiquities of Boston.*

children, empowering the "chosen-men" [i.e., the selectmen] in every town

to take accompt from time to time of their parents and masters, and of their children, concerning their calling and impliment of their children, especiallity of their ability to read and understand the principles of religion and the capital lawes of the country, and to impose fines upon all those who refuse to render such accompt to them when required; and they shall have power (with consent of any Court or magistrates) to put fourth apprentice the children of such as shall not be able and fitt to employ and bring them up, . . .

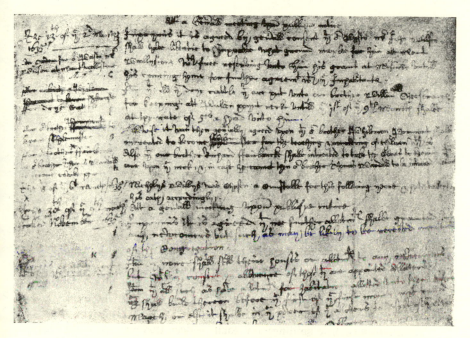

RECORD OF A TOWN VOTE TO CHOOSE A SCHOOLMASTER

Reduced facsimile of part of page of *Boston Town Records, 1634-1661*, dated "The 13th of the 2d moneth, 1635," containing the town vote to choose a schoolmaster. The third paragraph reads: "Likewise it was then generally agreed upon yt or brother Mr Philemon Pormort shalbe intreated to become scholemaster for the teaching & nourtering of children wth us."

From the original in the office of the City Clerk, City Hall, Boston, by courtesy of Mayor Frederick W. Mansfield.

This famous law of 1642 is remarkable in that for the first time in the English-speaking world the State ordered that all children should be taught to read. In 1647 the General Court, after recounting in a preamble that it had in the past been "one cheife piect [project] of yt ould deluder, Satan, to keepe men from the knowledge of ye Scriptures, . . . by keeping ym in an unknowne tongue," ordered every township of fifty householders to appoint a Master "to teach all such children as shall resort to him to write & reade" and further ordered every township of one hundred householders to establish "a grāmer schoole" [Latin Grammar School], the Master "being able to instruct youth as farr as they may be fited for yᵉ university," subject to a fine of five pounds "if any towne neglect yᵉ pformance." According to the preamble of this act, the object of instruction in the classics was to prepare young men for college[8] and to secure a body of learned scholars and ministers, who, by acquaintance with Latin, Greek, Hebrew, and Syriac, could obtain a knowledge of the Scriptures in their original languages, and through such knowledge become qualified to discern "yᵉ true sence & meaning of yᵉ originall."

In 1648 the act of 1642 was revised with respect to both additions and omissions.[9] The act of 1648 empowered the selectmen of every town to have

... a vigilant eye over their brethren and neighbours, to see first that none of them shall suffer so much barbarism in any of their families as not to indeavour to teach by themselves or others, their children and apprentices so much learning as may inable them perfectly to read the english tongue, and knowledge of the Capital lawes; upon penaltie of twentie shillings for each neglect therein. Also that all masters of families doe once a week (at the least) catechize their children and servants in the grounds and principles of Religion, . . . And further that all parents and masters do breed and bring up their children and apprentices in some honest lawful calling, labour or imployment, . . . if they will not or can not train them up in learning to fit them for higher imployments. . . .

These school laws of 1642, 1647, and 1648 embodied the unprecedented policy of universal, tax-supported, and state-controlled education and, in the light of later developments,

[8] Harvard College, established in 1636 by a vote of the General Court, opened in 1637-1638. See Samuel Eliot Morison, *The Founding of Harvard College*, pp. 193-209. See also Arthur Orlo Norton, *Harvard College, 1636-1660*, published in *Commonwealth History of Massachusetts*, Vol. I, pp. 325-359, edited by Albert Bushnell Hart.

[9] The Huntington Library of California owns the only known extant copy of the code of laws enacted by the General Court of Massachusetts in 1648. The Harvard Law School Library owns a photostat copy. For a full discussion of the code of 1648 see Marcus Wilson Jernegan, *Laboring and Dependent Classes in Colonial America, 1607-1783*, pp. 91-95.

represented the foundations upon which our American state public-school systems have been built. It should be emphasized, however, that our present school system is secular, whereas the aim of classical education, according to the Colonial legislation of 1647, was largely religious. Having come to America to secure religious freedom, the Puritans naturally desired to perpetuate their particular ideas by means of education.

The significant fact to note is that the town of Boston had as early as 1635 established the Latin Grammar School, more than a decade before the 1647 law requirement. Later school legislation,[10] moreover, had little to do with the Boston Latin School, since its policies and practices were usually ahead of the law.

The General Court, in 1645, ordered that all youths between ten and sixteen years of age should receive instruction "in ye exercise of armes, as small guns, halfe pikes, bowes & arrowes, ec." Later records show that the Boston Latin School boys received their military training on Boston Common. The schools were closed on the general training days. Military drill was introduced in 1864, although the legislature refused to pass bills authorizing it. The Boston Latin School Battalion was organized in 1865, at the close of the Civil War. Military drill has continued as a part of the prescribed curriculum and today, as in olden days, the annual exhibition is held on historic Boston Common.

On October 10, 1683, the General Court ordered towns of five hundred families to maintain "two gramar schooles and

[10] For a discussion of educational legislation see Arthur Orlo Norton, *Educational Legislation in Massachusetts from 1642 to 1837*, mimeographed in 1920 by the Department of Education of Wellesley College. This unpublished chronology contains not only the text of the laws but also comments and interpretations. For a discussion of educational legislation for poor children and apprentices from 1642 to 1776 see Marcus Wilson Jernegan, *Laboring and Dependent Classes in Colonial America, 1607-1783*, pp. 84-115.

two wrighting schooles." Four years previous to this time, on March 10, 1678/79, the town of Boston had referred to the selectmen the consideration of a "Free Schoole to teach the Children of poore people." On December 18, 1682, the town voted that a committee of five, with the selectmen, "consider of & pvide one or more Free Schooles for the teachinge of Children to write & Cypher...." The selectmen and the committee voted, on April 30, 1683, to establish two schools "for teachinge of children to write and cipher," allowing twenty-five pounds per year for each school.[11] It appears from later records that one of these schools was established in the "Centre" of the town on Queen Street [now Court Street], called the Queen Street Writing School,[12] and the other, in the North End, later called the North Writing School.[13]

It was not until March 11, 1711/12, that Boston voted to establish a second Latin Grammar School "at the North end of this Town," in reply to a "Proposition for a Free Gramer School at the North End of Boston,"[14] which was dated the preceding day to be presented to the "Inhabitants of Boston ... in the Next General Meeting." As early as 1685 Cotton Mather recorded in his *Diary*: "Never bee at Rest, while our Island here, the North part of Boston is without a good Schoolmaster, and a florishing School." This school, called the North Grammar School[15] [Latin Grammar] to distinguish it from the original Boston Latin School, was built in 1712 on Bennet Street [now North Bennet Street] on the land where the Eliot School was later constructed in 1792. On the front façade of the North Grammar School was the Hutchinson

[11] See page 11 for facsimile of manuscript record.

[12] See Appendix I for the history of the Queen Street Writing School.

[13] See Appendix II for the history of the North Writing School.

[14] The original manuscript paper, dated March 10, 1711/12, was found as late as 1859 in a hand cart near the door of a junk shop in Boston. See Appendix III.

[15] See Appendix III for the history of the North Grammar School.

RECORD OF A VOTE TO ESTABLISH TWO FREE SCHOOLS

Facsimile of part of page of *Boston Town Records, 1660-1701*, dated April 30, 1683, containing the vote to establish two free schools "for teachinge of Children to write & Cipher."

From the original in the office of the City Clerk, City Hall, Boston, by courtesy of Mayor Frederick W. Mansfield.

coat of arms, in honor of Captain Thomas Hutchinson [father of Governor Hutchinson], who had offered to build the school at his own expense. On March 30, 1713, Mr. Recompense Wadsworth was appointed the first Master, to begin his services on April 20 of that year. Under the "New System of Education," adopted in 1789, the North Grammar School

Samuel Sewall

Benj^a Simpson

Saml. Adams

Danl Henchman

SOUTH-END PETITIONERS FOR ANOTHER SCHOOL, 1715/16
From Justin Winsor's *The Memorial History of Boston.*

was discontinued.[16]   The scholars afterwards attended the original Boston Latin School [called the South Grammar School from 1713 to 1789], which has remained since then the only public Latin School for boys in Boston.

As the population increased, the town of Boston established new writing schools to meet the needs of the growing colony.   Boston maintained a writing school at Muddy River[17] from 1700 until 1705, when the "Hamlet of Muddy

[16] The assumption of some historians that the North Grammar School at no time in its existence (1713-1789) offered anything but the usual program of instruction in Latin and Greek is incorrect, as is evidenced by the following manuscript document, dated November 1, 1789, now in the possession of the Boston School Committee: "Master Nathan Davies reports that in the North Grammar School he had two scholars for Latin and Greek, seventeen for Latin and English, and twenty-one for reading and spelling."

[17] See Appendix IV for the history of the Muddy River Writing School.

River" was named Brookline and established as a separate village. Boston also supported a writing school at Rumney Marsh[18] from 1708 until 1738, when the district was incorporated as the town of Chelsea.

On March 13, 1715/16, the town of Boston voted to erect a writing school "at the Southerly part of this Town," and on May 15, 1717, the town voted to have the selectmen "Sett out a convenient Peice of Land accordingly, vizt upon ye Comon adjoyning to Cowells Lott over ag^t m^r Wainrights." The first Master of this South Writing School[19] was Mr. Ames Angier, who on March 15, 1719/20, was appointed "School master at ye new writing School House at ye South." The most famous writing Master of this school was Abiah Holbrook, who was the Master for twenty-seven years from March 23, 1742/43, until 1769. The records testify that in the eighteenth century the Boston Latin School boys were dismissed each day[20] to attend this South Writing School "to learn to write and cypher."

[18] See Appendix V for the history of the Rumney Marsh Writing School.

[19] See Appendix VI for the history of the South Writing School.

[20] Harrison Gray Otis, who entered the Latin School in 1773, has recorded that he attended Mr. Holbrook's school "in private hours (from 11 A. M. and 5 P. M.) to write and cypher." Henry Roby, who attended the North Grammar School from 1772 to 1775 and entered the Boston Latin School in 1776, has recorded that he "used to go out of the Latin School" to attend Mr. James Carter's Writing School "in Scollay's Building at the head of Court Street . . . to learn to write." [See Mr. T. Franklin Currier's interleaved copy of Henry F. Jenks's *Catalogue of the Boston Public Latin School* for Henry Roby's account.] Dr. James Jackson, who entered the Latin School in 1784, has recorded: "During this time, however, or after arriving in the third class, I believe they went twice a week, half a day, to an English public, or private, school, where they were taught writing and arithmetic, etc." After 1789, according to the "New System of Education," the first class of the Latin School attended the Writing School "from half past Nine o'clock, A. M. 'till Eleven, or from half past Three P. M. as shall be found most convenient" and the second class "in the same manner for the first half of that year."

The TOWN of BOSTON
IN
New England
by
Capt John Bonner
1722
Ætatis Suæ 60.

Engraved from a copy in the possession of Wm Taylor Esq.
and published by
GEORGE G. SMITH, Engraver
1867. No 94 Washington, opposite State Street Boston.
1835.

I have examined this plan and find it a
copy of the original
Boston July 2 1835 —

Roxbury Flats

Welt Hill

Fox Hill

Beacon Hill

PowderHoufe
Watch Houfe

COMMON

School

From Town H.
One Mile

Orange Str

Fortification

Orange Str

Rainford

Cools
Garden

Pond

Marlb

Sum Str

Hills Wharf

Wind Mill Point

Derby W.

Butts W.

Scale of ⅛ a Mile.

BOSTON: N.E
Planted An. Dom. 1630

A. *The Old Church*	1630
B. *Old North*	1650
C. *Old South*	1660
D. *Annabaptist*	1680
E. *Ch. of England*	1688
F. *Brattle St Church*	1699
G. *Quakers*	1710
H. *New North*	1714
I. *New South*	1716
K. *French*	1716
L. *New Br Brick*	1721

EXPLANATION.
a. *Town Houfe*.
b. *Governours Houfe*.
c. *South Gramar School*.
d. *North Gramar School*.
e. *Writing School*.
f. *Writing School*.
g. *Alms House*.
h. *Bridewell*.
Streets 42 Lanes 36 Alleys 22
Houses near 3000.
1000 Brick reft Timber.
Near 12000 People.

Great Fires.
First ... 1653
Second ... 1676
Third ... 1679
Fourth ... 1683
Fifth ... 1690
Sixth ... 1691
Seventh ... 1702
Eigth ... 1711

Genll
Small Pox.
First ... 1640
Second ... 1660
Third ... 1677
Fourth ... 1690
Fifth ... 1702
Sixth ... 1721

Engraven and Print

BONNER'S

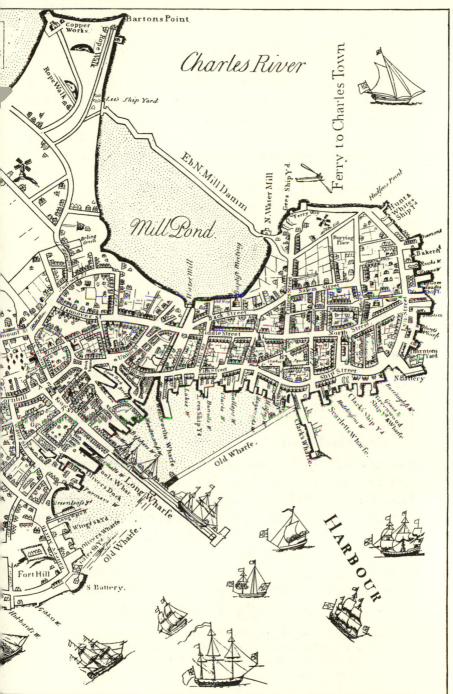

Charles River

Bartons Point

Copper Works

Rope Walk

Lee's Ship Yard

Eb N. Mill Damm

Mill Pond

N. Water Mill

Gees Ship Yd

Burying Place

Ferry to Charles Town

Hudsons Point

Hunt & Whites Ship Yd

Bakers

Bowling Green

Middle Street

Union Street

Fish Street

Sun Street

North Street

N Battery

Clarks Ship Yard & Wharfe

Thorntons Yard

Scarletts Wharf

Old Wharfe

Clarks Wharf

Long Wharfe

Old Wharfe

Wings Yd

Olivers Wharfe

Fort Hill

S Battery.

HARBOUR

Boston N E. 1722. Sold by Capt. John Bonner and Willm Price against ÿ TownHouse where may be had all sorts of Prints &c.

ON, 1722

Before the Revolutionary War spinning schools[21] were established in Boston. As early as 1718 a company of Scotch-Irish from Londonderry, Ireland, arrived in Massachusetts, bringing with them implements for manufacturing linen. In 1720 the town of Boston chose a committee "to Consider ab^t promoting of a Spinning School or Schools for the Instruction of the children of this Town, in Spinning." Again in 1769 the town voted to establish spinning schools for poor children "to learn such Children to Spin (free of Charge)."

The Revolutionary War absorbed the energies and the resources of the Province; there was little time for attention to educational matters. It is a school tradition that the Boston Latin School boys and their friends won the first victory of the Revolution. They protested to General Haldimand that his servant had destroyed their School Street coast by putting ashes on the street. The General ordered his servant to repair the damage, and then "acquainted the Governor with the affair, who observed that it was impossible to beat the notion of Liberty out of the people, as it was rooted in 'em from their childhood."[22]

The schools were closed on April 19, 1775, and were not reopened until the following year, after the British had evacuated Boston. Harrison Gray Otis, who entered the Boston Latin School in 1773, has recorded that on the morning of April 19, 1775, the British line was drawn up a few yards from the schoolhouse on School Street, preparing to march to Lexington. John Lovell, the Master of the School and a loyalist, excitedly cried to his pupils, "War's begun—school's done. *Deponite libros!*"[23] Since many of the families had left Boston during its occupancy by the British red-coats, the only

---

[21] See Appendix VII for the history of the spinning schools.

[22] Henry F. Jenks's *Catalogue of the Boston Public Latin School, established in 1635. With an Historical Sketch*, Part I, p. 40.

[23] *Ibid.*, Part I, pp. 35-37.

BOSTON BOYS PROTESTING TO GENERAL HALDIMAND, WHOSE SERVANT HAD
PUT ASHES ON THEIR SCHOOL STREET COAST
From *The Eighteen Fifties and The Boston Five Cents Savings Bank,* by George A. Kyle. By
courtesy of the Boston Five Cents Savings Bank.

schools to reopen, on June 5, 1776, were the Boston Latin
School and the North Writing School. The South Writing
School was reopened on the Monday following July 17, 1776,
as the following record of the selectmen on that date testifies:
"The Town Clerk directed to give the Cryer a Notification,
that the Writing School in the Common will be opened . . .
on Monday next . . . and that the same be published on Satturday next, from the Towns house to the Fortification." The
Queen Street Writing School was not reopened until November 8, 1776, and the North [Latin] Grammar School, not until
March 10, 1779.

After the Revolutionary War the families slowly returned to Boston, and in 1784 the town found it necessary to establish another writing school in the South End. This new school, on the south side of Pleasant Street, was called the Southermost Writing School,[24] to distinguish it from the South Writing School. The next year, in 1785, another writing school was established in the North End, on Middle Street [now Hanover Street], and this new school was called the New North Writing School,[25] to distinguish it from the North Writing School.

In 1780 the people adopted a State Constitution establishing the Commonwealth of Massachusetts. This Constitution, which is still in force, recognized the importance of education to a democracy, devoting an entire chapter to education.[26] The first school law, enacted under the Constitution, was the law of June 25, 1789: "An Act to provide for the Instruction of Youth, and for the Promotion of good Education." This act was a consolidated school law, containing the substance of all the educational laws prior to 1780, with modifications, changes, and additions. This general school law of 1789 continued in force until 1827, when it was repealed.

A committee, including the distinguished Samuel Adams and other eminent citizens appointed by the town of Boston, drew up a recommendation[27] for a new educational program, which was presented to the town meeting on October 15, 1789, and adopted on October 16, 1789, as the "New System of Pub-

[24] See Appendix VIII for the history of the Southermost Writing School.

[25] See Appendix IX for the history of the New North Writing School.

[26] In contrast to this we note that nine of the thirteen original states made no mention of education in their first Constitutions. The four states which mentioned education in their Constitutions were: Pennsylvania, 1776; North Carolina, 1776; Georgia, 1777; and Massachusetts, 1780. The first three of these, however, devoted but a few lines each to the subject. For a full discussion of education legislation see Arthur Orlo Norton, *Educational Legislation in Massachusettts from 1642 to 1837*, mimeographed in 1920 by the Department of Education of Wellesley College.

[27] The original manuscript is in the possession of the Boston School Committee.

lic Education."[28] This reform completely reorganized the school system of Boston, by providing for only one Latin School, three writing schools, and three reading schools, namely, the original Boston Latin School, the North Writing School, the North Reading School, the Centre Writing School, the Centre Reading School, the South Writing School, and the South Reading School.[29] Another significant change, marking a departure from the English precedent, was the reducing of the Latin School curriculum from a seven-year to a four-year course.

This reform of 1789, furthermore, is very significant because it made the first provision for the education of girls in the public writing and reading schools, during the summer

[28] See Appendix X for the full text of "The System of Public Education, Adopted by the Town of Boston, 15th Octob. 1789." This is the first printed Boston school document. Samuel Hunt's copy has the following vote appended in manuscript: "December 28, 1789. Voted, That the several Schoolmasters instruct the children under their care, or cause them to be instructed, in the Assemblie's Catechism, every Saturday, unless the Parents request that they may be taught any particular catechism of the religious Society to which they belong; and the Masters are directed to teach such Children accordingly. Order, John Scollay, Chairman." Samuel Hunt's copy also has the following manuscript note on the margin of page 6: "Aug'st 24th, 1802. From the 3d Monday in Ap. to y⁰ 3d Monday in Oct. the Schools will begin at 8 o'Clock, A. M. and continue ('till) eleven. In the Afternoon they will begin at 2 o'Clock and continue 'till 5. From y⁰ 3d Monday in Oct. to the 3d Monday in April, the Schools will begin at 9 o'Clock, A. M. and continue 'till 12 o'Clock. In the Afternoon they will begin at 2 o'Clock and continue untill 5, excepting the Months of November, December, and January, when the Schools shall be closed at ½ past four."

[29] The North Writing School was continued as the North Writing School and the New North Writing School was continued as the North Reading School. The Queen Street Writing School, near the site of the present subway [south] entrance at Scollay Square, was continued as the Centre Writing School and the town voted to rent a "Building" for the Centre Reading School. In 1790 the Centre Reading and Writing School was built on the north side of School Street, where the City Hall now stands. The South Writing School on West Street was continued as the South Writing School and the Southermost Writing School was continued as the South Reading School.

months from April 20 to October 20, and also provided for a regular school committee of twelve members to be elected annually by the town.[30]

According to the "New System of Public Education," adopted in 1789, candidates for admission into the Boston Latin School were required to be at least ten years of age, "having been previously well instructed in English Grammar." This preparation they received at the public writing and reading schools, which they could enter at the age of seven years, "having previously received the instruction usual at Women's [Dame] Schools."

These seven schools—the Boston Latin School, the three writing schools, and the three reading schools—accommodated all the children of Boston until 1803, when it was necessary to establish an elementary school in the West End, at the corner of Chardon Street and Hawkins Street. In 1821 this West Writing and Reading School was named the Mayhew School,[31] in honor of the Reverend Jonathan Mayhew, minister of the West End Church.

A part of Dorchester, now South Boston, was annexed to Boston in 1804 by an act of legislature. On March 14, 1811, the inhabitants of South Boston sent a petition to Boston, stating that they paid $1000 in taxes and yet had no public school. The town of Boston approved this petition on May 27, 1811, and appropriated $300 for the support of a school for one year. Boston finally appointed Mr. Zephaniah Wood the Master of the South Boston School. A new building, named the Hawes School[32] for Mr. John Hawes, the donor of the land, was erected in 1823, on Broadway, South Boston.

[30] See Appendix XI for the list of the members of the School Committee from 1789 through 1822, compiled by the writer from the *Town Records*. See Appendix XII for a chronological list of the Boston School Committee manuscript documents from 1789 through 1822, compiled by Professor Arthur Orlo Norton and the writer.

[31] See Appendix XIII for the history of the Mayhew School.

[32] See Appendix XIV for the history of the Hawes School, South Boston.

The Smith School[33] for colored children was established in 1812, when the town of Boston voted "that the sum of Two hundred Dollars be appropriated towards maintaining a School for African children, under the direction of the School Committee." On February 25, 1818, at a meeting of the selectmen, the chairman reported that he had "viewed the school for people of colour in Belknap street" and that he had agreed with Mr. James Walter to take the school on trial "the Board to allow him (out of the donation of Abiel Smith Esq. deceased) such sum as they shall think he deserves in addition to the $200 allowed by the School Committee." In 1834 a new schoolhouse was erected on Belknap Street [now Joy Street], which in 1835 was named the Smith School after its benefactor.

The Boylston Reading and Writing School,[34] named for Thomas Boylston, was established on May 25, 1818, when the town voted that

. . . the Town Treasurer be authorized to borrow . . . a sum not exceeding twenty thousand Dollars for the express purpose of erecting two additional School houses in the Town for the use of the Town; which schools shall be called the Boylston town Schools and that the like sum of twenty thousand Dollars from the money secured to be paid to the Town by Ward N. Boylston Esqr. arising out of the will of the late Thomas Boylston of London Esqr. deceased, with the Interest accuring thereon, be appropriated to the discharge of this debt.

In 1819 the Boylston School was built in Washington Place, Fort Hill, to accommodate both the Reading School, under the mastership of Mr. John J. Stickney, and the Writing School, under the mastership of Mr. Ebenezer E. Finch.

It was not until 1816 that Sunday Schools [Schools on

[33] See Appendix XV for the history of the Smith School for colored children.

[34] See Appendix XVI for the history of the Boylston School.

Sunday] were established in Boston by the Society for the Moral and Religious Instruction of the Poor, the object being to teach poor, neglected children to read and write, thus laying a foundation for subsequent religious and moral training. It is interesting to note that as early as April 25, 1791, the "Proprietors of the Duck Manufactory" [manufacturers of cotton duck] requested the selectmen to permit them to open a Sunday School, but this was refused on the ground that "the Law respecting Schools had not in contemplation such as is requested." The establishment of these private Sunday Schools in Boston in 1816 brought out the fact that a large proportion of children could neither read nor write, and to them, therefore, under the law of 1789, the doors of the public schools were closed. This was one of the causes which led to the establishment of primary schools in 1818.

Since primary schools[35] for children between four and seven years of age were not established until 1818, it was necessary for parents to send their children to private schools or to teach them themselves, a fact which accounts for the great number of such private schools[36] in Boston prior to this time. In 1820 the first intermediate school was established for illiterate children over seven years of age, who were too old to be admitted into the primary schools and, under the law of 1789, because of their illiteracy, could not be admitted into the English grammar schools.

In 1821 the School of Mutual Instruction[37] was established to accommodate those boys and girls who were too old for the primary schools and unqualified to enter the grammar schools. The school committee engaged Mr. Dale, who was "principal teacher of the Lancastrian schools in Albany," to organize and establish the school.

[35] See Appendix XVII for the history of the primary schools.
[36] See Appendix XVIII for the history of private schools.
[37] See Appendix XXII for the history of the School of Mutual Instruction.

Recognition of the need of a more democratic system of education to benefit boys not preparing for college is shown in the establishment, in 1821, of the English Classical School,[38] which has the distinction of being the first public high school in the United States. The school was classical in name only, for the classics properly so-called were not taught; the name was accordingly changed in 1824 to the English High School.

It was not until 1826, four years after Boston became a city, that the High School for Girls was established; this school has the distinction of being the first public high school for girls in the United States. The number of girls applying was so great that it was given up in 1828, when the school committee recommended putting most of the curriculum into the English Grammar and Writing Schools.

From 1821 to 1848 fourteen elementary schools were established to meet the requirements of a rapidly increasing population. They were the following: the Bowdoin School, established in 1821; the Hancock School, in 1822; the Wells School, in 1833; the Johnson School, in 1836; the Winthrop School, in 1836; the Lyman School, in 1837; the Endicott School, in 1839; the Mather School, in 1842; the Brimmer School, in 1843; the Phillips School, in 1844; the Otis School, in 1844; the Dwight School, in 1844; the Quincy School, in 1847; and the Ingraham School, in 1848.

In 1852 the Normal School was established for the purpose of preparing young women to become teachers. This was the second oldest city normal school in the United States. In 1854 high-school courses for girls were introduced in the Normal School, and the name was changed to the Girls' High and

[38] See Appendix XXIII for the history of the English Classical School. Boston now maintains the following suburban high schools: The Brighton High School, Charlestown High School, Dorchester High School for Boys, Dorchester High School for Girls, East Boston High School, Hyde Park High School, Jamaica Plain High School, Roxbury Memorial High School for Boys, Roxbury Memorial High School for Girls, and South Boston High School.

Normal School. In 1872 the two departments separated and each was established as an independent institution. In 1922 the curriculum of the Normal School was reorganized upon a collegiate basis, and later the name was changed to the Teachers College of the City of Boston.

The first public kindergarten[39] in Boston, based on the system of Froebel, was established in 1870, with the understanding that "if successful it should be continued and others established." The school committee, although satisfied with the results of this experiment, were so alarmed at the prospective cost of adopting more kindergartens that they discontinued the system altogether in 1879. Fortunately for Boston, in 1878, Mrs. Pauline Agassiz Shaw [Mrs. Quincy A. Shaw] and other public-spirited citizens contributed the necessary means for establishing several free kindergartens for poor children. Mrs. Shaw continued her generous work for fourteen years, at one time supporting thirty such kindergartens. It was not until 1888 that Boston reëstablished public kindergartens by taking over the maintenance of the fourteen kindergartens which at that time were supported by Mrs. Shaw.

In 1877 a petition was sent to the school committee to admit girls into the Boston Latin School. This resulted in the establishment in 1878 of a separate school for girls, called the Girls' Latin School, which was strictly a college-preparatory school. Mr. John Tetlow was appointed the first Master.[40] It is interesting to recall here that the Boston Latin School for boys had been in continuous existence since 1635, 243 years previous to the establishment of equal opportunities for girls.

---

[39] "Infant Schools" had been established in Boston by private societies and individuals as early as 1830. In 1859 Miss Elizabeth Peabody of Boston became interested in the writings of Froebel. In 1867 she studied in Germany with Froebel's widow and, after returning to America in 1868, she induced philanthropists to contribute to the support of the kindergarten movement.

[40] Mr. Ernest G. Hapgood, the present Master, was appointed in 1910.

In the last half century additional public schools[41] have been established in Boston to meet the needs of a growing democracy and the economic demands of a new civilization. Conspicuous among the schools for boys are the following: the Mechanic Arts High School, established in 1893 "to meet the needs of boys whose dominant interests are in science, mathematics, drawing and the mechanic arts"; the High School of Commerce, established in 1906 "to train boys for business life"; and the Boston Trade School, established in 1911 and opened in 1912 "to train boys who are to enter industrial life in the essentials of the chosen trade." Conspicuous among the schools for girls are the High School of Practical Arts, established in 1907, the Trade School for Girls,[42] established in 1909, and the Boston Clerical School, established in 1914— all three of which offer exceptional opportunities for training in vocational subjects.

Additional opportunities have been provided for handicapped children in the establishment of the Horace Mann School for the Deaf,[43] in 1869, and the first special class for mentally retarded children, in 1899. Boston now maintains lip-reading classes for hard-of-hearing children, hospital classes, special improvement classes, a disciplinary day school for boys, and classes for the conservation of eyesight.

Some of the more recent developments, established to meet the requirements of a growing democracy, have been the

[41] For a full discussion see the article on education, written by Jeremiah E. Burke and Louis J. Fish, in *Fifty Years of Boston,* published in 1932 by the Subcommittee on Memorial History of the Boston Tercentenary Committee.

[42] The Trade School for Girls was accepted by the Boston School Committee in 1909, making it the first State-aided industrial school in Massachusetts. The School was first opened in July, 1904, under the auspices of the Massachusetts Association of Women Workers.

[43] The Horace Mann School for the Deaf was established by the Boston School Committee, in coöperation with the State Board of Education, which was established in 1837.

Evening Schools for adolescents and adults, the Day School for Immigrants, the Continuation School for Boys, and the Continuation School for Girls. To meet the economic results of the present depression the Boston school system has adjusted its program to help those young citizens who are affected by the consequences of unemployment.

Having traced the growth of public education in Boston during the last three hundred years, we look into the future and wonder what new developments will take place a few generations hence. From the history of the last three centuries it appears that the schools have been established to meet the needs of a changing civilization. What, then, will be the future civilization and what educational program will Boston pursue to maintain that civilization?

CHAPTER II

THE DEVELOPMENT OF SUPPORT OF THE BOSTON LATIN SCHOOL IN THE COLONIAL AND PROVINCIAL PERIODS

Our free Schools seem to have been interested for the Benefit of the Poor and the Rich; that the Children of all, partaking of equal Advantages and being placed upon an equal Footing, no Distinction might be made among them in the Schools on account of the different Circumstances of their Parents, but that the Capacity & natural Genious of each might be cultivated & improved for the future Benefit of the whole Community.

—A committee report presented to the town on April 5, 1784.

THE Puritan founders of Boston, under the leadership of John Winthrop, appreciated the value of education and considered that money appropriated for schools was a wise investment, essential not only to the welfare of the individual but also to the welfare of the State and Church. The Colonial beginnings of school support in New England[1] eventually, in the nineteenth century, developed into the policy of universal, tax-supported, and state-controlled education.

The name "free school," which was applied not only to the Latin School but to the writing schools, meant a democratic, public institution not restricted to any class of children. Secondary education was declared at once not to be the privilege of any aristocratic class; the governor's son and the poor man's son were, in this sense, both "free" to enter the school. The schools were also free, in the modern connotation of the term, because tuition fees were not charged to residents of

[1] For a discussion of the beginnings of free public schools in New England see Marcus Wilson Jernegan, *Laboring and Dependent Classes in Colonial America, 1607-1783,* pp. 69-83. See also George Leroy Jackson, *The Development of School Support in Colonial Massachusetts.* For a discussion of the support of Boston schools in the Colonial and Provincial periods see Robert Francis Seybolt, *The Public Schools of Colonial Boston, 1635-1775,* pp. 33-42.

the town but only to non-residents. A small amount was expected for "entrance and fire money," but this fee was not required.

In successive stages of its development the Boston Latin School was supported from the following sources: voluntary contributions; income from town property, including the rental of islands in Boston Harbor and other town lands; and general town taxation. Additional income was provided from one or a combination of two or more of the following sources: personal gifts and legacies of land and money, fines from Colonial law-breakers, tuition fees of non-residents, and "entrance" and "fire money."

Voluntary Contributions

The first record of support of the School is on August 12, 1636, when the "richer inhabitants," forty-five in number—including Governor Henry Vane, Deputy-Governor John Winthrop, Mr. Richard Bellingham, Mr. Robert Keayne, Mr. Cotton [John Cotton], Mr. Edward Hutchinson, and others—made generous voluntary contributions, totaling between forty and fifty pounds, "towards the maintenance of a free school master."[2] It is to be noted that this was not a town meeting but rather a meeting of the "richer inhabitants." The support of the School by voluntary contributions is not town support and, therefore, at this early period, the School was not strictly public according to the present significance of public education.

Indication that the town was beginning to assume responsibility for the support of the School, before the close of the

[2] See page 89 for facsimile of manuscript record. See Appendix XXIV for the printed record, as transcribed by the Boston Record Commissioners. The total sum cannot be accurately determined because of the incompleteness and the illegibility of the record. Experts in chirography disagree as to whether Richard Bellingham contributed ten pounds, eleven shillings, or forty shillings. The amounts contributed by William Brenton, Nicholis Willys, William Hudson, and Mr. Cotton [*sic*] were not listed.

first decade after its establishment, is the following vote of the selectmen on December 2, 1644: "Its ordered that the Constables shall pay unto Deacon Eliot[3] for the use of mr Woodbridge eight pounds due to him for keeping the Schoole the Last yeare." Marcus W. Jernegan[4] states that it is possible that this represents a voluntary contribution, collected by the constables, but he also states that, "since the order indicates some contract with the schoolmaster made by the town perhaps in part payment for his services," it is more probable that the selectmen "decided on the town rate and then gave orders to the constables to pay certain sums due, out of the money collected." George Leroy Jackson[5] suggests that this vote is a probable instance of "rating" of those who refused to support the School by voluntary contributions.

Some historians, quoting a statement in Governor John Winthrop's *Journal* under date of July 3, 1645, have asserted that the second stage in the development of school support in Boston was the yearly contribution of "50 pounds to the master and an house, and 30 pounds to an usher, . . . either by voluntary allowance, or by rate of such as refused, etc., and this order was confirmed by the general court. . . ." Professor Jernegan states that there is doubt concerning Winthrop's statements since "neither the town records of Boston nor those of the selectmen contain any such order, nor is there any such reference in the records of the General Court at this date; nor is there any evidence of the appointment of an usher, or more than one teacher, until 1666."[6] Professor Seybolt states that "such a practice may have been considered at the meeting of August 12, 1636, at which Winthrop was

[3] Jacob Eliot was one of the selectmen.
[4] Marcus W. Jernegan, *op. cit.,* pp. 71-72. Quoted by permission of the University of Chicago Press.
[5] George Leroy Jackson, *op. cit.,* p. 36.
[6] Marcus W. Jernegan, *op. cit.,* p. 72.

present, but it was not established."[7]   The Massachusetts school legislation of 1647, enacted by the General Court, allowed each town to determine its own policy for school support.

INCOME FROM TOWN PROPERTY

Income from the Rental of Islands in Boston Harbor— Seventeenth-century records show that the town of Boston secured income for the support of the Boston Latin School from the rental of islands[8] in Boston Harbor, granted to the town by the General Court on March 4, 1634/35.   This was one of the earliest of the permanent endowments for education in America.

On January 10, 1641/42, at a "general Townsmeeting," the town of Boston ordered that "Deare-Island shall be Improoved for the maintenance of a free schoole for the Towne, and such other Occasions as the Townsmen For the time being shall thinke meet, the sayd schoole being sufficiently Provided for."   Exactly three weeks later, on January 31, 1641/42, the selectmen voted:

It's Agreed for the satisfaction of John Ruggle, senior, concerning 7l. 15s. 5d. charges in building expended at Deare Island, That Capt. Gibones (who hath undertaken it) shall pay the sayd sume to our Bro. Ruggle, and in liew thereof shall have the present use of the sayd Iland untill the Towne doe let the same, and then the said sume of 7l. 15s. 5d. is againe to be repayd unto him by the Towne.

It was not until December 30, 1644, that the island was

---

[7] Robert Francis Seybolt, *op. cit.*, p. 33.

[8] See *Records of the Governor and Company of the Massachusetts Bay in New England,* edited by Nathaniel B. Shurtleff, Vol. I, p. 139. "Deere Iland, Hogg Iland, Longe Ileland, & Spectacle Ileland are graunted to the inhabitants of Boston, to enioy to them, their heires & successors, that shall inhabite there, for eu[r], payeing to the Tresurer for the tyme being the yearly rent of iiij[s], & the former rent of iij[t] is remitted them."

rented to James Penn and John Oliver for three years "paying unto the Use of the Schoole seaven pounds per yeare, In part whereof they are to repay according to former order on 31 st of 11 th mo., 1641, unto Major Gibons the mony payd by him unto John Ruggle, and that before the 1st of 3d mo., 1645." Three years later, on January 31, 1647/48, Deer Island was let to Edward Bendall for seven years,

In Consideration whereof hee is to pay to the Towne of Boston the sum of fourteen pounds per annum for the scooles use of the sayd Towne in provision and clothing, provided their be reserved a liberty for the Inhabitants of the towne of Boston to cutt wood for their own use, nott bringing a draught upon the Iland to cart withall, except it be with the consent of the sayd Edward Bendall.

The next year, on February 26, 1648/49, "Bro. Bendall's" seven-year lease was "made up twenty and one years payinge his rent of 14 1. per annum." The town evidently had difficulty in collecting the rent due, as is evidenced by the following vote of the selectmen, on April 27, 1655: "Itt is ordered that the Constable shall distrayne upon Deare Iland for the rent that is due to the towne to the first of March last past." On February 23, 1662/63, the lease of Deer Island was renewed by Sir Thomas Temple "Knight & Baronight" for thirty-one years "att £14 rent to be payed yearly every first day of March to the Towne Treasuerer, for the use of the Free schoole, ..." At the town meeting on March 9, 1684/85, Ezekiel Cheever, the Master of the Boston Latin School, made a motion that "the lease of Deare Island may be renewed to Mr. Sam[ll.] Shrimpton the present Tenant." It was then voted to refer the matter to the selectmen "to agree with s[d] M[r.] Shrimpton or any other about a longer lease or renewinge the former." On May 25, 1685,[9] Mr. Samuel Shrimpton renewed his lease of Deer Island

[9] See Robert Francis Seybolt, *op. cit.*, p. 35. Professor Seybolt states: "Although Deer Island continued to be leased, the school was not designated as the beneficiary of the income after May 25, 1685."

. . . for the terme of 18 yeares, to comence from the 1st of March 1693/94 (when his present lease will expire) at ye rent of 14ld mony p ann, to be paid on every 1st. day of March yearelie to the use of the Free schoole, alsoe in consideration of 19ld mony pd by him in the behalfe of the Towne unto Josiah Sachen & other Indians for the ratification of theire predecessors grant of all the Lands within the Necke of Bostone & other out Lands within the precincts thereof.

Lands on Long Island and Spectacle Island in Boston Harbor were also rented to several gentlemen on condition that they pay a certain sum yearly "for the Schools Use." On March 12, 1648/49, the town ordered that "the select men of the towne shall take order aboute Longe Iland and Spectacle Iland, with them that now hold it, to instate it on them for Inheritance, upon paying a yearly rent upon evrye accre for the Schols use." The next month, on April 9, 1649, the selectmen recorded the names of fifteen men, who "doth bind themselves and their successors to pay six pence an accre per yeare for their land at Spectacle Iland for ever to the use of the schole, that so it may be proprietye to them for ever, . . . or else there land is forfiet into the towne's dispossinge." Six years later, on June 25, 1655, the selectmen ordered that the "present renters" of Long Island and Spectacle Island "shall within ten dayes . . . come in and cleare their severall payments due for the said land, to the towne's treasurer upon the forfeiture of the said lands as by former agreement, ..." Almost twelve years later, on March 11, 1666/67, the town voted that the "annuall rent" from these two islands [six pence per acre per annum by agreement on April 9, 1649] "is made voyde, provided that what is short payed in of there rent be forthwith payed to the Towne Tresuere."

Income from the Rental of a Tract of Land in Braintree— Land in Braintree, owned by the town of Boston, was rented to certain inhabitants on condition that they pay a yearly sum

to the town of Boston forever "for the use of the school."
On April 19, 1649, the selectmen recorded that "Moses Paine,
of Braintry, hath let to him 500 Accers of land, to be layd
out at Braintry, painge forty shillings per annum for ever, for
the schols use, . . . in corne or porke at the prize curant, and
that to be payd into the towne treasuree successivlye." The
town of Boston, on March 11, 1649/50, voted that all the
land at Braintree "undespossed of, besides the 2,000 acers
that was set apart for the schools use, is not from this time
forward to be alotted to any particular persons, but to be
improved for the publike service of the Towne of Boston."
After the "wast Lands at Brantree" were sold, Boston voted
on January 24, 1708/9, that the income of the five hundred
pounds be forever "impropriated and improved for a School
or Schools for writeing and Arithmetick."[10]   On March 13,
1710/11, the town voted that the Selectmen sell "the Townes
Lands in Brantree, and that they have full power to Sign &
execute Deeds for ye same, & yt they Lay out ye Sd money
in Some Real Estate for the use of the Publick Lattin School,
that ye Stock be not Exhausted Provided ye Town be advised
wth before ye money be disposed of. . . ."   In less than two
months, on May 9, 1711,[11] the town voted that thirteen hundred pounds "part of the Purchase money for the Towns Land
in Brantrey . . . (Together with the Two hundred pounds

[10] For a discussion of the support of the writing schools from 1684 to
1789, the North Grammar School from 1713 to 1789, and the writing and
reading schools from 1789 to 1822 see Pauline Holmes, *Chapters in the History
of Boston Schools, 1635-1822*, in the possession of the Wellesley College
Library (Unpublished M. A. thesis, written in 1923).

[11] On this same day the town voted to release Samuel Sewall from "an
Annual Quit claim of Forty Shillings. Issueing out of a Ceader Swamp . . .
in Brooklyne [Brookline], Appropriated to the use of the Grammar School,"
as recompense for an abatement of seventy pounds on a sale to the town
of "a parcell of Land for Enlargeing ye North burying place, at the price
of One hundred and Twenty pounds." The town also voted to invest the
seventy pounds for "the use of the Free Grammar School, in liew of the
afore said Quit Rent."

already received towards the S^d purchace) Be Invested and Layd out in Some Real Estate for the use of the Publick Lattin School, . . . The Annual Rent and Incomes . . . to be imployed to and for the Support of the Publick Grammar School. . . ."

Income from Town Lands, Docks, Ferries, and House Rents—On June 26, 1649, land in Bendalls Cove was rented to a group of eight men with the understanding that they and their successors are "indebted to the Towne of Boston, . . . for ever for the schols use . . . which some that is to be payd yearly is 3 l. 3s. 2d." On November 31, of that year, the selectmen recorded that they had sold "the Reversion of the Dock or Cove Called by the name of Bendall Docke, together with the flats thereto belonginge" to James Evirill, with the agreement that he should forever pay "to the School's use sixe pounds sixteene shillings ten pence p. Anum for ever, . . ."

In the *Town Records* and in the *Suffolk Deeds* appear the names of several individuals who contributed to the support of the "free school" through the sale and rent of lands and houses. On June 26, 1649, the selectmen leased to Benjamin Ward "a parcill of land by his howse," for which he and his successors were to pay to the town forever three pounds a year "to be for the schols use." Richard Cooke was granted a permit, on March 29, 1652, to build a house on the town's ground between "the towne's house in which M^r. Woodmansy now liveth, and the town skoole house" on the north side of the present School Street, "paying quarterly into the tresurer for the towne the sum of seaven shillings and six penc, in merchtll good pay which sum maketh the sum of thirtie shillings per annum to be paid for ever; . . . alsoe if the towne shall see cause to inlarg the skoolehouse at any time hearafter, the town hath reserved libertie soe to doe." There is the name of William Blanton,[12] who on March 30,

---

[12] In the *Town Records* the name is often spelled "Blantan."

1655, bought "a parcell of land," for which he was to pay "six shillings per annum for ever . . . for the schooles use." In the same year, on July 30, 1655, Edward Greenliff was granted a piece of land on which to build a house, "paying two shillings, six pence per annum to the schooles use, as long as hee improves itt for a dying house"; the records show that this same lot of land "by the spring" was let the next year, on March 31, 1656, to Mathew Coy, "for two shillings, sixe pence, per yeare for the schooles use."   Richard Staines, a sailmaker, bought a house and shop of Leonard Buttles, a bricklayer, on February 22, 1655/56, with the agreement that he "doe yearely pay unto the free Schoole of Boston Sixe shillings three pence, . . .[13] Then appears the name of Captain James Johnson, who, on February 23, 1656/57, was granted the lease of "all the wast land belonging to the towne on the southside of the Creeke . . . to enjoy the same for ever, hee paying foure pounds, ten shillings per annum for ever to the schoole of Boston."   Later, on January 30, 1681/82, there appears the name of John Woodmansey, who agreed to pay the selectmen for a "peece with another peece of like land on the other side of the docke . . . for the use of the free schoole of Boston."

Eighteenth-century records show that the town of Boston continued its policy of securing additional income for school support from rentals.   On May 9, 1711, it was proposed that the income from the "Townes Wharfe & Dock at Merryes Point, ye Rent of Winisimit Ferry & the wharfe at ye end of Cross Street" be appropriated "for the Support of a Free School or Schols at the North end of the Town."   Again, on March 11, 1711/12, the town voted that "the Townes Wharfe, Dock and Flatts at the North Battree, be Appropriated to-

---

[13] *Suffolk Deeds*, Vol. II, p. 259. The writer is indebted to Arthur Wellington Brayley, *Schools and Schoolboys of Old Boston*, p. 12, for information concerning this document.

wards the Support of the Free Grammar School at the North end of Boston."[14]

More names are recorded as the years pass. On April 19, 1720, the selectmen voted that the town give a deed to Colonel Joshua Lamb for the marsh formerly leased to John Alcock, "upon his paying . . . Seventy pounds . . . to be Invested in some Real Estate for the use of the first Gramer School in Boston forever." The next week, on April 27, 1720, the town granted this marsh to Colonel Joshua Lamb, "upon his paying unto the Town Treasury . . . the Sume of Seventy pounds. And S[d] money to be invested in Some Real Estate, for the use of the First Free Gramer School in Boston."

Provision Made for Support of the Free School in Boston from Land Granted to Boston by the General Court—One thousand acres of land in Haverhill, Massachusetts, "in the wildernesse on the North of merimack River,"[15] were granted to the town of Boston by the government of Massachusetts Bay Colony, following an order of the General Court on October 16, 1660: "In ans[r] to the petition of the toune of Boston, the Court judgeth it meete to graunt y[e] s̃d toune of Boston one thousand acres of land, for their furtheranc & helpe to dischardg y[e] chardg of a free schoole there."[16] The first reference to this grant in the *Town Records* is the vote of the selectmen on April 25, 1664, to appoint Mr. John Hull "to looke after the layeing out the 1000 Ackers of land for the vse of the Free Schole, and to make returne thereof."

[14] Later records show that this school was opened in 1713 and was named the North [Latin] Grammar School, to distinguish it from the original Latin Grammar School established in 1635.

[15] *Massachusetts Archives*, LVIII, No. 53. See page 37 for facsimile of manuscript record.

[16] *Records of the Governor and Company of the Massachusetts Bay in New England*, Vol. IV, Part I, p. 444. For a discussion of land grants for the support of schools see Arthur Orlo Norton, *Educational Legislation in Massachusetts from 1642 to 1837*, mimeographed in 1920 by the Department of Education of Wellesley College.

GENERAL COURT LAND GRANT

Location of the tract of 1000 acres "in the wilderness on the North of merimack River," granted by the General Court in 1660 to the town of Boston "in reference to their free schoole."

From the original in the Massachusetts State Archives Division, State House, by courtesy of Mr. Frederic W. Cook, Secretary of The Commonwealth.

The next month, on May 13, 1664, the General Court determined the position of the grant of land "in the wildernesse on the North of merimack River."[17]   Over three and a half

[17] *Massachusetts Archives*, LVIII, No. 53.

decades passed before the selectmen, on January 1, 1701/2, ordered the "Town Clark" to procure a record "out of the Secretaryes office of the Gen^ll Courts grant of a thousand Acres of Land to the Free Schooll of the Town of Boston." Another decade passed and, on June 14, 1714, the selectmen voted that Mr. Edward Hutchinson "Imploy one or more meet persons to find out the thousand Acres of Land on the North Side of Merimeck a River, formerly Granted by ye Gen^ll Court to this Town wth Refference to ye Free School. and to make return to the Sel men in order that they may know where to find the Same hereafter." Almost two years passed before the selectmen, on April 17, 1716, voted to employ a surveyor.[18] After almost five years the selectmen again voted, on December 3, 1720, to appoint Mr. John Gardiner and Mr. Samuel Danforth "to renew the bounds of ye Farm granted to the Free-School of Boston by the Gen^ll Court Several years past, the Auntient boundaryes being now difficult to be found. And if in the Town grant of Haveril, to notify them to run wth them." Over two months later, on February 20, 1720/21, the selectmen voted that at least two selectmen should accompany the surveyors, Captain John Gardiner of Salem and Mr. Samuel Danforth of Billerica, to Haverhill to survey the thousand acres of land and "new mark the S^d Tract of Land agreeable to the Grant & return wch was accepted by ye Government Anno 1664/65." Fourteen years later, on May 21, 1735,[19] the town recorded that "The Committee have also obtained Copys of the Grant, Survey and Return of One Thousand Acres of Land for the Free School of Boston which are also herewith laid before the Town."

[18]*Thirteenth Report of the Record Commissioners,* p. 3: "The T. Treasu^r is directed to Supply m^r Danforth wth money not exceeding three pounds towards his Expences in case he undertake to find out & Survey ye 1000 Acres of Land belonging to this Town on ye North Side of Merrimack River."

[19] Professor Seybolt states: "After May 21, 1735, the grant disappears from the records, leaving no trace of income for the school."

GENERAL TOWN TAXATION

The support by general taxation, by a "rate"[20] on the inhabitants, was the final stage in the development of support of the schools. At the town meeting, on March 11, 1649/50, it was voted that "M^r. Woodmansey, the Schoolmaster, shall have fiftye pounds per annum for his teachinge the schollers, and his proportion to be made up by ratte." This is the first reference in the *Town Records* to the appropriation by the town of a definite yearly salary to the schoolmaster, although this policy was probably established prior to this date.[21] As early as 1644, as has been said above, the selectmen assumed responsibility for the support of the School by ordering that "the Constables shall pay unto Deacon Eliot for the use of m^r Woodbridge eight pounds due to him for keeping the Schoole the Last yeare."

The schools were listed with other town expenses in the general town tax.[22] An illustration of this policy is the following interesting report of Edward Willis, Treasurer, dated June 2, 1686, which is copied into the *Town Records*, following a meeting of the "freemen of Bostone" on May 14, 1686:

Whereas the president & Councill June ye 2^d 1686 in answer to the motion of the Select men of Bostone for the supply of mony to maintain the poore, mendinge of the high wayes & other necessary Towne occasions . . . It is found . . . that ratinge the Towne about 600^{ld}. rate pay, beinge customarie to abate one third pte if paid in mony, which brings it to 400^{ld}. & abatem^t for such as haue beene rated, and found not able to pay, & for such as haue dyed

---

[20] The General Court, in 1646, fixed the tax on property at the rate of one penny per pound. The various rates were often paid in "country pay" which meant whatever kind of produce or live stock the tax-payer had to offer. For a discussion of rates see George Leroy Jackson, *op. cit.*, pp. 34-35. See also Marcus Wilson Jernegan, *op. cit.*, p. 83.

[21] See Appendix XXV for the salaries and house rent of Masters and Ushers of the Boston Latin School from 1636 to 1796.

[22] See Robert Francis Seybolt, *op. cit.*, p. 39.

& such as haue gone to sea, remoued to other places before they haue paid, & such as haue beene abated on complaint of beinge ouer rated, comonlie brings it to 340ld or 350ld. And the standinge charge of this towne at this time is about 400ld. p. ann—aboue 200ld. of which is in mainetaineinge three Free Schooles, mendinge the high wayes in Bostone, Rumny Marsh & Muddie riuer, The rest to severall yt. haue standinge salerie for service in ye Towne & to poore people that are not like to get theire liueings as longe as they doe liue, besides clothinge & buryinge ye poore, and giueinge to peoples necessities transientlie, repaire the Towne house & schoole houses, maintaineinge basterds & poor people when they are sicke, and nurses for them and powder for the townes occasions paying house rent for it and blowinge up of houses and findinge powder for the towne as the Law requires.

Another illustration of the policy of listing the schools, with other town expenses, in the general town tax[23] is the following vote of the town on May 12, 1701: "It was voted that One Thousand and fifty pounds be raised upon the Inhabittants and Residents of this Towne for the defraying the necessary charges of the Town for the year Ensueing, viz. for the relief of the poor Schoolmasters Saleryes &c. the charge of the watch, the building a House for the Lattin Schoolmaster, and the charge of Representitives, Select men, &c." The next year, at the May meeting, it was voted that "the Sum of One Thousand pounds be assessed by the Select men on the Inhabitants & residents of this Town to be imployed in defraying the necessary charges of this Town for the year Ensueing, the charge of the watch being included."

[23] The general town tax raised on the inhabitants in 1701 was £1050; in 1702, £1000; in 1703, £700; in 1704, £1200; in 1705, £1000; in 1706, £1300; in 1707, £1600, including £300 for watch; in 1708, £1450; in 1709, £1350; in 1710, £1400; in 1711, £1600, including £300 for watch and £300 for streets; in 1712, £3300, including £300 for watch; in 1713, £3230; in 1714, £2400; in 1715, £1750, including £300 for streets and £250 for watch; in 1716, £2700, including £400 for streets and £300 for watch; in 1720, £2400, including £300 for watch and £100 for streets; in 1721, £2700; in 1722, £2500; in 1750, £4000 "lawful money"; in 1757, £5000 "lawful money"; in 1795, £12000; and in 1809, $70,000.

On March 13, 1703/4, the town voted "that a New School House be build in Stead of the Old School House in wch m^r Ezekiell Chever Teacheth, and it is Left wth the Select men to get the Same accomplished."[24] The paragraph which immediately follows this vote is "Voted that the Sum of Twelve hundred pounds be Assessed by the Select men on the Inhabitants and Estates of this Town, to be imployed in defraying the necessary Charges there of." It should be noted that this tax of £1200 was the general annual tax to defray the total charges of the town, and not a special tax to defray the cost of the proposed new schoolhouse, as a casual reading might suggest.

On March 13, 1710/11,[25] the selectmen offered a "Memorial" to the town, suggesting an improvement in the methods of teaching at the Latin School. The "Free School," according to this report, was "maintained cheifly by a Town Rate on the Inhabitants." The appropriation for school support was included in the total town taxation; the word "cheifly" suggests that additional income was provided from tuition fees from non-residents.

In the eighteenth century, as to-day, some of the citizens of Boston rebelled against the high taxes. A committee was appointed by the town on March 12, 1750/51, to investigate the causes of the town's great expenses, in answer to a petition[26] of some of the inhabitants requesting the town to consider "the great Expence occasion'd by the Publick Schools." This committee reported, on May 14, 1751, that, although the school expenses were more than one third of the total sum drawn by the selectmen, they strongly disapproved economizing by cutting the school appropriation. Their argument is so significant, in view of the present day agitation for and

---

[24] See page 238 for facsimile of manuscript record.

[25] The regular March meeting was held on the preceding day, on March 12, 1710/11. The adjournment was held on March 13, 1710/11.

[26] The petition was presented to the town on March 11, 1750/51.

against school expenditure because of the depression, that it is quoted in full as follows:

That the Charge of supporting the several Publick Schools amounted the last Year to more than ½ part of the whole Sum drawn for by the Selectmen; but altho. this Charge is very Considerable, & the number of Schools is greater than the Law requires, Yet as the Education of Children is of the greatest Importance to the Community; the Committee cannot be of Opinion that any Saving can be made to Advantage on that head; except the Town should think it expedient to come into Methods to oblige such of the Inhabitants who send their Children to the Publick Schools and are able to Pay for their Education themselves, to ease the Town of that Charge by assessing some reasonable Sum upon them for that purpose.[27]

During the Revolutionary War, the town found it difficult to collect taxes. A committee reported to the town on November 27, 1776, that the money granted for each year should be "applied to defray Expenses of that year only, & that it be made a Rule, that the first Draughts should be first paid." The committee urged the adoption of this regulation so that every man would "be assured of his Money in his Turn, without any needless Attendance, & the Punctuality would prevent those useful Servants of the Town, the Schoolmasters, from appearing, by their Heirs, as Creditors of the Town." Many of our big cities to-day could profit by this commendable policy of our ancestors.

On December 7, 1781, the town voted to raise money for the payment of the schoolmasters and other "necessary charges" because the "Tax laid in March last" had been collected almost entirely "in Monies of the New Emmission, now out of circulation." On December 24, of this same year, the town voted "to enquire and Ascertain what losses the Schoolmasters may have sustained by the depreciation of the Paper

---

[27] After discussion the town voted not to change its policy of free public education, and this paragraph of the report was not accepted.

Money comparing the Salaries received from year to year with the Grants made in 1774—the Committee to have no respect to any Sums granted to the Schoolmasters on Account of the high prices of the Necessaries of Life." This depreciation of money during and after the Revolutionary War was a natural consequence of that war, just as a depression was indirectly the result of the World War.

Even as late as 1795, more than a decade after the close of the Revolutionary War, the town treasurer had extreme difficulty in collecting the taxes, to meet the expenses of the town, including the salaries of the schoolmasters. In the *Columbian Centinel* of December 16, 1795, is recorded the treasurer's very polite and gracious announcement to the tax payers:

The Town Treasurer presents his most respectful compliments to those citizens who have tax-bills unpaid, and requests the favor of them to pay the same to the collectors immediately, as he has large drafts from the Selectmen and Overseers of the Poor in favor of mechanics, schoolmasters, and others, to whom, especially at the present season, money would be very acceptable.

In 1796, because of the continued high cost of living and the low salaries paid to the schoolmasters, the school committee prepared a comparison of the salaries of the Latin School Master with the prices of food, house rent, and the wages of the common laborer, for the years 1794 and 1796.[28] From 1794 to 1796 the cost of the "necessaries of life" had more than doubled. Foodstuffs, such as flour, meal, and meat, were twice as high in 1796 as in 1794; house rent was exactly three times as high; wood was almost three times as high; and the wages of "Labourers" had increased from a range of two to four shillings to a range of six to twelve shillings, exactly three times as much. However, the salary and house

[28] The original manuscript document, a facsimile of which appears on page 44, is in the possession of the Boston School Committee.

COMPARISON OF SALARIES OF GRAMMAR MASTER AND OF PRICES OF FOOD IN
1794 AND 1796

By courtesy of the Boston School Committee.

rent of Mr. Samuel Hunt, Master of the Boston Latin School, had increased from £150 to only £200, an increase of only 33 1/3 per cent. Mr. Hunt, accordingly, petitioned the town, on April 26, 1797, for an increase in salary and again, on August 22, 1798, he headed a petition of the seven Masters of the public schools requesting a grant.[29]

The Ushers of the public schools, headed by Charles Cutler, Usher of the Boston Latin School, had previously in April, 1796, and again in August, 1797,[30] petitioned the select-

[29] The original petition, a facsimile of which appears on page 45, is in the possession of the Boston School Committee.

[30] The original petition, a facsimile of which appears on page 46, is in the possession of the Boston School Committee.

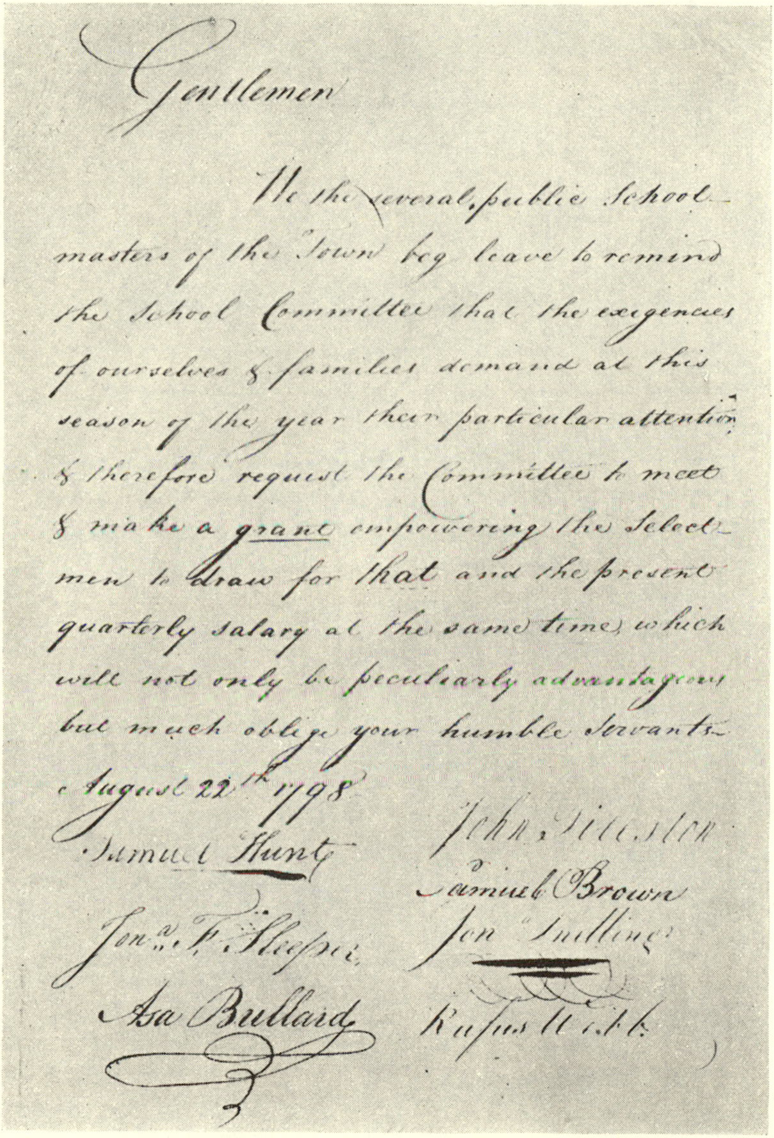

Gentlemen

We the several, public School-masters of the Town beg leave to remind the School Committee that the exigencies of ourselves & families demand at this season of the year their particular attention & therefore request the Committee to meet & make a grant empowering the Select-men to draw for that and the present quarterly salary at the same time, which will not only be peculiarly advantageous but much oblige your humble Servants

August 22ʰ 1798

Samuel Hunt

Jon⁴ F. Sleeper

Asa Bullard

John Tileston

Samuel Brown

Jon Snelling

Rufus Webb

MASTERS' REQUEST FOR INCREASE IN SALARY, IN 1798
By courtesy of the Boston School Committee.

USHERS' REQUEST FOR INCREASE IN SALARY, IN 1797
By courtesy of the Boston School Committee.

men for an increase in salary. It appears from the records that the petitions of the Masters and Ushers were granted, and the town of Boston in 1797 increased the appropriation for the salaries of the seven Masters[31] and six Ushers of the public schools to $10,000, $600 more than in 1796. In 1800 the appropriation for salaries[32] was increased to $11,100.85.

If the income from taxation proved to be inadequate to meet the current expenses, the town of Boston sometimes borrowed money. On May 11, 1762, the town voted that the treasurer be directed "to borrow upon Interest of any Person or Persons, a Sum not exceeding Fifteen hundred Pounds lawful Mony, for the payment of the School Masters Salarys now due; the Wages of the Watch, . . ." and "to allow the several School-masters Interest on the Sums due to them from the date of their Warrants to the time of payment." This is an early instance of the dangerous policy of borrowing money to pay debts.

ADDITIONAL INCOME FOR SCHOOL SUPPORT PROVIDED FROM VARIOUS SOURCES

Personal Gifts and Legacies of Land and Money—The records show that another source of income for school support was provided from personal gifts and legacies of land and money. The "Great and General Court" in 1671 ordered County Courts to supervise the trustees of gifts and legacies for the college [Harvard] and schools of learning. The earliest record of a bequest to the Boston Latin School is that of Christopher Stanley,[33] a tailor and an owner of extensive property in the old North End, who willed in 1646 "to the

[31] The Boston Latin School, the three writing schools, and the three reading schools.

[32] See Appendix XXVII for the appropriation for salaries from 1789 to 1821.

[33] For Christopher Stanley's will, dated March 27, 1646, see *Suffolk County Probate Records*, Vol. I [Original], p. 57. The writer is indebted to Arthur Wellington Brayley, *op. cit.*, p. 12, for information concerning this document. Christopher Stanley's property is recorded in *The Book of Possessions*. His widow, Susannah, married William Phillips, who confirmed to her the house Stanley left her "with the great pasture."

maintenance of the free schoole at Boston a pcell of land lying neere to the water side & foure rodds in length backward." In the *Town Records,* under the date April 19, 1649, the selectmen recorded: "Wm. Philips hath agreed to give 13s. 4d. per annum for ever to the use of the schole for the land that Christopher Stanley gave in his will for the schols use; the rent day began the 1 of March, 1649." On February 25, 1666/67, the selectmen voted that "the s^d rent of 13s. 4d. is remitted to the said Will Phillips and his heyres for ever."

Mrs. Mary Hudson, [34] who died in 1651, willed "to the use of the schoole in Boston tenn pounds." On March 30, 1655, the selectmen ordered "that the ten pounds left by legacy to the use of the schoole of Boston by mis. Hudson, deceased, shall bee lett to Capt. James Olliver for sixteen shillings per annum, so long as hee pleases to improve itt, the which he is to pay in wheate, pease and Indian [corn] . . ."

The Reverend John Cotton,[35] who died in 1652, willed his "ffarme & grounds at Muddy River by two equall Moityes the one Moitye to Harvard Colledge at Cambridge for ye use of ye Colledge forever, according to ye wisedome of ye Inspectors, with ye President & fellows, & ye other Moity . . . forever to ye Deacons of ye church at Boston, towards ye maintenance of ye free Schoole in Boston forever."

[34] For Mrs. Mary Hudson's will, dated September 26, 1651, see *Suffolk County Probate Records,* Vol. I, pp. 60-61. The writer is indebted to Justin Winsor, *The Memorial History of Boston,* Vol. II, Introduction, p. xv, for information concerning this document. Mrs. Hudson had two houses on a lot on the present State Street near Washington Street.

[35] For the Reverend John Cotton's will, dated November 30, 1652, see *Suffolk County Probate Records,* Vol. I, pp. 72-73. The bequest to Harvard College and to the Boston Latin School is prefaced by the following: "But if it shall please ye Lord to take my wife & children by death, without heires discending fro^m me, or if they shall Transplant y^m selves from hence into old England, then my will is (& I trust acceptable to ye will of God) & I doe hereby bequeath & Devise my ffarme. . . ."

Captain Robert Keayne,[36] who died on March 23, 1655/56, bequeathed "fivety pounds with the increase there of . . . to the use of the free schoole at Boston, to helpe on the Trayning up of some poore mens Children of Boston. . . ." He was one of the "richer inhabitants" who, in 1636, contributed to the support of the Boston Latin School.

Thomas Gunter, a well-to-do merchant, offered in 1748 to build, at his own expense, a cellar under the new schoolhouse on School Street, "which will preserve said School from Rotting." In his petition to the town he requested that he be allowed "a term of Years in said Cellar, as shall be adequate to the Expence of Building the same."

Income from Fines—Fines exacted in punishment from law-breakers added to school revenue in the Provincial period. The General Court passed a law on June 29, 1700, to be in force for one year only, requiring that all who sold "wine, brandy, rhum, or other distilled liquors, beer, ale, perry or cyder, by retail, without having licence . . . shall forfeit and pay the sum of four pounds, one-half thereof to the informer, and the other half to and for the use and support of a free grammar- or writing school or schools in the town where the offence shall be committed."[37] This law was reënacted in subsequent years. On March 17, 1702/3, the General Court passed a law requiring that those who failed "to give a true list of their estate and polls" should pay a fine of forty shillings, one half of which was "to be paid for and towards the support of the Schoolmaster in said town."[38] Again, in

---

[36] For Robert Keayne's will, dated December 28, 1653, see *Suffolk County Probate Records*, Vol. I [Original], p. 145, and Vol. I [Transcribed in 1892], p. 167.

[37] *The Acts and Resolves of the Province of the Massachusetts Bay*, Vol. I, p. 435.

[38] *Ibid.*, p. 516.

1720, an act was passed that certain fines were to go towards the support of the town schoolmaster.[39]

Income from Tuition of Non-Residents—It seems more than probable that from the very beginning of the Boston Latin School the Master's salary was provided for without any supplementary tuition fees, since there is no extant record of tuition prior to 1711 and then only from non-residents of Boston. The selectmen, on June 18, 1711, directed the school-masters to demand "the accustomed recompense" of parents of "other Townes or Precincts" who sent their children to the free school of Boston. This vote is so significant that it is now quoted in full:

> Where as the Support of the Free Schools of this Town hath been, and Still is, at ye Cost & charge of the Inhabitants of ye Said Town and the Select men being informed of Several Instances, of Children Sent to ye Sd Schools, whose parents, or others who of Right ought to defray the Charge of their Education, do belong to other Townes or Precincts.
>
> Where fore they ye Sd Select men do direct the Sd School masters to demand & receive of the persons Sending any Such children the accustomed recompence for their Schooling, and to Return unto ye Select men a List of their names, once (at ye Least) every year.

There is no reference in the *Town Records* of the amount of tuition charged to non-residents, but manuscript letters reveal the fact that in 1718 Nathaniel Williams, Master of the Boston Latin School, received forty shillings a year for the tuition of one Richard Hall,[40] who was sent to Boston from Barbados to be educated at the "best Grammar School." His grandmother, Madam William Coleman, a resident of

[39] For a chronology of these laws, with comments, see Arthur Orlo Norton, *Educational Legislation in Massachusetts from 1642 to 1837*, mimeographed in 1920 by the Department of Education of Wellesley College.

[40] The name of Richard Hall is not recorded in Henry F. Jenks's *Catalogue of the Boston Public Latin School*.

Boston, wrote home to Richard's family: "I delivered Richard's Master, Mr. Williams, 25 lbs. Cocoa. I spoke with him a little before and asked him what he expected for Richard's schooling. He told me 40 shillings a yeare."[41]

Income from "Entrance" and "Fire Money"—Nonresident pupils also paid a small supplementary fee to the Master for "entrance" and "firing."[42] The amount of the entrance fee is not recorded in the *Town Records*. Entrance and firing fees were often paid by resident pupils, but this charge was not ordered by the town. In 1751 entrance charges for children of the town were forbidden, as is evidenced by the following vote passed at the town meeting on May 14, 1751:

On a Motion made and Seconded, Voted that the several Masters of the Publick Grammer Schools and Writing Schools in the Town be directed not to refuse taking into their respective Schools, any Child or Children that may be brought to 'em for Education, in case Enterance money (so called) is not paid said Masters, and also that they shall not demand any Pay or Allowance for Instructing such Children, as belong to the Town, and that attend in School hours only.

[41] From Alice Morse Earle, *Child Life in Colonial Days*, p. 87, by permission of The Macmillan Company, publishers. See also *Ibid.*, p. 88, for Richard's letter to his father, dated July 1, 1719, in which he states: "My Master is very kind to me. I am now in the Second Form, am Learning Castalio and Ovid's Metamorphosis & I hope I shall be fit to go to College in two Years time. . . ."

[42] In the early eighteenth century the annual fee for fuel per pupil was six shillings. See *Suffolk County Probate Records,* Vol. XIX, p. 253. [The writer is indebted to Henry F. Jenks's *Catalogue of the Boston Public Latin School,* Part II, p. 41, footnote 8, for information concerning this document.] In the account of "Martha Balston late Ballard," dated April 27, 1716, in which she charges her husband's estate for the cost of three children's schooling, is listed the following: "To Cash p^d. for 7 years Schooling my Son Robert Ballard at the Writing Schoole at 40^s / p Annum with 3^s / a year for Firing. . . . 15£ 1s. To cash p^d Mr Cheivers for firing him at 6^s. . . . 2£ 2s. To Cash p^d Mr Rawlings for learning him the French tong . . . 3£." According to Henry F. Jenks's *Catalogue,* Robert Ballard entered the Boston Latin School in 1701 under the mastership of the famous Ezekiel Cheever.

Also Voted that the Selectmen for the time being give Directions to said Masters what money they may receive from the Scholars, for defraying the Expence of Firing.

It was not until April 5, 1784, that Boston voted to abolish the system of "Entrance & Fire Money," because such a practice was "inconsistant with that Freedom of Education which was originally intended in the Institution of the Publick Schools and introductory of such Distinction as injure the Minds of the Scollars & tending to deprive many Poor Children of the Benefit of the s^{d.} Schools." At this same meeting the town voted that "the Publick Schools be provided with Fire wood at the Discretion of the Selectmen to be paid for by their Draft on the Town Treasury."

Provision was made for poor parents who could not afford even a small fee for entrance and firing. Robert Keayne, who died on March 23, 1655/56, willed fifty pounds "to the use of the free schoole at Boston, to helpe on the Trayning up of some poore mens Children of Boston (that are most towardly & hopefull) in the knowledge of God & of Learning, not only in the Latine Tongue but also to write & cypher, as farr as the profitt of it will reach . . . as the Townesmen or ffeoffees of the free schoole from time to time shall Judge best. . . ."

The records show that further provision was also made for poor parents who could not afford the small entrance fee to the writing schools.[43] The town voted, on May 9, 1744, that the overseers of the poor "in the most prudent & frugal manner to take Care that the Poor Children within their respective Wards be put to such Schools as are proper for

[43] Primary schools for children between four and seven years of age were not established until 1818. Since "reading a few verses in the Bible" was a prerequisite for admission into the Latin School and ability to "read in the Psalter" was also a requirement for admission into the writing schools, it was necessary for parents to send their children to private Dame schools or to teach them themselves.

teaching them to Read & that the Town be at the Expence of the same." Later, on May 9, 1749, the selectmen recommended that the town provide "suitable Books" in reading and spelling "to be given to such Poor Children as they may think proper."[44] On April 5, 1784, the overseers of the poor were again authorized to give certificates to those parents who could not finance their children's education "in the early Stage" and to allow "such Schoolmasters & Schoolmistresses as they shall direct, the usual Sum given Per Week for the Instruction of each of such Children."

SUMMARY

In successive stages of its development the Boston Latin School was supported from the following sources: voluntary contributions; income from town property, including income from the rental of islands in Boston Harbor granted to Boston by the General Court, income from the rental of a tract of land in Braintree owned by the town of Boston, and income from town lands, docks, ferries, and house rents; and general town taxation.

Additional income was provided from one or a combination of two or more of the following sources: personal gifts and legacies of land and money; fines from Colonial lawbreakers; tuition fees of non-residents; and "entrance" and "fire" money.

[44] It was not until 1826 that the law required that textbooks be free to all pupils unable to pay and to those pupils able to pay "at such prices merely to reimburse to the town the expense of procuring the same." It was as late as 1884 that the free textbook bill was passed by the Massachusetts legislature, due largely to the influence of Patrick D. Dwyer.

CHAPTER III

ADMINISTRATION AND SUPERVISION

Train up a child in the way he should go; and when he is old,
he will not depart from it.

—Proverbs: 22:6.

SELECTMEN, 1635-1789

Selectmen, 1635-1789—From an examination of the *Town
Records* and the *Selectmen's Minutes* it appears that the Boston Latin School and the writing schools in the Colonial and
Provincial periods were under the supervision of the town, or
the selectmen appointed by the town. It was not until 1789,
under the "New System of Education," that the regular school
committee was first established.

From 1686 until 1689 the governor of New England, acting directly under authority of the Crown, assumed the management of the "affaires of the free schools" of Boston. In
1686 James II appointed first Joseph Dudley and second, a
few months later, Sir Edmund Andros as governor of New
England. Thus the independence of the Colony was lost.
In 1689 James II was dethroned in favor of William and
Mary; on receipt of this news, the Colony revolted and de-
posed Andros, and government under the charter of 1629
was temporarily restored. The town of Boston, on June 24,
1689, voted "that the former Custome & practice in managing
the affaires of the free schools be restored & continued."

The selectmen in most instances managed the schools on
their own responsibility, such as granting licenses to private
teachers, regulating the fees which public-school teachers
could charge scholars "at Private hours," appointing and dis-
missing public-school teachers, introducing teachers to the
scholars on "induction days," acquainting the masters of the
schools with the by-laws, settling disputes between teachers

and parents, visiting the schools, building and repairing school-houses, and ordering school materials. The selectmen issued warrants for town meetings for general discussion of school problems, at which the town either made definite decision or voted to refer the questions back to the selectmen. This policy naturally resulted in great waste of time. It is interesting to note, however, that the schoolmasters' salaries[1] were voted by the "freeholders and other inhabitants" at the town meeting.

The Reverend Cotton Mather, the famous pastor of the North Church, Boston, following the example of his father, the Reverend Increase Mather, and of his maternal grandfather, the Reverend John Cotton, always maintained an active interest in the schools. In his *Diary*, under the date June 7, 1699, he wrote: "I proposed . . . That I would more concern myself to promote Schools for Children, in my Neighborhood. And what if I should visit all the Schools; and endeavour to speak such things both to the Teachers and the Scholars, as they may all bee the better for."

The origin of the regular school committee, established in 1789, was the town vote of December 19, 1709, "That a Committee be chosen to consider of the affaires relateing to the Gramer Free School of this Town, & to make report thereof at the Town meeting in March next." On March 13, 1709/10, this committee reported recommending that the town, "Agreeably to the Usage in England, and (as we understand) in Some time past practiced here," appoint learned gentlemen, together with some of the ministers, to be inspectors of the School and to visit the School notifying the Master in advance.[2] The town, accordingly, voted that one of the min-

---

[1] See Appendix XXV and Appendix XXVI for the salaries of the Master and Usher of the Boston Latin School and of the North Grammar School. For the salaries of the Masters and Ushers of the writing schools see Pauline Holmes, *Chapters in the History of Boston Schools, 1635-1822*, in the possession of the Wellesley College Library (Unpublished M.A. thesis).

[2] See page 57 for facsimile of manuscript record.

A PETITION OF 1687 OR 1688

Ezekiel Cheever's petition addressed to Governor Edmund Andros, requesting that he be continued as schoolmaster and that he receive "about fifty five pounds" due him for past services.

From the original in the Massachusetts State Archives Division, State House, by courtesy of Mr. Frederic W. Cook, Secretary of The Commonwealth.

isters should pray with the scholars and "Entertain 'em with Some Instructions of Piety Specially Adapted to their age and Education." At this town meeting the town elected five distinguished gentlemen to be inspectors for one year, namely,

A TOWN VOTE FOR SCHOOL INSPECTORS

Facsimile of part of page of *Boston Town Records, 1700-1728*, dated March 13, 1709/10, containing the town vote to appoint school inspectors. This vote was the origin of the Boston School Committee, which was definitely established in 1789.

From the original in the office of the City Clerk, City Hall, Boston, by courtesy of Mayor Frederick W. Mansfield.

Wait Winthrop, Samuel Sewall, Elisha Cooke, Isaac Addington, and Thomas Brattle. It is to be noted that no minister was included in this committee of inspectors. This movement was disapproved by some of the ministers, who had grown to think that they had an ordained right to control the schools.

The Reverend Increase Mather sent the following letter to Samuel Sewall on April 24, 1710, in which he stated that the ministers are "the fittest persons in the World to be the Visitors of the School":

Sir,—I understand that there is a discourse about Visitors for the School, and that your self intends to speak with me about that Affair, and to desire that I would be concernd. I therefore send this to prevent you from that trouble; for I am not willing to be concerned; for 2 Reasons; 1. I have no Call to that Service. I cannot but judge that the Ministers of the Town are the fittest persons in the World to be the Visitors of the School. But the Town (I hear) has left them out of their Vote; which has been a great disrespect, and Contempt put upon (not me but) all the Ministers in Boston. They must be very fond of the Office (which, I am sure, I am not) who shall now run before they are called. A Secondary call from T.B. &c. I esteem as none at all. 2. I am stricken in years. That which was a Recreation to me formerly, is now a Burden. I may not then concern my self with a new office. . . .

Nevertheless, I purpose (if the Lord will) to goe to the School-house, and preach a Sermon to the children; but not as a Visitor. And therefore I am not willing that any one should goe with me. (especially not any of the Visitors chosen by the Town.) For which cause I shall conceal the day of my doing that Service from everybody, untill the work is over.[3]

Judge Samuel Sewall immediately answered, on the following day, urging the Reverend Increase Mather to visit the school on the day appointed by the inspectors. His reply follows:

Reverd. Sir, I am favour with yours of yesterday. The purpose therein mentioned, I Entreat you to Review, and alter; . . .

As for the business of the Visitation, the Town also came into that, with this caution, that the Visitors should stand but one year. And I am confident, they designd not to offend, much less contemn any of their honoured Pastors. But many times you know, *In vitium ducit culpae fuga.* For which, in their behalf, I ask your Pardon.

[3] "The Letter-Book of Samuel Sewall," reproduced in *Collections of the Massachusetts Historical Society*, Sixth Series, Vol. I, pp. 393-94. The writer is indebted to an article by Charles Knapp Dillaway [Master of the Boston Latin School from 1831 to 1836], published in Justin Winsor's *The Memorial History of Boston*, Vol. IV, p. 238, for information concerning the correspondence between Mather and Sewall.

SAMUEL SEWALL

Judge Samuel Sewall (1652-1730) was appointed one of the School inspectors on March 13, 1709/10.

From Justin Winsor's *The Memorial History of Boston.*

Four of this year's Visitors were bred and born in the Town, and bear a considerable part of its charge. Mr. Brattle is a good Scholar, and excels in Mathematical Learning, upon which Account Respect is due to him. As for any Exorbitances of his, the Town is far from liking them and much farther from abetting him in them. And therefore I humbly entreat you to do what Service you shall chuse, for the School; only condescend to do it upon the Tenth of May, the Time apointed by the Visitors: your work will thereby be much more Beautifull, much more Honorable, much more profitable. Boston of the Massachusets invites you, calls you, Courts you.[4]

It was not long before the ministers were appointed with the selectmen as inspectors of the free grammar schools, as is evidenced by the following vote of the town on March 16, 1713/14: "Voted. That ye Sel: men together with the Reverend Ministers of this Town be desired to be the Inspectors of the Free Grammar Schools for the year ensuing." This policy continued until March 9, 1718/19, when Samuel Sewall, John Clark, Elisha Cooke, Addington Davenport, Adam Winthrop, Habijah Savage, and John White "together with the R^d ministers of this Town" were appointed to be inspectors of the grammar schools "for the year ensuing."[5]

The selectmen, on February 8, 1724/25, invited the Reverend Benjamin Wadsworth, the Reverend Joseph Sewall, and the Reverend Samuel Checkley to accompany them on the "visitation" of the Boston Latin School. On June 26, 1738, the selectmen, with five inspectors and two ministers, the Reverend William Hooper and the Reverend Samuel Mather, visited the public schools. They reported that in general the scholars "perform'd to the great Satisfaction of the Visitors." We wonder if the visitors performed to the satisfaction of the scholars!

There is ample evidence, official and unofficial, that the regular "visitations" were very grand affairs, for the visitation of the schools often meant the arrival of more than fifty of

---

[4] "The Letter-Book of Samuel Sewall," reproduced in *Collections of the Massachusetts Historical Society*, Sixth Series, Vol. I, pp. 391-93. The quotation *"In vitium ducit culpae fuga, si caret arte"* [The avoiding of error, if unrestrained by sense of art, leads to imperfection.] is from Horace, *De Arte Poetica*, Line 31.

[5] The next year the same inspectors were re-elected. There is no record that the ministers were also appointed.

Boston's great and near-great. The governor, lieutenant-governor, members of the Council, representatives to the General Court, overseers of the poor, the selectmen, ministers, doctors, lawyers, leading citizens of Boston, and sometimes the parents were invited to attend the exercises. The picture presented by these celebrities, with their powdered wigs, cocked hats, lace ruffles, parsons' robes, and lawyers' gowns must have been most impressive. Probably the poor little school boys were frightened to death, and the teachers themselves suffered more than one qualm when faced by such an imposing array of dignitaries.

An interesting description of Governor Jonathan Belcher's attendance at the "visitation" of the schools in 1734 is recorded in the *Boston Gazette*,[6] for June 17-24, 1734:

Last Wednesday being the Day appointed by the Select Men for the Visitation of the Free Schools in this Town, they resolved to attend that Service with some of the Ministers of the Town as usual. His Excellency Governor Belcher being appraised of their Resolution, took that opportunity of paying the Schools a Visit, at the same time to shew his Respect to the Town, and to give his Countenance and Encouragement to Learning among us. At the two Grammar Schools his Excellency was Saluted by the two Masters in Latin Orations, to which his Excellency returned his Answer in Latin, as elegantly as kindly. His Excellency being gratified with the Reception which he had met with at these and the other Schools, and pleas'd with the Improvement of the Children in them, directed the Masters respectively to allow their Scholars a Play Day; and then Invited the Masters, together with the Visitors of the Schools, to an Entertainment in the Evening.

After the visitation, the gentlemen and the schoolmasters had a dinner at the expense of the town, with the understanding that they pay for their own liquor. Their favorite resort seems to have been "The Orange-Tree,"[7] an old hostelry on

---

[6]The writer is indebted to the Massachusetts Historical Society for information concerning this document.

[7] The first hackney coach stand in Boston was set up at "The Orange-Tree."

EXERCISES
In the Boston Public Latin School,
At the Semi-annual Visitation,
Friday, Jan. 22, 1813.

Salutatory Address in Latin, by
Thomas Thompson.
Extract from Addison's Cato, by
Thomas S. English,
Frederic A. Farley,
Samuel B. Tuck,
William Austin,
Constant F. Minns.
Essay in English Verse, by
Richard G. Parker.
Extract from Sallust, by
George W. Gardner.
Extract from Xenophon, by
John S. Wood.
Latin Translation, by
Francis Jenks, &
Thomas B. Coolidge.
Extract from Lucian, by
Thomas H. Oliver,
& William H. Bass.
Essay in English Verse, by
George S. Bulfinch.
Essay in English Prose, by
William Emerson.

PROGRAM FOR A VISITATION
By courtesy of the Boston Latin School Association.

Hanover Street kept by Jonathan Wardwell in 1712 and by
Mrs. Wardwell in 1724. It is recorded in the *Town Records*
that on several occasions they had a dinner at Faneuil Hall.
On July 6, 1764, the selectmen voted "that a Dinner be provided at Faneuil Hall for about 50 Gentlemen the Day for
visiting the Schools and that Mr. Ballard shall have the dress-

ORDER OF EXERCISES

AT THE

LATIN GRAMMAR SCHOOL,

August, 21, 1816.

—

I.   A Salutatory Oration in Latin.

W. H. FURNESS.

II.   An English Dialogue, " Edward and Warwick."

F. CUNNINGHAM, & T. STEVENSON.

III.   A Greek Oration, Περι της παιδειας."

F. P. LEVERETT.

IV.   A Latin Dialogue, " Decius and Cato."   Translated from *Addison.*

T. C. HALE, & L. P. CURTIS.

V.   A Poetical translation from *Ovid.*

S. B. TUCK.

VI.   A Greek Dialogue, " Lucian and Herodotus."   Translated from *Fenelon.*

J. L. GARDNER, & G. A. OTIS.

VII.   An English Poem on " Eloquence."

R. W. EMERSON.

VIII.   A Latin Poem, " De Autumno."   Imitation of *Thomson*

T. G. BRADFORD.

IX.   An English Dialogue, " Tamerlane and Bajazet."

G. R. M. WITHINGTON, & E. G. LORING.

X.   A Valedictory Oration in English.

ALEXANDER YOUNG.

—

THE performances are all original except the English Dialogues. The performers' names are in the order in which they will speak.

ORDER OF EXERCISES AT THE BOSTON LATIN SCHOOL ON AUGUST 21, 1816

The students who performed are the following: William Henry Furness; Francis Cunningham; Thomas Stevenson; Frederic Percival Leverett; T. C. Hale; Loring Pelham Curtis; Samuel Barrett Tuck; John Lowell Gardner; George Alexander Otis; Ralph Waldo Emerson; Thomas Gamaliel Bradford; George Richards Minot Withington; Edward Greeley Loring; and Alexander Young. Alexander Young, who delivered the Valedictory Oration, later became the minister of the New South Church, Boston.

Reduced from the original in the possession of the Boston Latin School, by courtesy of the Boston Latin School Association.

LATIN SCHOOL.

ORDER OF DECLAMATION.

JUNE 19, 1830.

1. Extract from a Speech of Mr. Canning, J. H. WRIGHT.
2. Extract from Gilchrist, - - G. H. CUTTER.
3. Speech of Rienzi,—Miss Mitford, W. M. EVARTS.
4. Extract from a Speech of Mr. Quincy, W. H. S. JORDAN.
5. The last Song of the Greek Patriot,—Percival, G. B. SARGENT.
6. An English Dialogue, F. E. WHITE & H. C. KINGSLEY.
7. The exile at rest,—Pierpont, - S. L. ABBOTT.
8. Extract from Dr. Channing's Election Sermon, J. F. W. LANE.
9. Description of an ancient Battle in Scotland,—Scott, C. H. A. DALL.
10. Extract from an Oration of Mr. Everett, J. FIELD.
11. Extract from the siege of Valencia,—Mrs. Hemans, B. S. OTIS.
12. An English Dialogue, J. H. WRIGHT & C. H. PARKER.
13. Soliloquy of Jugurtha,—C. Wolfe, W. V. THACHER.
14. Extract from a Speech of Mr. Phillips, J. I. T. COOLIDGE.
15. Extract from an Oration of Mr. Church, J. L. LINCOLN.
16. Extract from a Speech of Patrick Henry, F. E. WHITE.
17. Speech of Raab Kiuprili,—Coleridge, H. C. KINGSLEY.
18. Extract from a Speech of Mr. Plunket, S. PARKMAN.
19. An English Dialogue, G. CABOT & W. V. THACHER.
20. Extract from a Speech of C. Wolfe, C. H. PARKER.
21. Extract from a Speech of Mr. Burke, G. F. HOMER.
22. Speech of Catiline—Croly's Catiline, W. S. CRUFT.
23. Extract from Byron's Marino Faliero, C. A. BUCKINGHAM.
24. Speech of Ringan Gilhaize,—Galt, G. CABOT.

ORDER OF DECLAMATION AT THE BOSTON LATIN SCHOOL ON JUNE 19, 1830

ing thereof, and also furnish the Liquors that may be Wanted." On June 11, 1765, the selectmen voted "that a Dinner be provided at Faneuil Hall on the Day[8] for visiting the Schools as usual" and they also voted to invite the fathers "of those Children who are in their highest Forms." The reader will note that the mothers were not invited! In 1774 the selectmen voted not to have the dinner after the visitation, on account of the "present distress." On June 30, 1783, the selectmen

---

[8] The day determined for the school "visitation" was June 26, 1765.

agreed with Mr. Woart "to dine about 70 or 80 Persons on the Day when the publick Schools are to be Visited at 3/6 P Man [3 shillings, 6 pence], and all the Liquors that shall be drank are to be paid for."

One document, printed in 1765 at the "Heart and Crown," bearing the impressive title *The Seasons: an Interlocutory Exercise at the South Grammar School, June 26, 1765. Being the Day of the annual Visitation of the Schools in Boston*[9] contains the dialogue between Jonathan Williams Austin and Daniel Jones, members of the graduating class of the Boston Latin School. The *Town Records* reveal the fact that the fathers of these boys were present at this great occasion.

SCHOOL COMMITTEE, 1789-1935

The act of 1789, enacted by the Massachusetts Legislature, ordered that the selectmen and ministers, "or such other persons as shall be especially chosen by each town or district for that purpose," supervise the schools and once in every six months, at least, visit and inspect them. At the town meeting on October 20, 1789, the first regular school committee[10] of twelve members was chosen, one from each ward, "who in addition to the Selectmen are to carry the new System of Education which has been adopted by the Town into operation."

On December 7, 1789, the committee passed the following votes:

Voted, That the Committee be divided into seven equal parts, as Sub-Committees for the purpose of inspecting the respective Schools, and examining the scholars; so that one Committee be assigned to each School. And the Committee was divided accordingly.

[9] According to Joseph Sabin's *Bibliotheca Americana*, this "Interlocutory Exercise" was written by John Lovell, the Master of the School from 1734 until 1775.

[10] See Appendix XI for the list of the members of the Boston school committee from 1789 until 1822, when Boston became a city.

JOHN THORNTON KIRKLAND
Member of the Boston School Committee, 1797-1811, and president of Harvard
College, 1810-1828.
From Justin Winsor's *The Memorial History of Boston.*

Voted, That the inspecting Committees be enjoined to visit their respective Schools at least once every month, and as much oftener as they may think proper.

JOHN PHILLIPS

Member of the Boston School Committee, 1803-1812, and first mayor of the
City of Boston, 1822.

From Justin Winsor's *The Memorial History of Boston.*

Voted, That the inspecting Committees make the laws of the
State respecting Schools, the votes of the Town, and of this Committee, the rule of their conduct in visiting the Schools.

WILLIAM E. CHANNING
Member of the Boston School Committee, 1808-1813.
From Justin Winsor's *The Memorial History of Boston.*

Voted, That the first Monday in January 1790 be the time assigned for putting into operation the new System of Education, as adopted by the Town, and regulated by this Committee.

JOSEPH S. BUCKMINSTER
Member of the Boston School Committee, 1811-1812.
From Justin Winsor's *The Memorial History of Boston.*

On December 14, 1789, the committee passed the following vote:

Voted, That it be the indispensable duty of the several School-Masters, daily to commence the duties of their office by prayer and reading a portion of the sacred Scriptures, at the hour assigned for opening the School in the morning; and close the same in the evening with prayer.

The next week, on December 21, 1789, the committee passed the two following votes:

LEMUEL SHAW
Chief Justice and member of the Boston School Committee, 1820-1821.
From Justin Winsor's *The Memorial History of Boston.*

Voted, That the Masters never expel any boy from School, but with the consent, and in the presence of the inspecting Committee.

Voted, That the Instructor of the Latin School be entitled The Latin Grammar Master; the Instructors of the Reading Schools be entitled English Grammar Masters; the Instructors of the Writing Schools be entitled Writing Masters.

The following vote, passed on December 28, 1789, is appended in manuscript to Samuel Hunt's copy of *The System of Public Education, Adopted by the Town of Boston, 15th Octob. 1789*:

Voted, That the several Schoolmasters instruct the children under their care, or cause them to be instructed, in the Assemblie's Catechism, every Saturday, unless the Parents request that they may be taught any particular catechism of the religious Society to which they belong; and the Masters are directed to teach such Children accordingly.[11]

The school committee in 1790 appointed sub-committees of three members each, whose duty it was to visit each of the seven schools [The Boston Latin School, the North Writing School, the North Reading School, the Centre Writing School, the Centre Reading School, the South Writing School, and the South Reading School] and to file written reports with the school committee.

It appears from the records that great preparations were made by Masters and pupils for the "visitation" but, in spite of this, the unexpected often happened, as in the case of the luckless boy and the absent-minded schoolmaster, Mr. William Biglow. One Latin School boy, having been drilled in the declining of *duo*, was inadvertently called upon to decline *tres*. He faltered, looked towards Master Biglow, and then in utter despair cried out, "That's not my word, Sir!" The mistake was instantly corrected, and the boy declined *duo* to perfection.[12]

The next important development in the administration

---

[11] The "Assemblie's Catechism," entitled *The humble advice of the Assembly of Divines, now by authority of Parliament sitting at Westminster, concerning*, i. *A confession of faith*. ii. *A larger catechism*. iii. *A shorter catechism*, was published in London in 1648.

[12] From an article by Rufus Dawes entitled "Boyhood Memories," published in the *Boston Miscellany* for February, 1843, and reproduced in Henry F. Jenks's *Catalogue of the Boston Public Latin School*, Part I, pp. 49-50. Rufus Dawes entered the Boston Latin School in 1811.

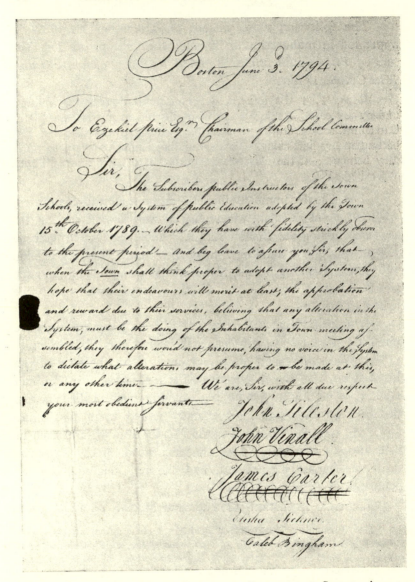

LETTER OF MASTERS TO SCHOOL COMMITTEE, DECLINING TO SUGGEST ALTERA-
TIONS IN THE "NEW SYSTEM OF EDUCATION"
By courtesy of the Boston School Committee.

and supervision of the public schools was the establishment of the office of superintendent of schools in 1851. Nathan Bishop, who had been superintendent of schools in Providence, Rhode Island, since 1839, was appointed the first superintendent of schools in Boston in 1851. Another important development in the educational system of Boston was the establishment, in 1876, of the board of supervisors, consisting of six members, and the reduction of the school committee from 116 members to 25, elected at large instead of by districts. In 1906 the school committee was completely reorganized and the number of members was reduced to five.

APPOINTMENT OF TEACHERS

On May 3, 1654, the General Court of the Massachusetts Bay Company ordered the selectmen of the towns not to employ teachers "that haue mannifested themselves vnsound in the faith or scandalous in theire liues, and not giving due sattisfaction according to the rules of Christ . . . for as much as it greatly concerns the welfare of this countrye that the youth thereof be educated, not only in good literature, but sound doctrine."

The General Court of the Province, on June 28, 1701, ordered that the Master of every grammar school [Latin Grammar School] "be approved by the minister of the town, and the ministers of the two next adjacent towns, or any two of them, by certificate under their hands." At the same time it was ordered "That no minister of any town shall be deemed, held or accepted to be the school-master of such town within the intent of the law." It was not until 1811 that this latter order was repealed.

Again, on March 19, 1711/12, the General Court ordered that teachers of elementary schools of reading and writing be approved by the selectmen of each town and also that Masters of grammar schools [Latin Grammar Schools] be approved

LETTER OF JOSEPH WILLARD, PRESIDENT OF HARVARD, 1781-1804
By courtesy of the Boston School Committee.

by ministers, as by the act of 1701 above. The preamble of this order is so human and universally true that it is now quoted in full:

And, forasmuch as the well educating and instructing of children and youth in families and schools are a necessary means to propogate religion and good manners; and the conversation and example of heads of families and schools having great influence on those under their care and government to an imitation thereof, . . .

That no person or persons shall or may presume to set up or keep a school . . . in reading, writing, or any other science, but such as are of sober and good conversation.

In the *Town Records* and *Selectmen's Minutes* are found

LETTER OF TIMOTHY DWIGHT, PRESIDENT OF YALE, 1795-1817

By courtesy of the Boston School Committee.

several instances in which the Masters of the Boston Latin School, before their appointment, were recommended by ministers. The earliest record is dated May 11, 1703, when the selectmen agreed to appoint Mr. Nathaniel Williams to assist Mr. Ezekiel Cheever at the Latin School, since he had been recommended by "sundry of the ministers in this Town."

The required intellectual and moral qualifications of candidates for teaching and the required recommendations by ministers are dealt with in *Section V* of the *Act of 1789*, enacted by the Massachusetts legislature. A candidate for the mastership of the Grammar School [Latin Grammar School] must have had "an education at some College or University" or must be able to produce a certificate from a learned minister, who was "well skilled in the Greek and Latin languages." The candidate was also required to produce a certificate from a minister or from the selectmen as to his "good moral character." *Section X* required that every teacher should be a naturalized citizen of the United States.

An additional ruling was passed by the Boston school committee, on February 6, 1801, that no law or medical student could be appointed Master or Usher of the Boston Latin School without special permission of the school committee. Throughout the files of the school committee are manuscript recommendations of teachers, the most interesting and valuable of which are those written by President Joseph Willard[13] of Harvard, President John Thornton Kirkland of Harvard, and President Timothy Dwight[14] of Yale.

A careful study of these early laws governing education reveals the conscientious effort to give the children of Boston a good education. Not only was the ability of the teacher considered but also his moral standing.

[13]See page 74 for facsimile of manuscript letter of President Joseph Willard.
[14]See page 75 for facsimile of manuscript letter of President Timothy Dwight.

CHAPTER IV

DISCIPLINE AND CORPORAL PUNISHMENT

He that spareth his rod hateth his son: but he that loveth him chasteneth him betimes.

—Proverbs: 13:24

"Spare the rod and spoil the child" was the theory believed and practised by our forefathers, not only in the home but also in the school. The old schoolmasters ruled and feruled in a vain attempt to administer law and order. A study of the early documents proves again and again that human nature never changes, either in the case of the boys or their masters; the records present many instances of truly human reactions.[1] It is only our methods of dealing with children that have changed, owing to our better understanding of child psychology.

What were the offences committed by these boys three hundred years ago? We find in the records complaints about not knowing lessons, tardiness, playing "hookey," fooling in class, whispering, firing a pistol, shooting with popguns, cheating, laziness, gambling, and even the use of bad language. How very modern this sounds!

The earliest record of discipline in the Latin School is during the mastership of the famous Ezekiel Cheever, an account of which is in the autobiography of the Reverend John Barnard, of Marblehead, who entered the Boston Latin School in 1689, when he was eight years old. Imagine a boy eight years of age being forced to study Latin and Greek! Mr. Barnard writes:

[1] The anecdotes quoted in this chapter are from Henry F. Jenks's *Catalogue of the Boston Public Latin School*, published in 1886 by the Boston Latin School Association.

Though my master advanced me as above, yet I was a very naughty boy, much given to play, insomuch that he at length openly declared, "You, Barnard, I know you can do well enough if you will; but you are so full of play that you hinder your classmates from getting their lessons; and therefore, if any of them cannot perform their duty I shall correct you for it." . . . I remember once, in making a piece of Latin, my master found fault with the syntax of the word, . . . and therefore I told him there was a plain grammar rule for it. He angrily replied, there was no such rule. I took the grammar and showed the rule to him. Then he smilingly said, "Thou art a brave boy; I had forgot it." And no wonder; for he was then above eighty years old.

In 1734 Mr. John Lovell was appointed Master of the Latin School. The following vivid description of Master Lovell and of his son, James Lovell, has been recorded by Harrison Gray Otis, who entered the School in 1773:

I attended school from that time until April, 1775, (the day of Lexington battle), being then on the second form. . . . The discipline of the school was strict but not severe. The Master's—Old Gaffer, as we called him—desk was near the south-west corner of the room; Master James's desk was in the north-west corner. I remember to have seen no other instrument of punishment but the ferule in Master Lovell's day. Gaffer's ferule was a short, stubbed, greasy-looking article, which, when not in use, served him as a stick of sugar candy. The lightest punishment was one clap, the severest four—the most usual was two, one on each hand. The inflictions of the old gentleman were not much dreaded; his ferule seemed to be a mere continuation of his arm, of which the centre of motion was the shoulder. It descended altogether with a whack, and there was the end of it, after blowing the fingers. But Master James's fashion of weilding his weapon was another affair. He had a gymnastic style of flourishing, altogether unique—a mode of administering our experimentum ferules that was absolutely terrific. He never punished in Gaffer's presence, but, whenever the old gentleman withdrew, all began to contemplate the "day's disaster," and to tremble, not when he "frown'd," for he did not frown, nor was he an ill-tempered person, but rather smiled sardonically as if preparing for a pugilistic effort and the execution as nearly resembled the motion of a flail in the hands of an expert thrasher as could be acquired by long practice. . . .

Mr. Samuel Hunt,[2] Master of the Latin School from 1776 to 1805, was very rigid in his discipline; for this reason, he became involved in difficulties with the parents, and, after 1789, with the school committee. In 1786 Mr. Samuel Whitwell and Mr. Thomas Walley, fathers of two of the Latin School boys, complained to the selectmen against Mr. Hunt's "unjustifiable severity" in the government of his school. The selectmen, after investigation, voted, on August 15, 1786, that "it appears to them that Mr. Samuel Hunt . . . has repeatedly practiced undue severity in the Correction of several of the Children under his Tuition—That they Highly disapprove of the same, and that Master Hunt be Admonished therefore and cautioned against such Conduct in Future. . . ."

In August, 1789, some publications appeared detrimental to the moral character of Master Hunt. The selectmen, having advised him to clear himself "from the aspersions," recorded, on September 23, 1789, that "Master Hunt has done it so effectually, that his character now appears in as fair a point of light, as it did before said publications." A few years later, in 1796, another father, the Reverend Joseph Eckley, complained to the school committee against Master Hunt and his Usher, Mr. Charles Cutler, because of "the maltreatment" of his son. On March 4 of that year the father again complained, giving details regarding the punishment. These manuscript documents are still extant in the files of the committee.

The school committee, soon after their appointment in 1789, held a conference with the schoolmasters and made recommendations concerning discipline and corporal punishment. The report of the interview with Samuel Hunt follows:

[2] Samuel Hunt was Master of the North Grammar School from 1767 until 1775. On May 27, 1771, ten of his pupils "engaged" with ten other pupils "to observe the Rules of this School for three Weeks," with the understanding that each should receive "peaceably the punishment" given to his contracted partner.

. . . always endeavored to use as little corporal punishment as possible. After the revolution he endeavor'd to do wᵗʰ out any & did not introduce either ferrile or rod & made use of argument & persuasion to operate upon yᵉ ingenuous & meritorious boys—but eventually found it necessary to bring both the rod and ferrile into use—but supposes the former is not used much more than once in a twelvemonth. His rewards for attention & good performance are the letting them leave yᵉ school soner than usual. He sometimes endeavord to operate upon the boys by praising them & often found it produce good effects—but found degradations were much more lasting & operated longer upon their minds to produce good behaviour. If any boy is more inattentive to his lesson than other he is put back.

One of Samuel Hunt's pupils, Charles Winston Green, who entered the Latin School in 1794, receiving the Franklin medal for scholarship in 1798, has described his master's rigid discipline, in the following very amusing account:

Your allusions to your old Teachers, Masters Emerson and Snelling, . . . reminds me of good old Master Hunt's ferule and my escape from it. He whipped me often and hard, and hurt confoundedly. One day I could not help crying bitterly. He called me up and seemed willing to console me. He said: "You know one Christopher Gore?" (afterwards Gov. Gore) "Yes, Sir." "He's a great man isn't he?" "Yes, Sir." "Do you know one Harrison Gray Otis?" "Yes, Sir." "He is a great man, is he not?" "Oh yes Sir," said I. "I whipped it into them both!" said Master Hunt. I replied, "guess you mean to make a plaguey great man of me." I was in a roaring passion, but the boys in the school laughed outright, and the old man smiled, and patted me on the head, and said, "Go to your seat, you rogue, I will not touch you again." And he never did.

It is only fair, in this connection, to hear Master Hunt's own defense. In the following rather pathetic letter, sent to Charles Bulfinch, chairman of the school committee, dated October 26, 1804, Mr. Hunt has left us this testimony:

That the Latin-Grammar School in this Town is not on such a respectable establishment, as the Town of Boston ought to support, has been for a long time my opinion, and I am happy, that the Committee are fully sensible of it, hoping that it may be the means of its regaining the rank it ought to hold in Society, and ever will when ancient learning is duly appreciated—but how or in what respect, is Mr. Hunt an obsticle to the melioration of its condition? Wherein is he deficient, either in the mode of his government or manner of tuition? Is it not possible, that you may have imbibed an erroneous opinion of Mr. Hunt's abilities to teach and govern?

Does not forty Year's experience rather increase than diminish his Respectability? Has he not given full proof of his ability to teach, when he has been lately been called upon to make use of Latin & Greek authors, not formerly read in our Schools? Does not the extraordinary success, he has met with, in the discharge of one of the most arduous duties, assigned to man, give him reason to hope for countenance & Support? Does not his long, his zealous, alass! too zealous services demand your solemn, your serious & deliberate Attention?

Will not a young, a numerous, a rising family, whose dependence is upon the daily exertions of their father, ever be a powerful stimulus to excite his unremitted Attention to duty? Will you not pause a moment before you deprive him of his usefulness by destroying the confidence of the Public in his talents? Is it not possible, that you should doubt, whether the step, you are contemplating, will not eventually prove injurious to the cause, you mean to serve?

These questions are humbly submitted, feeling confidence in their meeting your candid consideration, and your affording me all that aid and support which will by your influence secure my future usefulness and respectability. I am,

Gentlemen,
with the highest respect & esteem,
Your most humble Servant
SAMUEL HUNT

Charles Bulfinch, Esqr, Chairman of the School Committee.

It appears from the above records that Samuel Hunt did not have an easy time as Master of the Latin School. In justice to him it must be said that the town did not carry out its contract. He understood that he had a life appointment, on a good salary, with certain perquisites and house rent. A grant of money was substituted for his perquisites, but later his house was taken away. After some controversy with the school committee he left office in 1805. The town, on May 27, 1805, voted "to grant Master Hunt $2500 . . . to be in full of all demands against said town."

Mr. William Croswell, who in 1780 was appointed Usher in the Latin School under Master Hunt, also had a difficult experience with a parent, one Mr. Clark, but the selectmen this time upheld the Usher in his discipline. The story of this incident, as recorded in the *Selectmen's Minutes*, is very human and amusing, as well as tragic. Three sons of Mr. Clark, having behaved improperly, were corrected by the Usher, Mr. Croswell. The father, resenting the punishment, later entered the School and "insulted him before the Scholars by striking him." Both parties were required to appear before the selectmen, who agreed that the parent's behavior "had a direct tendency to destroy the influence of his Usher & the good order & Government of the Schools." The selectmen further ordered that the sons could not enter any of the public schools unless their father made a public apology at the Latin School in the presence of the scholars; however, no record of such an apology has been found. As late as April 10, 1782, the selectmen agreed to send a letter to each of the schoolmasters "relative to Mr. Clark's Children."

The next Master of the Latin School was William Biglow, who held the office from 1805 until 1814. His pupils have described him as hard and severe; the boys rebelled at his rule and resisted his authority. He, too, was reported to the school committee by one of the fathers, a Mr. Caleb Loring, who resented the severe flogging of his son.

Rufus Dawes, who entered the School in 1811, has described Master Biglow's government and dramatic methods of teaching, in the following very amusing account:

Somewhere about 1811, the public Latin School was under the charge of a man, whose soubriquet was "Sawney," an extremely original and eccentric character, who lorded it over four or five classes of the most intractable and turbulent fellows, sixty or seventy in number, that ever met together to have Latin and Greek hammered into them. . . .

"Well!" continues Sawney switching the air with his cane, "well, mutton-head, what does an active verb express?"

After a little delay—"I'll tell you what it expresses," he resumes, bringing the stick down upon the boy's haunches with decided emphasis, "it expresses an action and necessarily supposes an agent, (flourishing the cane, which descends again as before) and an object acted upon, As *castigo te*, I chastise thee; do you understand now, hey?"

"Yes, sir! yes, sir!" replies the boy, doing his best to get out of the way of the rattan. But Sawney is not disposed to let him off so.

"Now tell me when an active verb is also called transitive."

"I don't know, sir," drawls Bangs, doggedly.

"Don't you?" follows Sawney: "then I'll inform you. An active verb is called transitive, when the action passeth over (whack, whack) to the object. You (whack) are the object. I am (whack) the agent. Now take care how you go home and say, that I never taught you anything. Do you hear?" (whack)

In the same article Rufus Dawes has described the rebellion at the Latin School under a new tutor, in the absence of Mr. Biglow. Mr. Dawes testifies that the boys shot at the new tutor with popguns, and, during the recess, filling their pockets with stones, hurled them about the room "till the floor was like the upper part of a sea-beach."

Ralph Waldo Emerson, who entered the Latin School in 1812, has given us this account of a rebellion at the School under Master Biglow:

In Mr. William Biglow's reign the boys discovered his habit of drinking, and one day when he was giving orders to the boys on one side of the School there was a sudden shout on the opposite side. He turned around amazed to them, and instantly the boys on the eastern side roared aloud. I have never known any rebellion like this in the English Schools to surpass it. I think the School was immediately dismissed and I think Mr. Biglow never entered it again. I remember on the following morning the prayer was simply these words: "Father, forgive them, for they know not what they do."

In his *Essays*, however, Emerson has paid a tribute to his

Latin School days, testifying that "the regular course of studies, the years of academical and professional education, have not yielded me better facts than some idle books under the bench at the Latin School."

According to the *Letters and Journals of Samuel Gridley Howe*, edited by his daughter, Laura E. Richards, Samuel Howe entered the Boston Latin School in 1812, where he met with rough and cruel treatment.

The principal belonged to a class of headmasters now seldom met with, in this country at least, the class that gives pain for the pleasure of giving it. One day my father was called up to be feruled for some slight offence; and the master, probably seeing something not wholly submissive in the child's demeanor, told him that he was "going to make him cry." He did not succeed, though the little hand was beaten nearly to a jelly.[3]

Robert Treat Paine, who entered the School in 1813 under Master Biglow, has left us an account of his school days, in which he describes the "atrocious disorder" of the School. He tells us that one boy fired a pistol "under the form in the upper room in the new School-house, near the middle window on the side next Cook's Court."

In 1814 Master Biglow resigned his office and Benjamin A. Gould, then a senior at Harvard College, recommended by President Kirkland, was appointed to fill the sudden vacancy. He gave such satisfaction that he was continued as Master of the Latin School, and was allowed his degree from Harvard College. He remained the Master of the Latin School until 1828, when he resigned to go into business. His kind and just government gained the reverence and love of all who came under his discipline.

Ralph Waldo Emerson describes Mr. Gould's introduction to the School and his reception by the scholars as follows:

[3] Laura E. Richards, *Letters and Journals of Samuel Gridley Howe*, Vol. I, pp. 14-15. See also Laura E. Richards, *Samuel Gridley Howe*, published by D. Appleton-Century Company.

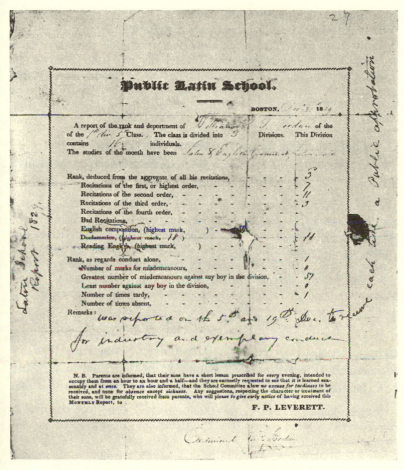

A Latin School Report Card of 1829
Report card of William Hamilton Stewart Jordan, who entered the Boston
Latin School in 1829.
*Reduced from the original in the possession of the Boston Latin School, by courtesy of the
Boston Latin School Association.*

The School Committee, Mr. Bulfinch, the famous architect who built our State House and the Capitol at Washington, Mr. Thacher, Mr. Wells, and the rest of the Committee if there were more, or their friends, came to school and introduced Mr. Benjamin Gould as the new Master. Mr. Thacher addressed us, and expressed every confidence in the high merit of Mr. Gould as a scholar and a gentleman, and congratulated the boys upon his appointment. As soon as the Committee took their hats and turned from the door, the boys began to buzz their opinions of the new Master in low tones. Mr. Gould turned towards them and lifted his finger to command silence, which was instantly accorded, and from that moment he ruled. He was an excellent Master, and loved a good scholar and waked his ambition.

The Reverend James Freeman Clarke, once minister of the Church of the Disciples in Boston, has described his Latin School days under Master Gould:

I am sure I have every reason to be grateful to the Latin School and its Masters for what they did for me, for the influence they have exerted on my life. I am sure the benefits of the public school can hardly be overrated. I was a poor, puny, insignificant child when I went to the Latin School, brought up at home, knowing nothing about boys; but I soon learned a great deal about them. Good Master Gould used to flog us in a noble way, but it was over very soon.[4]

The ferule was hard medicine, but it was apparently effective at times. The records testify that our ancestors literally believed that "Foolishness is bound up in the heart of a child; but the rod of correction shall drive it far from him."

[4] From James Freeman Clarke's *Autobiography, Diary and Correspondence*, edited by Edward Everett Hale, by permission of Houghton Mifflin Company, publishers.

CHAPTER V

BIOGRAPHICAL SKETCHES OF THE MASTERS AND USHERS
OF THE BOSTON LATIN SCHOOL

> Wisdom is the principal thing; therefore get wisdom: and with
> all thy getting get understanding.
>
> —*Proverbs*: 4:7.

THE history of the School is, in a certain sense, the history
of the Masters.[1] It is significant to note, as a testimony of
long-continued service, that in three hundred years the Boston
Latin School has had only twenty-one Head Masters.

The Boston Latin School Association, in 1886, published
a *Catalogue of the Boston Public Latin School, with an Historical Sketch,* prepared by Henry F. Jenks. This work, based
largely on the original sources, represents a long and painstaking collection of materials relating to the School. In this
same year, the *Sixteenth Report of the Boston Record Commissioners* was published. Since that time twenty-three more
reports have been issued. In these *Town Records* and *Selectmen's Minutes* the writer has found many additional references which have enabled her to revise the list of Masters and
Ushers of the Boston Latin School, with their respective dates
in office.

REVISED LIST OF THE MASTERS FROM 1635 TO 1935

PHILEMON PORMORT, 1635(?)-1638(?)

On April 13, 1635 [O.S.], the town of Boston voted,
"Likewise it was then generally agreed upon y^t o^r brother
Mr Philemon Pormort shalbe intreated to become schole-

---

[1] See Appendix XXXI for the teaching staff from 1635 to 1935.

master for the teaching & nourtering of children wth us."[2]
Although there is no extant record whether or not Pormort
accepted, there is indirect evidence that he did accept.[3] Pormort[4] came to Boston from Alford, England, in 1634; on
August 28, 1634, he united with the First Church; on May 6,
1635, he was admitted a freeman; and on January 8, 1638,
he was allotted thirty acres of land at Muddy River [now
Brookline]. There is no record of the year he left office, but,
in 1638, when the Reverend John Wheelwright led a colony
of the friends and sympathizers of Mrs. Anne Hutchinson to
settle the town of Exeter, New Hampshire, Mr. Pormort enrolled himself with that colony. Both Mrs. Anne Hutchinson
and Philemon Pormort came from the same town in England.
There is no record of his death, but he died before 1656, as
is evidenced by a record of the marriage of Elizabeth, daughter "of the late Philemon Pormorte of Boston."

DANIEL MAUDE, 1636-1643(?)

On August 12, 1636, the town clerk recorded in the back
of the *Town Records*:[5] "At a general meeting of the richer

[2] See page 7 for a facsimile of this manuscript record.

[3] On August 12, 1636, at a "general meeting of the richer inhabitants,"
forty-five persons subscribed between forty and fifty pounds "towards the
maintenance of a free school master. . . . M^r. Danyel Maud being now also
chosen thereunto." The word "also" may possibly indicate that Mr. Pormort
was continued in the School or it may connote that the richer inhabitants
not only voted to support the School but also voted to appoint the Master.

[4] See Rev. Charles H. Purmort, *Purmort Genealogy*, published by the
Homestead Company, Des Moines, Iowa, in 1907. Philemon Pormort is recorded as "under age" in the year 1603. He married Susan Bellingham in
1627.

[5] See page 89 for facsimile of manuscript record. See also Appendix XXIV
for the printed document, as transcribed by the Boston Record Commissioners.
The total sum cannot be accurately determined because of the incompleteness and the illegibility of the record. Experts in chirography disagree as to
whether Richard Bellingham contributed ten pounds, eleven shillings, or forty
shillings. The amounts contributed by William Brenton, Nicholis Willys,
William Hudson, and Mr. Cotton [*sic*] were not listed.

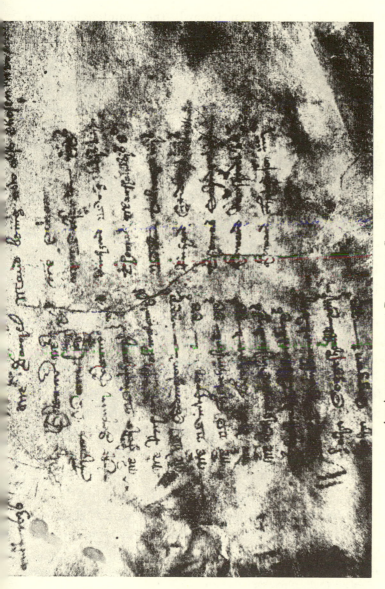

An Appointment and Record of Contributions

Facsimile of part of page of *Boston Records, 1634-1660*, dated August 12, 1636, containing the appointment of Daniel Maude and some of the voluntary contributions of the "richer inhabitants."

From the original in the office of the City Clerk, City Hall, Boston, by courtesy of Mayor Frederick W. Mansfield.

inhabitants there was given towards the maintenance of a free school master for the youth with us, Mr. Danyel Maud being now also chosen thereunto: . . ." Daniel Maude[6] (1586-1655) was graduated from Emmanuel College, Cambridge, in 1606/7, and in 1610 he received the degree of M.A. from the University. This education would well qualify him to teach Latin and Greek. The word "also," in the above record, may possibly indicate that Mr. Pormort was continued in the School, probably to teach the elementary subjects. The records show that Mr. Maude left office in 1643, when he went to Dover, New Hampshire, to be the minister of the church in that town. He died in Dover on July 3, 1655.

JOHN WOODBRIDGE, 1643(?)- (?)

There is no definite record of the appointment of Mr. Woodbridge, but the following record testifies that he was in office in 1643: "This 2d of 10th mo., 1644. . . . Its ordered that the Constables shall pay unto Deacon Eliot for the use of mr Woodbridge eight pounds due to him for keeping the Schoole the Last yeare." There is no definite record of the year he left office. He is supposed to have been the same as the John Woodbridge[7] who was ordained the first minister of Andover about 1645. He was born in Stanton in 1613, probably attended Magdalen Hall, came to New England in 1633/34, and died on March 17, 1695.

ROBERT WOODMANCY, 1649/50 (?)-1667(?)

On March 11, 1649/50, the town recorded: "It is alsoe agreed on that Mr. Woodmansey, the Schoolmaster, shall have fiftye pounds per annum for his teachinge the schollers, and

---

[6] See Henry F. Jenks's *Catalogue of the Boston Public Latin School*, Part I, pp. 19-22, and Part II, pp. 3-4. See also Samuel Eliot Morison, *The Founding of Harvard College*, p. 389.

[7] See Henry F. Jenks, *op. cit.*, Part I, p. 22, and Part II, p. 4. See also Samuel Eliot Morison, *op. cit.*, pp. 409-10.

BENJAMIN TOMPSON WAS MASTER FROM 1667 TO 1670.

-Benj. Tompson-

EZEKIEL CHEEVER WAS MASTER FROM 1670 TO 1708.

Ezekiel Cheever

NATHANIEL WILLIAMS WAS USHER FROM 1703 TO 1708 AND MASTER FROM 1708 TO 1734.

Nathl. Williams

JOHN LOVELL WAS USHER FROM 1729 TO 1734 AND MASTER FROM 1734 TO 1775.

Johne Lovell

DANIEL HENCHMAN WAS USHER FROM 1666 TO 1670.

Henchman.

JAMES LOVELL WAS USHER FROM 1760 TO 1775.

James Lovell

AUTOGRAPHS OF MASTERS AND USHERS OF THE BOSTON LATIN SCHOOL
From Justin Winsor's *The Memorial History of Boston.*

his proportion to be made up by ratte." Robert Woodmancy[8] (?-1667) was graduated from Magdalene College, Cambridge, in 1612/13, and in 1616 he received the degree of M.A. from the University. He came to New England in 1635, settled in Ipswich, and later moved to Boston in 1644. It appears that he probably held the position as Master of the Latin School until shortly before his death on August 13, 1667.

[8] See Henry F. Jenks, *op. cit.*, Part I, pp. 22-23, and Part II, p. 4. See also Samuel Eliot Morison, *op. cit.*, p. 410.

On March 14, 1669/70, the town voted to allow Mrs. Margeret Woodmansey [*sic*] eight pounds per year for house rent "dureinge her widdowhood . . . if she remoueth from the schoole house."

BENJAMIN TOMPSON, 1667-1670/71

Benjamin Tompson[9] (1642-1714) was born in Braintree, Massachusetts, and was graduated from Harvard College in 1662. He was appointed Master of the Latin School on August 26, 1667, when the selectmen voted that Mr. Hull "agree for tearmes, what to allow hime p. Annū." Mr. Tompson was also a preacher, physician, and the first native poet[10] of New England. On December 29, 1670, the selectmen appointed Ezekiel Cheever the Master and invited Mr. Tompson "to be an assistant." Benjamin Tompson accepted "a call to Charlestowne" on January 3, 1670/71, and resigned from the Boston Latin School on January 6 of that year.[11] He then taught at Charlestown and later at Braintree. In 1700 he became Master of the Latin Grammar School in Roxbury. He died on April 13, 1714.

EZEKIEL CHEEVER, 1670/71-1708

Ezekiel Cheever [12] (1614/15-1708) was born in London on January 25, 1614/15. He was admitted to Emmanuel Col-

[9] See Henry F. Jenks, *op. cit.*, Part I, pp. 23-24, and Part II, p. 4. See also Samuel Eliot Morison, *op. cit.*, p. 402.

[10] See page 93 for facsimile of a broadside poem, entitled *The Grammarians Funeral*, written by Benjamin Tompson. See *Collections of the Massachusetts Historical Society*, Fourth Series, Vol. VIII, p. 635, for a letter of Benjamin Tompson addressed to the Reverend Increase Mather. [The writer is indebted to Henry F. Jenks's *Catalogue* for information concerning this document.]

[11] See page 94 for facsimile of this manuscript record.

[12] See Henry F. Jenks, *op. cit.*, Part I, pp. 24-31, and Part II, p. 5. See also Samuel Eliot Morison, *op. cit.*, p. 371. See also Robert Francis Seybolt, *op. cit.*, p. 14. According to the *Dictionary of American Biography*, edited by Dumas Malone and published by Charles Scribner's Sons, Ezekiel Cheever was born on January 25, 1614/15. Contemporary historians disagree as to the date of his birth.

The Grammarians Funeral.

OR,

An ELEGY composed upon the Death of Mr. *John Woodmancy,*
formerly a School-Master in *Boston* : But now Published upon
the DEATH of the Venerable

Mr. Ezekiel Chevers,

The late and famous School-Master of *Boston* in *New-England* ; Who Departed this Life the
Twenty-first of *August* 1 7 0 8. Early in the Morning. In the Ninety-fourth Year of his Age.

EIghtParts of *Speech* thisDay wear *MourningGowns*
Declin'd *Verbs, Pronouns, Participles, Nouns.*
And not declined, *Adverbs* and *Conjunctions,*
In *Lillies* : orch they stand to do their functions.
With *Prepofition* ; but the most affection
Was still observed in the *Interjection.*
The *Subftantive* seeming the limbed best,
Would set an hand to bear him to his Rest.
The *Adjective* with very grief did say,
Hold me by strength, or I shall faint away.
The Clouds of Tears did over-caft their faces,
Yea all were in most lamentable *Cafes.*
The five *Decleufions* did the Work decline,
And *Told* the *Prenoun Tu,* The work is thine :
But in this cafe those have no call to go
That want the *Vocative,* and can't fay O!
The *Pronouns* faid that if the *Nouns* were there,
There was no need of them, they might them fpare :
But for the fake of *Emphafis* they would,
In their Difcretion do what ere they could.
Great honour was confer'd on *Conjugations,*
They were to follow next to the *Relations.*
Amo did love him beft, and *Doceo* might
Alledge he was his Glory and Delight.
But *Lego* faid by me he got his skill,
And therefore next the *Herfe* I follow will.
Audio faid little, hearing them fo hot,
Yet knew by him much Learning he had got.
O *Verbs* the *Active* were, Or *Paffive* fure,
Sum to be *Neuter* could not well endure:
But this was common to them all to Moan
Their load of grief they could not foon *Depone.*
A doleful Day for *Verbs,* they look fo *moody,*
They drove Spectators to a Mournful Study.
The *Verbs* irregular, 'twas thought by fome,
Would break no rule, if they were pleas'd to come.
Gaudeo could not be found ; fearing difgrace
He had with-drawn, fent *Mæreo* in his Place.
Poffum did to the utmoft he was able,
And bore as Stout as if he'd been A *Table.*

Volo was willing, *Nolo* fome-what ftout,
But *Malo* rather chofe, not to ftand out.
Poffum and *Volo* wifh'd all might afford
Their help, but had not an *Imperative Word.*
Edo from Service would by no means Swerve,
Rather than fail, he thought the *Cakes* to Serve.
Fio was taken in a fit, and faid,
By him a Mournful *POEM* fhould be made.
Fero was willing for to bear a part,
Altho' he did it with an aking heart.
Feror excus'd, with grief he was fo Torn,
He could not bear, he needed to be born.
Such *Nouns* and *Verbs* as we defective find,
No *Grammar* Rule did their attendance bind.
They were excepted, and exempted hence,
But *Supines,* all did blame for negligence.
Verbs Offspring, *Participles* hand-in-hand,
Follow, and by the fame direction ftand :
The reft Promifcuoufly did croud and cumber,
Such Multitudes of each, they wanted Number.
Next to the Corps to make th' attendance even,
Jove, Mercury, Apollo came from heaven.
And *Virgil, Cato,* gods, men, Rivers, Winds,
With *Elegies,* Tears, Sighs, came in their kinds
Ovid from *Pontus* haft's Apparrell'd thus,
In Exile-weeds bringing *De Triftibus :*
And *Homer* fure had been among the Rout,
But that the Stories fay his Eyes were out.
Queens, Cities, Countries, Iflands, Come
All Trees, Birds, Fifhes, and each Word in *Um.*
What *Syntax* here can you expect to find ?
Where each one bears fuch difcompofed mind.
Figures of Diction and Conftruction,
Do little : Yet ftand fadly looking on.
That fuch a Train may in their motion *chord,*
Profodia gives the meafure Word for Word.

Sic Mæftus Cecinit,

Benj. Tompfon.

A BROADSIDE

Facsimile of broadside, entitled *The Grammarians Funeral*, written by Benjamin Tompson.

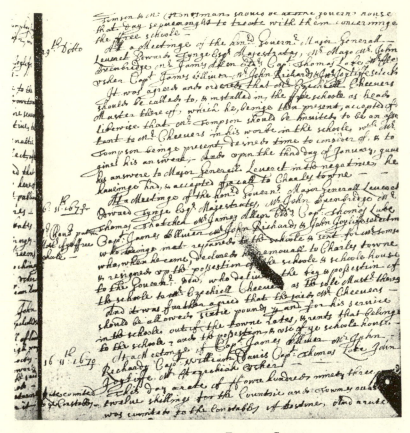

THE APPOINTMENT OF EZEKIEL CHEEVER

Reduced facsimile of part of page of *Boston Records, 1660-1701*, dated "29th of the 10th month, 1670," containing the vote of the selectmen to appoint Ezekiel Cheever the Master of the Boston Latin School, followed by the vote of "6:11th:1670/1" to allow Ezekiel Cheever sixty pounds per annum for his service.

From the original in the office of the City Clerk, City Hall, Boston, by courtesy of Mayor Frederick W. Mansfield.

lege, Cambridge, on January 12, 1632/33, but he was not graduated. He came to Boston, New England, in June, 1637. The next year he settled in New Haven, where he was appointed Master of the Grammar School. Here he remained until 1650, when he became Master of the school in Ipswich. Eleven years later, in 1661, he was appointed Master of the school in Charlestown. The first mention of the celebrated Ezekiel Cheever, in the Boston *Town Records,* is on December 22, 1670, when the selectmen order that "M^r. Ezachiell Cheuers, M^r. Thomson and M^r. Hinksman should be at the Gouern^rs. house that day seauen-night to treate with them concerninge the free schoole." On December 29, one week later, the selectmen appointed Ezekiel Cheever the Master and, on January 6, 1670/71, he was installed and received "the key & possestion of the schoole."[13] He continued as Master of the Latin School for thirty-eight years, until the illness which preceded his death on August 21, 1708. The Reverend Cotton Mather preached the funeral sermon.[14]

Cheever was the author of *Scripture Prophecies Explained,* which was published in 1757. He has also been credited, by some historians, with the authorship of the famous Latin grammar, popularly known for over a century as Cheever's *Accidence.*[15]

[13] See page 94 for a facsimile of this manuscript record.

[14] The Reverend Cotton Mather's funeral sermon on Ezekiel Cheever, entitled *Corderius Americanus,* was printed in Boston in 1708. Cotton Mather testifies: "He [Cheever] was not a Meer Grammarian; yet he was a Pure One. And let no Envy Misconstrue it, if I say, It was noted, that when Scholars came to be Admitted into the Colledge, they who came from the Cheeverian Education, were generally the most unexceptionable. What Exception shall be made, Let it fall upon him, that is now speaking of it."

[15] As a matter of fact the earliest edition was not published until 1709, one year after Cheever's death. The name of the author does not appear on the title-page. The title suggests, however, that the printed textbook was "Abbridg'd and Compiled" from Cheever's manuscript *Accidence.* The manuscript *Accidence* is not extant. Evidence that Cheever was not the author of the published *Accidence* in its final form is the following statement on the title-page of the 1724 edition: "The Third Edition revised and corrected by the Author." Ezekiel Cheever had been dead for sixteen years! For a discussion of possible authors see p. 316 *infra.*

NATHANIEL WILLIAMS, 1708-1734

After the death of Ezekiel Cheever in 1708, Mr. Nathaniel Williams[16] (1675-1738/39), who had been the Usher of the School since 1703 and acting Master during Mr. Cheever's illness, was officially appointed the Master. He perhaps entered the Boston Latin School in 1682, was graduated from Harvard College in 1693, received the degree of A.M. in 1696, and, in 1698, was ordained as an evangelist for one of the islands of the West Indies. Here he studied medicine and, after his return to Boston, he practised as a physician and a teacher.

On September 6, 1708, the selectmen ordered "that mr Nathll Williams be invited to remove into ye House where mr Cheever dwelt." That the town appreciated Mr. Williams's quality of teaching is evidenced by the following committee report presented to the town on March 13, 1709/10: "Wee have discoursed wth mr Williams the present master of whose qualifications and fitness for that imployment we take for granted every body must be abundantly Satisfied." On March 13, 1733/34, he informed the selectmen "that he intends in a short time to resign his Care of the South Grammar School." On December 10, 1735, the selectmen granted him a license to open a private school. He died on January 10, 1738/39.[17]

[16] See Henry F. Jenks, *op. cit.*, Part I, pp. 31-34, and Part II, p. 6 and p. 280. See Thomas Prince, *A Funeral Sermon on the Rev. Nathanael Williams* and the *Boston Weekly News-Letter*, from Thursday, Jan. 5th, to Thursday, Jan. 12th, 1738. [The writer is indebted to Henry F. Jenks's *Catalogue* for information concerning these two sources.] See also Robert Francis Seybolt, *op. cit.*, pp. 14-15. Professor Seybolt states: "Williams was chosen Rector (president) of Yale, but declined the honor."

[17] According to Henry F. Jenks's *Catalogue*, he died January 15, 1738. According to the *Boston Weekly News-Letter*, from Thursday, Jan. 5th, to Thursday, Jan. 12th, 1738 [O.S.], he died "Last Tuesday in the afternoon."

JOHN LOVELL
The original, by Smibert, hangs in Memorial Hall, Harvard University.
From Justin Winsor's *The Memorial History of Boston.*

JOHN LOVELL, 1734-1775

John Lovell[18] (1710-1778) was appointed the Master on May 21, 1734. He probably entered the Boston Latin School as a pupil in 1717, was graduated from Harvard College in 1728, and received the degree of A.M. in 1731. Since 1728/29 he had been the Usher of the School. He continued to be

---

[18] See Henry F. Jenks's *Catalogue,* Part I, pp. 35-41, and Part II, p. 6. See also the *Dictionary of American Biography,* edited by Dumas Malone and published by Charles Scribner's Sons.

PAGE OF JAMES LOVELL'S CATALOGUE OF STUDENTS OF THE BOSTON LATIN SCHOOL

John Lovell was Master of the School from 1734 to 1775 and James Lovell, his son, was Usher from 1760 to 1775. In the right column, note the name of Samuel Adams who "left school July 1766." This Samuel Adams, who entered the School in 1759, was the son of the distinguished patriot, Samuel Adams.

Reduced from the original in the possession of the Boston Latin School, by courtesy of the Boston Latin School Association.

the Master for over forty years, closing the School on April 19, 1775, the day of the battle of Lexington, with the following words: "War's begun—School's done. *Deponite libros*." He delivered the public address in Faneuil Hall, on March 14, 1742, at the town meeting called on occasion of the death of Peter Faneuil. He was a rigid loyalist during the Revolutionary War and in March, 1776, he went with the British troops to Halifax, where he died in 1778. His son, James Lovell (1737-1815), a strong patriot, was appointed Usher of the School in 1760.

SAMUEL HUNT, 1776-1805

Samuel Hunt[19] (1745-1816), who had been the Master of the North Grammar School since 1767, was appointed the Master of the South Grammar School [Boston Latin School] on June 5, 1776, when the School was re-opened after the evacuation of Boston by the British troops. He probably entered the Boston Latin School as a pupil in 1753, was graduated from Harvard College in 1765, and received the degree of A.M. in 1768. As a teacher he was very conscientious but perhaps too rigid in his discipline. During his mastership the "New System of Education of 1789" was adopted. He left office in 1805, receiving a pension from the town, after which he retired to Watertown, where for several years he educated private pupils for college. In 1816 he went to Lexington, Kentucky, where he died on October 8, 1816.

SAMUEL COOPER THACHER
JANUARY, 1805-APRIL, 1805

Samuel Cooper Thacher, who had been the Usher of the Boston Latin School since his graduation from Harvard College in 1804, was the acting Master from January to April 15, 1805. He was later appointed minister of the New South Church, Boston, and was a fellow of Harvard College.

[19] See Henry F. Jenks's *Catalogue*, Part I, pp. 41-45, and Part II, p. 7.

WILLIAM BIGLOW

William Biglow was Master of the Boston Latin School from 1805 to 1814.

From the original in the possession of the Essex Institute, Salem.

WILLIAM BIGLOW, 1805-1814

William Biglow[20] (1773-1844) was appointed the Master
on April 15, 1805. He was graduated from Harvard College

[20] See Henry F. Jenks's *Catalogue,* Part I, pp. 45-50, and Part II, p. 8.

in 1794 and received the degree of A.M. in 1804. Previous to this appointment he taught school in Salem. Besides his teaching he preached occasionally and wrote for periodicals. In 1801 he published a textbook entitled *Introduction to the Making of Latin*. He continued as Master of the Boston Latin School for nine years, resigning in March, 1814. Afterwards he taught a village school in Maine and later was proof reader in the University Printing Office, Cambridge. He also taught school in Cambridge, where Oliver Wendell Holmes was one of his pupils. He died on January 12, 1844.

NATHANIEL KEMBLE GREENWOOD OLIVER, MARCH, 1814-MAY, 1814

Nathaniel Kemble Greenwood Oliver, who had been the Usher of the Boston Latin School since his graduation from Harvard College in 1809, was the acting Master from March to May, 1814. He died in 1832.

BENJAMIN APTHORP GOULD, 1814-1828

Benjamin Apthorp Gould[21] (1787-1859), a member of the graduating class of Harvard College in 1814, was appointed the Master of the Boston Latin School in May, 1814, to fill a sudden vacancy. President Kirkland of Harvard College allowed him his A.B. degree in 1814, and he received the degree of A.M. in 1817. Under his mastership the curriculum was extended from a four-year course, which had been adopted in 1789, to a five-year course. Mr. Gould published six numbers of *The Prize Book*, from 1820 to 1826, published an edition of Alexander Adam's *Latin Grammar* in 1825, and also published annotated editions of Ovid, Virgil, and Horace, which were the standard editions for several years. His kind and just government gained the love and respect of all his pupils. Mr. Gould began the practice of declamations by the

---

[21] See Henry F. Jenks's *Catalogue*, Part I, pp. 50-52, and Part II, p. 8. The portrait of Mr. Gould by Albert Gallatin Hoit is in the Assembly Hall of the School.

students, introduced the system of "misdemeanor marks," and issued report cards to be sent to the parents. He continued as Master for fourteen years, resigning in 1828 because of poor health. In 1830 he became a shipowner in the China and East Indian importing business. He died in Boston on October 24, 1859.

FREDERIC PERCIVAL LEVERETT
MAY, 1828-SEPTEMBER, 1831

Frederic Percival Leverett[22] (1803-1836) was appointed the Master of the Boston Latin School in May, 1828. He was graduated from the School in 1817, was graduated from Harvard College in 1821, and received the degree of A.M. in 1824. He had been the Usher of the Boston Latin School from 1821 to 1824 and the Sub-Master from 1824 to 1828. He was a remarkable student of Latin, Greek, and mathematics. He edited the *Latin Lexicon,* a monumental piece of work, bearing his name, and also edited the *Satires of Juvenal* and the *Commentaries of Caesar,* with excellent notes. In the course of study for 1860, Leverett's *Latin Lexicon* (or Gardner's *Abridgment* of the same) is listed as a required book of reference. After resigning his position in 1831, he established a school for boys in Boston. He died on October 5, 1836.

CHARLES KNAPP DILLAWAY
SEPTEMBER, 1831-NOVEMBER, 1836

Charles Knapp Dillaway[23] (1804-1889) was appointed the Master of the Boston Latin School in 1831. He was graduated from the School in 1821, was graduated from Harvard College in 1825, and received the degree of A.M. in

[22] *Ibid.,* Part I, pp. 52-54, and Part II, p. 9.
[23] See Henry F. Jenks's *Catalogue,* Part I, pp. 53-54, and Part II, p. 9. The portrait of Mr. Dillaway by J. Harvey Young is in the Assembly Hall of the School.

CHARLES KNAPP DILLAWAY

Charles Knapp Dillaway was Master of the Boston Latin School from 1831 to 1836.

By courtesy of the Boston Latin School Association.

1829. He had been the Usher of the School from 1827 to 1830 and Sub-Master from 1830 to 1831. He published the following textbooks: Eight volumes of Cicero; Plautus; Terence; Quintilian; Tacitus; Erasmus's *Colloquies;* and *Roman Antiquities and Ancient Mythology.* He assisted John Pickering in preparing his *Greek Lexicon* and assisted Joseph Emerson Worcester in his *English Dictionary.* He resigned his position as Master in 1836, owing to poor health, and for several years afterwards taught a private school for boys in Boston and, later, for young ladies in Roxbury. In 1860 he was elected the president of the Boston Latin School Association. He died in Roxbury on May 2, 1889.

FREDERIC PERCIVAL LEVERETT

After the resignation of Mr. Dillaway, Mr. Leverett was reappointed the Master in August, 1836. He died on October

EPES SARGENT DIXWELL

Epes Sargent Dixwell was Master of the Boston Latin School from 1836
to 1851.

By courtesy of the Boston Latin School Association.

5, 1836, soon after his reappointment, before assuming the
office. He was succeeded by Mr. Epes Sargent Dixwell.

EPES SARGENT DIXWELL, 1836-1851

Epes Sargent Dixwell[24] (1807-1899) was appointed the
Master of the Boston Latin School on November 8, 1836,
and was inducted into office on December 5, 1836. He was
graduated from the School in 1823 and from Harvard College
in 1827. He received the degree of A.M. in 1830. Previous

[24] See Henry F. Jenks's *Catalogue,* Part I, pp. 54-55, and Part II, p. 9.
The writer is indebted to Mary Dixwell Wigglesworth (Mrs. George Wigglesworth), the youngest daughter of Epes Sargent Dixwell, for permission to
quote from her father's unpublished sketch of his life written for his children.
The portrait of Mr. Dixwell by Mr. H. O. Walker is in the Assembly Hall
of the School.

to this appointment he had been an Usher of the English High School from 1827 to October, 1828, and afterwards a Sub-Master of the Boston Latin School until the summer of 1830, when, according to his unpublished sketch, he resigned and entered his name "as student at Law in the office of C. G. Loring and Charles Jackson." He was admitted to the bar in 1833. He resigned from the Boston Latin School in 1851, when "a law was passed by both chambers of the City Council requiring all those who received salaries from the city to reside within its precincts." He then opened a private Latin School for boys in Boston on Boylston Place, leading from Boylston Street. This was very successful and continued until 1872. He died in Cambridge on December 1, 1899. Mr. Dixwell was a member of the American Academy of Arts and Sciences and of other learned bodies. In 1844 he founded the Boston Latin School Association.

FRANCIS GARDNER, 1851-1876

Francis Gardner[25] (1812-1876) was appointed the Master of the Boston Latin School in 1851. He was graduated from the School in 1827, and from Harvard College in 1831; he received the degree of A.M. from Harvard College in 1834 and the degree of LL.D. from Williams College in 1866. Ever since his graduation from Harvard College he had been connected with the Boston Latin School, first as Usher from 1831 to 1836, and afterwards as a Sub-Master from 1836 to 1850. He resigned in 1850 and then returned to the School in 1851 after a year abroad. He was the editor of an *Abridgment of Leverett's Latin Lexicon* and associate editor of a series of Latin School Classics. In 1867 the Master became the Head Master and the teachers were raised to the grade of Masters. Mr. Augustine Milton Gay, the Sub-Master under Dr. Gardner, took charge of the School in November, 1875, as acting Head Master, during Dr. Gardner's illness.

[25] See Henry F. Jenks's *Catalogue*, Part I, pp. 55-58, and Part II, p. 10.

FRANCIS GARDNER
Francis Gardner was Master of the Boston Latin School from 1851 to 1876.
By courtesy of the Boston Latin School Association.

Dr. Gardner died two months later, on January 10, 1876. Wendell Phillips, a classmate of Francis Gardner at the Latin School, has recorded the following tribute to Gardner: "He was, from mere boyhood and life long, eminently a just man, only claiming fair play, and more than willing to allow it to others. I never knew the time, even in his boyhood, when he did not detest or despise a sham." Dr. Edward Southworth Hawes, who entered the School in 1870, has recorded this testimony of his Master: "Francis Gardner was Head Master, a remarkable man, terrifying to me as a little boy (I entered the school before I was ten) austere in appearance, gruff in manner, but with a kindly human heart showing sometimes through his rough husk."

AUGUSTINE MILTON GAY
JUNE, 1876-NOVEMBER, 1876

Augustine Milton Gay[26] (1827-1876) received the degree of A.B. from Amherst College in 1850 and the degree of A.M. in 1853. He became the Head Master of the Charlestown High School and later conducted a private school for girls in Louisburg Square, Boston. He was appointed an Usher of the Boston Latin School in 1865, a Master in 1867, and the Head Master in June, 1876. He was taken ill soon after the close of the summer vacation and died suddenly on November 3, 1876. He was an associate editor of several Latin textbooks, of which the best known are the Latin School Series, of two volumes, containing extracts from Phædrus, Justin, Nepos, Ovid, Curtius, and Cicero.

MOSES MERRILL, 1877-1901

Moses Merrill[27] (1833-1902), a man of high character and strong moral influence, was appointed the Head Master in June, 1877, having been acting Head Master for six months following the death of Mr. Gay in 1876. He was graduated from Harvard College in 1856, received the degree of A.M. in 1859, and the honorary degree of Ph.D. from Amherst College in 1880. Previous to his appointment as Head Master he had been an Usher from 1858 to 1867, a Sub-Master from 1867 to 1869, and a Master from 1869 to 1876. He resigned because of ill health in December, 1901. Arthur Irving Fiske, then a Master of the School, was appointed acting Head Master. Dr. Merrill died in Boston on April 26, 1902.

[26] See Henry F. Jenks's *Catalogue,* Part I, p. 58, and Part II, p. 10.
[27] See *Ibid.,* Part I, p. 58, and Part II, p. 10.

MOSES MERRILL

By courtesy of the Boston Latin School Association.

ARTHUR IRVING FISKE
By courtesy of the Boston Latin School Association.

ARTHUR IRVING FISKE, 1902-1910

Arthur Irving Fiske[28] (1848-1910) was officially appointed Head Master of the Boston Latin School on January 6, 1902. He was graduated from Harvard College in 1869, received the degree of A.M. in 1872, and the degree of Litt.D. from Williams College in 1908. Previous to his appointment as Head Master he had been a Master from 1873 to 1901, and acting Head Master from December, 1901, to 1902. He continued as Head Master from 1902 until his resignation in 1910. He died in Portland, Connecticut, on February 18, 1910, soon after his resignation. Dr. Fiske was distinguished as a Greek scholar and was loved and respected by his pupils.

[28] The writer is indebted to Mr. Lee J. Dunn, librarian of the Boston Latin School, for information concerning the lives of the recent Masters. The portrait of Arthur Irving Fiske by Wilton Lockwood is in the Assembly Hall of the School.

HENRY PENNYPACKER, 1910-1920

Henry Pennypacker[29] (1866-1934), who was graduated from Harvard College in 1888, was appointed Head Master of the Boston Latin School in 1910. Previous to this appointment he had been a Junior Master from 1891 to 1905 and a Master from 1905 to 1909. He was acting Head Master for the year 1909-1910. He continued as Head Master until 1920, when he was appointed Chairman of the Committee on Admission of Harvard College. He died in 1934. Mr. Pennypacker was a very successful administrator and is held in loving remembrance by his pupils.

PATRICK THOMAS CAMPBELL, 1920-1929

Patrick Thomas Campbell[30] (1871—*ad multos annos*), "a second father to several generations of Latin School boys," was appointed Head Master of the Boston Latin School in 1920. He was graduated from the School in 1889 and from Harvard College in 1893. Previous to this appointment he had been a Junior Master of the School from 1897 to 1908, and a Master and head of the department of history from 1908 to 1920. He continued as Head Master from 1920 to 1929, when he was appointed assistant superintendent of the Boston public schools. Since 1931 he has been superintendent of the Boston public schools. In 1934 he received the honorary degree of Ed.D. from Colby University.

[29] The portrait of Mr. Pennypacker by W. W. Churchill is in the Assembly Hall of the School.

[30] The portrait of Mr. Campbell by H. E. Smith is in the Assembly Hall of the School.

HENRY PENNYPACKER
By courtesy of the Boston Latin School Association.

PATRICK THOMAS CAMPBELL

Photograph by Bachrach.

JOSEPH LAWRENCE POWERS
Photograph by J. E. Purdy and Co.

JOSEPH LAWRENCE POWERS
1929—*ad multos annos*

Joseph Lawrence Powers[31] (1878—*ad multos annos*) was appointed the Head Master of the Boston Latin School in 1929. He had been a pupil of the School from 1891 to 1895, was graduated from Boston College in 1899, and received the

[31] The portrait of Mr. Powers by C. B. Moulton is in the Assembly Hall of the School.

degree of A.M. in 1921. Previous to his appointment as Head Master he had been a Junior Master from 1906 to 1914, and a Master and head of the department of mathematics from 1914 to 1929. Mr. Powers continues to maintain the high standard of scholarship for which the School has long been distinguished.

Revised List[32] of the Ushers from 1645 to 1789

DANIEL HENCHMAN
1665/66-1668; 1669/70-1670/71

On March 26, 1665/66, the selectmen agreed with "Mr Dannell Hincheman for 40 £ p Annm to asist Mr Woodmancy in the grammer Schoole & teach Childere to wright, the Yeare to begine the 1th of March: 65/6."[33] In November, 1668, the General Court appointed Mr. Daniel Hinckman [sic], with three other gentlemen, to arrange about the location of the town [afterwards called Worcester] "about twelue miles westward from Marlborough, neare the road to Springfeild." He served again, from March 1, 1669/70, to March 1, 1670/71, according to the agreement of the selectmen, on November 27, 1671, to pay "Capt Daniell Hinksman £ 10. over & above his yeares sallery ending the first of March last as a gratuity from the towne for not haveing suffitient warning to provide otherwise for him selfe." He was a captain in King Philip's War, and later was appointed major.[34]

EZEKIEL LEWIS, 1699-1703 (?)

On May 8, 1699, the town voted "That the Selectmen shall agree wth Mr Ezekiel Lewis, for his Salary as an Assis-

---

[32] The writer has made several corrections and additions to Henry F. Jenks's *Catalogue of the Boston Public Latin School,* published in 1886.

[33] See page 115 for facsimile of manuscript record.

[34] See Henry F. Jenks's *Catalogue,* Part II, p. 16.

VOTE OF SELECTMEN TO APPOINT ASSISTANT

Reduced facsimile of part of page of *Boston Records, 1660-1701*, dated "26: 1: 1666," containing the following vote of the selectmen: "Agreed with Mr Dannell Hincheman for 40 £ p. Ann^m to asist Mr Woodmancy in the grammer Schoole & teach Childere to wright, the Yeare to begine the 1th of March: 65/6:"

From the original in the office of the City Clerk, City Hall, Boston, by courtesy of Mayor Frederick W. Mansfield.

tant to his Grandfather Mr Ezekiel Cheever in the Latine School, not exceeding 40^{ld}. p. year." On August 31, 1702, the selectmen voted: "M^r. Ezekiell Lewis is allowed £ 22. 10 s for his halfe years Sallery as an Assist^t to M^r. Cheever in the free School." It appears from the records that he probably left office in 1703 or earlier. The town on April 27, 1703, voted to have the selectmen "procure Some meet person to be an assistant to M^r. Ezekiell Chever."

NATHANIEL WILLIAMS, 1703-1708

Nathaniel Williams, a former pupil of the Boston Latin School and a graduate of Harvard College in 1693, was recommended as Usher of the School on May 13, 1703, was approved by the town on June 25, and began his services on July 12 of that year. On July 26 of this same year the selectmen voted "to Provide a desk & Seat in the Lattin School for Mr. Williams." After Ezekiel Cheever's death in 1708, Mr. Williams was appointed the Master.

EBENEZER THAYER, 1709(?)-1709/10(?)

Ebenezer Thayer, who was graduated from Harvard College in 1708, was appointed the Usher of the Boston Latin School probably in 1709. On December 19, 1709, the town voted to defray the charge of an assistant for the School until the March town meeting, at which time [March 13, 1709/10] the town voted "to Introduce an Usher into ye Sd School" and "to agree wth mr Thayer for his past Service in that worke." There is no further record of his service. In 1712 he was appointed pastor of the Second Church in Roxbury.

EDWARD WIGGLESWORTH, 1713(?)-1718/19(?)

Edward Wigglesworth, who was graduated from Harvard College in 1710, served as Usher earlier than October, 1713, as is evidenced by a certificate[35] of Nathaniel Williams, dated February 3, 1713/14, in the office of the city clerk, Boston. The only reference to his service at the School, in the *Town Records*, is the town vote of June 13, 1715, to add "Ten pounds p Annum to mr Wigglesworths Sallery as Usher of the

---

[35] The writer is indebted to Mr. T. Franklin Currier, assistant librarian of the Harvard College Library, for information concerning this certificate. Mr. Currier received the information from Mr. Grenville H. Norcross.

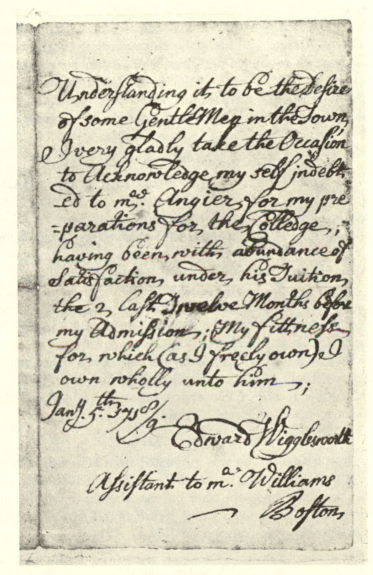

LETTER OF EDWARD WIGGLESWORTH, DATED JANUARY 5, 1718/19
By courtesy of the Harvard College Library.

Gramer School." A manuscript letter,[36] dated January 5, 1718/19, and signed "Edward Wigglesworth Assistant to m^r. Williams Boston," is the only extant record that Edward Wigglesworth continued as Usher of the Latin School as late as 1718/19, under the mastership of Nathaniel Williams. Edward Wigglesworth was the first occupant of the Hollis Professorship of Divinity at Harvard College and he was also a fellow of the college.

BENJAMIN GIBSON, 1720-1722(?)

Benjamin Gibson, who was graduated from Harvard College in 1719, was appointed Usher of the Latin School in 1720, according to the following record in Samuel Sewall's *Diary* under the date March 29, 1720: "The Inspectors of the Grammar Schools met at the Council-Chamber; Sewall, Davenport, Cooke, Savage, and with Mr. Williams the Master, approv'd of Mr. Benjamin Gibson, Bachelour, to be the Usher in School-street. Mr. White came in, and ratified what we had done. Dr. Clark told me he was for it, a little before the Meeting."[37] The next year, on March 14, 1720/21, the town voted to allow him "the Sum of fifty Pounds for his Services as Usher of the Gramer School. . . . Ending the Second of May next." There is no further record of his service, but on July 14, 1722, the selectmen appointed Joseph Green the Usher.

JOSEPH GREEN, 1722-1724

Joseph Green, who was graduated from Harvard College in 1720, was appointed Usher of the Latin School on July 14, 1722, "to Enter upon the Said busynes the Sixteenth of July Current." There is no further record of his service in the *Town Records*. He resigned on July 17, 1724.

[36] This letter, in the possession of the Harvard College Library, is a testimonial of Mr. Ames Angier's teaching ability. It is inclosed in a letter of Mr. Ames Angier, dated March 9, 1718/19, which he sent to the moderator of the town of Boston.

[37] The writer is indebted to Henry F. Jenks's *Catalogue*, Part I, p. 34, for information concerning this document.

SAMUEL DUNBAR, 1724-1727(?)

Samuel Dunbar, who was graduated from Harvard College in 1723, was "approved of by the Selectmen as Usher to m^r. Nath^ll. Williams" on September 12, 1724, having been recommended by the latter "from July 17th." There is no further record of his service, but he probably continued until October 17, 1727, when Jeremiah Gridley was appointed the Usher.

JEREMIAH GRIDLEY, 1727-1733/34(?)

Jeremiah Gridley, who was graduated from Harvard College in 1725, was appointed the Usher in 1727. The selectmen, on October 26, 1727, recorded: "M^r. Jeremiah Gridley is admitted Usher or asistant to m^r Nathan^ll Williams at the Gramer School from the 17th octo^r Instant." He continued as Usher probably until February 4, 1733/34, according to the following vote of the selectmen on January 9, 1733/34: "Upon a Motion of Mr. Nathanael Williams . . . for an Usher in the Room of Mr. Jer. Gridley Mr. Nathanael Oliver Junr . . . having been recommended . . . Voted, That the said Oliver be Usher . . . To Commence from ye 4th. Feb."

JOHN LOVELL, 1728/29-1734

John Lovell, who was graduated from Harvard College in 1728, was appointed Usher of the Latin School probably a few days after March 11, 1728/29,[38] when the town voted to allow "the Sum of Eighty Pounds for another Usher of the Said School, when A Sutable Person is Provided to the Satisfaction of the Selectmen as usual." On May 10, 1732, John Lovel [*sic*] presented a petition to the town at the "Publick Town Meeting." The next week, on May 17, the town voted that the consideration of John Lovell's petition "be Continued

---

[38] The regular town meeting, held on March 10, 1728/29, was adjourned "untill tomorrow-Morning at Eight of the Clock," at which time this vote was passed.

to the Next Meeting to be Debated." On July 28, of this year, the town voted "In Answar to the Petition of m^r John Lovell" to add twenty pounds to his salary "as one of the Ushers of the South Gramer School." On May 21, 1734, the town "by Written Votes" unanimously appointed John Lovell the Master of the School.

NATHANIEL OLIVER, JR., 1733/34-1734

Nathaniel Oliver, Jr., who was graduated from Harvard College in 1733, was appointed Usher by the selectmen on January 9, 1733/34, at a salary of eighty pounds per year "To Commence from ye 4th. Feb." He continued as Usher until September 10, 1734, according to the following vote of the selectmen on August 14, 1734: "Voted. That Mr. Samuel Gibson be accepted as Usher of the South Grammar School, in the room of mr. Nathanael Oliver jun^r. Who is to enter into that Service, the 10th. of Sept^t. next." On March 4, 1734/35, the selectmen licensed "Capt. Nathanael Oliver" to keep a school "for the teaching and Instructing of Children Or youth in Reading, Writing, Or any Other Science, agreeable to the Law of this Province made in the Eleventh year of Queen Anne."

SAMUEL GIBSON, 1734-1749/50

Samuel Gibson, who was graduated from Harvard College in 1730, was appointed Usher of the Latin School on August 14, 1734, "to enter into that Service, the 10th. of Sept^t. next." On March 11, 1734/35, Samuel Gibson petitioned for an increase of salary and the town voted to add twenty pounds "which will make his whole Salary to be One Hundred Pounds." On May 4, 1743, the town voted to add "Twenty five Pounds Old Tenor" to his salary "to Commence from his next Quarters Payment." On several occasions he petitioned for an

---

[39] The regular town meeting, held on March 12, 1749/50, was adjourned "to nine a Clock tomorrow morning," at which time this vote was passed.

increase in salary and finally, on March 13, 1749/50,[39] the town voted "that the Sum of One hundred pounds old tenor bills be and hereby is allowed unto M^r. Gibson in full for past Services, . . ." He continued in office until the illness which preceded his death in 1750. On April 4, 1750, Mr. John Lovell, the Master of the School, informed the selectmen that "his late Usher m^r Samuel Gibson decēd a few days since, that there was a necessity of Having another to Succeed him, as he now has a large number of Scholars to Educate."

ROBERT TREAT PAINE, APRIL, 1750-AUGUST, 1750

Robert Treat Paine,[40] who was graduated from Harvard College in 1749, was appointed Usher of the Latin School on April 4, 1750, "to Enter on that Service on Monday next the ninth instant." On May 15, 1750, the town voted "that the Sum of Fifty Pounds, lawful money be allowed and paid unto M^r. Robert Treat Paine, for his Salary, as Usher of the South Grammar School." He continued only a few months, as is evidenced by the following record of the selectmen, dated August 27, 1750: "M^r. John Lovell Master of the South Grammar School appeared and informed that M^r. Robert Treat Paine his Usher left that Employment this Day fortnight." He was succeeded by Nathaniel Gardner, Jr.

NATHANIEL GARDNER, JR., 1750-1759/60(?)

Nathaniel Gardner, Jr., who was graduated from Harvard College in 1739, was appointed Usher of the Latin School on August 27, 1750, "until further Orders." It appears from the records that he continued in office until the illness which preceded his death in March, 1760. He was succeeded by James Lovell, the son of John Lovell.

---

[40] Robert Treat Paine later became distinguished as one of the signers of the Declaration of Independence.

JAMES LOVELL, 1760(?)-1775

James Lovell, who was graduated from Harvard College in 1756, was appointed the Usher in 1760, or possibly earlier. The earliest reference to his service, in the *Town Records,* is the town vote of May 16, 1760, "that the Sum of Sixty Pounds be allowed and paid unto M^r. James Lovel for his Salary as Usher in the South Grammar School the ensuing Year, to be paid him quarterly and to Commence from the time he entered upon that Service." On August 10, 1764, a number of the inhabitants petitioned the town to raise his salary, "representing that the Usher of the South Grammar School is about leaving the Town for want of a competent support." On August 16, of that year, the town voted to grant him fifty pounds "as a Gratuity for his services the present Year, and as an encouragement to remain in the service of ye Town." On February 5, 1767, James Lovell was appointed temporary Master of the North Grammar School, during the emergency following the resignation of Peleg Wiswall. He continued as acting Master of that School until April, of that year, after which he was reappointed Usher of the South Grammar School, remaining in office until April 19, 1775, the day of the battle of Lexington. After the battle of Bunker Hill he was imprisoned in the Boston Gaol by General Howe, and, after the evacuation of Boston in March, 1776, he was taken to Halifax as a prisoner with the British troops. After his return to Boston, the citizens of Massachusetts elected him a delegate to the Continental Congress in December, 1776.

WILLIAM BENTLEY, 1777-1779

After the Revolutionary War, the Latin School was reopened on June 5, 1776, under the mastership of Samuel Hunt. At first the small enrollment did not necessitate an Usher but later, on July 30, 1777, Mr. Hunt applied to the selectmen for an Usher. They immediately appointed William Bentley, who was graduated from Harvard College in 1777. He was re-appointed annually until March 17, 1779, when he was promoted as the Master of the North Grammar School, with the understanding that he could "enter upon that charge in one month from this day, or sooner if an Usher can be provided for the South Grammar School." It appears from the records that an Usher was temporarily provided, although there is no record of his name. On December 6, 1779, the town voted to pay Samuel Hunt, the Master of the Boston Latin School, four hundred and seventy-five pounds "in full for an Assistant for the Nine Months past." It is to be noted that this amount was not as large as it would appear, due to the great depreciation of currency after the war.

AARON SMITH, JANUARY, 1780-MARCH, 1780

Aaron Smith was appointed the Usher on January 19, 1780. On February 23, 1780, he applied for the position of Master of the North Grammar School. He received the appointment and on March 11, 1780, he was "inducted as Master thereof."

WILLIAM CROSWELL, 1780-1782

William Croswell was appointed the Usher on March 29, 1780, "for four months from his entring upon the business," and on August 2, 1780, he was officially appointed the Usher, "he having acted in that capacity for about four months past to the approbation of the Selectmen." He was reappointed annually until 1782, when he resigned.

SAMUEL PAYSON, 1782-1786

Samuel Payson was appointed the Usher on August 7, 1782, having applied for the position on July 22, 1782. He was reappointed annually until 1786, when he was succeeded by Amasa Dingley.

RESIGNATION OF JOSEPH DANA
By courtesy of the Boston School Committee.

AMASA DINGLEY, 1786-1790

Amasa Dingley, of Duxbury, was appointed the Usher on September 14, 1786. On May 16, 1787, the town voted that "M^r. Amasa Dingley Usher of the South Grammer School be Allowed and paid the Sum of Ninety Seven pounds ten shillings the same to be paid him Quarterly." He was reappointed annually until 1790.

CHAPTER VI

BIOGRAPHICAL SKETCHES OF SOME FAMOUS PUPILS OF THE
BOSTON LATIN SCHOOL

THE Boston Latin School Association in 1886 published *Catalogue of the Boston Public Latin School, with an Historical Sketch, prepared by Henry F. Jenks.* This work lists the names of the pupils from 1635 to 1884, with the date of entrance to the School.

In 1918 Thomas Franklin Currier, Assistant Librarian of the Harvard College Library, edited *Catalogue of Graduates of the Public Latin School in Boston, 1816-1917.*

From these two sources Mr. Joseph L. Powers, the Head Master of the Boston Latin School, and Mr. Lee J. Dunn, the librarian, have prepared *A Partial List of Eminent Latin School Men,* no one of whom is now living. To this list the writer has added other distinguished pupils. The following biographical sketches[1] are arranged in chronological order of entrance to the School.

JOHN HULL

John Hull, the famous mint-master, was born in Market Hareborough, in the County of Leicester, England, on December 18, 1624. His father, Robert Hull, moved with his family to New England, arriving in Boston on November 7, 1635. John Hull probably entered the Boston Latin School in 1635, one of its first pupils. In his diary he recorded that "after the little keeping at scoole, I was taken to help my father plant corne, which I attended for seven yeares together." He then practised the trade of a goldsmith and silversmith. In 1652 the Court ordered shillings, sixpences, and threepences

---

[1] See the bibliography for the list of encyclopædias and biographical dictionaries from which material has been obtained for these biographical sketches.

to be struck to take the place of paper bills. John Hull and Robert Sanderson were placed in charge of the minting. In 1652 Hull was appointed a sergeant of the militia of Boston. In 1657 he was chosen by the town "to be one of the seven men to looke after the Townes affaires." He was chosen town treasurer in 1660/61. In 1668, 1671, 1672, and 1673 he was chosen deputy to the General Court. In 1671 he was promoted to captain of the artillery company. In 1675, at the beginning of Philip's War, he was appointed by the council to be a member of the "Committee of War" and also "Treasurer for the War." In the same year he was chosen "Treasurer for the Countrey," which office he held until 1680. He was then chosen one of the assistants, which office he held until his death on October 1, 1683.

John Leverett

John Leverett, governor of the province of Massachusetts Bay, was born in England in 1616. He came to Boston, New England, with his father, Thomas Leverett, and, according to Henry F. Jenks's *Catalogue,* he may have entered the Boston Latin School in 1635. Later he was captain of a militia company and a successful merchant. He returned to England in 1644, taking the side of parliament in the struggle between parliament and the king. As a commander of a company of foot soldiers he gained military distinction and the friendship of Cromwell. After his return to Boston he was a delegate to the General Court from 1651 to 1653 and again from 1663 to 1664. He was one of the governor's council from 1665 to 1671, major general from 1663 to 1673, and deputy governor from 1671 to 1673. He was appointed governor of the province of Massachusetts Bay in 1673, holding office until 1679. In 1676 he was knighted by Charles II, in acknowledgment of his services to the New England colony during King Philip's War. He died in Boston on March 16, 1679.

JOHN LEVERETT
John Leverett may have entered the Boston Latin School in 1635.
From Samuel G. Drake's *The History and Antiquities of Boston.*

WILLIAM STOUGHTON

William Stoughton entered the Boston Latin School in 1640.

From Samuel G. Drake's *The History and Antiquities of Boston.*

WILLIAM STOUGHTON

William Stoughton, chief justice and lieutenant-governor of the province of Massachusetts Bay, was born in England on May 30, 1632. He entered the Boston Latin School in 1640 and was graduated from Harvard College in 1650. After studying theology he went to England where he became a fellow at New College, Oxford, but he was ejected from that office on the restoration. He returned to New England in 1662. He served as an assistant from 1671 until the dissolution of the government in 1686. From 1677 to 1679 he was in England as agent for the Colony. In 1692 he was appointed lieutenant-governor, holding the office until his death. After the death of Sir William Phips he became acting governor. In 1692 he was appointed chief justice of the Superior Court of the Colony and presided at the trial of the Salem witches. He gave to Harvard College property that cost one thousand pounds, and by his will he made a bequest of land to the College. Stoughton Hall at Harvard College is named for him. He died in Dorchester, Massachusetts, on July 7, 1701.

Elisha Hutchinson

Elisha Hutchinson, the father of the Honorable Thomas Hutchinson (1674-1739) and the grandfather of Governor Thomas Hutchinson (1711-1780), was born in Boston in 1640 and was baptized on November 29, 1641. He probably entered the Boston Latin School in 1648. He was the first chief justice of the Court of Common Pleas, a councillor of the province, a colonel commanding the militia of the province of Massachusetts Bay, and one of the commissioners of Boston. He died on December 10, 1717, at the age of seventy-seven.

John Leverett

John Leverett, president of Harvard College, was born on August 25, 1662. He was the grandson of Governor John Leverett. He entered the Boston Latin School in 1669 and was graduated from Harvard College in 1680. He received the degree of A.M. in 1683 and the degree of S.T.B. in 1692. In 1685 he was chosen fellow and tutor of Harvard College. In 1700 Mr. Leverett was dropped as the result of a college government shake-up. In 1699 he was appointed justice of the peace. In 1700 he was appointed speaker of the House and in 1702 he was appointed judge of the Superior Court of the province of Massachusetts Bay and judge of probate for

COTTON MATHER, D.D.
Cotton Mather entered the Boston Latin School in 1669.
From Samuel G. Drake's *The History and Antiquities of Boston.*

Middlesex County. In 1706 he was elected to the Provincial
Council. He was president of Harvard College from 1707 to
1724. In 1713 he was elected a fellow of the Royal Society,
an honor rarely given to the colonists. He died on May 3,
1724.

COTTON MATHER

The Reverend Cotton Mather, son of the Reverend
Increase Mather and grandson of the Reverend John Cotton,
was born in Boston on February 12, 1662/63. He entered
the Boston Latin School probably in 1669, under Ezekiel

BENJAMIN LYNDE
Benjamin Lynde entered the Boston Latin School in 1680.
From Justin Winsor's *The Memorial History of Boston.*

Cheever, and was graduated from Harvard College in 1678. He became a teacher and in 1685 he was ordained his father's colleague over the North Church, Boston. In 1710 he received the degree of S.T.D. from Glasgow University and in 1717 he was elected a fellow of the Royal Society. He succeeded his father as minister of the Second Church. He was also a fellow of Harvard College. He was the author of 382 works, among which are the following: *Wonders of the Invisible World,* published in 1693; *Magnalia Christi Americana,* published in 1702; and *Essays to Do Good,* published in 1710. He died in Boston on February 13, 1727/28. The *Life of Cotton Mather* was written by his son, Samuel Mather, in 1729.

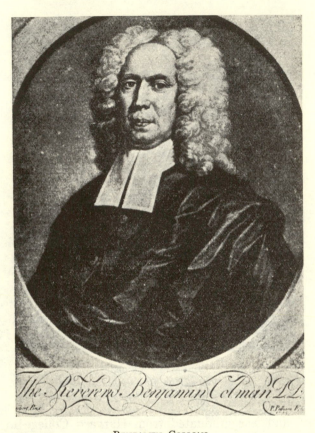

BENJAMIN COLMAN
The Reverend Benjamin Colman entered the Boston Latin School in 1681.
From Justin Winsor's *The Memorial History of Boston.*

BENJAMIN LYNDE

Benjamin Lynde, chief justice of the Supreme Court of Massachusetts, was born in Salem, Massachusetts, on September 22, 1666. He entered the Boston Latin School in 1680, or earlier, and was graduated from Harvard College in 1686. He received the degree of A.M. from Harvard College in 1689. He studied law at the Temple, London, from 1692 to 1697. He was judge of the Superior Court of Massachusetts from

1712 to 1728 and chief justice of the Supreme Court from 1728 to 1746. He died in Salem on March 28, 1745.

BENJAMIN COLMAN

The Reverend Benjamin Colman, the first minister of the Manifesto Church in Brattle Square, was born in Boston on October 19, 1673. He entered the Boston Latin School in 1681 and was graduated from Harvard College in 1692. He began his teaching in Medford. In 1695 he embarked for England but was captured by a privateer and kept some time a prisoner in France. He returned to Boston in 1699, and became the pastor of the Brattle Street Church. He was chosen president of Harvard College in 1724, but he declined. In 1731 he received the degree of S.T.D. from Glasgow University. He died in Boston on August 29, 1747.

SAMUEL MATHER

Samuel Mather, the youngest son of Increase Mather and the brother of Cotton Mather, was born in Boston on August 28, 1674. He probably entered the Boston Latin School in 1681 and was graduated from Harvard College in 1690. He went to England and established a Congregational Church at Witney, in Oxfordshire. He wrote several religious works, including *The Godhead of the Holy Ghost,* published in London in 1719, and *A Vindication of the Holy Bible,* published in 1723. He died in Witney and was buried in the churchyard of Saint Mary on March 14, 1733.

JONATHAN BELCHER

Jonathan Belcher was born in Cambridge, Massachusetts, on January 8, 1681/82. According to Henry F. Jenks's *Catalogue* he entered the Boston Latin School in 1689 and was graduated from Harvard College in 1699. After travelling abroad, he returned to Boston as a merchant and became a representative and councillor. He was royal governor of

JONATHAN BELCHER
Governor Belcher entered the Boston Latin School in 1689.
From Justin Winsor's *The Memorial History of Boston.*

Massachusetts and New Hampshire from 1730 to 1741. Having been removed from office, he went to England to vindicate himself and was appointed governor of New Jersey in 1747, holding the office until his death. He became the devoted friend of Princeton College and its chief patron and benefactor. He died in Elizabethtown, New Jersey, on August 31, 1757.

WILLIAM COOPER
The Reverend William Cooper entered the Boston Latin School in 1701.
From Justin Winsor's *The Memorial History of Boston.*

JOSEPH SEWALL

The Reverend Joseph Sewall, minister of the Old South Church, was born in Boston on August 26, 1688. He was the son of the famous Judge Samuel Sewall (1652-1730). He entered the Boston Latin School in 1696 and was graduated from Harvard College in 1707. He studied theology and was ordained colleague pastor of the Old South Church in 1713. In 1724 he declined the presidency of Harvard College and in 1728 he was chosen a fellow of the College. In 1731 he received the degree of D.D. from the University of Glasgow. He published many sermons. He died in Boston on June 27, 1769.

WILLIAM COOPER

The Reverend William Cooper, the eminent minister of the Church in Brattle Square, was born in Boston in 1694. He entered the Boston Latin School in 1701 and was graduated from Harvard College in 1712. In 1715 he was appointed colleague pastor of the Church in Brattle Square. In 1737 he declined the presidency of Harvard College. He published many sermons. He died in Boston on December 12, 1743.

CHARLES CHAUNCY

The Reverend Charles Chauncy, the great-grandson of Charles Chauncy (1592-1672), who was president of Harvard College from 1654 to 1672, was born in Boston on January 1, 1705. He entered the Boston Latin School in 1712, at the age of seven, and was graduated from Harvard College in 1721. In 1727 he was appointed the colleague of the Reverend Thomas Foxcroft in the pastorate of the First Church of Boston, continuing as minister until his death. He received the degree of S.T.D. from Edinburgh University in 1742. Theologically he has been classed as a precursor of the New England Unitarians. He died in Boston on February 10, 1787.

SAMUEL MATHER

Samuel Mather, the son of Cotton Mather, was born in Boston on October 30, 1706. According to Henry F. Jenks's *Catalogue,* he entered the Boston Latin School in 1712. According to the *Dictionary of American Biography,*[2] edited by Dumas Malone and published by Charles Scribner's Sons, he

---

[2] The article was written by K.B.M. (Professor Kenneth B. Murdock), to whom the writer acknowledges her indebtedness for this information. See also the *Diary* of Cotton Mather.

CHARLES CHAUNCY

The Reverend Charles Chauncy entered the Boston Latin School in 1712.

From Justin Winsor's *The Memorial History of Boston.*

attended the North Grammar School. He was graduated from Harvard College in 1723. In 1736 he received the degree of S.T.D. from Harvard College. In 1732, four years after his father's death, he was ordained as colleague pastor of the North Church. Differences arose in the congregation in 1742 concerning the subject of revivals and a separate church was established under Samuel Mather in North Bennet Street.

Mather Byles

MATHER BYLES

The Reverend Mather Byles probably entered the Boston Latin School in 1714.

From Justin Winsor's *The Memorial History of Boston.*

Among his published works are the following: *The Life of Cotton Mather,* in 1729; *Essay on Gratitude,* in 1732; and *An Apology for the Liberties of the Churches in New England,* in 1738. He died in Boston on June 27, 1785.

MATHER BYLES

The Reverend Mather Byles, first pastor of the Hollis Street Church, was born in Boston on March 15, 1706/7. He probably entered the Boston Latin School in 1714 and was graduated from Harvard College in 1725. He was ordained the first pastor of the Hollis Street Church in 1733. He received the degree of S.T.D. from Aberdeen College in 1765. He maintained his loyalty to the king during the Revolutionary War and, accordingly, was forced to sever his connection with his parish in 1776. In 1777 he was denounced at the town meeting as an enemy. He died in Boston on July 5, 1788.

BENJAMIN FRANKLIN

Benjamin Franklin, a signer of the Declaration of Independence and Minister to France, was born in Boston on January 17, 1706. His father, intending to train him for the ministry, sent him to the Boston Latin School in 1714. Within a year he left the School and attended a private school kept by George Brownell; here he remained for about one year and then "his school days were ended forever." He was a member of the first American Congress. From 1776 to 1785 he was employed in the diplomatic service of the United States, chiefly at Paris. He signed the treaty of alliance with France and the treaty of peace with England. He died in Philadelphia on April 17, 1790. He willed one hundred pounds sterling to the Boston public schools, the interest of which was to be spent in silver medals to be awarded to the best scholars. These medals are called the Franklin Medals.

THOMAS HUTCHINSON

Thomas Hutchinson, the last royal governor of the province of Massachusetts Bay, was born in Boston on September 9, 1711. According to Henry F. Jenks's *Catalogue,* he entered the Boston Latin School in 1716; according to

BENJAMIN FRANKLIN
Benjamin Franklin entered the Boston Latin School in 1714.
From Justin Winsor's *The Memorial History of Boston.*

the *Dictionary of American Biography*, edited by Dumas Malone and published by Charles Scribner's Sons, he entered Harvard College at the age of twelve from the North Gram-

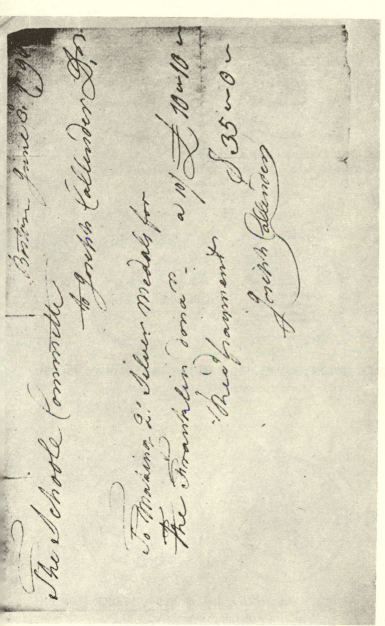

JOSEPH CALLENDER'S RECEIPT FOR MAKING TWENTY-ONE FRANKLIN MEDALS
By courtesy of the Boston School Committee.

ORIGINAL DESIGN.
THOUGH DATED 1792, FIRST DISTRIBUTED JANUARY, 1793.

DEVICE ESPECIALLY PREPARED FOR THE LATIN SCHOOL IN 1794.
FROM AN ORIGINAL, AWARDED 1809.

DEVICE OF 1851.   THE FIRST FRANKLIN MEDAL STRUCK FROM DIES.
USED IN ALL THE SCHOOLS FOR BOYS.

THE FRANKLIN MEDALS

By courtesy of the Boston Latin School Association.

THOMAS HUTCHINSON
Thomas Hutchinson probably entered the Boston Latin School in 1716.
From Justin Winsor's *The Memorial History of Boston*.

mar School. He was graduated from Harvard College in 1727. In 1737 he was appointed a member of the Boston board of selectmen and a few weeks later he was elected to

PAGE OF LATIN ORATION WRITTEN BY ANDREW ELIOT IN 1733

Andrew Eliot entered the Boston Latin School in 1726 and was graduated in 1733. He was graduated from Harvard College in 1737. He later became pastor of the New North Church, Boston.

From the original in the possession of the Boston Latin School, by courtesy of the Boston Latin School Association.

the General Court of Massachusetts Bay, of which he was a member until 1740 and again from 1742 to 1749, serving as speaker in 1747, 1748, and 1749. In 1740 he went to England as the representative of Massachusetts in a boundary dispute with New Hampshire. He was a member of the Massachusetts council from 1749 to 1756. In 1752 he was appointed judge of probate and from 1761 to 1769 he was chief justice of the Superior Court of the province. He was lieutenant-governor from 1758 to 1771, acting as governor in 1770 and 1771, and from 1771 to 1774 he was royal governor. In 1774, upon the appointment of General Thomas Gage as military governor, he went to England. In 1776 he received the degree of J.C.D. (Doctor of Civil Law) from Oxford University. Governor Hutchinson is the author of *History of the Province of Massachusetts*. He died at Brompton, now a part of London, on June 3, 1780. The Hutchinson manuscripts are in the archives of the Massachusetts State House.

Andrew Eliot

The Reverend Andrew Eliot was born in Boston on December 28, 1718. He entered the Boston Latin School in 1726 and was graduated from Harvard College in 1737. He received the degree of S.T.D. from Edinburgh University in 1767. In 1742 he became the associate pastor of the New North Church, Boston, and in 1750 he was appointed the sole pastor. He was a fellow of Harvard College. In 1773 he declined an election to the presidency of Harvard College. He died in Boston on September 13, 1778.

Samuel Adams

Samuel Adams, the distinguished patriot and one of the signers of the Declaration of Independence, was born in Boston on September 27, 1722. He was a second cousin of President John Adams. He entered the Boston Latin School in 1729 and was graduated from Harvard College in 1740. He began

Samuel Adams

SAMUEL ADAMS
Samuel Adams entered the Boston Latin School in 1729.
From Samuel G. Drake's *The History and Antiquities of Boston.*

the study of law but discontinued it in response to his mother's disapproval. He became a merchant but, not being successful in business, he soon abandoned it. About 1748 he began to take an important part in the affairs of the town of Boston and became a leader in the debates of a political club, to whose weekly publication, the *Independent Advertiser,* he contributed many articles. From 1756 to 1764 he was one of Boston's tax collectors. He came into wide prominence at the beginning of the Stamp Act episode, in 1764, when he urged opposition to taxation by act of parliament. In 1765 he was elected to the lower house of the General Court, where he served as clerk from 1766 to 1774. In 1768 he drafted the state papers sent by the Massachusetts legislature to members of the cabinet and to the provincial agent in London. In 1773 he managed the proceedings of the Boston Tea Party and later he was moderator of the convention of Massachusetts towns called to protest against the Boston Port Bill of 1774. He was a delegate to the Continental Congress from 1774 to 1781. In 1779 he was a member of the convention which framed the Constitution of Massachusetts, adopted in 1780. In 1788 he was a member of the Massachusetts convention to ratify the Constitution of the United States. From 1789 to 1794 he was lieutenant-governor of Massachusetts and from 1794 to 1797 he was governor, after which he retired to private life. He died in Boston on October 2, 1803.

SAMUEL LANGDON

The Reverend Samuel Langdon, president of Harvard College, was born in Boston on January 12, 1723. He entered the Boston Latin School in 1729 and was graduated from Harvard College in 1740. In 1762 he received the degree of S.T.D. from the University of Aberdeen. In 1745 he was appointed chaplain of a regiment and was present at the capture of Louisburg. On his return he was ordained pastor of the North Church of Portsmouth, New Hampshire, in 1747. He was president of Harvard College from 1774 to 1780, when his resignation was virtually compelled because of his ardent patriotism, which was obnoxious to Tory students. In 1781 he became pastor of the Congregational Church at Hampton Falls, New Hampshire. In 1788 he was a delegate to the New Hampshire convention which adopted the Constitution of the United States. He was a member of the American Academy

SAMUEL COOPER

The Reverend Samuel Cooper entered the Boston Latin School in 1732.

From Justin Winsor's *The Memorial History of Boston*.

of Arts and Sciences from its foundation. He published many books and sermons. He died in Hampton Falls, New Hampshire, on November 29, 1797.

SAMUEL COOPER

The Reverend Samuel Cooper, the son of the Reverend William Cooper, was born in Boston on March 28, 1725. He entered the Boston Latin School in 1732 and was graduated from Harvard College in 1743. He was elected colleague pastor of the Church in Brattle Square in 1744 and was ordained in 1746. In 1767 he received the degree of S.T.D. from the University of Edinburgh. He declined the presidency of Harvard College in 1774. He was first vice-president of the American Academy of Arts and Sciences in 1780. He published many sermons. He died in Boston on December 23, 1783.

JAMES BOWDOIN

James Bowdoin, governor of Massachusetts, was born in Boston on August 8, 1727. He entered the Boston Latin School in 1734 and was graduated from Harvard College in 1745. In 1775 he was president of the Colonial Council. In 1778 he was president of the Massachusetts constitutional convention which formed the state Constitution. In 1784 he was appointed the first president of the Massachusetts Bank [now the First National Bank of Boston]. He was elected governor of Massachusetts in 1785 and again in 1786. He suppressed Daniel Shays's rebellion in 1786. He promised pardon to all rebels who would submit before January 1, 1787, but the disturbances continued and Governor Bowdoin ordered out 4400 militia under General Benjamin Lincoln. He was a member of the convention which ratified the federal Constitution in 1789. He received the degree of LL.D. from Harvard College in 1783. He was a fellow of Harvard College, president of the American Academy, and a fellow of the Royal Society, London. Bowdoin College in Brunswick, Maine, was named in honor of Governor Bowdoin, whose

JAMES BOWDOIN
Governor James Bowdoin entered the Boston Latin School in 1734.
From *Commonwealth History of Massachusetts*, edited by Albert Bushnell Hart.   By courtesy
of the States History Company, New York City.
After the original by Robert Feke, Bowdoin College, reproduced by courtesy of the Society for
the Preservation of New England Antiquities.

son, James Bowdoin, was a benefactor of the College.   He died in Boston on November 6, 1790.

Robert Treat Paine

Robert Treat Paine (1731-1814), one of the signers of the Declaration of Independence, was born in Boston on March 11, 1731. He entered the Boston Latin School in 1738 and was graduated from Harvard College in 1749. He was Usher of the Boston Latin School from April to August, 1750. Subsequently he studied law and was admitted to the bar in 1759, settling at Taunton, Massachusetts. In 1768 he was a delegate to the provincial convention which was called to meet in Boston. In 1770, in the absence of the king's attorney-general, he conducted the prosecution of Preston and his men in the Boston Massacre trial. As a result of the trial Preston was acquitted. He was a member of the Massachusetts General Court from 1773 to 1774, a member of the Provincial Congress from 1774 to 1775, and a delegate to the Continental Congress from 1774 to 1778. He was speaker of the Massachusetts House of Representatives in 1777, a member of the executive council in 1779, a member of the committee which drafted the Constitution of 1780, attorney-general of Massachusetts from 1780 to 1790, and judge of the Supreme Court of Massachusetts from 1790 to 1804. With others he founded the American Academy of Massachusetts in 1780. He died in Boston on May 11, 1814.

James Lovell

James Lovell, the patriot, was born in Boston on October 31, 1737. He was the son of John Lovell, who was Master of the Boston Latin School from 1734 to 1775. James entered the Boston Latin School in 1744 and was graduated from Harvard College in 1756. He was appointed Usher of the Boston Latin School in 1760, or possibly earlier. In 1767 he was appointed temporary Master of the North [Latin] Grammar School. He continued as acting Master of that School until April, 1767, after which he was reappointed Usher of the Boston Latin School, remaining in office until April 19,

ROBERT TREAT PAINE
Robert Treat Paine entered the Boston Latin School in 1738.
From *Commonwealth History of Massachusetts*, edited by Albert Bushnell Hart. By courtesy
of the States History Company, New York City.
After a copy, in the Copley Gallery, of the portrait by Edward Savage.

1775. He delivered the official address before the city authorities on April 2, 1771, in commemoration of the Boston Massacre. He was imprisoned by General Gage after the battle of Bunker Hill and was exchanged in November, 1776. He

JOHN HANCOCK
John Hancock entered the Boston Latin School in 1745.
From Samuel G. Drake's *The History and Antiquities of Boston.*

was a member of the Continental Congress from 1776 to 1782, receiver of taxes from 1784 to 1788, collector of the port of Boston in 1788 and 1789, and naval officer from 1790 to

1814. He published several tracts. He died in Windham, Maine, on July 14, 1814.

John Hancock

John Hancock, the first of the signers of the Declaration of Independence, was born in that part of Braintree, Massachusetts, now called Quincy, on January 12, 1736/37. He entered the Boston Latin School in 1745 and was graduated from Harvard College in 1754. In 1764 he inherited the business and the greater part of the large fortune of his Uncle Thomas Hancock, in whose counting-house he had been trained to business. From 1766 to 1772 he was a member of the Massachusetts General Court. In 1770 he delivered a fearless address at the funeral of those slain at the Boston Massacre. In 1774 he was appointed president of the Provincial Congress. The arrest of John Hancock and Samuel Adams was one of the objects of the expedition to Concord. Both escaped but were excepted from the general pardon issued to the rebels by General Gage, on June 12, 1775. He was a member of the Continental Congress from 1775 to 1780 and again from 1785 to 1786. From 1775 to 1777 he was president of the General Congress. In 1778, as major-general of the Massachusetts militia, he took part in the expedition against Rhode Island under Sullivan. He was governor of Massachusetts from 1780 to 1785 [the first governor under the new state Constitution] and again from 1787 to 1793. In 1788 he was president of the Convention which met to consider the new federal Constitution. He died in Braintree on October 8, 1793.

Nathaniel Gorham

Nathaniel Gorham, president of Congress, was born in Charlestown, Massachusetts, on May 27, 1738. He entered the Boston Latin School in 1746. He later engaged in mercantile business. He was a member of the colonial legislature from 1771 to 1775, a delegate to the Provincial Congress from 1774 to 1775, and a member of the Board of War from 1778 to 1781. In 1779 he was a member of the state Constitutional Convention. He was a delegate to the Continental Congress from 1782 to 1783 and also from 1785 to 1787, serving as president in June, 1786. For several years he was judge of the Court of Common Pleas. He died in Charlestown on June 11, 1796.

WILLIAM HOOPER

William Hooper, one of the signers of the Declaration of Independence, was born in Boston on June 17, 1742. He entered the Boston Latin School in 1749 and was graduated from Harvard College in 1760. He studied law under James Otis. In 1767 he removed to North Carolina, where he held many important public positions. He was a member of the Continental Congress from 1774 to 1777. He died at Hillsborough, North Carolina, in October, 1790.

JONATHAN JACKSON

Jonathan Jackson, a member of the Continental Congress and state senator, was born in Boston on June 4, 1743. He was the son of Edward and Dorothy Quincy Jackson. His granddaughter was the wife of Dr. Oliver Wendell Holmes. He entered the Boston Latin School in 1750, was graduated from Harvard College in 1761, and received the degree of A.M. in 1764. He moved to Newburyport where he engaged in mercantile business. He was a delegate to the Provincial Congress in 1775, a representative in the state legislature in 1777, a delegate to the Continental Congress in 1782, and state senator in 1789. He was United States marshall for the district of Massachusetts under President Washington from 1789 to 1791, treasurer of Massachusetts from 1802 to 1806, treasurer of Harvard College from 1807 to 1810, and first president of the Boston Bank from 1803 to 1810. He was a fellow of the American Academy of Arts and Sciences from 1807 to 1810. He died in Boston on March 5, 1810.

JONATHAN JACKSON
Jonathan Jackson entered the Boston Latin School in 1750.
From Justin Winsor's *The Memorial History of Boston.*

FRANCIS DANA

Francis Dana, son of Judge Richard Dana and father of
the poet, Richard Henry Dana, was born in Charlestown,
Massachusetts, on June 13, 1743. He entered the Boston
Latin School in 1751 and was graduated from Harvard College in 1762, receiving the degree of LL.D in 1792. He studied

law and was admitted to the bar in 1767. In 1774 he was a member of the first Provincial Congress of Massachusetts. He was a member of the Massachusetts Executive Council from 1776 to 1780 and a delegate to the Continental Congress from 1776 to 1778. In 1778 he was chairman of the committee to submit plans for the reorganization of the army and a member of the committee to consider the offer of conciliation of Lord North. From 1779 to 1781 he was the official secretary abroad to John Adams. He was United States minister to Russia from 1781 to 1783, but he was not recognized by Catherine. In 1784 he was elected to the Continental Congress. In 1785 he was appointed justice of the Supreme Court of Massachusetts and in 1786 he was a delegate to the Annapolis Convention. In 1787 he was appointed a delegate to the Constitutional Convention at Philadelphia, but poor health prevented his attendance. From 1791 to 1806 he was chief justice of the Massachusetts Supreme Court. He died in Cambridge on April 25, 1811.

Josiah Quincy, Jr.

Josiah Quincy, Jr., son of Josiah Quincy (1709-1784) and father of Josiah Quincy (1772-1864), who was president of Harvard College from 1829 to 1845, was born in Boston on February 23, 1744. He entered the Boston Latin School in 1754, and after graduation from Harvard College in 1763 he studied law in the office of Oxenbridge Thacher, to whose large practice he succeeded. In 1767 he contributed to the *Boston Gazette* two bold papers declaiming against British oppression. With John Adams, in 1770, he defended Captain Preston and the soldiers implicated in the Boston Massacre and secured their acquittal. In 1773 he went south for his health, and as a result of his influence the southern patriots were brought into closer relations with the popular leaders in Massachusetts. In May, 1774, he published his *Observations on the Act of Parliament, commonly called the Boston Port Bill*. In September, 1774, he left for England where he con-

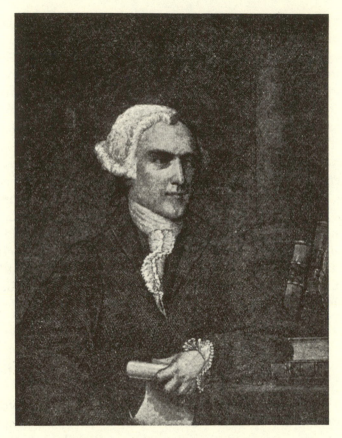

JOSIAH QUINCY
Josiah Quincy entered the Boston Latin School in 1754.
From Justin Winsor's *The Memorial History of Boston*.

sulted with leading Whigs as to the political situation in
America. He died on the return voyage, off Gloucester,
Massachusetts, on April 26, 1775.

Sir William Pepperell

Sir William Pepperell, the loyalist, was born in 1746. His name at birth was William Pepperell Sparhawk, the son of Colonel Nathaniel Sparhawk and the grandson of the first Sir William Pepperell (1696-1759) of Kittery, Maine. He entered the Boston Latin School in 1755 and was graduated from Harvard College in 1766. He assumed his grandfather's name and his great estates in 1774 and was subsequently created Baronet. He lost everything in consequence of his Tory principles. He was a member of the governor's council of Massachusetts. He went to England in 1775 and in 1778 he was proscribed, banished, and had his estates confiscated. He was the first president of an association of loyalists formed in London in 1779. He died in London on December 17, 1816.

Henry Knox

Henry Knox, the Revolutionary soldier, was born in Boston on July 25, 1750. He entered the Boston Latin School in 1758. He enlisted in the Continental army and fought in the Revolutionary War. He was present at the battle of Bunker Hill in 1775, acting as aide to Major-General Artemus Ward. He was then placed in command of the artillery in New York. Because of his brilliant work in the battles of Trenton and Princeton, he was elected by Congress brigadier-general and chief of artillery in 1776. In the battles of Brandywine, Germantown, and Monmouth the artillery under General Knox played a prominent part. He was at the battle of Yorktown, after which he was made major-general in 1782. He received the surrender of New York City from Sir Guy Carleton in 1783. He was appointed commander-in-chief of the army in 1783 and 1784. He was secretary of war in Washington's cabinet. In 1795 he moved to St. George's, in Maine, finally settling at Thomaston, Maine, where he died on October 25, 1806.

HENRY KNOX

General Henry Knox entered the Boston Latin School in 1758.

From *Commonwealth History of Massachusetts*, edited by Albert Bushnell Hart. By courtesy of the States History Company, New York City.

From the portrait by Stuart in the Museum of Fine Arts, Boston

WILLIAM TUDOR

William Tudor, the distinguished lawyer and secretary of state, was born in Boston on March 28, 1750. He entered the Boston Latin School in 1758 and was graduated from Harvard College in 1769. He studied law with John Adams and was admitted to the Suffolk bar in 1772, rising to a high rank in his profession. He was attached to General Washington's staff from 1775 to 1778 as judge-advocate with the rank of colonel. He was a member of both houses of the Massachusetts legislature and was secretary of state from 1809 to 1810. Colonel Tudor was vice-president of the Massachusetts Society of the Cincinnati in 1816. He was one of the founders of the Massachusetts Historical Society. He died in Boston on July 8, 1819.

WINTHROP SARGENT

Winthrop Sargent, Revolutionary soldier and governor of Mississippi Territory, was born in Gloucester, Massachusetts, on May 1, 1753. He entered the Boston Latin School in 1759 and was graduated from Harvard College in 1771. During the Revolutionary War he was navy-agent at Gloucester and captain of artillery at the siege of Boston. Congress appointed him surveyor-general of the Northwest Territory in 1786, its secretary in 1787, and its governor from 1798 to 1801. He was governor of Mississippi Territory in 1790 and again in 1801. He was a member of the American Academy of Arts and Sciences and was an original member of the Society of the Cincinnati. He died in New Orleans on June 3, 1820.

JAMES BOWDOIN

James Bowdoin, the son of Governor James Bowdoin, was born in Boston on September 22, 1752. He entered the Boston Latin School in 1760 and was graduated from Harvard College in 1771. In 1805 he was sent on a mission to Spain to procure the cession of Florida to the United States and to obtain indemnity for injuries to United States commerce. He was a benefactor of Bowdoin College, to which he gave 6000 acres of land, 1100 pounds, his valuable library, and collection of paintings. He was a fellow of Harvard College. He died on October 11, 1811, at his summer residence on the island of Naushon, in Buzzard's Bay.

WILLIAM EUSTIS

William Eustis, secretary of war, minister to Holland, and governor of Massachusetts, was born in Cambridge, Massachusetts, on June 10, 1753. He entered the Boston Latin School in 1761, was graduated from Harvard College in 1772, and received the degree of A.M. in 1784. After studying medicine under Dr. Joseph Warren, he entered the Revolutionary army as surgeon. After the war he practised medicine in Boston and was a surgeon in the expedition against the insurgents in Shays's rebellion. He was a member of the Massachusetts legislature from 1788 to 1794, a representative to Congress from 1801 to 1805 and again from 1820 to 1823, secretary of war from 1807 to 1813, minister to Holland from 1814 to 1818, and governor of Massachusetts from 1823 to 1825. In 1823 he received the degree of LL.D. from Harvard College. He died in Boston on February 6, 1825.

WILLIAM DUMMER POWELL

William Dummer Powell,[3] first judge at Detroit and the fifth chief justice of Upper Canada, was born in Boston on November 5, 1755. He entered the Boston Latin School in 1762, at the age of seven, and after three years went to England with his father. He then entered a school at Tunbridge, Kent, where he remained until 1769. He later studied the French and Dutch languages in Holland. In 1772 he returned to Boston. In 1775, at the beginning of the Revolutionary War, he joined the British garrison at Boston. In 1776 he went to England and entered the Middle Temple to study law. Returning to America, he moved to Quebec in 1779 to practise law. Later he became the foremost advocate at the Montreal bar. He was appointed judge at Detroit and

---

[3] The writer acknowledges her indebtedness to the Honorable William Renwick Riddell's *The Life of William Dummer Powell*, published by the Michigan Historical Commission in 1924.

WILLIAM DUMMER POWELL
William Dummer Powell entered the Boston Latin School in 1762.
From *The Life of William Dummer Powell*, by Hon. William Renwick Riddell. By courtesy
of the Michigan Historical Commission.

in 1794 he was appointed the first Puisne justice of the Court
of the King's Bench of Upper Canada. He died in Toronto on
September 6, 1834.

JONATHAN MASON

Jonathan Mason, representative and senator, was born in Boston on September 12, 1756. He entered the Boston Latin School in 1763 and was graduated from the College of New Jersey [now Princeton] in 1774. He studied law under John Adams and in the office of Josiah Quincy, and was admitted to the bar of Suffolk County in 1779. On March 5, 1780, he delivered the official oration before the authorities of Boston on the tenth anniversary of the Boston Massacre. From 1786 to 1796 he was a member of the Massachusetts House of Representatives. In 1797 and 1798 he was a member of the executive council. In 1799 and 1800 he was state senator and, from 1800 to 1803, United States senator from Massachusetts. He was elected to the lower house of Congress as a federalist, serving from 1817 until his resignation in 1820. He died in Boston on November 1, 1831.

ALFRED MOORE

Alfred Moore, the Revolutionary soldier and associate justice of the United States Supreme Court, was born in New Hanover County, North Carolina, on May 21, 1755. His parents sent him to Boston to be educated, where he entered the Boston Latin School in 1763. He returned home before the Revolution, studied law under his father, and was licensed to practise in 1775. He left his profession to join the army. He was made captain in the first North Carolina regiment in 1775 and participated in the battles of Charleston and Fort Moultrie. In 1792 he was elected state attorney-general by the North Carolina legislature. He was elected judge of the Superior Court in 1798 and in 1799 he was appointed by President Adams an associate justice of the United States Supreme Court. He resigned in 1804, due to poor health. He died in Bladen County, North Carolina, on October 15, 1810.

CHRISTOPHER GORE

Christopher Gore entered the Boston Latin School in 1765.

From Justin Winsor's *The Memorial History of Boston.*

CHRISTOPHER GORE

Christopher Gore, the son of John Gore, was born in Boston on September 21, 1758. He entered the Boston Latin School in 1765, attended the North Latin Grammar School from 1770 to 1772, and after his graduation from Harvard

College in 1776 studied law with Judge Trowbridge. He was United States district attorney for Massachusetts from 1789 to 1796, the first to hold the office. From 1796 to 1804 he was a commissioner to England, to settle the claims of the United States on Great Britain for spoliations. In 1803 and 1804 he was *chargé d'affaires* at London. He was governor of Massachusetts in 1809 and 1810 and United States senator from 1814 to 1817. He was a fellow of Harvard College and president of the Massachusetts Historical Society. He died in Waltham, Massachusetts, on March 1, 1827. Gore Hall at Harvard College was built from the fund of nearly $100,000 bequeathed by Christopher Gore.

Samuel Sewall

Samuel Sewall, chief justice of Massachusetts and a member of Congress, was born in Boston on December 11, 1757. He entered the Boston Latin School in 1765, was graduated from Harvard College in 1776, and received the degree of A.M. in 1779. He studied law and practised in Marblehead, Massachusetts. He was a representative in the state legislature for several terms, a representative in the fifth and sixth Congresses from 1797 to 1801, a judge of the Supreme Court of Massachusetts from 1801 to 1813, and chief justice from 1813 to 1814. He was a member of the Electoral College of 1801 from the second Massachusetts district. In 1808 he received the honorary degree of LL.D. from Harvard College. He was a fellow of the American Academy of Arts and Sciences. He died in Wiscasset, Maine, on June 8, 1814.

Royall Tyler

Royall Tyler, the jurist, dramatist, and novelist, was born in Boston on July 18, 1757. He entered the Boston Latin School in 1765 and was graduated from Harvard College in 1776. He studied law under John Adams. In 1790 he settled in Guilford, Vermont. He was judge of the Vermont Supreme

Court from 1794 to 1800 and chief justice from 1800 to 1806. He was also professor of law in the University of Vermont. He was one of the earliest dramatists in America. Among his dramas are *The Contrast,* produced in 1787; *May Day, or New York in an Uproar,* produced in 1787; and *The Georgian Spec, or Land in the Moon,* produced in 1797. He was also a novelist and a contributor of humorous verse and prose. He died in Brattleboro, Vermont, on August 16, 1826.

JAMES FREEMAN

The Reverend James Freeman, the Unitarian clergyman and minister of King's Chapel, was born in Charlestown, Massachusetts, on April 22, 1759. He entered the Boston Latin School in 1766 and was graduated from Harvard College in 1777. He received the degree of D.D. from Harvard College in 1811. In 1780 he went to Quebec, where he was captured and detained until 1782, when he returned to Boston and became lay-reader of King's Chapel. This was originally an Episcopal Church founded in 1686. He was the first minister in the United States to avow the name of Unitarian, and through his means the first Episcopal Church in New England became the first Unitarian Church in this country. He was consecrated by his own wardens and people in 1787. He continued as the minister of King's Chapel until 1826. He was a member of the Boston school committee from 1789 to 1792, a member of the Academy of Arts and Sciences, and was one of the founders of the Massachusetts Historical Society. He published several books and sermons. He died in Newton, Massachusetts, on November 14, 1835.

ISAAC COFFIN

Sir Isaac Coffin was born in Boston, of a Nantucket family, on May 16, 1759. His father was a Tory and collector of the port of Boston. Isaac entered the Boston Latin School in 1766. He entered the Royal English Navy in 1773, at the

JAMES FREEMAN
The Reverend James Freeman entered the Boston Latin School in 1766.
From Justin Winsor's *The Memorial History of Boston.*

age of fourteen, and was advanced rapidly, attaining the rank
of lieutenant in 1778.   In April, 1804, he was appointed rear
admiral and the following month was created a baronet.   By
regular seniority he became a full admiral in 1814.   In 1826
he visited Nantucket, where he founded and endowed the
Coffin School.   He died in Cheltenham, England, on July 23,
1839.

THOMAS DAWES

Thomas Dawes, the distinguished jurist, was born in Boston on July 8, 1757.   He was the son of Thomas Dawes (1731-

ISAAC COFFIN
Isaac Coffin entered the Boston Latin School in 1766.
From Justin Winsor's *The Memorial History of Boston*.

1809). He entered the Boston Latin School in 1766 and was graduated from Harvard College in 1777. He received the degree of A.M. from Harvard College in 1791. He was a member of the state Constitutional Conventions of 1780 and 1820 and of the convention that ratified the federal Constitu-

CHARLES BULFINCH
Charles Bulfinch entered the Boston Latin School in 1770.
From Justin Winsor's *The Memorial History of Boston.*

tion in 1789. He was judge of the Supreme Court of Massachusetts from 1792 to 1802, of the Municipal Court of Boston from 1803 to 1823, and of the Probate Court from 1823 to 1825. He was a fellow of the American Academy of Arts and

Sciences and an overseer of Harvard College from 1810 to 1823. He died in Boston on July 22, 1825.

CHARLES BULFINCH

Charles Bulfinch, the famous architect, was born in Boston on August 8, 1763. He entered the Boston Latin School in 1770 and was graduated from Harvard College in 1781. After travel and study in Europe from 1784 to 1786 he returned to Boston, where he was the first to practise as a professional architect. He was chairman of the board of selectmen of Boston for twenty-one years, from 1797 to 1818. Among his early works in Boston were the old Federal Street Theatre, in 1793, and the new State House, in 1798. After the Capitol at Washington was burned by the British in 1814 Mr. Bulfinch was applied to by President Monroe to superintend its re-erection. In 1830 he returned to Boston. He died in Boston on April 15, 1844.

HARRISON GRAY OTIS

Harrison Gray Otis, son of Samuel Allyne Otis and nephew of James Otis, was born in Boston on October 8, 1765. He entered the Boston Latin School in 1773, was graduated from Harvard College in 1783, and was admitted to the bar in 1786. He was a member of the Massachusetts House of Representatives in 1796 and 1797 and a member of the United States House of Representatives from 1797 to 1801. He was district attorney for Massachusetts in 1801, speaker of the Massachusetts House of Representatives from 1803 to 1805, a member of the Massachusetts Senate from 1805 to 1811, and president of the Massachusetts Senate from 1805 to 1806 and from 1808 to 1811. He was a member of the United States Senate from 1817 to 1822 and mayor of Boston from 1829 to 1832. He died in Boston on October 28, 1848.

HARRISON GRAY OTIS
Harrison Gray Otis entered the Boston Latin School in 1773.
From *Commonwealth History of Massachusetts*, edited by Albert Bushnell Hart. By courtesy
of the States History Company, New York City.
After the original by Chester Harding, by courtesy of Samuel Eliot Morison.

JOHN LOWELL

John Lowell entered the Boston Latin School in 1776 or 1777.

From Justin Winsor's *The Memorial History of Boston.*

JOHN LOWELL

John Lowell, son of John Lowell (1743-1802), was born in Newburyport, Massachusetts, on October 6, 1769. He entered the Boston Latin School in 1776 or 1777, was graduated from Harvard College in 1786, and was admitted to the bar in 1789. He retired from practice in 1803, after which he visited Europe. Upon his return he wrote for the press and published many pamphlets. He was a founder of the Massachusetts General Hospital, the Boston Athenæum, the Savings Bank and the Hospital Life Insurance Company. For many years he was president of the Massachusetts Agricultural Society. He received the degree of LL.D. from Harvard College in 1814. He died in Boston on March 12, 1840.

ISAAC PARKER

Isaac Parker, chief justice of the Supreme Court of Massachusetts, was born in Boston on June 17, 1768. He entered the Boston Latin School in 1777, was graduated from Harvard College in 1786, and received the degree of A.M. in 1789. After teaching for a time at the Boston Latin School he studied law. He was federal representative in the fifth Congress from 1797 to 1799, was United States marshall for the district of Maine from 1799 to 1801, and was chief justice of the Supreme Court of Massachusetts from 1814 to 1830. He was Royall professor of law at Harvard College from 1816 to 1827 and an overseer of the College from 1810 to 1830. He was a trustee of Bowdoin College from 1799 to 1810 and president of the Massachusetts Constitutional Convention in 1820. He received the honorary degree of LL.D. from Harvard College in 1814. He died in Boston on May 26, 1830.

THOMAS W. THOMPSON

Thomas W. Thompson, United States senator, was born in Boston on March 15, 1766. He entered the Boston Latin School in 1779 and was graduated from Harvard College in 1786. He studied law, was admitted to the bar, and practised in Salisbury from 1790 to 1810, when he removed to Concord, New Hampshire. He was a member of the State House of Representatives and its speaker in 1813 and 1814, a member of Congress from 1805 to 1807, and state treasurer in 1809. He was appointed United States senator to fill the unexpired term of Nicholas Gilman and served from 1814 to 1817. He died in Concord, New Hampshire, on October 1, 1821.

CHARLES JACKSON

Charles Jackson, judge of the Supreme Court of Massachusetts, was born in Newburyport, Massachusetts, on May 31, 1775. He was the son of Hon. Jonathan Jackson and father-in-law of Dr. Oliver Wendell Holmes. He entered the Boston Latin School in 1784 and was graduated from Harvard College in 1793. He studied law and was admitted to the bar in 1796. He practised in Newburyport from 1796 to 1803 and in Boston from 1803 to 1813. He was judge of the Supreme Judicial Court of Massachusetts from 1813 to 1824. He was overseer of Harvard College from 1816 to 1825 and was a fellow of the College from 1825 to 1834. In 1821 he received the degree of LL.D. from Harvard College. He was a fellow of the American Academy of Arts and Sciences and a member of the Massachusetts Historical Society. He died in Boston on December 13, 1855.

JAMES JACKSON

Dr. James Jackson, the distinguished physician and professor, was born in Newburyport, Massachusetts, on October 3, 1777. He was the son of Hon. Jonathan Jackson and the grandson of Edward and Dorothy Quincy Jackson. He entered the Boston Latin School in 1784, was graduated from Harvard College in 1796, and received the degree of A.M. in 1799. He studied medicine at the Harvard Medical School, receiving the degree of M.B. in 1802 and the degree of M.D. in 1809. In 1854 he received the degree of LL.D. He was Hersey professor of the theory and practice of physics in Harvard Medical School from 1812 to 1836 and professor emeritus from 1836 to 1867. He was the first physician of the Massachusetts General Hospital from 1812 to 1835. He was an overseer of Harvard College from 1844 to 1846 and was president of the American Academy of Arts and Sciences. He died in Boston on August 27, 1867.

JOHN C. WARREN

Dr. John Collins Warren entered the Boston Latin School in 1786.

JOHN COLLINS WARREN

Dr. John Collins Warren, the distinguished surgeon and president of the Massachusetts Medical Society, was born in Boston on August 1, 1778. He entered the Boston Latin School in 1786 and was graduated from Harvard College in 1797. He studied medicine with his father, Dr. John Warren, at London, Edinburgh, and Paris. He began practice in Boston in 1802. In 1819 he received the degree of M.D. from Harvard College. He was assistant professor of anatomy and surgery in the Harvard Medical School from 1806 to 1815, professor of anatomy and surgery from 1815 to 1847, and professor emeritus from 1847 to 1856. He was one of the founders of the Massachusetts General Hospital. In 1846 he carried into effect the successful application of ether in a surgical operation at the Massachusetts General Hospital. He died in Boston on May 4, 1856.

JAMES TRECOTHICK AUSTIN

James Trecothick Austin, lawyer and author, was born in Boston on January 7, 1784. He was the son of Jonathan Loring Austin. He entered the Boston Latin School in 1795 and was graduated from Harvard College in 1802. He studied law and rose to eminence in his profession. In 1806 he married the daughter of Elbridge Gerry, vice-president of the United States. He was town advocate in 1809, a member of the state legislature, attorney for the county of Suffolk from 1812 to 1832, and attorney-general of Massachusetts from 1832 to 1843. For a time he edited a literary periodical entitled *The Emerald* and delivered several popular orations. His principal work is *The Life of Elbridge Gerry*, published in Boston in 1828. In 1838 he received the degree of LL.D. from Harvard College. He died in Boston on May 8, 1870.

THOMAS BULFINCH

Thomas Bulfinch, the distinguished author, was born in Boston in 1796. He entered the Boston Latin School in 1805 and was graduated from Harvard College in 1814. He was Usher of the Boston Latin School from August, 1814, to August, 1815. He then entered upon a mercantile life in Boston. He is the author of *The Age of Fable*, a perennial favorite, which was revised by Edward Everett Hale in 1881. He also published *Hebrew Lyrical History, The Age of Chivalry, Oregon and Eldorado, The Boy Inventor, Poetry of the Age of Fable,* and *Legends of Charlemagne.* He died in 1867.

EDWARD EVERETT

Edward Everett, the celebrated statesman, orator, and educator, was born in Dorchester, Massachusetts, on April 11, 1794. After his father's death in 1802 he moved to Boston with his mother. He entered the Boston Latin School in 1805 and was graduated from Harvard College in 1811. After graduation he was a tutor at Harvard College, pursuing at the same time his studies in divinity. In 1813 he was called to the ministry of the Brattle Street Unitarian Church in Boston. In 1815 he resigned and was appointed Eliot professor of Greek literature in Harvard College. After nearly five years spent in Europe in preparation, he entered on his duties in 1819 as professor at Harvard. From 1820 to 1824 he was editor of the *North American Review* and also established a reputation as an orator. He was a member of the United States House of Representatives from 1825 to 1835. In 1835 he was elected governor of Massachusetts, holding the office for four years. In 1841 he was named United States minister to Great Britain. From 1846 to 1849 he was president of Harvard College. In 1852 he succeeded his friend, Daniel Webster, as secretary of state in President Fillmore's cabinet. In 1853 he entered the Senate as one of the representatives of

EDWARD EVERETT
Edward Everett entered the Boston Latin School in 1805.
From *Commonwealth History of Massachusetts,* edited by Albert Bushnell Hart. By courtesy
of the States History Company, New York City.
From a photograph in the possession of Harvard College Library.

Massachusetts. He was a celebrated orator, his better-known orations being the one on Washington and the Gettysburg Oration, delivered in 1863. His orations have been collected in four volumes. He died on January 15, 1865.

GEORGE HAYWARD

Dr. George Hayward, a prominent physician and president of the Massachusetts Medical Society, was born in Boston on March 9, 1791. He entered the Boston Latin School in 1805, was graduated from Harvard College in 1809, and received the degree of M.D. from the University of Pennsylvania in 1812. From 1835 to 1849 he was professor of clinical surgery in Harvard Medical School. He was president of the Massachusetts Medical Society, a member of the Academy of Arts and Sciences of Boston, and a fellow of Harvard College. He wrote several books, among them *Outlines of Physiology*, published in Boston in 1834. He spent several years in Europe and acquired a continental reputation as a surgeon. He died in Boston on October 7, 1863.

GEORGE EUSTIS

George Eustis, chief justice of the Supreme Court of Louisiana, was born in Boston on October 20, 1796. He entered the Boston Latin School in 1806 and was graduated from Harvard College in 1815. He became private secretary to his uncle, Governor William Eustis, then minister to The Hague, where he began his legal duties. He went to New Orleans, Louisiana, in 1817, and was admitted to the bar in 1822. He served several terms in the state legislature. He was afterwards secretary of the State and commissioner of the Board of Currency. He was attorney-general of Louisiana, member of the Constitutional Convention of 1845, and chief justice of the Supreme Court of Louisiana until 1852. In 1849 he received the degree of LL.D. from Harvard College. He died in New Orleans on December 23, 1858.

SAMUEL ATKINS ELIOT

Samuel Atkins Eliot, mayor of Boston and treasurer of Harvard College, was born in Boston on March 5, 1798. He entered the Boston Latin School in 1809 and was graduated

SAMUEL A. ELIOT
Samuel Atkins Eliot entered the Boston Latin School in 1809.
From Justin Winsor's *The Memorial History of Boston.*

from Harvard College in 1817. He became a merchant in Boston. He served several terms in the state legislature and was mayor of Boston from 1837 to 1839. He was treasurer of Harvard College from 1842 to 1853. He was elected to Congress as a Whig, to fill the vacancy caused by the appointment of Robert Charles Winthrop to the United States Senate, and served from 1850 to 1851. He published *Sketch of the History of Harvard College and of its Present State*, in Boston, in 1848. He died in Cambridge on January 29, 1862. His son, Charles William Eliot, was president of Harvard College from 1869 to 1909.

RUFUS DAWES

Rufus Dawes, the lawyer and American poet, was born in Boston on January 26, 1803. He was the son of Thomas Dawes. He entered the Boston Latin School in 1811 and attended Harvard College from 1820 to 1823. He was refused his diploma as punishment for a supposed breach of discipline, afterwards disproved. He studied law and was admitted to the bar, but he did not practise. He devoted his time to literature and was editor of *The Emerald*, published in Baltimore. Among his writings are: *The Valley of Nashaway and Other Poems*, in 1830; *Geraldine, and Miscellaneous Poems*, in 1839; and *Nix's Mate*, in 1840. He died in Washington on November 30, 1859.

RALPH WALDO EMERSON

Ralph Waldo Emerson, the philosopher and essayist, was born in Boston on May 25, 1803. He entered the Boston Latin School in 1812 and was graduated from Harvard College in 1821. He became an assistant in his brother William's school for young ladies in Boston and taught for three years. In 1825 he entered the Divinity School at Cambridge to train for the Unitarian ministry. In 1829 he was installed as associate minister of the Second Church (Unitarian) in Boston, soon becoming the sole pastor. He afterwards abandoned his profession and, retiring to Concord, devoted himself to the study of philosophy. He became one of the most eminent American philosophers of the transcendental school. In 1832 he travelled in Italy, France, Scotland, and England, where he met Lan-

RALPH WALDO EMERSON
Ralph Waldo Emerson entered the Boston Latin School in 1812.
From *Commonwealth History of Massachusetts*, edited by Albert Bushnell Hart. By courtesy of the States History Company, New York City.

dor, Coleridge, Carlyle, and Wordsworth. After his return from England in 1833 he lived in Concord and began his career as a lecturer in Boston. In 1866 he received from Harvard College the degree of LL.D. and in 1867 he was elected an overseer. Among his published works are the following: *Nature*, in 1836; *Essays*, in 1841 and 1844; *Poems*, in 1846; *Representative Men*, in 1850; *English Traits*, in 1856; *The Conduct of Life*, in 1860; *May Day and Other Pieces*, in 1867; *Society and Solitude*, in 1870; and *Letters and Social Aims*, in 1876. He died on April 27, 1882, and was buried in Sleepy Hollow Cemetery, Concord, Massachusetts.

SAMUEL GRIDLEY HOWE

Dr. Samuel Gridley Howe, the husband of Julia Ward Howe, was born in Boston on November 10, 1801. According to the *Letters and Journals of Samuel Gridley Howe*, edited by his daughter, Laura E. Richards, he entered the Boston Latin School in 1812 and later entered Brown University, from which he was graduated in 1821. In 1824 he received the degree of M.D. from Harvard College. He later spent six years in Greece administering to the suffering people during the Revolution. In 1829, when Massachusetts incorporated the Perkins Institution and Massachusetts Asylum for the Blind, Dr. Howe was engaged to open and carry it on. He went abroad, where he inspected such schools. After returning to America, he started a school for the blind in his father's house in August, 1832. He was interested in many humanitarian and philanthropic causes. He died on January 9, 1876.

EDWARD GREELEY LORING

Edward Greeley Loring, judge of probate and judge of the United States Court of Claims, was born in Boston, on January 28, 1802. He entered the Boston Latin School in 1812 and was graduated from Harvard College in 1821. He studied law and practised in Boston in 1824. He was appointed United States commissioner of Massachusetts in 1841 and judge of probate for Suffolk County in 1847. In 1852 he became a lecturer at the Harvard Law School. In 1854 Anthony Burns, an escaped slave, was arrested in Boston and was brought before Judge Loring. As United States commissioner he was called upon to execute the fugitive slave law and ordered Burns's return to slavery. This was one of the cases which aroused the strong anti-slavery feeling in Massachusetts. In 1858, because of his unpopularity, he was removed from the position of probate judge. Two months later, however, President Buchanan appointed him judge of the United States Court of Claims. He retired in 1877 and died in Winthrop, Massachusetts, on June 18, 1890.

ELLIS GRAY LORING

Ellis Gray Loring, the distinguished lawyer and distant relative of Edward Greeley Loring, was born in Boston in 1803. He entered the Boston Latin School in 1814 and later attended Harvard College, leaving in his senior year. He studied law and was admitted to the Suffolk bar in 1827. He enrolled himself as a Garrison abolitionist and was one of the "immortal twelve" who formed the first anti-slavery society in Boston in 1831. He was elected counsellor of the anti-slavery society in 1833. He died in Boston on May 24, 1858.

CHARLES FRANCIS ADAMS

Charles Francis Adams, the distinguished diplomatist, was born in Boston on August 18, 1807. He was the son of John Quincy Adams and the grandson of John Adams. He entered the Boston Latin School in 1817, was graduated from Harvard College in 1825, and was admitted to the bar in 1828. He was the editor of the Boston *Whig* from 1846 to 1848. In 1848 he was nominated for vice-president of the United States by the Freesoilers, who nominated ex-President Martin Van Buren for the presidency. General Zachary Taylor and Millard Fillmore, the Whig candidates, were elected. Having joined the Republican party, he was elected a member of Congress in 1858 and in 1860. In 1861 he was appointed United States minister to Great Britain, serving until 1868, when he returned home. He received the degree of LL.D. from Harvard College in 1864. In 1871 and 1872 he was a member of the Geneva Court of Arbitration for the settlement of the Alabama claims. In 1872 he received the degree of D.C.L. from Yale College. He was vice-president and president of the American Academy of Arts and Sciences and vice-president of the Massachusetts Historical Society. He published *Life and Works of John Adams*. He died on November 21, 1886.

George Goldthwaite

George Goldthwaite, lawyer and United States senator, was born in Boston on December 10, 1809. He entered the Boston Latin School in 1818 and entered the United States Military Academy in 1822, where he remained two years. In 1826 he removed to Montgomery, Alabama. Here he studied law with his brother, Henry, and was admitted to the bar in 1827. In 1843 he was elected circuit judge. He was appointed justice of the Supreme Court in 1852 and in 1856 he became chief justice, resigning after thirteen days. He was appointed adjutant-general of Alabama at the beginning of the Civil War. In 1868 he was elected judge of the Circuit Court but he was disqualified by an act of Congress. In 1870 he was elected United States senator and in 1877 he retired. He died in Montgomery, Alabama, on March 16, 1879.

George Tyler Bigelow

George Tyler Bigelow, chief justice of the Supreme Court of Massachusetts, was born in Watertown on October 6, 1810. He entered the Boston Latin School in 1820 and was graduated from Harvard College in 1828. In 1839 he was elected a representative from Boston and entered the legislature in 1840. He served in the Lower House for five years. In 1860 Judge Bigelow was appointed to succeed Lemuel Shaw as chief justice of the Supreme Court of Massachusetts. He was a fellow of Harvard College. He died on April 12, 1878.

SAMUEL FRANCIS SMITH

Samuel Francis Smith, the author of the national hymn, *My Country, 'tis of Thee*, was born in Boston on October 21, 1808. He entered the Boston Latin School in 1820 and was graduated from Harvard College in 1829, in the same class with Oliver Wendell Holmes and James Freeman Clarke. He studied theology at Andover Seminary in 1831 and 1832 and became a Baptist clergyman in 1832. While at Andover he wrote *My Country, 'tis of Thee*, which was first used at a children's Fourth of July celebration at the Park Street Church in 1832. He edited *The Baptist Missionary Magazine* in Boston in 1832 and 1833. He was the pastor of the Baptist Church at Waterville, Maine, in 1834, and professor of modern languages in Waterville College (Colby University) from 1834 to 1842. In 1853 he received the degree of S.T.D. from Waterville College. He was pastor of a Baptist Church in Newton, Massachusetts, from 1842 to 1854. He edited *The Christian Review* from 1842 to 1849, and for many years was editor of the publications of the Baptist Missionary Union. He later devoted himself to private teaching and to writing. He is the author of many well-known songs and hymns, including *My Country, 'tis of Thee* and *The Morning Light is Breaking*. On April 3, 1895, he was given a very enthusiastic reception in Music Hall, Boston. He died in Boston on November 16, 1895.

JONATHAN MASON WARREN

Dr. Jonathan Mason Warren, the noted physician and son of Dr. John Collins Warren, was born in Boston in 1811. He entered the Boston Latin School in 1820, was graduated from the medical department of Harvard College in 1832, and afterwards studied in London and Paris. He established him-

SAMUEL FRANCIS SMITH
Samuel Francis Smith entered the Boston Latin School in 1820.
By permission of the Perry Pictures Company.

self in Boston, where for twenty years he was attending physician to the Massachusetts General Hospital. He received the
degree of A.M. from Harvard College in 1844. His chief work

was *Surgical Observations* . . . published in Boston in 1867. He died in Boston on August 19, 1867.

JAMES FREEMAN CLARKE

The Reverend James Freeman Clarke, the Unitarian preacher and author, was born in Hanover, New Hampshire, on April 4, 1810. He entered the Boston Latin School in 1821 and was graduated from Harvard College in 1829, and from the Cambridge Divinity School in 1833. He settled in Louisville, Kentucky, from 1833 to 1840. From 1841 until his death he was pastor of the Church of the Disciples in Boston. He was professor of natural theology at Harvard College from 1867 until 1871. Among his many works are the following: *Service-book and Hymn-book for the Church of the Disciples*, in 1844; *Life and Military Services of General William Hull*, in 1848; *Eleven Weeks in Europe*, in 1851; *Christian Doctrine of Forgiveness*, in 1852; *Christian Doctrine of Prayer*, in 1854; *The Hour Which Cometh and Now Is*, in 1862; *Orthodoxy: Its Truths and Errors*, in 1866; *Steps of Belief*, in 1870; *Ten Great Religions*, in 1871 and 1883; *Common Sense in Religion*, in 1873; *Exotics*, in 1874; *Go Up Higher*, in 1877; *Essentials and Non-Essentials in Religion*, in 1878; *Self Culture*, in 1880; *The Legend of Thomas Didymus*, in 1881; *Events and Epochs in Religious History*, in 1881; *Anti-Slavery Days*, in 1884; and *The Ideas of the Apostle Paul*, in 1884. He is also the author of many religious poems. He died in Boston on June 8, 1888. His *Autobiography to 1840, Diary, and Correspondence* was edited by Edward Everett Hale in 1891.

JAMES JACKSON, JR.

Dr. James Jackson, Jr., son of Dr. James Jackson (1777-1867), was born in 1810. He entered the Boston Latin School in 1821 and was graduated from Harvard College in 1828. In 1834 he received the degree of M.D. After his graduation

JAMES FREEMAN CLARKE

The Reverend James Freeman Clarke entered the Boston Latin School in 1821.

From James Freeman Clarke's *Autobiography, Diary and Correspondence*, edited by Edward Everett Hale, by permission of Houghton Mifflin Company, publishers.

CHARLES SUMNER
Charles Sumner entered the Boston Latin School in 1821.
From Justin Winsor's *The Memorial History of Boston.*

he went to Paris to study medicine under the famous teacher,
Louis. He made observations on a cholera epidemic in Paris,
an account of which he published in 1832 in Boston. He re-

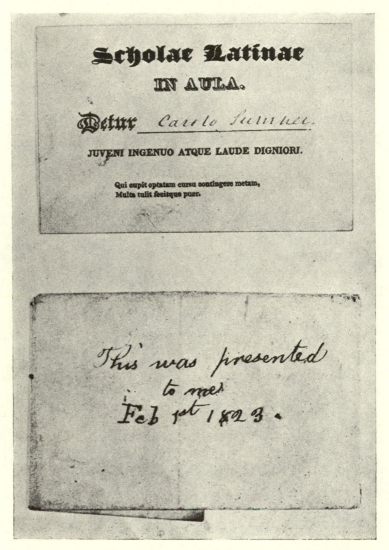

APPROBATION CARD PRESENTED TO CHARLES SUMNER ON FEBRUARY 1, 1823
Charles Sumner entered the Boston Latin School in 1821 and was graduated
in 1826.
*From the original in the possession of the Boston Latin School, by courtesy of the Boston
Latin School Association.*

turned to America to practise with his father. He died in Boston on March 27, 1834, at the age of twenty-four.

Charles Sumner

Charles Sumner, the famous senator and anti-slavery advocate, was born in Boston on January 6, 1811. He entered the Boston Latin School in 1821 and was graduated from Harvard College in 1830. He entered the Harvard Law School in 1831, under Judge Joseph Story, and was admitted to the bar in 1834, after which he practised at Boston. He was appointed, by Judge Story, reporter to the Circuit Court and wrote three volumes of Story's *Decisions,* known as *Sumner's Reports.* He was a lecturer at Harvard Law School from 1835 to 1837, and again in 1843. From 1837 to 1840 he travelled in Europe. Returning in 1840, he again opened a law office and, with J. C. Perkins, edited twenty volumes of Vesey's *Reports.* In 1845 he was chosen by Boston to give the Fourth of July oration. In 1851 he was elected to the United States Senate, succeeding Daniel Webster. In 1852 he began his congressional assault on slavery. He was violently assaulted in 1856 by Preston S. Brooks, a nephew of Senator Butler and a member of Congress from South Carolina, and was so severely beaten with a bludgeon that it was seven years before his health was fully restored. In 1857 he was reëlected to the Senate but he was not able to take his seat permanently until 1859. He was reëlected in 1863 and again in 1869. During the Civil War and afterwards he was chairman of the Senate Committee on Foreign Relations, from which he was removed in 1871. He died in Washington on March 11, 1874.

Robert Charles Winthrop

Robert Charles Winthrop, the distinguished orator and statesman, was born in Boston on May 12, 1809. He was a descendant of Governor John Winthrop. He entered the Boston Latin School in 1821 and was graduated from Harvard

THE FRANKLIN MEDAL FOR SCHOLARSHIP GIVEN TO CHARLES SUMNER

From the original in the possession of the Boston Latin School, by courtesy of the Boston Latin School Association.

College in 1828.   He studied law with Daniel Webster from 1828 to 1831 and was admitted to the bar in 1831.   He was a Whig member of the Massachusetts House of Representatives from 1836 to 1840 and speaker of the House from 1838 to 1840.   From 1840 to 1850 he was a member of the United

ROBERT CHARLES WINTHROP

Robert Charles Winthrop entered the Boston Latin School in 1821.

From *Commonwealth History of Massachusetts*, edited by Albert Bushnell Hart. By courtesy of the States History Company, New York City.

After the original by Huntington, by courtesy of the Massachusetts Historical Society.

States House of Representatives, with a short intermission from April to December, 1842. He was speaker of the Thirtieth Congress from 1847 to 1849. He was appointed to the Senate in July, 1850, to fill the unexpired term of Daniel Webster, and served only until February, 1851. He received a large plurality of popular votes for governor of Massachusetts in 1851, but he was defeated in the legislature. He was president of the Massachusetts Historical Society from 1855 until his resignation in 1885. From 1867 until his death he was president of the Peabody Trust for the advancement of education in the Southern states. He died in Boston on November 16, 1894.

GEORGE STILLMAN HILLARD

George Stillman Hillard, the distinguished lawyer and author, was born in Machias, Maine, on September 22, 1808. He entered the Boston Latin School in 1822 and was graduated from Harvard College in 1828. He taught in the Round Hill School at Northampton, Massachusetts, after graduation. He then entered Harvard Law School, from which he received the LL.B. degree in 1832. In 1833 he was admitted to the bar in Boston, where he entered into partnership with Charles Sumner. He was elected a member of the Massachusetts House of Representatives in 1836. In 1846 he visited Europe and upon his return he delivered a course of lectures upon Italy before the Lowell Institute of Boston. He was elected a member of the Massachusetts Senate in 1850 and a member of the Massachusetts Constitutional Convention in 1853. In 1857 he received the degree of LL.D. from Trinity College. He was United States district attorney for Massachusetts from 1867 to 1870. He devoted a great deal of time to literature. He was a member of the editorial staff of the *Christian Register* in 1833, editor of the *American Jurist* in 1834, and associate editor of the *Boston Courier* from 1856 to 1861. He published several books, prepared a series of school readers, and delivered many addresses. He died in Boston on January 21, 1879.

WENDELL PHILLIPS

Wendell Phillips entered the Boston Latin School in 1822.

From *Commonwealth History of Massachusetts*, edited by Albert Bushnell Hart. By courtesy of the States History Company, New York City.

After a photograph in the possession of Harvard College Library.

WENDELL PHILLIPS

Wendell Phillips, the orator and anti-slavery leader, was born in Boston on November 29, 1811. He was the son of John Phillips, the first mayor of Boston in 1822. He entered the Boston Latin School in 1822 and was graduated from Harvard College in 1831, receiving the degree of LL.B. in 1834. He was admitted to the Suffolk bar in 1834. In 1835 occurred the attack on William Lloyd Garrison by a Boston mob and two years later the murder of Lovejoy, the editor of an anti-slavery newspaper in Alton, Illinois. At a meeting held in Boston to condemn Lovejoy's murder Phillips delivered a speech of great fire and eloquence. From this time he was the foremost orator of the abolitionists. He was also an advocate of women's rights and a supporter of the temperance movement. He died in Boston on February 2, 1884.

NATHANIEL BRADSTREET SHURTLEFF

Dr. Nathaniel Bradstreet Shurtleff, the physician, antiquary, and mayor of Boston, was born in Boston on June 29, 1810. He entered the Boston Latin School in 1822, was graduated from Harvard College in 1831, and from the Medical School in 1834. He became a prominent physician in Boston. He was mayor of Boston from 1868 to 1870. He was the author of *A Topographical Description of Boston* in 1871, and was the editor of the series of *Records of the Governor and Company of Massachusetts Bay 1628-1686*, besides many other publications. He died in Boston on October 17, 1874.

EPES SARGENT

Epes Sargent, the journalist and author, was born in Gloucester, Massachusetts, on September 27, 1813. After studying at the Boston Latin School, which he entered in 1823, he attended Harvard College. He was editorially connected at different times with the *Boston Advertiser*, the *Atlas*, the *New York Mirror*, the *New Monthly Magazine*, and the *Boston Evening Transcript*. Among his dramas are *The Bride of Genoa, Velasco, Change Makes Change,* and *The Priestess.* Among his other works are *Wealth and Worth, Fleetwood, Songs of the Sea and Other Poems, Arctic Adventure by Sea*

GEORGE EDWARD ELLIS
The Reverend George Edward Ellis entered the Boston Latin School in 1824.
From *Massachusetts of To-day, A Memorial of the State Historical and Biographical, Issued for the World's Columbian Exposition at Chicago,* edited by Thomas C. Quinn in 1892. Published by the Columbia Publishing Company, Boston.

and Land, Peculiar, The Woman Who Dared, Planchette, and *Life of Henry Clay.* He also compiled a series of *Readers for Schools* and edited *Harper's Cyclopaedia of British and*

American Poetry. He died in Roxbury, Massachusetts, on December 31, 1880.

GEORGE EDWARD ELLIS

The Reverend George Edward Ellis, Unitarian clergyman and historian, was born in Boston on August 8, 1814. He entered the Boston Latin School in 1824, was graduated from Harvard College in 1833, and from the Divinity School in 1836. After travelling two years in Europe, he returned home and was ordained pastor of Harvard Unitarian Church in Charlestown, Massachusetts, in 1840. From 1857 to 1863 he was professor of systematic theology in Harvard Divinity School. He delivered courses of lectures before the Lowell Institute in 1864, 1871, and 1879. He was vice-president and then president of the Massachusetts Historical Society and a member of the board of overseers of Harvard College. He received the degree of D.D. from Harvard College in 1857 and the degree of LL.D. in 1883. He published many books and sermons. He died in Boston on December 20, 1894.

JOHN LOTHROP MOTLEY

John Lothrop Motley, the distinguished historian, novelist, and minister to Austria and England, was born in Dorchester, Massachusetts, on April 15, 1814. He entered the Boston Latin School in 1824 and was graduated from Harvard College in 1831. He studied in the German Universities of Berlin and Göttingen, where he became associated with Bismarck. He returned to America in 1834 and continued his legal studies. He was admitted to the bar in 1836. In 1839 he published his first novel, entitled *Morton's Hope.* In 1841 he was appointed secretary of the legation at Saint Petersburg, Russia, but he resigned within three months. Returning to America, he entered upon a literary career. In 1849 he published another novel, entitled *Merry Mount.* In 1851 he went to Europe, where he spent the next five years at Dresden, Brus-

JOHN LOTHROP MOTLEY
John Lothrop Motley entered the Boston Latin School in 1824.

sels, and The Hague in research work, preparatory to the publication of *The Rise of the Dutch Republic,* in London in 1856. He published *The History of the United Netherlands,* in four volumes, from 1860 to 1867, and the *Life of John van Barneveld* in 1874. In 1861 he was appointed United States minister to Austria, resigning in 1867. In 1869 he was appointed United States minister to England, but in November, 1870, he was recalled by President Grant for political reasons. He died at Frampton Court, near Dorchester, England, on May 29, 1877.

HENRY WARD BEECHER

The Reverend Henry Ward Beecher, the clergyman, orator, and reformer, was born in Litchfield, Connecticut, on June 24, 1813. He was the son of Dr. Lyman Beecher (1775-1863) and brother of Harriet Elizabeth Beecher-Stowe (1811-1896). He entered the Boston Latin School in 1826 and was graduated from Amherst College in 1834. In 1837 he was graduated from Lane Theological Seminary, Cincinnati, Ohio, of which his father was president. From 1837 to 1839 he was pastor of a missionary Presbyterian Church in Lawrenceburg, Indiana, and from 1839 to 1847 he was pastor of the Presbyterian Church in Indianapolis, Indiana. From 1847 to 1887 he was pastor of Plymouth Church, Brooklyn, a new Congregational organization. His speeches delivered in England in 1863 changed English public opinion in favor of the North. His writings are extensive in number and scope. He died in Brooklyn on March 8, 1887.

JOHN BERNARD FITZPATRICK

The Reverend John Bernard Fitzpatrick was born in Boston on November 1, 1812. He entered the Boston Latin School in 1826, was graduated from the College of Montreal in 1833, and later was educated at the Seminary of Saint Sulpice, in Paris. He received the degree of S.T.D. from Har-

HENRY WARD BEECHER

Henry Ward Beecher entered the Boston Latin School in 1826.

From *Saints, Sinners and Beechers,* by Lyman Beecher Stowe, copyright 1934, used by special permission of the publishers, the Bobbs-Merrill Company.

vard College in 1861. In 1840 he was ordained a Roman Catholic priest. In 1844 he was consecrated bishop-coadjutor of Boston, *cum jure successionis,* and in 1846 he succeeded Bishop Fenwick in the bishopric. He died in Boston on February 13, 1866.

FREDERICK OCTAVIUS PRINCE

Frederick Octavius Prince, lawyer and mayor of Boston, was born in Boston on January 18, 1818. He entered the Boston Latin School in 1827 and was graduated from Harvard College in 1836. He studied law and was admitted to the Suffolk bar in 1840. He was a member of the House of Representatives from 1851 to 1853, was a member of the Constitutional Convention of 1853, and served one term in the State Senate in 1854. He was mayor of Boston in 1877 and from 1879 to 1881. He was a trustee of the Boston Public Library. He died on June 16, 1899.

WILLIAM MAXWELL EVARTS

William Maxwell Evarts, the famous lawyer and statesman, was born in Boston on February 6, 1818. He entered the Boston Latin School in 1828 and was graduated from Yale College in 1837. He studied law and was admitted to the bar in New York in 1840. In 1860 he was chairman of the New York delegation to the Republican national convention. In 1861 he was an unsuccessful candidate for the United States senatorship from New York. He was chief counsel for President Andrew Johnson during the impeachment trial before the Senate in 1868. He was attorney-general of the United States from July, 1868, to March, 1869. In 1872 he was one of three lawyers for the United States, appointed by President Ulysses S. Grant, before the Court of Arbitration at Geneva, Switzerland, convened to settle on the Alabama claims. He was secretary of state during President Rutherford B. Hayes's administration from 1877 to 1881. In 1881 he was United States delegate to the international monetary conference at Paris. He was one of the United States senators from New York from 1885 to 1891. As an orator Senator Evarts stood in the foremost rank. He died in New York on February 28, 1901.

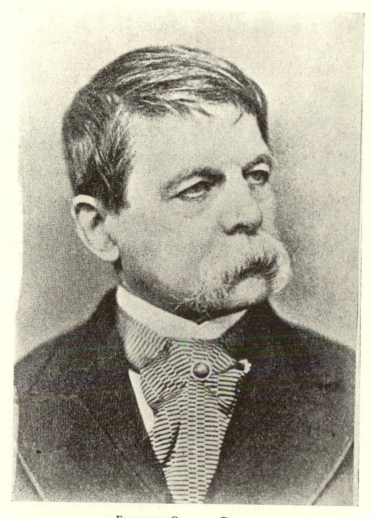

FREDERICK OCTAVIUS PRINCE
Frederick Octavius Prince entered the Boston Latin School in 1827.

From *Massachusetts of To-day, A Memorial of the State Historical and Biographical, Issued for the World's Columbian Exposition at Chicago*, edited by Thomas C. Quinn in 1892. Published by the Columbia Publishing Company, Boston.

Thomas William Parsons

Thomas William Parsons, dentist, poet, and translator of Dante, was born in Boston on August 18, 1819. He entered the Boston Latin School in 1828. In 1836 he visited Italy and after returning to Boston in 1837 he entered the Harvard Medical School. Although he received no medical degree he practised dentistry in Boston and later in London. In 1843 he translated the first ten cantos of Dante's *Inferno* and in 1867 he published the completed translation. In 1853 he received the honorary degree of M.A. from Harvard College. Among his published works are a volume of poems entitled *Ghetto di Roma*, published in Boston in 1854; *The Magnolia*, privately printed in 1867; *The Old House at Sudbury*, published in 1870; and *The Shadow of the Obelisk*, published in London in 1872. He died in Scituate, Massachusetts, on September 3, 1892.

Charles Devens

Charles Devens, the lawyer and jurist, was born in Charlestown, Massachusetts, on April 4, 1820. He entered the Boston Latin School in 1829 and was graduated from Harvard College in 1838 and from Harvard Law School in 1840. He was admitted to the bar in 1841. In 1848-1849 he was a Whig member of the Massachusetts Senate and from 1849 to 1853 he was United States marshall for Massachusetts. He practised law at Worcester from 1853 until 1861. Throughout the Civil War he served in the federal army, attaining the rank of brigadier general and that of major general. He was associate justice of the Superior Court of Massachusetts from 1867 to 1873, and associate justice of the Supreme Court of Massachusetts from 1873 to 1877. From 1877 to 1881 he was attorney-general of the United States, in the cabinet of President Rutherford B. Hayes. From 1881 until his death he was again associate justice of the Supreme Court of Massachusetts. He died in Boston on January 7, 1891.

RICHARD SALTONSTALL GREENOUGH

Richard Saltonstall Greenough, the eminent sculptor, was born in Jamaica Plain, Massachusetts, on April 27, 1819. He entered the Boston Latin School in 1829. In 1859 he received the honorary degree of A.M. from Harvard College. Among his works are the following: the familiar statue of Benjamin Franklin on School Street, executed in 1853; the marble statue of Governor John Winthrop, erected in Scollay Square in 1880 and now in the grounds of the First Church on Marlborough Street; a colossal statue of Governor John Winthrop in the Capitol at Washington; the *Boy and Eagle* in Boston Athenæum; *Carthaginian Girl* in the Museum of Fine Arts; and *Alma Mater* in the main corridor facing the entrance of the Boston Latin School. He died in Rome on April 23, 1904.

CHARLES SMITH BRADLEY

Charles Smith Bradley,[4] chief justice of Rhode Island, was born in Newburyport, Massachusetts, on July 19, 1819. He entered the Boston Latin School in 1830 and was graduated from Brown University in 1838. He was a tutor at Brown University for two years, after which he studied law at Harvard Law School in 1840 and 1841. He was admitted to the Rhode Island bar. In 1854 he was elected to the Rhode Island Senate. In 1866 he was elected chief justice of Rhode Island. In 1870 he was appointed lecturer at the Harvard Law School and in 1876 he became Bussey professor of law. He resigned in 1879 and returned to private practice. He died in New York on April 29, 1888.

EDWARD EVERETT HALE

The Reverend Edward Everett Hale, the Unitarian clergyman, author, and reformer, was born in Boston on April 3,

[4] The writer acknowledges her indebtedness to *The Centennial History of the Harvard Law School, 1817-1917*, published by The Harvard Law School Association in 1918.

CHARLES SMITH BRADLEY
Charles Smith Bradley entered the Boston Latin School in 1830.
From *The Centennial History of the Harvard Law School, 1817-1917*, published by The Harvard Law School Association in 1918. By courtesy of the Harvard Law School Association. After a portrait by Sir Hubert von Herkomer.

EDWARD EVERETT HALE

The Reverend Edward Everett Hale entered the Boston Latin School in 1831.

From *Commonwealth History of Massachusetts*, edited by Albert Bushnell Hart. By courtesy of the States History Company, New York City.

From a photograph by Garo, Boston.

1822. He was the son of Nathan Hale and nephew of Edward Everett. He entered the Boston Latin School in 1831 and was graduated from Harvard College in 1839. He was an Usher at the Boston Latin School from 1839 to 1841. He was pastor of the Church of the Unity, Worcester, Massachusetts, from 1846 to 1856, and minister of the South Congregational [Unitarian] Church, Boston, from 1856 to 1899. He first came into notice as a writer in 1859, when he contributed to the *Atlantic Monthly* the short story, "My Double and How He Undid Me." In 1863, at a time appropriate to develop loyalty to the Union, he published in the *Atlantic Monthly* his well-known "The Man Without a Country." He promoted the Chautauqua movement and assisted in organizing "lend-a-hand" clubs. He was the founder and editor of *The Christian Examiner* and *Old and New*, which were finally merged into the original *Scribner's Monthly*. In 1903 he became chaplain of the United States Senate, serving until his death. He died at Roxbury, Massachusetts, on June 10, 1909.

Thomas Ruggles Pynchon

Thomas Ruggles Pynchon, president of Trinity College, Hartford, Connecticut, was born in New Haven on January 19, 1823. He entered the Boston Latin School in 1832 and was graduated from Trinity College, Hartford, in 1841. He received the degree of M.A. in 1844. He was tutor at Trinity College from 1843 to 1847. In 1848 he was ordained a deacon at New Haven and, in 1849, a priest at Boston. From 1849 to 1855 he was rector of Stockbridge and Lenox. In 1854 he was elected Scovill professor of chemistry in Trinity College. He was president of Trinity College from 1874 to 1883. He received the degree of D.D. from Saint Stephen's College, New York, in 1865 and the degree of LL.D. from Columbia College in 1877. He was the author of *Introduction to Chemical Physics,* published in New York in 1869, and of various sermons, scientific papers, and pamphlets. He died in New Haven on October 6, 1904.

Charles Keating Tuckerman

Charles Keating Tuckerman, the author and United States minister to Greece, was born in Boston on March 11, 1821. He entered the Boston Latin School in 1834. He was United States minister to Greece from 1868 to 1872 and after his retirement resided in Europe. He edited A. R. Rongabe's *Greece: Her Progress and Present Position*, in New York in 1867. Among his works are *The Greeks of Today*, published in 1873; *Poems*, published in London in 1885; and *Personal Recollections of Notable People*, published in 1895. He died in Florence, Italy, on February 26, 1896.

Benjamin Apthorp Gould

Benjamin Apthorp Gould, the distinguished astronomer, was born in Boston on September 27, 1824. He was the son of Benjamin Apthorp Gould (1787-1859), who was the Master of the Boston Latin School from 1814 to 1828. He entered the Boston Latin School in 1835 and was graduated from Harvard College in 1844. He later studied astronomy at the observatories of Greenwich, Paris, Berlin, Göttingen, and Altona, returning home in 1848. From 1852 to 1867 he was in charge of the longitude department of the United States coast survey. From 1855 to 1859 he was director of the Dudley Observatory, in Albany, New York. In 1848 he received the degree of Ph.D. from Göttingen University and in 1885 he received the degree of LL.D. from Harvard College, and in 1887 from Columbia University. In 1868 he was appointed to organize the National Observatory of the Argentine Republic in Cordoba. He died in Cambridge on November 26, 1896.

Francis James Child

Frances James Child, the distinguished scholar, author, and educator, was born in Boston on February 1, 1825. He entered the Boston Latin School in 1840 and was graduated from Harvard College in 1846. He was tutor at Harvard from

REPORT CARD OF BENJAMIN APTHORP GOULD, JR., WHO ENTERED BOSTON LATIN
SCHOOL IN 1835

Benjamin Apthorp Gould, Jr., the noted astronomer, was the son of Benjamin Apthorp Gould, who was the Master of the Boston Latin School from 1814 to 1828.

Reduced from the original in the possession of the Boston Latin School, by courtesy of the Boston Latin School Association

1846 to 1848. In 1849 and 1850 he travelled in Europe and studied at Göttingen. In 1851 he returned to Harvard College and became Boylston professor of rhetoric and oratory, holding the position for twenty-five years. In 1857 he published eight volumes of *English and Scottish Ballads,* with critical notes. He was recognized in England and America as an authority on Anglo-Saxon and Old English. In 1876 he became professor of English literature. In 1854 he received the degree of Ph.D. from Göttingen. He died in Boston on September 11, 1896. In 1897 the Child Memorial Library was established in his honor at Harvard College.

FREEMAN JOSIAH BUMSTEAD

Dr. Freeman Josiah Bumstead, the famous physician, was born in Boston on April 21, 1826. He entered the Boston Latin School in 1841 and was graduated from Williams College in 1847. He then studied medicine in Paris. He became a practitioner in New York City, where he was appointed professor of venereal diseases in the College of Physicians and Surgeons. He was also surgeon at the Eye and Ear Hospital and the Charity Hospital. He published *Pathology and Treatment of Venereal Diseases,* in 1861, and valuable translations from Ricord and Cullerier. He died in New York City on November 28, 1879.

PAUL JOSEPH REVERE

Colonel Paul Joseph Revere was born in Boston on November 10, 1832. He entered the Boston Latin School in 1842 and was graduated from Harvard College in 1852. In July, 1861, he was appointed major of the Twentieth Massachusetts Volunteers. In September, 1862, he was promoted to the rank of lieutenant-colonel, and in April, 1863, to colonel of the Twentieth Massachusetts Volunteers. He was mortally wounded on July 2, 1863, at Gettysburg and died on July 5, 1863. He is buried in Mount Auburn Cemetery.

CHARLES WILLIAM ELIOT

Charles William Eliot, the distinguished president of Harvard University, was born in Boston on March 20, 1834. He

PAUL J. REVERE
Colonel Paul Joseph Revere entered the Boston Latin School in 1842.
From Justin Winsor's *The Memorial History of Boston.*

entered the Boston Latin School in 1844 and was graduated from Harvard College in 1853. He was tutor in mathematics and chemistry at Harvard College from 1854 to 1858, assistant professor of mathematics and chemistry from 1858 to 1861, and assistant professor of chemistry from 1861 to 1863. He studied chemistry and foreign educational methods in Europe from 1863 to 1865. He was professor of analytical chemistry at the Massachusetts Institute of Technology from 1865 to

CHARLES WILLIAM ELIOT
Charles William Eliot entered the Boston Latin School in 1844.
From *Commonwealth History of Massachusetts*, edited by Albert Bushnell Hart. By courtesy
of the States History Company, New York City.

1869, being absent fourteen months in Europe in 1867 and 1868. He was appointed president of Harvard University in 1869, resigning in November, 1908, and retiring from the position early in 1909. He was then elected president emeritus, when he was succeeded by Abbott Lawrence Lowell. In December, 1908, he was elected president of the National Civil Service Reform League. In 1910, at the age of seventy-six, he took a journey around the world. He died in 1927 at the age of ninety-three. Some of his published works are *The Working of the American Democracy, Educational Reform, Essays*, and *Addresses*. He published, in conjunction with F. H. Stover, *Manual of Inorganic Chemistry*, in 1866, and *Manual of Qualitative Chemical Analysis*, in 1869 and 1874.

SAMUEL PIERPONT LANGLEY

Samuel Pierpont Langley, the astronomer, physicist, and pioneer in aviation, was born in Roxbury, Massachusetts, on August 22, 1834. He entered the Boston Latin School in 1845 and then attended the English High School, from which he was graduated in 1851. From 1851 to 1864 he was engaged in engineering and architecture. In 1864 and 1865 he travelled in Europe with his brother, visiting observatories and learned societies. In 1865 he was an assistant in the Harvard College observatory and later he was appointed assistant professor of mathematics in charge of the observatory of the United States Naval Academy at Annapolis. In 1867 he became director of the Allegheny observatory and professor of physics and astronomy in the Western University of Pennsylvania, in Pittsburgh where he remained twenty years. In 1881 he organized an expedition to occupy the summit of Mount Whitney, California, in order to study the sun's rays. From 1887 to 1906 he was secretary of the Smithsonian Institution. He was the pioneer in research concerning solar radiation and human flight in heavier-than-air machines. He died in Aiken, South Carolina, on February 27, 1906.

SAMUEL PIERPONT LANGLEY

Samuel Pierpont Langley entered the Boston Latin School in 1845.

From *Fifty Years of Boston, A Memorial Volume Issued in Commemoration of the Tercentenary of 1930.* By courtesy of the Subcommittee on Memorial History of the Boston Tercentenary Committee.

JUSTIN WINSOR

Justin Winsor, the distinguished librarian and historian, was born in Boston on January 2, 1831. He entered the Boston Latin School in 1845 and was graduated from Harvard College in 1853. In 1866 he was appointed a trustee of the Boston Public Library and, in 1868, its superintendent. In 1877 he was appointed the librarian of Harvard University, retaining the position until his death. In 1880 he began the editing of the *Memorial History of Boston* in four volumes. In 1889 he published eight volumes of *The Narrative and Critical History of America*. He was one of the founders of both the American Library Association and the American Historical Association; he was president of the former from 1876 to 1885 and president of the latter from 1886 to 1887. He died in Cambridge on October 22, 1897.

PHILLIPS BROOKS

The Reverend Phillips Brooks, Bishop of Massachusetts, was born in Boston on December 13, 1835. He entered the Boston Latin School in 1846 and was graduated from Harvard College in 1855. After graduation he was Usher of the Boston Latin School for a few months and, in 1856, he began to study for the ministry of the Protestant Episcopal Church in the Episcopal Theological Seminary at Alexandria, Virginia. In 1859 he was graduated, was ordained deacon, and became rector of the Church of the Advent, Philadelphia. In 1860 he was ordained priest and in 1862 he became rector of the Church of the Holy Trinity, Philadelphia, where he remained seven years. In 1869 he was appointed rector of Trinity Church, Boston. In 1891 he was consecrated Bishop of the Protestant Episcopal Church of Massachusetts. In 1878 he published his first volume of sermons and later he issued other volumes. Among his other works are *Lectures on Preaching* and *The Influence of Jesus*. In 1885 he received from Oxford University the degree of S.T.D. In 1886 he was elected assis-

JUSTIN WINSOR
Justin Winsor entered the Boston Latin School in 1845.
From *Commonwealth History of Massachusetts,* edited by Albert Bushnell Hart. By courtesy
of the States History Company, New York City.

PHILLIPS BROOKS
The Reverend Phillips Brooks entered the Boston Latin School in 1846.

tant bishop of Pennsylvania, but he declined the offer. He died on January 23, 1893. Five of his brothers were also pupils of the Boston Latin School, three of whom later entered the ministry of the Episcopal Church.

HENRY LEE HIGGINSON

Henry Lee Higginson,[5] the banker and founder and patron of the Boston Symphony Orchestra, was born in New York City on November 18, 1834. His father, who was for a time a merchant in New York City, returned to Boston with his family after the panic of 1837. Henry Lee Higginson entered the Boston Latin School in 1846 and, after his graduation in 1851, he entered Harvard College, from which he was withdrawn in his freshman year because of eye trouble. He was sent to Europe in charge of a clergyman and returned home in 1853. He served in the Civil War, attaining the rank of major and brevet lieutenant-colonel in the first Massachusetts cavalry, and was wounded in 1863. After the war he engaged in banking in Boston. He devoted much of his income to the promotion of music and especially to the organization of the Boston Symphony Orchestra. He died in Boston on November 14, 1919.

ROBERT TREAT PAINE

Robert Treat Paine, the distinguished philanthropist, was born in Boston on October 28, 1835. He was the great-grandson of Robert Treat Paine, the signer of the Declaration of Independence. He entered the Boston Latin School in 1846 and was graduated from Harvard College in 1855. After studying law at the Harvard Law School and in Europe, he was admitted to the bar in 1859. He was the first president of the Associated Charities of Boston. He organized the Wells Memorial Workingmen's Institute and the Workingmen's Loan Association. In 1891 he was elected president of the American Peace Society. He was a member of the vestry of Trinity Church, a member of the Society for the Suppres-

[5] The writer acknowledges her indebtedness to Mark Antony De Wolfe Howe's *A Great Private Citizen*, published in 1920, and to Bliss Perry's *Life and Letters of Henry Lee Higginson*, published in 1921.

HENRY LEE HIGGINSON
Henry Lee Higginson entered the Boston Latin School in 1846.
From *Fifty Years of Boston, A Memorial Volume Issued in Commemoration of the Tercentenary of 1930.* By courtesy of the Subcommittee on Memorial History of the Boston Tercentenary Committee.

ROBERT TREAT PAINE
Robert Treat Paine entered the Boston Latin School in 1846.
From *Massachusetts of To-day, A Memorial of the State Historical and Biographical, Issued for the World's Columbian Exposition at Chicago*, edited by Thomas C. Quinn in 1892. Published by the Columbia Publishing Company, Boston.

sion of Vice, and vice-president of the Children's Aid Society. He died in Boston on August 11, 1910.

CHARLES FRANCIS ADAMS, JR.

Charles Francis Adams, Jr., the son of the distinguished diplomatist, was born in Boston on May 27, 1835. He entered the Boston Latin School in 1848 and was graduated from Harvard College in 1856. He was admitted to the bar in 1858. He served as an officer of cavalry in the Civil War, rising to the rank of brigadier-general. He was a member of the Massachusetts Board of Railroad Commissioners from 1869 to 1879 and chairman of the Board from 1872 to 1879. For several years he was president of the Union Pacific Railroad, from which office he resigned in 1890. He published *Chapters on Erie*, in 1871, and *Three Episodes of Massachusetts History*, in 1892. He contributed articles in the *North American Review* on railroad management, and wrote two chapters in *The Memorial History of Boston*, edited by Justin Winsor, one chapter on "The Earliest Explorations and Settlement of Boston Harbor," and the other on "The Canal and Railroad Enterprise of Boston." In 1911 he published *Studies Military and Diplomatic*. He died in Washington, D. C., on March 20, 1915.

CYRUS COBB

Cyrus Cobb, artist and sculptor, was born in Malden, Massachusetts, on August 6, 1834. He was the twin brother of the artist, Darius Cobb. He entered the Boston Latin School in 1849. Both brothers studied art together and refused opportunity for European study, wishing to have no master but nature. Cyrus began the study of law in 1869 and was graduated from Boston University Law School in 1873. He practised until 1879 and then resumed his art work. Among his sculptures are the Cambridge Soldiers' Monument in 1869 and a bust of Theodore Parker in 1886. He died in 1903.

CHARLES FRANCIS ADAMS
Charles Francis Adams entered the Boston Latin School in 1848.
From *Massachusetts of To-day, A Memorial of the State Historical and Biographical, Issued for the World's Columbian Exposition at Chicago*, edited by Thomas C. Quinn in 1892. Published by the Columbia Publishing Company, Boston.

CYRUS COBB
Cyrus Cobb entered the Boston Latin School in 1849.
From *Massachusetts of To-day, A Memorial of the State Historical and Biographical, Issued for the World's Columbian Exposition at Chicago*, edited by Thomas C. Quinn in 1892. Published by the Columbia Publishing Company, Boston.

DARIUS COBB
Darius Cobb entered the Boston Latin School in 1849.

From *Massachusetts of To-day, A Memorial of the State Historical and Biographical, Issued for the World's Columbian Exposition at Chicago,* edited by Thomas C. Quinn in 1892. Published by the Columbia Publishing Company, Boston.

DARIUS COBB

Darius Cobb, the portrait and landscape painter, was born in Malden, Massachusetts, on August 6, 1834. He was the twin brother of Cyrus Cobb. He entered the Boston Latin School in 1849. He then studied art from nature without instruction. Both brothers served in the Civil War from 1861 to 1865. Among his portraits are those of Governor Andrew of Massachusetts and Professor Agassiz, both at Harvard University. He died in 1919.

EDWARD GREELY LORING

Dr. Edward Greely Loring, the distinguished ophthalmologist, was born in Boston on September 28, 1837. He entered the Boston Latin School in 1850 and later attended Harvard College, leaving at the end of his sophomore year. He then went to Italy, where he spent three years studying medicine at Florence and Pisa. He entered Harvard Medical School, from which he received the degree of M.D. in 1864. After a year of training with Dr. Henry Willard Williams, Boston's pioneer ophthalmologist at the Boston City Hospital, and at the Massachusetts Charitable Eye and Ear Infirmary, he practised in Baltimore one year and later settled in New York City. He was one of the founders of the Manhattan Eye and Ear Hospital and later was surgeon to the New York Eye and Ear Infirmary. He made the first practical ophthalmoscope and published *Text-book of Ophthalmoscopy* in New York, in 1886. He died in New York City on April 23, 1888.

HORACE ELISHA SCUDDER

Horace Elisha Scudder, the distinguished author and editor, was born in Boston on October 16, 1838. He entered the Boston Latin School in 1853 and was graduated from Williams College in 1858. He then went to New York City, where he taught until 1861. He returned to Boston and pursued a literary career. He was editor of *The Riverside Magazine for Young People* from 1867 to 1871, and then became connected with Houghton, Mifflin and Company. In 1890 he succeeded Thomas Bailey Aldrich as editor of the *Atlantic Monthly*. Among his published works are *Seven Little People and their Friends*, in 1862; *The Life and Letters of David Coit Scudder*, in 1864; *Men and Manners in America*, in 1876; *Boston Town*, in 1881; *Life of Noah Webster*, in 1882; and *History of the United States*, in 1884. He died in Boston on January 11, 1902.

Edward Charles Pickering

Edward Charles Pickering, the distinguished astronomer, was born in Boston on July 19, 1846. He entered the Boston Latin School in 1857 and was graduated from the Lawrence Scientific School of Harvard College in 1865. He taught mathematics at the Lawrence Scientific School from 1865 to 1867. He was then elected Thayer professor of physics at the Massachusetts Institute of Technology and in 1876 he was appointed professor of astronomy and director of the Harvard College observatory. In 1877 he devised the meridian photometer. He died in Boston on February 2, 1919.

Matthew Harkins

Bishop Matthew Harkins, Roman Catholic bishop of Providence, was born in Boston on November 17, 1845. He entered the Boston Latin School in 1859 and was graduated from the School in 1862. From 1864 to 1869 he studied at the College of the Holy Cross, in Worcester, Massachusetts, at the English College at Douai, France, and at the Seminary of Saint Sulpice, in Paris. In 1869 he was ordained a priest at the Church of Saint Sulpice, Paris. He was curate of the Church of the Immaculate Conception, in Salem, Massachusetts, from 1871 to 1876; rector of Saint Malachis Church, in Arlington, Massachusetts, from 1876 to 1884; and rector of

Horace E. Scudder

HORACE E. SCUDDER

Horace Elisha Scudder entered the Boston Latin School in 1853.

Saint James's Church, in Boston, from 1884 to 1887. In 1887 he was consecrated bishop of the diocese of Providence, Rhode Island. He died on May 25, 1921.

HENRY MARION HOWE

Henry Marion Howe, the distinguished metallurgist and son of Dr. Samuel Gridley Howe and Julia Ward Howe, was born in Boston on March 2, 1848. He entered the Boston Latin School in 1859 and after his graduation from Harvard College in 1869 took graduate work at the Massachusetts Institute of Technology. From 1883 to 1897 he was consulting metallurgist in Boston and also lecturer in metallurgy at Massachusetts Institute of Technology. In 1897 he was appointed a professor at Columbia University, retiring in 1913 with the title of professor emeritus. From 1918 to 1922 he was consulting metallurgist to the United States Bureau of Standards. In 1919 he was scientific attaché of the American embassy at Paris. He died at Bedford Hills, New York, on May 14, 1922.

MARTIN MILMORE

Martin Milmore, the distinguished sculptor, was born in Sligo, Ireland, on September 14, 1844. In 1851 he came to Boston with his family. He entered the Boston Latin School in 1859. In 1860 he entered the studio of Thomas Ball, and several years later he established his own studio in Boston. He received in 1864 a commission to execute granite statues of Ceres, Flora, and Pomona for the Horticultural Hall in Boston. In 1867 he designed a bronze statue for the soldiers' monument at Forest Hills Cemetery, Roxbury. After receiving the contract from the city of Boston to execute an army and navy monument on the Common, he went to Rome for further study. The monument was unveiled in 1877. Among his notable works are busts of Pope Pius IX, Charles Sumner, Wendell Phillips, Ralph Waldo Emerson, Henry Wadsworth Longfellow, Theodore Parker, George Ticknor, and other distinguished citizens. He died in Boston on July 21, 1883.

CHAPTER VII

LOCATION OF THE BOSTON LATIN SCHOOL BUILDINGS

DURING the first decade after its establishment until 1645, or perhaps earlier, the "free school" in Boston was undoubtedly kept in the home of the Masters.[1] The success of a school does not depend upon the expense and excellence of its architecture, but upon the quality of its teaching, as the illustrious history of the Latin School testifies.

Philemon Pormort, who was appointed the Master in 1635, came to Boston in 1634. He is not listed in *The Book of Possessions* of 1643(?) as the owner of property, but in 1645, according to a deed of sale[2] from Valentine Hill to William Davies, he lived on the west side of a square [later called Church Square,[3] 1708], near the south corner of a lane [now Court Avenue] leading to Court Square.[4]

[1] For information concerning the exact location of the Masters' homes and of the schoolhouses on School Street the writer is indebted to Mr. Samuel C. Clough, a member of the Colonial Society of Massachusetts and an accepted authority on land titles in Colonial Boston.

[2] See *Suffolk Deeds*, Vol. I, p. 60, for the following: "Valentine Hill of Boston granted to William Davies a house & garden bounded wth the ordinary now in possession of James Pen on the south: the prison garden on the west: Philemon Permort on the North & also the meeting house: & the high street on the east: & this was by an absolute deed of sale dated the 20th (3°) 1645."

[3] Church Square was an open space around the First Church, constructed in 1640 on Cornhill [now Washington Street]. Church Square was named Cornhill Square in 1809 and Cornhill Court in 1814. It should be noted, to avoid confusion, that the first building of the First Church was constructed in 1632 on the south side of State Street.

[4] The house in which Pormort lived is listed in *The Book of Possessions* as Richard Truesdale's property, bounded on the north by Richard Parker, on the south by Valentine Hill, on the west by the Prison Yard, and on the east by the meeting-house. This house is numbered 109 on Samuel C. Clough's *Map of the Book of Possessions*, published in the *Transactions of the Colonial Society of Massachusetts*, March, 1927.

Daniel Maude, appointed the Master in 1636, is listed in *The Book of Possessions* as owning one house and garden "bounded with M^r. Bellingham south and west: M^r. Cotton north: and the streete east." This house was on the site of the present location of the Suffolk Bank on the corner of Pemberton Square and Tremont Street.[5] Daniel Maude was also granted a garden plot in 1637 on Long Acre [now Tremont Street], between Winter Street and School Street.

John Woodbridge succeeded Daniel Maude, probably in 1643. He is not listed in *The Book of Possessions* and his home is not recorded in the *Suffolk Deeds*. He was ordained the first minister of Andover about the year 1645.

On March 31, 1645, Thomas Scottow sold to the town of Boston for the town's use his "Dwelling howse, and yard, and garden" [the present City Hall lot], on the north side of the present School Street.[6] The Scottow home was later occupied by the Master of the Boston Latin School, as the following record in the *Selectmen's Minutes*, dated October 27, 1645, testifies: "It's Ordered that the Constables shall sett off six shillings of Henry Messenger's Rates, for mending the Schoole Master [probably Mr. Woodbridge] his part of the partition fence betweene their gardens." Mr. and Mrs. Robert Woodmancy later lived in this Scottow home, during the years in which Woodmancy was Master of the School. After Mr. Woodmancy's death on August 13, 1667, his widow continued to live in this home, provided by the town, as is evi-

[5] This property is numbered 36 on Samuel C. Clough's *Map of the Book of Possessions*, published in the *Transactions of the Colonial Society of Massachusetts*, March, 1927.

[6] See *Second Report of the Record Commissioners*, p. 83, for the following location of Thomas Scottow's property: ". . . bounded with the Lands of Henry Messenger towards the North; with the Land of M^r. Richard Hutchinson towards the East: with the Comon street toward the South: with the Burying place toward the west, and all for the sume of fifty-five pounds, . . ." Scottow's property is numbered 113 on Samuel C. Clough's *Map of the Book of Possessions*, published in the *Transactions of the Colonial Society of Massachusetts*, March, 1927.

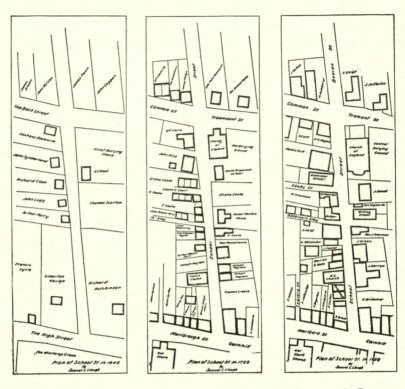

PLANS OF SCHOOL STREET IN 1643, 1722, AND 1798 BY MR. SAMUEL C. CLOUGH
From *The Eighteen Fifties and The Boston Five Cents Savings Bank*, by George A. Kyle. By courtesy of the Boston Five Cents Savings Bank.

denced by the following vote of the selectmen, on December 27, 1669: "Mr. Raynsford [one of the selectmen] to giue notice to Mᵣˢ Woodmansey that the towne occasions need the vse of the schoole house and to desire her to prouide otherwise for her selfe." She requested the town to provide her another house "if she remoueth from the schoole house" and, on March 14, 1669/70, the town voted "to allowe her £ 8. p. an for that end, dureinge her widdowhood."

Sometime between 1645 [or possibly earlier] and 1652 the town built the first schoolhouse on the north side of the present School Street,[7] in the southeast corner of the first burial ground. The first King's Chapel was later erected west of the schoolhouse between 1687 and 1689. This old King's Chapel, built of wood, covered the space now occupied by the tower and front part of the present stone King's Chapel erected in 1749. This first schoolhouse stood on the site now occupied by the rear of the present stone King's Chapel and a few feet adjacent to the east, but not at the rear of the site now occupied by King's Chapel, as some historians have asserted. According to Mr. Samuel C. Clough, King's Chapel covers more than one half of the site of the old schoolhouse.

The schoolhouse is first mentioned in the *Town Records* on March 29, 1652, when the selectmen granted "Libertie" to "Sarjt. Richard Cooke . . . for to set a house one the Towne's ground, which is betwixt the towne's house in which M[r]. Woodmansy now liveth, and the town skoole house; . . . alsoe if the towne shall see cause to inlarg the skoolehouse at any time hearafter, the town hath reserved libertie soe to doe." On March 14, 1655/56, the town ordered that the selectmen "shall have liberty to lay outt a peece of Ground outt of the townes land, which they give to the building of a house for instruction of the youth of the towne." According to Henry F. Jenks's *Catalogue of the Boston Public Latin School,* the word "give" is probably a clerical mistake for "gave." On December 29, 1656, the selectmen ordered that "care bee taken to pay Rich. Gridley for building the schoole house chimny."[8]

On January 30, 1664/65, the selectmen ordered that "John Hull and Petter Oliuer . . . take care about the inlardg-

[7]On May 3, 1708, "The way from Haugh[s] Corner Leading Northwesterly by the Lattin Free School extending as far as M[rs]. Whetcombs Corner" was officially recorded as School Street. See *Eighth Report of the Record Commissioners,* p. 51. As early as February 7, 1689/90, this way was mentioned in the *Town Records* as School House Lane. See *Seventh Report of the Record Commissioners,* p. 199.

[8]This chimney was probably a new chimney constructed on the old schoolhouse. There is no further evidence that a new schoolhouse was built at this early date, as some historians have asserted.

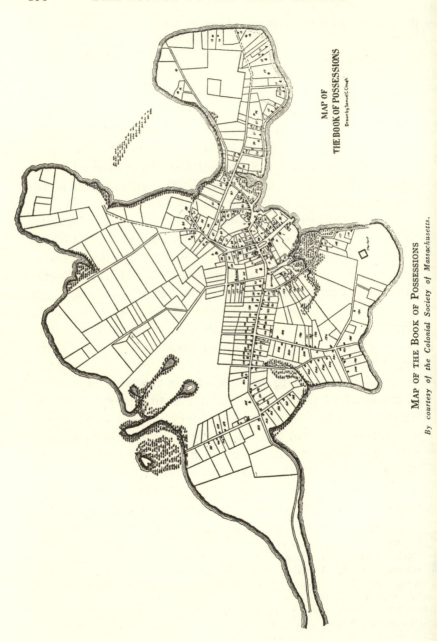

MAP OF
THE BOOK OF POSSESSIONS
Drawn by Samuel C Clough

Map of the Book of Possessions
By courtesy of the Colonial Society of Massachusetts.

ment of the Towne schoole-house." This enlarged schoolhouse accommodated the School until 1704, when a new building was constructed on the site of the original schoolhouse.

The old Scottow home east of the schoolhouse continued to be the Master's dwelling house, the rent of which was given to him in addition to his salary. On March 11, 1699/1700, the town voted that an appointed committee, with the selectmen, "shall Consider about repairing or Building, or hiring a House for Mr Ezek^ll Cheever, wch they Judge may be best." On March 10, 1700/1, the town voted that "a house be built for old M^r. Eze^k. Cheever the Latine Schoolmaster, and it was further voted that the Selectmen to take care about the building of it." The next month, on April 28, 1701, the selectmen voted "to provide a House for Mr Chever to dwell in untill a house be built for him." Later records prove that Ezekiel Cheever, on May 3, 1701, moved into a temporary dwelling house where he remained until the new dwelling was completed in the fall on the site of the old Scottow home, which had been the Master's home since 1645.

The description[9] and location of the new dwelling house, according to the agreement made by the selectmen with Captain John Barnerd, dated November 24, 1701, follows:

That the Said Barnet [*sic*] Shall Erect a House on the Land where Mr Ezekiell Chever Lately dwelt of forty foot long, Twenty foot wide and Twenty foot Stud wth four foot Rise in the Roof, to make a Cellar floor under one halfe of S^d house and to build a Kitchin of Sixteen foot in Length & twelve foot in bredth with a Chamber therein, and to Lay the floors flush through out the main house and to make three paire of Stayers in ye main house & one paire in the Kitchin and to Inclose S^d house & to do and compleat all carpenters worke and to finde all timber boards, Clapboards, nayles, glass and Glaziers worke & Iron worke. and to make one

---

[9] For the agreement with Mr. John Goodwin "to perform the masons worke" see *Eleventh Report of the Record Commissioners,* pp. 11-12. On June 3, 1702, the selectmen ordered that "Capt. John Barnerd do provide a Raysing Dinner for the Raysing the Schoolmasters House at the Charge of the Town not exceeding the Sum of Three pounds."

A TOWN VOTE TO BUILD A SCHOOLHOUSE

Reduced facsimile of part of page of *Boston Records*, 1700-1728, dated "March the 13th, 1703/4," containing the town vote to build a new schoolhouse for the Boston Latin School. It should be noted that the tax of £ 1200 "to be imployed in defraying the necessary Charges thereof" was the general annual assessment to defray the total charges of the town, including the cost of the proposed new schoolhouse.

From the original in the office of the City Clerk, City Hall, Boston, by courtesy of Mayor Frederick W. Mansfield.

Celler door and to finde one Lock for the Outer door of Said House, And also to make the Casemts for Sd house, and perform Sd worke and to finish Sd building by the first day of August next.

In consideration whereof the Select men do agree that the Sd Capt Barnet Shall have the Old Timbr, boards, Iron work & glass of the Old house now Standing on Sd Land and to pay unto him the Sum of One hundred and thirty pounds money that is to say forty pounds down in hand & the rest as the worke goes on.

A new schoolhouse was built in the summer of 1704 on the site of the old schoolhouse on the north side of School

Street. This new building was the result of the town vote on March 13, 1703/4, "that a New School House be build in Stead of the Old School House in wch m^r Ezekiell Chever Teacheth."[10] Three months later, on June 27, 1704, the selectmen voted "to proceed to the building of a new School house according to the Town vote" and then appointed a committee "to advise there about, and to promote the best methodes for the accomplishing there of, and to advise wth M^r. Cheever & M^r. Williams therein." There is no record where the School was temporarily held during the construction of the new building. It is the assumption of some historians that the pupils may have met in the Master's new dwelling house on School Street or they may have met in the Town House, on the site of the old State House.

The description of the plan of this new schoolhouse,[11] as recorded in the *Selectmen's Minutes* for July 24, 1704, follows:

Agreed wth M^r. John Bernerd as followeth, he to build a new School House of forty foot Long, Twenty-five foot wide & Eleven foot Stud, with eight windows below & five in the Roofe with wooden Casements to the eight Windows, to Lay the lower flowr with Sleepers & double boards So far as needfull, & the Chamber flowr with Single boards, to board below the plate inside & inside and out, to Clapboard the Out side and Shingle the Roof, to make a place to hang the Bell in, to make a paire of Staires up to the Chamber, and from thence a Ladder to the bell, to make one door next the Street, and a partition Cross the house below & to make three rows of benches for the boyes on each Side the room, to finde all Timber, boards, Clapboards, Shingles, nayles, hinges.

In consideration whereof the S^d. M^r. John Bernerd is to be paid One hundred pounds, and to have the Timber, Boards & Iron worke of the Old School House.[12]

---

[10] See page 238 for a facsimile of this manuscript record.

[11] See the frontispiece for a conjectural drawing of this 1704 schoolhouse by Mr. Samuel C. Clough. See also page 241 for the architectural plans drawn by Mr. Clough.

[12] See page 240 for a facsimile of this manuscript record.

CONTRACT FOR BUILDING THE SCHOOLHOUSE

Facsimile of page of *Records of Boston Selectmen, 1701-1715*, dated July 24, 1704, containing the contract with Mr. John Barnerd for building the new schoolhouse on the site of the old schoolhouse on the north side of School Street.

From the original in the office of the City Clerk, City Hall, Boston, by courtesy of Mayor Frederick W. Mansfield.

The Agreement

"Agreed wth Mr. John Barnerd as followeth, he to build a new School House of forty foot Long, Twenty-five foot wide & Eleven foot Stud, with eight windows below & five in the Roofe with wooden Casements to the eight Windows, to Lay the lower flowr with Sleepers & double boards So far as needfull, & the Chamber flowr with Single boards, to board below the plate inside & inside and out, to Clapboard the Outside and Shingle the Roof, to make a place to hang the Bell in, to make a paire of Staires up to the Chamber, and from thence a Ladder to the bell, to make one door next the Street, and a partition Cross the house below & to make three rows of benches for the boyes on each Side the room, to finde all Timber, boards, Clapboards, Shingles, nayles, hinges."

Record Commissioners Report, Vol. XI, p. 39

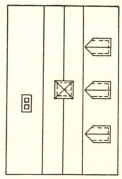

Roof Plan

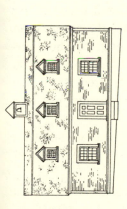

Front Elevation

Section A-B

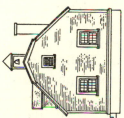

End Elevation

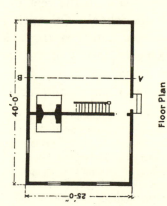

Floor Plan

Conjectural Drawing of the Boston Latin School in accordance with the contract between the Selectmen of Boston and Mr. John Barnerd, July 24, 1704.

Samuel C. Clough Del.

On June 30, 1707, the selectmen, "being Sencible of the necessity of setting up a House of Easment for the Lattin Free-School," ordered that "the same be set on the South Side of the wood House, joyning to the South Easterly Corner of S^d School House." On September 2, of that year, the selectmen directed Mr. Samuel Bridge "to place & Set up the House of Easement for the Latten School at the West^{ly} end of ye School-House."

During the height of the smallpox epidemic[13] in the late spring and early summer of 1721 the Boston Latin School, under the mastership of Nathaniel Williams, was held in the representatives' room at the Town House,[14] "in as much as there are three Several Persons in Distinct Houses in School Street near to the Publick Gramer Scholl Sick of the Small pox which may Prevent many of the youth attending the School at that Place." It is interesting to note, in this connection, that Nathaniel Williams also practised medicine and was known as "the beloved physician." He was the author of a tract on *Small Pox.*

On March 14, 1747/48, the proprietors of King's Chapel, desiring to reconstruct and enlarge their Church, petitioned the town for the land in the rear of the Church occupied by the Boston Latin School. On April 18, 1748, the town voted that the selectmen make "a legal Conveyance" to the Petitioners [of King's Chapel] of "a Peice of Land Fronting on School Street extending Thirty feet on said Street from the East end of Kings Chappel and includes the Passage way into

[13] Approximately six thousand persons had smallpox in Boston in 1721, of whom nearly one thousand died. Inoculation was then first introduced in Boston by Dr. Zabdiel Boylston, against strong opposition. This was the most important event in the medical history of the Province. The Reverend Cotton Mather favored inoculation, in spite of threats of personal violence.

[14] The original Town House, built of wood, was on the site of the old State House, at the head of the present State Street, and was destroyed by the great fire of 1711. In 1712 a new brick building was erected for the Town House, on the same site, which was later destroyed by the fire of 1747.

FIRST SCHOOLHOUSE ON SOUTH SIDE OF SCHOOL STREET
1748-1812

From Henry F. Jenks's *Catalogue of the Boston Public Latin School*, by courtesy of the Boston
Latin School Association.

the Burying Ground, and the westerly part of the School house
and of the Yard thereto belonging measuring Thirty Seven feet
back from the said Street together with the old School house
and other Buildings belonging to it, . . ." After much discussion, the town proposed that King's Chapel should have
this lot, on condition that a new schoolhouse should be built,
by the Church, on a convenient lot of land in the near vicinity.
Mr. Joseph Green, a prominent merchant and wit of the day,
sent to John Lovell, the Master of the School, who heartily
opposed the proposal of removing the School to accommodate
the Church, the following facetious poem:

> A fig for your learning! I tell you the Town,
> To make the church larger, must pull the school down.
> Unluckily spoken replied Master Birch,—
> Then learning, I fear, stops the growth of the church.

On July 20, 1748, the selectmen agreed that the Church should build a new brick schoolhouse on the south side of School Street, on the land purchased from Richard Saltonstall, on the corner of what was then Cook's Court, later called Chapman Place, where a corner of the Parker House was subsequently erected. A tablet, on the west side of Chapman Place, today marks the site. The plan of the new schoolhouse, as agreed by the selectmen on July 20, 1748, is as follows: "A Brick house of the Dimensions following, Vizt. Thirty four feet front towards School street, Thirty six feet deep on the Passage and twelve feet stud, with suitable Doors and Windows and Finished Workmanlike to the acceptance of the Select men with House of Office, Wood house &c."

It appears, from later records, that "further Conveniences & Ornaments" had been added to the School, which were made possible by subscriptions procured by John Lovell, the Master. Mr. Lovell sent a "Memorial" to the town on May 20, 1772, in which he described the schoolhouse as follows:

The Effects of which appear in the hight of the Walls of the Room two feet above what the Masons were to build them by Contract in the Carvings round the top, the Frontispeice of the Door, the Cornish round the Pediment & Eves; the Cupola for the Bell with the Vane upon the top, & the large and commodious Stone Steps at the Entrance of the School; the cost of all which amounted to a much larger sum than that of the Cellar.[15]

[15]See page 245 for a facsimile of this manuscript record. See also the *Fourteenth Report of the Record Commissioners,* p. 208, under the date March 9, 1751/52: "Voted that a Porch be built at the South Entrance of the Grammer School whereof M^r. John Lovel is Master, and the Selectmen are desired to Effect the same in the best manner they can."

A TOWN VOTE CONCERNING THE SCHOOLHOUSE CELLAR

Reduced facsimile of page of *Boston Town Records, 1770 -1777*, dated May 20, 1772, containing town vote to allow Mr. John Lovell the use of the cellar of the Latin schoolhouse. It appears that "further Conveniences & Ornaments" had been added to the schoolhouse constructed in 1748 on the south side of School Street.

From the original in the office of the City Clerk, City Hall, Boston, by courtesy of Mayor Frederick W. Mansfield.

SECOND SCHOOLHOUSE ON SOUTH SIDE OF SCHOOL STREET
1812-1844
From Justin Winsor's *The Memorial History of Boston.*

The Boston Latin School, under the mastership of John Lovell, moved into the new schoolhouse on Monday, May 8, 1749, as the following vote of the selectmen, on May 3, 1749, testifies: "Voted, That m^r. Lovell, Master of the South Grammar School, be directed to remove his Scholars into the New School house, on Monday morning next being the Eighth of May instant."

In 1785 this schoolhouse was repaired and the Latin School was temporarily kept in Faneuil Hall. About 1812 there was a fire in the schoolhouse, after which the old building was pulled down, and a new building of three stories with a granite front was built on the same site.[16] This schoolhouse for several years accommodated both the Boston Latin School and the Centre Reading and Writing School.

While this new schoolhouse was being rebuilt, the School, according to Henry F. Jenks's *Catalogue of the Boston Public*

[16]See picture above.

BEDFORD STREET SCHOOLHOUSE
1844-1881

The following is an extract from "Glimpses of Old Boston," written by George Santayana and published in the March 1932 issue of the *Boston Latin School Register*. George Santayana, the distinguished philosopher, poet, and essayist, entered the Boston Latin School in 1874 and was graduated in 1882.

"There is one image above all others that survives from the wreckage of my school days: the picture of the old Bedford Street Schoolhouse. There is no beauty in it, and little intrinsic interest; but for me it has become a symbol; a part of one of those Great Companions, one of those friendly worlds or countries of the imagination, which accompany a man through life. They become parts of himself, from which he draws his dreams, or his stories if he is a writer of stories; and in the style of those remembered episodes he may invent others, having the same homely flavour. The Bedford Street Schoolhouse was, or seemed, a vast rickety old shell of a building, bare, shabby, and forlorn to the point of squalor; not dirty exactly, but worn, shaky, and stained deeply in every part by time, weather, and merciless usage. The dingy old brickwall—everything in that world was dingy red brick—had none of those soft pink lights or mossy patina or plastic inequalities of surface which make some old brick walls so beautiful. They remained stark and unyielding in spite of time, thin and sharp like impoverished old maids; and the glassy expanse of those great rattling window-sashes, cut into many panes, and movable with difficulty, remained blank and vacant."

From Henry F. Jenk's *Catalogue of the Boston Public Latin School*, by courtesy of the Boston Latin School Association.

THE BOSTON LATIN SCHOOLHOUSE ON WARREN AVENUE
By courtesy of the Boston Latin School Association.

Latin School, was kept for a time in an old barn in Cole Lane[17] [now Portland Street] and soon afterwards the School was removed to a building on Pemberton's Hill.[18]

From 1844 until 1881 the Boston Latin School was located on Bedford Street,[19] now the extension of Harrison Avenue. The English High School, established in 1821, occupied one half of the building. In 1844, according to a letter[20] from Epes Sargent Dixwell to Henry F. Jenks, dated January 29, 1887, the Latin School for over three weeks occupied the Washington Bank Building, situated opposite Boylston Market House at the corner of Washington and Beach Streets.

[17] In 1708 Cold Lane [*sic*] was recorded as "The way Leading from m[r]. Harrises Corner in Hanover Street North westerly down to the Mill pond."

[18] Pemberton's Hill was dug down in 1835. It was the site of the present Pemberton Square.

[19] See page 247.

[20] The writer is indebted to Mr. T. Franklin Currier for information concerning these letters sent to Henry F. Jenks after the publication of Henry F. Jenks's *Catalogue of the Boston Public Latin School* in 1886.

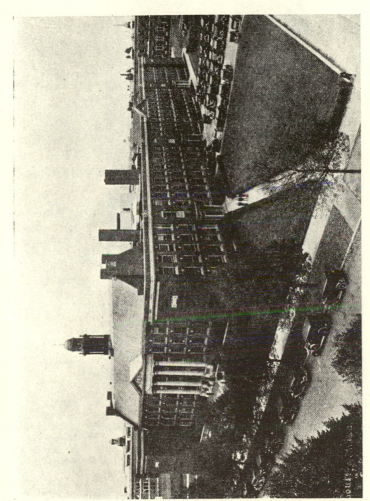

THE PRESENT BOSTON LATIN SCHOOLHOUSE ON AVENUE LOUIS PASTEUR
By courtesy of the Boston Latin School Association.

STATUE OF "ALMA MATER" BY RICHARD SALTONSTALL GREENOUGH

This statue, in the lower corridor facing the main entrance of the Boston Latin School, represents Alma Mater crowning her heroes who served in the Civil War. Those who died in the war are named on a shield which she is holding. Those who returned are named on two marble tablets near the statue. The wife of Dr. John Collins Warren posed for the studies of the statue when she was a young girl in Rome.

A bronze tablet, on the right wall of the main corridor of the Boston Latin School, has inscribed upon it the names of those Latin School boys who died in the World War. The tablet on the left wall is in honor of the 480 alumni and undergraduates who enlisted in the army and navy.

By courtesy of the Boston Latin School Association.

Dr. Benjamin Joy Jeffries, who entered the Boston Latin School in 1843, also wrote to Henry F. Jenks in 1887, stating that the Latin School "occupied the Boylston Bank Building [*sic*]." Dr. Jeffries also added: "For us boys there it was a memory."

From 1881 until 1922 the Latin School was located on Warren Avenue.[21] The English High School occupied the part of the building facing Montgomery Street.

The present building, into which the School moved in September, 1922, is located on Avenue Louis Pasteur in the Fenway. The School was dedicated on May 17, 1923, at which occasion President *Emeritus* Charles William Eliot was present. In the first year the building proved inadequate for the growing numbers and six extra classrooms were added. In 1932 and 1933 the building was enlarged[22] to about twice its original size.

[21]See page 248.
[22]See page 249.

CHAPTER VIII

THE DEVELOPMENT OF THE CURRICULUM OF THE BOSTON LATIN SCHOOL

One wonders . . . what is to be taught here in the years to come. He is sure that the books will change, that the sciences will change, that new studies will be developed, that new methods of interpretation will be discovered, that new kingdoms of the infinite knowledge are to be opened to the discerning eye of man, in the years that are to come. He knows it is impossible for any man to say what will be taught in these halls a hundred years hence; but yet, with that unknown development he is in deep sympathy, because he knows that the boys of a hundred years hence, like the boys of to-day, will be taught here to be faithful to the deep purposes of knowledge, will be trained to conscientious study, to the love of knowledge, to justice and generosity, to respect for themselves, and obedience to authority, and honor for man, and reverence for God.

—Phillips Brooks (*Address,* February 22, 1881)

It is assumed by other writers that the School established by vote of the town on "The 13th of the 2d moneth, 1635" was for the teaching of Latin and Greek. The assumption that the School from the beginning taught the classics may be, and probably is, correct. It is important, however, to state the exact facts as revealed by the documents, dividing sharply the established facts and those inferred.

The Curriculum from 1635 to 1708

From 1635 to 1708, the year in which Ezekiel Cheever died, no definite curriculum has been recorded. The inferences that, from the beginning, not only the classics but also the elementary subjects of reading, writing, "cyphering," and spelling were taught at the School are drawn from the following data: namely, the known curricula of English Latin grammar schools of the period; the scholarly qualifications of Daniel Maude, who was Master of the School from 1636 to 1643; the establishment of Latin grammar schools in neighboring towns; the entrance requirements of Harvard College in 1642, the testimony of Governor John Winthrop in 1645; the will of Robert Keayne, "executed and proved" in 1656; the evidence in the *Selectmen's Minutes*; and the identification of old textbooks belonging to boys who entered the "free school" in Boston.

We know that the free grammar schools in England were schools in which Latin and Greek were taught.[1] In Boston, Lincolnshire, England, there was a free grammar school, in which the classics were taught. The Reverend John Cotton had been appointed to the vicarage of that town in 1612 and, in 1613, he was nominated to examine an Usher for the free school. In 1633 he came to Boston, New England, with enthusiasm and wise plans for the new Colony. It is more than probable that he was influential in establishing in 1635 the first free school in Boston, New England, and it is reasonable to infer that this school was patterned after the Latin grammar school in Boston, England. It was the Reverend John Cotton who introduced in Boston the English custom of the Thursday lecture. For many years the School was dismissed early on that day and the school boys were required to attend the lecture.

Daniel Maude, who was appointed Master of the free school in Boston in 1636, had received the degree of Master of Arts from Cambridge University. This preparation would well qualify him to be a teacher of the classics; it is unlikely that he would be employed simply to teach reading, writing, and arithmetic.

We know that other Latin grammar schools were estab-

[1] See Foster Watson, *The English Grammar Schools to 1660: their Curriculum and Practice.*

The Wicked mans 'Portion.

OR

A SERMON

(Preached at the *Lecture* in *Boston* in *New-England* the
18 th. day of the 1 Moneth 1674. when two men
were *executed*, who had *murthered*
their Master.)

Wherein is shewed

*That excesse in wickednesse doth bring
untimely Death.*

By *INCREASE MATHER*, Teacher
of a Church of Christ.

Prov. 10. 27. *The fear of the Lord prolongeth dayes, but the years
of the wicked shall be shortned.*

Eph. 6. 2. 3. *Honour thy Father and thy Mother (which is the first
Commandment with promise) that it may be well with thee,
and thou mayst live long on the Earth.*

Pœna ad paucos, metus ad omnes.

BOSTON,
Printed by *John Foster.* 1675

TITLE OF THE FIRST BOOK PRINTED IN BOSTON
The Boston Latin School boys were required to attend the Thursday Lecture,
an English custom introduced by the Reverend John Cotton.
From Justin Winsor's *The Memorial History of Boston.*

lished in neighboring towns at this time.[2] It is, therefore,
reasonable to infer that the school established in Boston in
1635 was also a Latin grammar school.

Some indication of the ground covered at the free school
in Boston is furnished by the following Harvard College en-

[2] See Marcus Wilson Jernegan, *Laboring and Dependent Classes in Colonial
America, 1607-1783*, pp. 69-83.

trance requirements of 1642, under President Henry Dunster, which included Introductory Latin, Latin Grammar, Cicero, and Greek Grammar, a typical English Latin-grammar-school curriculum: "When any Schollar is able to understand *Tully*, or such like classicall Latine Author *extempore*, and make and speake true Latine in Verse and Prose, *suo ut aiunt Marte*; And decline perfectly the Paradigm's of *Nounes* and *Verbes* in the *Greek* tongue: Let him then and not before be capable of admission into the Colledge."[3]

That the elementary subjects were taught at this free school, in addition to the classics, is evidenced by the record in Governor Winthrop's *Journal,* under the date August 3, 1645, that in Boston "they made an order to allow forever fifty pounds to the master and an house, and 30 pounds to an usher, who should also teach to read and write and cipher."[4]

The earliest definite reference in the *Town Records* to the study of Latin at the School is in 1653, when Robert Keayne[5] signed a will, bequeathing fifty pounds "to the use of the free schoole at Boston, to helpe on the Trayning up of some poore mens Children of Boston (that are most towardly and hopefull) in the knowledge of God & of Learning, not only in the Latine Tongue but also to write & cypher. . . ."

In 1666 the School is called "the grammer Schoole"; the expression so used may fairly indicate a Latin grammar school. It was not until March 13, 1698/99, that this "free school" in Boston was definitely referred to in the *Town Records* as the "Latine School."

That the duty of the Usher of the School was to teach the elementary subjects is evidenced by the following record of the selectmen of Boston, dated the 26th of the first month,

---

[3] *New Englands First Fruits,* p. 13. In 1655 Harvard College introduced higher Greek requirements but, in 1692, the college went back to the original "paradigm" requirement.

[4] See Marcus W. Jernegan, *op. cit.,* p. 72. Professor Jernegan states that there is doubt concerning Winthrop's statement.

[5] Robert Keayne died on March 23, 1655/56.

1666: "Agreed with Mr Dannell Hincheman for 40 £ p Annm to asist Mr Woodmancy in the grammer Schoole & teach Childere to wright, the Yeare to begine the 1th of March: 65/6."[6]

The most interesting evidence of the classical curriculum is the Harvard College Library collection of Colonial textbooks, several of which have been identified by their dated autographs and inscriptions as belonging to boys who entered the "free school" in Boston.[7]

THE CURRICULUM OF 1708

The first printed record of subjects taught and of textbooks used at the Latin School is the Reverend Cotton Mather's *Corderius Americanus*,[8] printed in Boston "at the Sign of the Bible in Cornhill" in 1708, containing the funeral sermon, an elegy,[9] and a Latin epitaph on Ezekiel Cheever, who was the Master of the School from January 6, 1670/71, until his death in 1708. Cotton Mather says: "All the Eight parts of Speech he [Cheever] taught to them" and "We Learnt Prosodia." He also mentions the following: Ovid's *De Tristibus* and *Metamorphoses*; Tully's [Cicero's] *De Officiis* and *Orations;* Virgil; Homer; The Testament; "Lilly" [Lily's *Latin Grammar*]; *Sententiae Pueriles;* Cato; Corderius's *Colloquies;* and the "Making of Themes." Mather testifies, in his writings, that when he was young he studied Aesop and Terence. In the elegy, furthermore, Mather calls Cheever "A Christian Terence," which may be taken as indirect evidence that Terence was also read at the Latin School as early as the seventeenth century. The Reverend John Barnard, who entered the Latin School in 1689, under Ezekiel Cheever, has recorded

[6] See page 115 for a facsimile of this manuscript record. The printed record is not an accurate copy of this original.

[7] See Chapter IX for a discussion of Latin School textbooks.

[8] See page 257 for the title-page of *Corderius Americanus*.

[9] The elegy is entitled *An Essay on the Memory of my Venerable Master; Ezekiel Cheever.*

Corderius Americanus.

An Essay

UPON

The Good EDUCATION of CHILDREN.

And what may Hopefully be Attempted, for the *Hope of the FLOCK.*

IN A

FUNERAL SERMON

UPON

Mr. EZEKIEL CHEEVER.

The *Ancient* and *Honourable* MASTER of the FREE-SCHOOL in *Boston.*

Who left off, but when Mortality took him off, in *August,* 1708. the Ninety Fourth Year of his Age. With an ELEGY and an EPITAPH upon him.

By one that was once a Scholar to him.

Veter [CHEEVERUS,] *cum sic moritur, non moritur.*

By Cotton Mather

BOSTON, Printed by *John Allen,* for *Nicholas Boone,* at the Sign of the *Bible* in *Cornhill,* near the Corner of *School-street.* 1708.

TITLE-PAGE OF *Corderius Americanus*
By courtesy of the Harvard College Library.

that he studied "the accidence," translated "Æsop's Fables into Latin verse," and was "perfectly acquainted with prosody."

THE CURRICULUM OF 1712

The earliest extant full record of the Latin School curriculum and "acct of the Methods of Instruction" is that of 1712, written by Nathaniel Williams, Master of the School. This document was inclosed in a letter sent to Nehemiah Hobart, then senior fellow of Harvard College. The original manuscript curriculum is in the possession of Professor Kenneth B. Murdock of Harvard University, and, with his kind permission, a facsimile is here reproduced.[10] This curriculum of 1712, a seven-year course, includes the textbooks mentioned in the earlier records, with the exception of Terence, and adds the following: Erasmus's *Colloquies*; Garretson's *Exercises*; Cicero's *Epistles* ["Tullies Epistles"]; Lucius Florus; Justin; Greek Testament; Isocrates; Hesiod; Horace; Juvenal; Persius; Godwin's *Roman Antiquities*; William Walker's *Treatise on Particles*; and "Turning a Psalm or something Divine into Latin verse."

The full text of this 1712 curriculum of Nathaniel Williams follows:[11]

1. 2. 3.   The three first years are spent first in Learning by heart & then acc. to their capacities understanding the Accidence and Nomenclator in construing & parsing acc: to the English rules of Syntax Sententiae Pueriles Cato & Corderius & AEsops Fables.

4.   The 4th year, or sooner if their capacities allow it, they are entred upon *Erasmus* to which they are allou'd no English, but are taught to translate it by the help of the Dictionary and Accidence, which Eng-

---

[10] See page 261. For a detailed discussion of this curriculum see the article by Kenneth B. Murdock on "The Teaching of Latin and Greek at the Boston Latin School in 1712," in *Publications of the Colonial Society of Massachusetts*, Vol. 27, pp. 21-29.

[11] According to Professor Murdock, the "x" refers to the marginal notation, indicating that there were inclosed with the account of the curriculum samples of students' work. These papers have not been found.

lish translatiō of theirs is written down fair by each
of them, after the recital of the lesson, and then
brought to the Master for his observation and correction both as to the Translatiō & orthography: This
when corrected is carefully reserved till fryday, and
then render'd into the Latin of the Author exactly
instead of the old way of Repitition, and in the afternoon of that day it is (a part of it) varied for them
as to mood tense case number &c and given them to
translate into Latin, still keeping to the words of the
Author. an Example of which you have in the paper
marked on the backside A. These continue to read
AEsops Fables with yᵉ English translation, the better
to help them in the aforesᵈ translatg. They are also
now initiated in the Latin grammar, and begin to give
the latin rules in Propr: As in pres: & Syntax in their
parsing; and at the latter end of the year enter upon
Ovid de Tristibus (which is recited by heart on the
usual time of fryday afternoon) & upon translating
English into Latin, out of mᵣ Garretson's Exercises.

5.   The fifth year they are entred upon Tullies
Epistles (Still continuing the use of Erasmus in the
morning & Ovid de Trist: afternoon) the Elegancies
of which are remarkd and improv'd in the afternoon

x

of the day they learn it, by translating an English

x vid   which contains the phrase somthing altered, and besides
letter B   recited by heart on the repetition day. Ov: Metam:
is learn'd by these at the latter end of the year, so
also Prosodia Scanning & turning & making of verses,

x

& 2 days in the week they continue to turn Mᵣ Gar:
x v: Let. C Engl: Ex: into Latin, w̄ the afternoons exerc: is ended,

x

x v: I   and turn a fable into verse a distich in a day.

6.   The sixth year they are entred upon Tullie's
Offices & Luc: Flor: for the forenoon, continuing the
use of Ovid's Metam: in the afternoon, & at the end

x

x v: D.   of the Year they read Virgil: The Elegancies of Tull:
Off: are improved in the afternoon as is aforesᵈ of
Tull: Epistˡ· & withal given the master in writing when
the lesson is recited, & so are the phrases they can
vid letter   discover in Luc: Fl:. All which that have been mett
E   x

with in that week are comprehended in a Dialogue

x
x E   on Fryday forenoon, and afternoon they turn a Fable
into Lat: Verse. Every week these make a Latin
Epistle, the last quarter of the Year, when also they
begin to learn Greek, & Rhetorick.

7.   The seventh Year they read Tullie's Orations &
Justin for the Latin & Greek Testamᵗ Isocrates Orat:
Homer & Hesiod for the Greek in the forenoons &
Virgil Horace Juvenal & Persius afternoons. as to their
Exercises after the afternoon lessons are ended they
translate Mundays & Tuesdays an Engl: Dialogue

x
x v: F.   containing a Praxis upon the Phrases out of Godwin's
Roman Antiquities. Wensdays they compose a Praxis
on the Elegancies & Pithy sentences in their lesson in

x
x v: G.   Horace in Lat: verse. On Repition days, bec: that
x v: H.   work is easy, their time is improved in yᵉ Forenoon

x
in makeing Dialogues containing a Praxis upon a Par-
ticle out of Mʳ Walker, in the afternoon in Turning

x   x
x v: I.   a Psalm or something Divine into Latin verse. Every
x K.   fortnight they compose a Theme, & now & then turn
a Theme into a Declamation the last quarter of the
year.

THE CURRICULUM OF 1734

Some indication of the ground covered at the Boston
Latin School in 1734 is furnished by the Harvard College entrance requirements of that year, which included a thorough
study of both Latin and Greek. These requirements are as
follow:

Whoever upon examination by the President, and two at least
of the Tutors, shall be found able *extempore* to read, construe, and
parse Tully, Virgil, or such like common classical Latin authors,
and to write true Latin in prose, and to be skilled in making Latin
verse, or at least in the rules of Prosodia, and to read, construe, and
parse ordinary Greek, as in the New Testament, Isocrates, or such
like, and decline the paradigms of Greek nouns and verbs, having

NATHANIEL WILLIAMS'S ACCOUNT OF THE CURRICULUM OF THE BOSTON LATIN
SCHOOL IN 1712

By courtesy of Mr. Kenneth B. Murdock, Dean of Harvard University.

withal good testimony of his past blameless behaviour, shall be looked upon as qualified for admission into Harvard College.[12]

THE CURRICULUM OF 1749

On May 9, 1749, the town voted to "Recommend to the Masters of the Schools that they instruct their Scholars in Reading and Spelling. . . ." It is to be noted that this recommendation was to be given to the "Masters of the Schools," not specifying whether it was intended for the Masters of the two Latin grammar schools or for the Masters of the three writing schools; if so, it would appear that, in 1749, reading and spelling were added to the elementary subjects taught at the Latin School.

THE CURRICULUM FROM 1752 TO 1759

The next list of textbooks, from which we infer the curriculum, is that of Benjamin Dolbeare, Jr., who attended the Boston Latin School for seven years from 1752 to 1759, under Master John Lovell. This list of textbooks,[13] which indicates the studies but does not go farther in giving the curriculum, omits Cicero's *De Officiis*, Dionysius Cato, *Sententiae Pueriles*, Ovid's *De Tristibus*, Lucius Florus, Hesiod, Isocrates, Godwin, and Walker—all of which are listed in the 1712 course of study—but adds the following textbooks: Clarke's *Introduction to the Making of Latin*, Eutropius, Caesar's *Commentaries*, Castalio, King's *Heathen Gods, Gradus ad Parnassum*, and Terence. In Dolbeare's document appears the following item: "At his French School French Grammer, Telemachus." This proves that at least one Latin School scholar also attended a private French school. It is reasonable to infer that other scholars at this same period did likewise.[14]

---

[12] Benjamin Peirce, *A History of Harvard University, from its foundation, in the year 1636, to the period of the American Revolution*, Appendix, p. 125.

[13] See page 263 for facsimile of manuscript document. The original manuscript document is in the possession of the Boston Latin School Association and, with the permission of Mr. Patrick T. Campbell, president of the Association, this facsimile is reproduced.

[14] Robert Ballard's mother, in 1716, charged her husband's estate for the

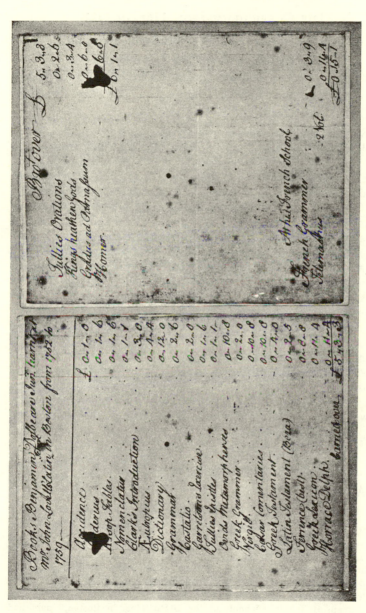

LIST OF TEXTBOOKS USED IN THE BOSTON LATIN SCHOOL FROM 1752 TO 1759,
BY BENJAMIN DOLBEARE, JR.

By courtesy of the Boston Latin School Association.

THE CURRICULUM FROM 1766 TO 1773

An account of the course of study at the Latin School from 1766 to 1773 has been recorded by the Reverend Jonathan Homer, who entered the Boston Latin School in 1766 and was graduated from Harvard College in 1777. The Reverend Jonathan Homer testifies:

> Entered Lovell's school at seven years. . . .
> We studied Latin from 8 o'clock till 11, and from 1 till dark. . . .
> The course of study was, grammar; Esop, with a translation; Clarke's Introduction to writing Latin; Eutropius, with a translation; Corderius; Ovid's Metamorphoses; Virgil's Georgics; AEneid; Caesar; Cicero. In the sixth year I began Greek, and for the first time attempted English composition, by translating Caesar's Commentaries. The master allowed us to read poetical translations, such as Trappe's and Dryden's Virgil. I was half way through Virgil when I began Greek with Ward's Greek Grammar.
> After Cheever's Latin Accidence, we took Ward's Lily's Latin Grammar. After the Greek Grammar, we read the Greek Testament, and were allowed to use Beza's Latin Translation. Then came Homer's Iliad, five or six books, using Clarke's Translation with notes, and this was all my Greek education at school. Then we took Horace, and composed Latin verses, using the Gradus ad Parnassum.
> I entered college at the age of fourteen years and three months, and was equal in Latin and Greek to the best in the senior class. Xenophon and Sallust were the only books used in college that I had not studied.[15]

THE CURRICULUM FROM 1773 TO 1789

An account of the curriculum of the School from 1773 to 1779 has been recorded by Harrison Gray Otis, a pupil of the School from 1773 to April 19, 1775, and from 1776 to 1779. The curriculum continued to be a seven-year course for the

education of their three children. Among other items she lists 3 pounds paid to "Mʳ Rawlings for learning him the French tong." See *Suffolk County Probate Records,* Vol. 19, p. 253.

[15] William B. Fowle, "Schools of the Olden Time in Boston," published in the *Common School Journal,* Vol. XII, pp. 311-12.

study of Latin and Greek. Mr. Otis testifies that Xenophon had been added to the course of study in 1779, if not earlier. The Latin School boys were dismissed for an hour each day to attend the South Writing School, and a few remained at the Latin School and "took lessons in writing of 'Master James,' son of the Preceptor."

Extracts from Mr. Otis's account follow:

Gentlemen,—I send you as requested some reminiscences connected with the old Latin School in Boston. I was a pupil—first of Master Lovell, afterwards of Master Hunt. I perfectly remember the day I entered the School, July, 1773, being then seven years and nine months old. Immediately after the end of Commencement week, I repaired, according to the rule prescribed for candidates for admission to the lowest form, to old Master Lovell's house, situate in School Street, nearly opposite the site of the old School House. I was early on the ground, anticipated only by Mr. John Hubbard, who lived near—it being understood that the boys were to take their places on the form in the same routine that they presented themselves at the house. The probationary exercise was reading a few verses in the Bible. Having passed muster in this, I was admitted as second boy on the lowest form.

I attended school from that time until April, 1775, (the day of Lexington battle), being then on the second form. The school was divided into seven classes. A separate bench or form was allotted to each, besides a skipping form, appropriated for a few boys who were intended to be pushed forward one year in advance. The books studied the first year were Cheever's Accidence, a small Nomenclature, and Corderius' Colloquies. The second year, Aesop's Fables, and towards the close of it, Eutropius and Ward's Lilly's Grammar. The third year Eutropius and Grammar continued, and a book commenced called Clarke's Introduction. In the fourth year, the fourth form, as well as the fifth and sixth, being furnished with desks, commenced "making Latin," as the phrase was, and to the books used by the third form Caesar's Commentaries were added. After this were read in succession by the three upper classes, Tully's Orations, the first books of AEneid, and the highest classes dipped into Xenophon and Homer. School opened at 7 in summer and 8 in winter, A. M., and at 1 P. M. throughout the year. It was ended at 11 A. M. and 5 P. M., . . .[16]

[16] Henry F. Jenks, *Catalogue*, Part I, pp. 35-37.

The Boston Latin School was closed during the siege of Boston and was reopened on June 5, 1776, under the mastership of Mr. Samuel Hunt.   An account of the curriculum of the School during the post-Revolutionary period has been left us by the famous physician, Dr. James Jackson, who entered the School in 1784, under Master Samuel Hunt.   Dr. Jackson testifies:

> The Latin School was then divided into seven classes, and the pupils spent seven years in it, usually entering it from seven to nine years of age. . . .
> We began our studies with Cheever's Latin Accidence, a book which I have always held in great veneration; next came 'quid agis,' which you will know means Corderius, his dialogues, if you had the happiness to study the book.   This book was made easy by the English translation of its short sentences, in columns opposite the Latin; and I am satisfied that this easy introduction to the reading of a foreign language is the most eligible mode, at least for little boys.   Several small works followed, among which I have always held in sweet remembrance Erasmus's Colloquies, more especially the Alchemist and the Shipwreck.[17]

THE CURRICULUM OF 1789

Under the "New System of Education," adopted in 1789, the Boston Latin School curriculum was reduced from a seven-year to a four-year course, a very significant change marking a departure from the English precedent.   Candidates for admission to the Boston Latin School were required, after 1789, to be at least ten years old, "having been previously well instructed in English Grammar."   The Harvard College entrance requirements of 1788 included, besides a thorough knowledge of Latin and Greek Grammar, the study of Virgil, Tully's [Cicero's] *Orations*, Caesar's *Commentaries*, and the Greek Testament.

The four-year curriculum of 1789[18] is as follows:

---

[17] *Ibid.*, Part I, pp. 42-43.
[18] See Appendix X for facsimile of document.

1st   Class—Cheever's Accidence.
            Corderius's Colloquies—Latin and English.
            Nomenclator.
            AEsop's Fables—Latin and English.
            Ward's Latin Grammar, or Eutropius.
2d   Class—Clarke's Introduction—Latin and English.
            Ward's Latin Grammar.
            Eutropius, continued.
            Selectae e Veteri Testamento Historiae, or,
            Castalio's Dialogues.
            The making of Latin, from Garretson's Exercises.
3d   Class—Caesar's Commentaries.
            Tully's Epistles, or Offices.
            Ovid's Metamorphoses.
            Virgil.
            Greek Grammar.
            The making of Latin from King's History of the
            Heathen Gods.
4th   Class—Virgil, continued.—Tully's Orations.
            Greek Testament.—Horace.
            Homer.—Gradus ad Parnassum.
            The making of Latin continued.

Under this "New System of Education," adopted in 1789, provision was made for the Latin School boys to attend the public writing schools in the following hours: "The 1st Class from half past Nine o'clock, A.M. 'till Eleven, or from half past Three P.M. as shall be found most convenient, and the 2d Class in the same manner for the first half of that year."

In the files of the school committee there is a manuscript document, written by Samuel Hunt, the Master of the Latin School, in which he says that the Latin School, in 1790, "consists of Six Classes, it being impossible to reduce it to four at present, . . . "

THE CURRICULUM OF 1808 (?)

In 1803 the former conditions of admission to Harvard College were repealed, and the following prerequisites were established: Dalzel's *Collectanea Graeca Minora*; the Greek

Testament; Virgil; Sallust; Cicero's *Select Orations*; Greek Grammar and Latin Grammar, including prosody; an ability to translate these languages correctly; and a knowledge of geography and of arithmetic to the rule of three.

The next extant curriculum of the Boston Public Latin School is that of 1808(?), under the mastership of William Biglow. In the Treasure Room of the Harvard College Library there is an undated pamphlet (1808 ?), which gives the following course of study for the "latin Grammar school" in Boston:

4th Class—1st Bigelow's Abridgement of Adam's Latin Grammar.
             2d New Latin Primer.
             3d Introduction to making of Latin.
3d Class—1, 2, 3, continued.
             4th Selectae e profanis scriptoribus historiae.
             5th Cicero de Officiis.
             6th Gradus ad Parnassum.
2d Class—3 and 6 continued.
             7 Adam's Latin Grammar.
             8 Heyne's Virgil.
             9 Sallust.
             10 Gloucester Greek Grammar.
             11 Caesar's Commentaries.
1st Class—3, 6, 7, 8, 9, 10, 11, continued.
             12 Cicero's Select Orations.
             13 Graeca Minora Collect.
             14 Greek Testament.
             15 Homer.

The above curriculum was undoubtedly introduced in 1803 or 1804, to meet the new Harvard College entrance requirements of 1803. We note that William Biglow's *Abridgement of Adam's Latin Grammar* was substituted for Ezekiel Cheever's *Accidence*, which had been the standard textbook for many years. We also note that Sallust and Andrew Dalzel's *Collectanea Graeca Minora*, published in 1789, were added to the curriculum. No mention is made of the introduction of geography and arithmetic, as listed in the 1803 Harvard College entrance requirements. These elementary subjects, however, were undoubtedly taught either at the Boston Latin School or at the South Writing School, which the Latin School boys were required to attend an hour each day, for special instruction in "writing and cyphering."

THE CURRICULUM OF 1814

After 1814, under the mastership of Mr. Benjamin A. Gould, the curriculum was extended to a five-year course, and further changes and additions were made. On June 28, 1814, the sub-committee for the Latin School, appointed by the school committee, made the following recommendations: (1) Five-year course; (2) Three lowest classes to be dismissed at 11 o'clock to attend writing schools at private hours; (3) Two highest classes to be taught arithmetic and geography as required for admission to Harvard College; and (4) Lads required to write in fair hand. These recommendations were adopted, as the following manuscript report of the school committee, dated June 21, 1819, testifies: "In addition to the Latin & greek languages, the boys at the latin School are now taught such branches of the Mathematics & geography, with the Elements of Geometry & algebra, as are requisite for admission to Harvard College."

THE CURRICULUM OF 1823

From Master Gould's description of the Boston Latin School in 1823 the writer has prepared the following outline of the curriculum:

First Year
Adam's *Latin Grammar*.
Liber Primus.

Second Year
Graeciae Historiae Epitome.
Viri Romae.
Phaedri Fabulae (From Burman's text, with English notes).
Cornelius Nepos.

Ovid's *Metamorphoses* (By Willymotte).
Scanning the rules of prosody.
Portions of Ovid committed to memory.
Valpy's *Chronology of Ancient and English History.*
Dana's *Latin Tutor for writing Latin.*
Tooke's *Pantheon.*

Third Year
Greek Grammar.
Caesar's *Commentaries.*
Electa ex Ovidio et Tibullo.
Delectus Sententiarum Graecarum.
Collectanea Graeca Minora.
Sallust.
Virgil.
Translations written in English from Latin and Greek.
Latin Tutor.
Valpy's *Elegantiae Latinae.*
Bradley's *Prosody.*
Colburn's *First Lessons in Arithmetic* (Later part of year).

Fourth and Fifth Years (Curriculum of respective years not specified)
Colburn's *First Lessons in Arithmetic* (Continued).
Cicero's *Orations, De Officiis, De Senectute,* and *De Amicitia.*
Horace Exp. (First book of Horace committed to memory).
Juvenal (Third and tenth *Satires* committed to memory).
Persius.
Greek Primitives.
Xenophon's *Anabasis.*
Maittaire's Homer (Many hundreds of verses committed to memory).
Greek Testament.
Wyttenbach's *Greek Historians.*
Themes in Latin and English.
Several books of Virgil committed to memory.
All the poetry in the *Graeca Minora* committed to memory.
Worcester's *Geography.*
Lacroix's *Arithmetic.*
Euclid's *Geometry.*
Euler's *Algebra.*

Mr. Gould adds the following:

Besides the books already mentioned, use is made of the following, viz.: Neilson's Greek Exercises for writing Greek, Schrevelius's Greek Lexicon, Hedericus, Scapula, Morell's Thesaurus, Walker's Classical Key, Lempriere's Classical Dictionary, Adam's Roman Antiquities, Entick's and Ainsworth's Latin Dictionary, etc.

On Saturdays the whole School comes together in the hall for declamation. . . .

The Curriculum of 1826

For admission to the Boston Latin School in 1826 boys were required to be at least nine years old. The five-year curriculum of 1826 follows:

First Year (Fifth Class)

1. Adam's Latin Grammar.
2. Liber Primus, or the Latin Reader. 1st Part.
3. Viri Romae, and reading English.

Second Year (Fourth Class)

1, and 3, continued.
4. The Fables of Phaedrus, ⎫ or the Latin Reader, 2d Part,
5. Cornelius Nepos;   ⎬ instead of these two.
6. Caesar's Commentaries.
7. Writing Latin Exercises, from Dana's Latin Tutor.
8. Declamation, Reading, and English Grammar.

Third Year (Third Class)

1, 7, 8, continued.
9. Mythology. (Tooke's Pantheon, or Irving's, or Pinnock's Catechisms.)
10. Arithmetic. (Colburn's Intellectual, Lacroix's written.)
11. Ovid's Metamorphoses, Expurg. Edition.
12. Greek Grammar. (Gloucester Gr.)
13. Valpy's Greek Delectus.
14. Sallust.

Fourth Year (Second Class)

1, 7, 8, 12, continued.
15. Grecian and Roman Antiquities.
16. Ancient and Modern Geography, with the use of Globes. (Worcester's Geog.)
17. Euler's and Colburn's Algebra.
18. Virgil.

19. Cicero's Select Orations.
20. Gr. Minora, and Jacob's Greek Reader, with Neilson's Greek Exercises.
21. Writing translations from Latin and Greek, into English and committing to memory select portions of Latin and Greek.

Fifth Year (First Class)
1, 8, 12, 17, 20, continued.
22. English Composition; Forensic Discussions; Geometry; Trigonometry, with its uses.
23. History and Chronology; Constitution of the U. S. A. and of Massachusetts.
24. Writing Latin, from Latinae Elegantiae; and composing Latin Themes and Verses.
25. Horace, Expurgated; Juvenal and Persius, Expurg.
26. Cicero De Officiis; De Senectute; De Amicitia; Tacitus's Germany and Life of Agricola.
27. Greek Testament; Xenophon's Anabasis; Mattair's Homer.

Books for reference and occasional use: The Greek Lexicons of Scapula, Hedericus, and Pickering; Morell's Thesaurus; Ainsworth's larger Dictionary, Lat. and Eng.; Adam's Lat. Dict.; Adam's and Kennett's Roman Antiquities; Potter and Robinson's Grecian Antiquities; Lempriere's Class. Dict. &c. &c.

The Curriculum of 1827 and 1828

For admission to the Boston Latin School in 1827 and 1828 boys were required to be at least nine years old, able to read correctly, to "write running hand," to have knowledge of all the stops, marks, and abbreviations, and to be able to parse common sentences in prose. The five-year curriculum follows:

First Year (Fifth Class)
1. Gould's Adam's Latin Grammar.
2. English Grammar, and Reading English.
3. The New Latin Tutor. Writing Exercises.
4. Liber Primus, or The Latin Reader, 1st Part.
5. Viri Romae.
6. Private Declamation.

Second Year (Fourth Class)
1, 2, 3, and 5, continued.

7. Roman Antiquities.
8. Phaedri Fabulae Expurgatae.
9. Cornelius Nepos.
10. Caesar's Commentaries.
11. Modern Geography. Worcester.
12. Intellectual Arithmetic. Colburn.
13. Writing Translations from Latin into English.
14. Public Declamation.

Third Year (Third Class)
1, 2, 3, 11, 13, and 14, continued.
15. Written Arithmetic. Colburn and Lacroix.
16. Excerpta ex Ovidio.
17. Popkin's Gloucester Greek Grammar.
18. Greek Delectus.
19. Sallust.
20. Ancient Geography and the use of the Globes. Worcester.

Fourth Year (Second Class)
1, 2, 3, 11, 13, 14, 15, 17, and 20, continued.
21. Grecian Antiquities.
22. Algebra. Colburn and Euler.
23. Cicero's Select Orations.
24. Gould's Virgil.
25. Jacob's Greek Reader.
26. Writing Translations from Greek into English, and committing to memory select portions of Latin and Greek.

Fifth Year (First Class)
1, 2, 3, 11, 13, 14, 15, 17, 20, 22, and 26, continued.
27. English Composition; Forensic discussions; Geometry; Trigonometry.
28. History and Chronology; Blair's Rhetoric.
29. Writing Latin, from Latinae Elegentiae, and composing Latin Themes and Verses.
30. Juvenal, Expurg.
31. Horace, Expurg.
32. Extracts from Cicero; Extracts from Tacitus.
33. Homer's Iliad.
34. Greek Testament; Xenophon's Anabasis.

THE CURRICULUM OF 1832

In the *Annual Catalogue of the Boston Latin School* of

1832 there is the following record that extra studies were introduced for the brightest pupils of the highest class:

It being however understood, that there must necessarily be different degrees of proficiency amongst different pupils, especially in the highest class, the following studies, viz. Blair's Rhetoric, Geometry and Trigonometry, Xenophon's Anabasis, Juvenal, Horace, Homer, Stansbury's Catechism, and Paley's Natural Theology, not being required for admission to the University, are allowed to be introduced at the discretion of the master, but are not absolutely required.

THE CURRICULUM OF 1834

First Year (Fifth Class)
1. Gould's edition of Adam's Latin Grammar.
2. English Grammar, Reading.
3. Liber Primus, as stereotyped in 1827.
4. Viri Romae, as published for this school in 1833.

Second Year (Fourth Class)
1, 3, 4, continued.
5. New Latin Tutor. and reading and writing exercises from it.
6. Latin Dictionary.
7. Dillaway's Roman Antiquities and Ancient Mythology.
8. Phaedri Fabulae Expurgatae.
9 Cornelius Nepos.
10. Caesar's Commentaries.
11. Worcester's Modern Geography.
12. Colburn's Intellectual Arithmetic.
13. Writing Translations from Latin into English.

Third Year (Third Class)
1, 2, 5, 6, 7, 11, 12, 13, continued.
14. Written Arithmetic, Colburn and Lacroix.
15. Excerpta ex Ovidio, Gould's edition.
16. Fisk's Greek Grammar and Exercises.
17. Greek Delectus.
18. Wilson's Sallust.
19. Worcester's Ancient Geography.
20. Lempriere's Classical Dictionary.

Fourth and Fifth Years (Second and First Classes)
1, 2, 5, 6, 11, 13, 14, 16, 19, continued.
21. Cleveland's Grecian Antiquities.
22. Colburn's and Euler's Algebra.

23. Cicero's Select Orations, Folsom's Edition.
24. Gould's Virgil, or any good edition, without an Interpretation, or an Order of construction.
25. Jacob's Greek Reader.
26. Greek Lexicon.
27. Writing translations from Greek into English, committing to memory portions of Latin and Greek.
28. English Composition.
29. History.
30. Geometry and Trigonometry.
31. Juvenal Expurgata, Leverett's edition.
32. Gould's Horace Expurgata, or any other good edition without an Order of construction.
33. Homer's Iliad.
34. Greek Testament, the Four Gospels.
35. Xenophon's Anabasis.
36. Writing and Composing Latin Themes and Verses.
37. Stansbury's Catechism on the Constitution of the United States.
38. Paley's Natural Theology, with Paxton's Illustrations.

THE CURRICULUM FROM 1835 TO 1852

From 1835 through 1851 the *Catalogue of the Boston Public Latin School* was not published. We have record, however, from the following testimony[19] of President Eliot of Harvard that the curriculum remained unchanged:

Sixty-six years ago, when I entered it [1844], the subjects of instruction were Latin, Greek, mathematics, English composition and declamation, and the elements of Greek and Roman history. There was no formal instruction in the English language and literature, no modern language, no science, and no physical training, or military drill. In short, the subjects of instruction were what they had been for two hundred years.

It is a matter of record that in 1843 Edward Seager was appointed an Instructor in drawing. He continued until 1850 when he was succeeded by Frederic Dickinson Williams.

[19] Address delivered in 1910 at the 275th anniversary of the Boston Latin School.

REPORT CARD OF SAMUEL LOTHROP THORNDIKE

Thorndike entered the Boston Latin School in 1845 and was graduated in 1848. The studies of the First Class (Senior Class) for the year 1847-1848 were the following: Virgil, Greek reader, Greek exercises, Latin exercises, Greek grammar, algebra, ancient geography, and declamation.

From the original in the possession of the Boston Latin School, by courtesy of the Boston Latin School Association.

THE CURRICULUM OF 1852

In the following curriculum of 1852 the study of French is listed, to be commenced in the third year of the six-year course. French was introduced, therefore, definitely in 1852 and possibly earlier, between 1844 and 1852, although there is no record that it was required for admission to Harvard College. In 1855, or earlier, Marie Bernard Montellier De Montrachy was appointed the Instructor of French.

The six-year curriculum of 1852[20] follows:

First Year (Sixth Class)
1. Andrews's and Stoddard's Latin Grammar.
2. English Grammar.

[20] The scholars had the option of completing the course in five years or less, "if willing to make due exertion."

3. Reading English.
4. Spelling.
5. Mental Arithmetic.
6. Mitchell's Geographical Questions.
7. Declamation.
8. Penmanship.
9. Andrews's Latin Lessons.
10. Andrews's Latin Reader.

Second Year (Fifth Class)
1, 2, 3, 4, 7, 8, continued.
11. Caesar's Commentaries.
12. Written Translations.
13. Colburn's Sequel.
14. Mitchell's Geography.
15. Cornelius Nepos.
16. Arnold's Latin Prose Composition.

Third Year (Fourth Class)
1, 2, 3, 4, 7, 8, 12, 13, 14, 16, continued.
17. Sophocles's Greek Grammar.
18. Sophocles's Greek Lessons.
19. Ovid's Metamorphoses.
20. Parker's Aids to English Composition.
21. Fasquelle's French Grammar.

Fourth Year (Third Class)
1, 2, 3, 4, 7, 8, 12, 13, 14, 16, 17, 20, 21, continued.
22. Sallust.
23. Arnold's Greek Prose Composition.
24. Felton's Greek Reader.
25. Sherwin's Algebra.
26. English Composition.
27. Le Grand-père.

Fifth Year (Second Class)
1, 2, 3, 4, 7, 8, 16, 17, 21, 23, 24, 25, 26, continued.
28. Virgil.
29. Elements of History.
30. Translations from English into Latin.
31. Somerville's Physical Geography.
32. Voltaire's Histoire de Charles XII.

Sixth Year (First Class)
1, 7, 16, 17, 21, 23, 24, 25, 26, 28, 30, 31, continued.
33. Geometry.
34. Cicero's Orations.
35. Composition of Latin Verses.
36. Bonnechose's Histoire de France.
37. Composition in French.
38. Exercises in Speaking and Reading French, with a native French Teacher.
39. Latham's English Grammar.
40. Ancient History and Geography.

The following books of reference shall be used in pursuing the above studies:—

Leverett's Latin Lexicon, or Gardner's Abridgment of the same.
Liddell and Scott's Greek Lexicon; or Pickering's Greek Lexicon, last edition.
Worcester's School Dictionary.
Anthon's Classical Dictionary.
Smith's Dictionary of Antiquities.
Baird's Classical Manual.

No translations of the foregoing Latin and Greek authors are allowed in the School; nor any Interpretation, Keys, or Orders of Construction.

THE CURRICULUM OF 1858

In the files of the Boston school committee there is a manuscript document which testifies that in 1858 music was introduced into the Boston public school system. A special instructor of music, Mr. Julius Eichberg, was appointed in 1872 for the Boston Latin School.

THE CURRICULUM OF 1860

For admission to the Boston Latin School in 1860 boys were required to be at least ten years old. The regular course continued to be a six-year course, with the option "of completing their course in five years or less, if willing to make due exertion."

The six-year curriculum of 1860 is as follows:

First Year (Sixth Class)
1. Andrews's and Stoddard's Latin Grammar.
2. English Grammar.
3. Reading English.
4. Spelling.
5. Mental Arithmetic.
6. Mitchell's Geographical Questions.
7. Declamation.
8. Penmanship.
9. Andrews's Latin Lessons.
10. Andrews's Latin Reader.

Second Year (Fifth Class)
1, 2, 3, 4, 6, 7, 8, continued.
11. Viri Romae.
12. Written Translations.
13. Colburn's Sequel.
14. Cornelius Nepos.
15. Arnold's Latin Prose Composition.

Third Year (Fourth Class)
1, 2, 3, 4, 7, 8, 12, 13, 15, continued.
16. Sophocles's Greek Grammar.
17. Sophocles's Greek Lessons.
18. Caesar's Commentaries.
19. Fasquelle's French Grammar.
20. Exercises in Speaking and Reading French, with a native French Teacher.

Fourth Year (Third Class)
1, 2, 3, 4, 7, 8, 12, 13, 15, 16, 19, 20, continued.
21. Ovid's Metamorphoses.
22. Arnold's Greek Prose Composition.
23. Felton's Greek Reader.
24. Sherwin's Algebra.
25. English Composition.
26. Le Grandpère.

Fifth Year (Second Class)
1, 2, 3, 4, 7, 8, 15, 16, 19, 20, 22, 23, 24, 25, continued.
27. Virgil.
28. Elements of History.
29. Translations from English into Latin.

Sixth Year (First Class)
1, 7, 15, 16, 19, 20, 22, 23, 25, 27, 28, 29, continued.
30. Geometry.
31. Cicero's Orations.
32. Composition of Latin Verses.
33. Composition in French.
34. Ancient History and Geography.

The following books of reference shall be used in pursuing the above studies:—

Leverett's Latin Lexicon, or Gardner's Abridgment of the same.
Liddell and Scott's Greek Lexicon; or Pickering's Greek Lexicon, last edition.
Worcester's School Dictionary.
Anthon's Classical Dictionary.
Smith's Dictionary of Antiquities.
Baird's Classical Manual.

No translations of the foregoing Latin and Greek authors are allowed in the School; nor any Interpretation, Keys, or Orders of Construction.

THE CURRICULUM OF 1869

For admission to the Boston Latin School in 1869 boys were required to be at least ten years old. The six-year curriculum of 1869, which differs from the 1860 curriculum only in the choice of textbooks, follows:

First Year (Sixth Class)
1. Harkness's Latin Reader.
2. English Grammar.
3. Reading English.
4. Spelling.
5. Mental Arithmetic.
6. Mitchell's Geographical Questions.
7. Declamation.
8. Penmanship.
9. Harkness's Latin Reader.

Second Year (Fifth Class)
1, 2, 3, 4, 6, 7, 8, continued.
10. Viri Romae.
11. Written Translations.

12. Colburn's Sequel.
13. Cornelius Nepos.
14. Arnold's Latin Prose Composition.

Third Year (Fourth Class)
1, 2, 3, 4, 6, 8, 11, 12, 14, continued.
15. Sophocles's Greek Grammar.
16. Sophocles's Greek Lessons.
17. Caesar's Commentaries.
18. Magill's French Grammar.
19. Exercises in Speaking and Reading French, with a native French teacher.

Fourth Year (Third Class)
1, 2, 3, 4, 7, 8, 11, 12, 14, 15, 18, 19, continued.
20. Ovid's Metamorphoses.
21. Arnold's Greek Prose Composition.
22. Xenophon's Anabasis.
23. Sherwin's Algebra.
24. English Composition.
25. Magill's French Reader.

Fifth Year (Second Class)
1, 2, 3, 4, 7, 8, 14, 15, 18, 19, 21, 22, 23, 24, continued.
26. Virgil.
27. Elements of History.
28. Translations from English into Latin.

Sixth Year (First Class)
1, 7, 14, 15, 18, 19, 21, 22, 24, 26, 27, 28, continued.
29. Geometry.
30. Cicero's Orations.
31. Homer's Iliad.
32. Composition in Latin Verses.
33. Composition in French.
34. Ancient History and Geography.

No translations of the foregoing Latin and Greek authors are allowed in the School; nor any Interpretation, Keys, or Orders of Construction.

The School session is from 9 A. M. to 2 P. M., throughout the year; excepting on Saturdays, when the School closes at one o'clock, unless a drill takes place on that day.

THE CURRICULUM OF 1870

In 1870, under the mastership of Francis Gardner, revolutionary changes were made in the curriculum of the Boston Latin School. A proposal to unite the Latin School and the English High School was rejected but, in spite of the protest of Francis Gardner, a "general broad culture" course, similar to that of the German gymnasium, was adopted for the Latin School, to prepare boys for professional life or for further study in "the higher branches of learning." The age for admission was raised from ten to twelve years. Another radical change was the introduction of the departmental system of instruction; the Master was raised to the grade of Head Master, the teachers were raised to the grade of Masters, Sub-Masters, and Instructors, and the quota of pupils for each Instructor was reduced to twenty-five. This "general culture" plan, which undertook the study of Latin, Greek, French, German, American literature, English literature, ancient history, mediaeval history, modern history, mathematics, geography, zoölogy, geology, botany, physics, astronomy, chemistry, physical philosophy, mechanics, drawing, penmanship, music, and gymnastics, proved impracticable as a college-preparatory course. This curriculum was modified in 1871 and was abolished in 1876. German, which was first introduced in 1870, was definitely established as a regular subject in 1874, when George Adam Schmidt was appointed Instructor.

The six-year curriculum of 1870 follows:

First Year (Sixth Class)
    Harkness's Latin Grammar (Rudiments).
    Harkness's Latin Reader.
    Viri Romae.
    Fables of Phaedrus.
    Scott, Goldsmith, Campbell, Wordsworth, Cowper, Tennyson, Leigh Hunt.
    Ancient History of the East.
    Review of General Geography.
    Geography of Asia.

Arithmetic reviewed and completed.
Eaton's Arithmetic, Crittenden's Calculations.
Elementary Algebra through Simple Equations, one unknown
quantity.
Ray's Elementary Algebra.
Zoölogy.
Drawing.
Penmanship.
Music.
Gymnastics.

Second Year (Fifth Class)
Nepos.
Justin.
Old English Ballads.
Sterne, Mrs. Thrale, Beattie, Cowper, Hawthorne, Tennyson,
Longfellow, Morris, Hazlitt.
History of Ancient Greece.
Geography of Europe and Africa.
Otto's French Grammar, first part, with exercises.
Ray's Elementary Algebra to the Binomial Theorem.
Geology (winter); Botany (spring and summer), Dana and
Gray, with specimens.
Drawing.
Music.
Gymnastics.

Third Year (Fourth Class)
Caesar, De Bello Gallico.
Ovid, Metamorphoses.
Quintus Curtius.
Virgil, Aeneid I, II.
Cicero, De Amicitia, De Senectute.
Greek Grammar (Rudiments).
Greek Lessons.
Xenophon, Anabasis begun.
Aelian, Extracts.
Lucian, Dialogues.
Plutarch, one life.
Gray, Addison, Moore, Burns, Irving, Bryant, Hood, Haw-
thorne, Shelley, Rogers.
History of Ancient Rome.
Revision of Geography of Asia, Europe and Africa.

Geography of America and Oceanica.

Le Grand Père, with applications of Syntax.

Exercises in translating and writing from a French treatise on Natural Science.

Plane Geometry.

Chauvenet's Elementary Geometry.

Geology and Botany, as in previous year.

Drawing.

Music.

Gymnastics.

Fourth Year (Third Class)

Latin Prosody.

Virgil, Aeneid III., IV., V.,—Eclogues.

Cicero, Archias, Marcellus.

Sallust, Catiline.

Horace, a few Odes.

Terence, Andria, Adelphi.

Homer, Iliad.

Isocrates, Panegyric on Athens.

Plutarch, Morals (one part).

Lucian, Art of Writing History.

Milton, Pope, Irving, Thompson, Collins, Prescott, Coleridge, Keats, Burke, Wordsworth, Holmes, Tyndall.

History of the Middle Ages, from the fifth century to the fourteenth.

Physical and Political Geography of Europe in minute detail.

French Comedy.

Translation.

Recitation.

Writing French.

Exercises in translating and writing from French Scientific Treatise.

Krauss's German Grammar, with Exercises in German.

Pure Algebra begun.

Algebraic Doctrine of Logarithms.

Loomis's Algebra, Bremiker's Logarithmic Tables.

Plane Trigonometry begun.

Chauvenet's Trigonometry.

A French Treatise on Physical Philosophy and Mechanics.

Drawing.

Music (optional).

Gymnastics.

Fifth Year (Second Class)
  Latin Verses.
  Virgil, Aeneid, VI., VII., VIII.,—Passages from the Georgics.
  Cicero, Verres, Catiline, Dream of Scipio.
  Horace, Odes, Epodes, Epistles.
  Tacitus, Agricola.
  Livy, one book.
  Quintilian.
  Greek Prosody.
  Homer, Iliad.
  Euripides, Alcestis.
  Demosthenes, Olynthiacs, Philippics.
  Plato, Crito, Apologia.
  Milton, Pope, Dryden, Spencer, Thackeray, Lamb, Tennyson, Lowell, Whittier, Ruskin, Shakespeare.
  History of the Middle Ages, and of Modern Times, from the fourteenth century to the middle of the seventeenth.
  Physical and political geography of Asia, Africa, America, Oceanica, in minute detail.
  Racine, Corneille, Molière, Rousseau.
  French Essay.
  Conversation in French.
  Krauss's Grammar, with German Reader.
  Plane Trigonometry finished, with applications.
  Chauvenet, Solid Geometry.
  Chauvenet's Elementary Geometry.
  Physics.
  Mechanics.
  Astronomy (French Treatise).
  Drawing.
  Music (optional).
  Gymnastics.

Sixth Year (First Class)
  Virgil, Parts of Aeneid.
  Cicero, De Republica.
  Tacitus, Annals.
  Livy.
  Horace continued, with Ars Poetica.
  Plautus.
  Lucretius, Extracts.
  Greek Verses.

Homer, Odyssey.

Thucydides, first book.

Demosthenes, Philippics, De Corona.

Sophocles, Oedipus.

Aristophanes, Birds, Clouds.

Macaulay, Junius, Emerson, Marvell, George Herbert, Byron, Carlyle, Robert Hall, Channing, Ben Jonson, Bacon, Shakespeare.

Modern History, from the accession of Louis the Fourteenth of France.

Geography reviewed.

Geography in relation to climate, soil, manufactures, commerce.

Cosmography.

French, as in previous year, a French Historical, or Scientific author.

German prose writers and poetry.

Spherical Trigonometry.

Chauvenet's Trigonometry.

Review of Trigonometric Formulae, Higher Algebra, etc.; Loomis's Algebra.

Chemistry.

Astronomy.

Music (optional).

Gymnastics.

THE CURRICULUM FROM 1876 TO 1879

A new eight-year course of study, founded on the advice of President Charles William Eliot of Harvard College and other leading educators, was adopted in 1876. A four-year course, called "the out-of-course," was offered to grammar-school graduates.

It was decided to abolish the "general culture" course of 1870 and to continue the Boston Latin School as a distinctly classical preparatory school, to prepare the student to enter college "with the kind of instruction which shall best enable him to pursue a college course." This new and improved curriculum of 1876 offered careful training in Latin, Greek, French, German, and mathematics, with general instruction

in the elements of the natural sciences, history, English literature, grammar and rhetoric, drawing, music, penmanship, and
gymnastics. This eight-year course continued until 1879
when it was again reduced to a six-year course, with a four-
year course for grammar school graduates.

The eight-year curriculum of 1876 is as follows:

First Year (Eighth Class)
  Latin.
  English.
  History.
  Geography.
  Natural Science.
  Mathematics.
  Drawing.
  Music.
  Penmanship.
  Gymnastics and military drill.
Second Year (Seventh Class)
  Latin.
  English.
  History.
  Geography.
  Natural Science.
  Mathematics.
  Drawing.
  Music.
  Penmanship.
  Gymnastics and military drill.
Third Year (Sixth Class)
  Latin.
  English.
  French.
  History.
  Geography.
  Natural Science.
  Mathematics.
  Drawing.
  Music.
  Penmanship.
  Gymnastics and military drill.

Fourth Year (Fifth Class)
    Latin.
    English.
    French.
    History.
    Geography.
    Natural Science.
    Mathematics.
    Drawing.
    Music.
    Penmanship.
    Gymnastics and military drill.
Fifth Year (Fourth Class)
    Latin.
    English.
    French.
    History.
    Geography.
    Natural Science.
    Mathematics.
    Drawing.
    Gymnastics and military drill.
Sixth Year (Third Class)
    Latin.
    Greek.
    English.
    French.
    History.
    Geography.
    Natural Science.
    Mathematics.
    Gymnastics and military drill.
Seventh Year (Second Class)
    Latin.
    Greek.
    English.
    French.
    German.
    History.
    Mathematics.
    Gymnastics and military drill.

Eighth Year (First Class)
  Latin.
  Greek.
  English.
  French.
  German.
  History.
  Mathematics.
  Gymnastics and military drill.
Supplementary Studies.
  Latin.
  Greek.
  English.
  French.
  German.
  History.
  Natural Science—Physics and Astronomy.
  Mathematics—Solid geometry, navigation, surveying, and plane
    analytic geometry.

THE CURRICULUM FROM 1880 TO 1891

In the latter part of the nineteenth century more emphasis
was placed on the study of English, due largely to the influence of President Charles William Eliot of Harvard University. In 1881 the *Latin School Register* was founded with
George Santayana, the distinguished poet, essayist, and philosopher, then a member of the class of 1882, as its editor. The
first issue, printed in September, 1881, contains the first in-
stallment of a parody on Virgil's *Aeneid*[21] and also a sonnet
on the Death of President Garfield, both written by Santayana
at the age of eighteen.

The *Literary Journal*, another publication by the students, first appeared in 1829 and the *Bedford Street Budget*,
in 1845. These School publications stimulated creative writing
and added a new interest to the study of English.

In the 1880 course of study of the Boston Latin School is
the following statement concerning the college entrance re-

---

[21] See Appendix XXXIII for *Æneas comes to land on Afric's torrid strand.*

quirements: "Two very marked features in the requirements for admission to college introduced within a few years ought to be noticed,—the increased emphasis laid upon the special study of the English language and literature, and the stress laid upon the student's ability to translate the classics at sight into good English."

Before 1887 both elementary Greek and elementary Latin were required for admission to Harvard College. In 1887 only one of the two was required. Under the "new plan" of 1910, every candidate for the A.B. degree at Harvard College had to offer elementary Greek or elementary Latin for admission.[22] It is significant that Greek continued to be a required subject at the Boston Latin School until the year 1913-1914, since which time the School has offered a choice between Greek and German.[23]

The six-year[24] curriculum of 1880 is as follows:

First Year (Sixth Class)
Latin.
English.
Geography and History.
Natural or Physical Science—Physiology and Hygiene.
Mathematics.
Penmanship.
Military drill.
Gymnastics.

Second Year (Fifth Class)
Latin.
English.
Geography and History.
Natural Science—Zoölogy.
Mathematics.
Penmanship.

[22] Samuel Eliot Morison, *The Development of Harvard University since the inauguration of President Eliot 1869-1929*, p. 36.

[23] A choice between Greek and German was offered from 1896 to 1900.

[24] A four-year course was offered to grammar-school graduates. According to the testimony of George Santayana, the class of 1882 formed a sort of debating society that met once a week in the evening.

Military drill.
Gymnastics.

Third Year (Fourth Class)
Latin.
English.
French.
Geography and History.
Natural Science—Zoölogy.
Mathematics.
Military drill.
Gymnastics.

Fourth Year (Third Class)
Latin.
Greek.
English.
French.
History.
Natural Science—Botany.
Mathematics.
Military drill.
Gymnastics.

Fifth Year (Second Class)
Latin.
Greek.
English.
French.
History.
Natural Science—Physics.
Mathematics.
Military drill.
Gymnastics.

Sixth Year (First Class)
Latin.
Greek.
English.
French.
Mathematics.
Military drill.
Gymnastics.

The Curriculum from 1891 to 1900

The curriculum for the year 1891-1892, although listed as a "revised course adopted on June 23, 1891," is practically the same as the curriculum of 1880, with emphasis on the classics and mathematics. In 1891 the students were offered a choice between German and French, and all students were given a course in moral training at the opening exercises.

The six-year curriculum of 1891[25] is as follows:

First Year (Sixth Class)
    English.
    Latin.
    American History.
    Geography.
    Elementary Science—Physiology and Hygiene.
    Mathematics.
    Physical Training.
Second Year (Fifth Class)
    English.
    Latin.
    English History.
    Geography.
    Elementary Science—Physiology, Hygiene, and Botany.
    Mathematics.
    Physical Training.
Third Year (Fourth Class)
    English.
    French or German.
    Latin.
    Greek. ("The study of Greek may be begun in March.")
    Greek History.
    Elementary Science—Astronomy, Physical Geography, and
        Botany.
    Mathematics.
    Physical Training—Gymnastics and Military Drill.
Fourth Year (Third Class)
    English.
    French or German.
    Latin.

[25] A four-year course was offered to grammar-school graduates.

Greek.
Roman History.
Mathematics.
Physical Training.
Fifth Year (Second Class)
English.
French or German.
Latin.
Greek.
Greek and Roman History.
Mathematics.
Physical Training.
Sixth Year (First Class)
English.
Latin.
Greek.
Elementary Science—Physics.
Mathematics.
Physical Training.

The Curriculum from 1900 to 1910

The course of study for the Boston Latin School was revised in 1900. The six-year curriculum for the year 1900-1901[26] is as follows:

First Year (Sixth Class)
English.
Latin.
History.
Geography.
Elementary Science—Physiology and Hygiene.
Mathematics—Arithmetic and Observational Geometry.
Physical Training.
Second Year (Fifth Class)
English.
Latin.
History.
Geography.
Elementary Science.
Mathematics—Arithmetic and Geometry.
Physical Training.

[26] A four-year course was offered to grammar-school graduates.

Third Year (Fourth Class)
    English.
    French.
    Latin.
    History.
    Elementary Science.
    Mathematics.
    Physical Training.
Fourth Year (Third Class)
    English.
    French.
    Latin.
    Greek.
    Roman History.
    Mathematics.
    Physical Training.
Fifth Year (Second Class)
    English.
    French.
    Latin.
    Greek.
    Greek and Roman History.
    Mathematics—Algebra and Plane Geometry.
    Physical Training.
Sixth Year (First Class)
    English.
    Latin.
    Greek.
    Elementary Science—Physics.
    Mathematics—Geometry.
    Physical Training—Military Drill.

THE CURRICULUM FROM 1910 TO 1913

In the First Class [Senior Class] of the 1910 course of study the pupils were allowed the choice between Greek and French. In all other respects the curriculum remained unchanged, as originally revised in 1900. The six-year curriculum of 1910[27] is as follows:

First Year (Sixth Class)
    English.
    Latin.

---

[27] A four-year course was offered to grammar-school graduates.

History.
Mathematics.
Geography.
Science—Physiology and Hygiene.
Physical Training.

Second Year (Fifth Class)
English, including Spelling and Penmanship.
Latin.
English History.
Mathematics—Algebra and Geometry.
Geography.
Science—Elementary physical ideas and Botany.
Physical Training.

Third Year (Fourth Class)
English.
Latin.
French.
Greek History.
Mathematics.
Science—Heating, Ventilating, and Constellations.
Physical Training.

Fourth Year (Third Class)
English.
Greek.
Latin.
French.
History.
Mathematics—Algebra and Demonstrative Geometry.
Physical Training.

Fifth Year (Second Class)
English.
Greek.
Latin.
French.
Roman and Greek History.
Mathematics—Geometry and Algebra.
Physical Training.

Sixth Year (First Class)
English.
Greek or French.
Latin.

Mathematics.
Physics.
Physical Training.

THE CURRICULUM FROM 1913 TO 1920

The year 1913 marks a significant change in the course of study in that the pupils were allowed the choice between Greek and German.

From 1913 to 1920 the First Class [Senior Class] was offered the choice of Greek, German, or French. The six-year curriculum for the year 1913-1914,[28] as adopted in October, 1913, is as follows:

First Year (Sixth Class)
    English.
    Latin.
    History.
    Mathematics.
    Geography.
    Science—Physiology and Hygiene.
    Physical Training.

Second Year (Fifth Class)
    English.
    Latin.
    History.
    Mathematics.
    Geography.
    Science—Elementary physical ideas and Botany.
    Physical Training.

Third Year (Fourth Class)
    English.
    Latin.
    French.
    History.
    Mathematics.
    Science.
    Physical Training.

Fourth Year (Third Class)
    English.

[28] A four-year course was offered to grammar-school graduates.

Greek or German.
Latin.
French.
History.
Mathematics.
Physical Training.
Fifth Year (Second Class)
English.
Greek or German.
Latin.
French.
History.
Mathematics.
Physical Training.
Sixth Year (First Class)
English.
Greek or German.
Latin.
French.
Mathematics.
Physics.
Physical Training.

THE CURRICULUM OF 1920

In the First Class [Senior Class] of the 1920 curriculum the pupils were allowed the choice of one of the following subjects: namely, Greek, German, French, or advanced mathematics. The six-year curriculum of 1920[29] is as follows:

First Year (Sixth Class)
English.
Latin.
History.
Mathematics.
Geography.
Science—Physiology and Hygiene.
Physical Training.
Second Year (Fifth Class)
English.
Latin.
French.
History.

[29] A four-year course was offered to grammar-school graduates.

Mathematics.
Geography.
Science.
Physical Training.
Third Year (Fourth Class)
English.
Latin.
French.
History.
Mathematics.
Science.
Physical Training.
Fourth Year (Third Class)
English.
Greek or German.
Latin.
French.
History.
Mathematics.
Physical Training.
Fifth Year (Second Class)
English.
Greek or German.
Latin.
French.
History.
Mathematics.
Physical Training.
Sixth Year (First Class)
English.
Latin.
Mathematics.
Physics.
Choice of Greek, German, French, or Advanced Mathematics.

THE CURRICULUM FOR THE YEAR 1934-1935

For three centuries the Boston Public Latin School has maintained a high standard of classical scholarship as a college-preparatory public school.[30]   The School offers a six-year

---

[30] Of the 132 members of the Harvard College class of 1935 who received honorable mention in all their college entrance examinations in June, 1931, 35 [almost one fourth] prepared at the Boston Public Latin School.

course, for students who have had the equivalent of six years of grammar-school preparation, and also offers a four-year course for grammar-school graduates. Both plans offer a choice between Greek and German.

In the First Class [Senior Class] the pupils are allowed the choice of one of the following subjects: namely, Greek, German, French, or advanced mathematics. Of the present graduating class, of the year 1934-1935, forty-six boys elected German; twenty-three boys elected Greek; ninety-nine boys elected French; and fifty-nine boys elected advanced mathematics.

As late as 1933 chemistry, which had been taught at various times since 1870, was introduced as a regular subject. The six-year course of study for the year 1934-1935 is as follows:

First Year (Sixth Class)
    English.
    Latin.
    History.
    Mathematics.
    Geography.
    Science: Physiology and Hygiene.
    Physical Training.
Second Year (Fifth Class)
    English.
    Latin.
    History.
    Mathematics.
    Geography.
    Science.
    Physical Training.
Third Year (Fourth Class)
    English.
    Latin.
    French.
    History.
    Mathematics.
    Physical Training.

Fourth Year (Third Class)
    English.
    Greek or German.
    Latin.
    French.
    Mathematics.
    Physical Training.
Fifth Year (Second Class)
    English.
    Greek or German continued.
    Latin.
    French.
    Mathematics.
    Physical Training.
Sixth Year (First Class)
    English.
    Latin.
    History.
    Mathematics.
    Physics.
    Chemistry.
    Choice of Greek, German, French, or Mathematics.
    Physical Training.

The four-year course for grammar-school graduates is as follows:

First Year (Class IV B)
    English.
    Latin.
    French.
    History.
    Mathematics: Algebra and Geometry.
    Physical Training.
Second Year (Class III B)
    English.
    Greek or German.
    Latin.
    French.
    Mathematics: Plane Geometry and Algebra.
    Physical Training.

Third Year (Class II B)
    Same as fifth year of six-year course.
Fourth Year (Class I B)
    Same as sixth year of six-year course.

SUMMARY

From 1635 to 1708, the year in which Ezekiel Cheever died, no definite curriculum has been recorded. From the indirect evidence available the conclusion is that from the beginning of the School not only the classics but also the elementary subjects of reading, writing, "cyphering," and spelling were taught. It was not until March, 1698/99, that the "free school" in Boston was definitely referred to in the *Town Records* as the "Latin School."

The first definite account of subjects taught and of textbooks used at the Latin School is recorded in the Reverend Cotton Mather's funeral sermon and essay on Ezekiel Cheever, who was Master from 1670 until his death in 1708. The curriculum at this time included a concentrated study of Latin and Greek.

The earliest extant full record of the Latin School curriculum is that of 1712, written by Nathaniel Williams, Master of the School from 1708 to 1734. This curriculum of 1712, a seven-year course, included the study of Latin, Greek, and "Roman Antiquities."

The next list of textbooks, from which we infer the curriculum, is that of Benjamin Dolbeare, Jr., who attended the Boston Latin School for seven years from 1752 to 1759, under Master John Lovell. This curriculum continued to be a seven-year course for the study of Latin and Greek and reading from King's *Heathen Gods*.

Under the "New System of Education" adopted in 1789 the Boston Latin School curriculum was reduced from a seven-year to a four-year course, a very significant change in that it marked a departure from the English precedent. Candidates for admission to the School were required after 1789 to be at least ten years old, "having been previously well instructed in English Grammar." The curriculum continued to be strictly classical, to meet the new Harvard College entrance requirements of 1788. Under this "New System of Education" provision was made for the Latin School boys to attend the public writing schools for instruction in penmanship.

In 1803 the former conditions of admission to Harvard College were repealed, and the following prerequisites were established: Dalzel's *Collectanea Graeca Minora*; the Greek Testament; Virgil; Sallust; Cicero's *Select Orations*; Greek grammar and Latin grammar, including prosody; an ability to translate these languages correctly; and a knowledge of geography and of arithmetic to the rule of three. The next extant curriculum of the Boston Latin School is that of 1808(?), which was undoubtedly introduced in 1803 to meet the above college requirements.

After 1814, under the mastership of Mr. Benjamin A. Gould, the curriculum was extended to a five-year course, and further changes and additions were made. A manuscript report of the school committee, dated June 21, 1819, testifies that "in addition to the Latin & greek languages, the boys at the latin School are now taught such branches of the Mathematics & geography, with the Elements of Geometry & algebra, as are requisite for admission to Harvard College."

From 1835 through 1851 the *Catalogue of the Boston Public Latin School* was not published. We have record, however, from the testimony of Charles William Eliot, who entered the School in 1844, that the curriculum remained unchanged. Drawing was introduced in 1843.

In 1852, or possibly earlier, the curriculum was extended to a six-year course. Another significant change was the introduction of French in 1852, although it was not required for admission to Harvard College. In 1855 a special Instructor of French was appointed.

In the files of the Boston school committee there is a

manuscript document which testifies that in 1858 music was introduced into the Boston public-school system. A special Instructor of Music was appointed for the Boston Latin School in 1872.

For admission to the Boston Latin School in 1860 boys were required to be at least ten years old. The regular course continued to be a six-year course, with the students allowed an option "of completing their course in five years or less, if willing to make due exertion."

In 1870, under the mastership of Dr. Francis Gardner, revolutionary changes were made in the curriculum of the Boston Latin School. A "general broad culture" course,[31] similar to that of the German gymnasium, was adopted for the Latin School. The age for admission was raised from ten to twelve years. This general culture plan, which undertook the study of Latin, Greek, French, German, American literature, English literature, ancient history, medieval history, modern history, mathematics, geography, zoölogy, geology, botany, physics, astronomy, chemistry, physical philosophy, mechanics, drawing, penmanship, music, and gymnastics, proved impracticable as a college-preparatory course. This curriculum was modified in 1871 and was abolished in 1876. German, which was first introduced in 1870, was definitely established as a regular subject in 1874.

A new eight-year course of study, founded on the advice of President Charles William Eliot of Harvard College and other leading educators, was adopted in 1876. A four-year course, called "the out-of-course," was also offered to grammar-school graduates. This new and improved curriculum of 1876 offered training in Latin, Greek, French, German, and mathematics, with general instruction in the elements of the

[31] Mr. Joseph L. Powers and Mr. Lee J. Dunn, in their "Brief History of the Boston Latin School" published in the *Catalogue of the Public Latin School in Boston for the year 1934-1935*, have appropriately described this general culture course as "an absurdly ambitious curriculum."

natural sciences, history, English literature, grammar and rhetoric, drawing, music, penmanship, and gymnastics. This eight-year course continued until 1879, when it was again reduced to a six-year course.

In June, 1891, a revised course of study was adopted for the year 1891-1892. This curriculum of 1891 is practically the same as the curriculum of 1880, with emphasis on the classics and mathematics. In 1891 the students were offered a choice between German and French, and all the students were given a course in moral training at the opening exercises.

The course of study for the Latin School was revised in 1900. All students were required to study French. German was not offered as an elective. The emphasis was placed on the study of Latin, Greek, English, history, science, and mathematics.

From 1910 to 1913 the boys in the First Class [Senior Class] were allowed the choice between Greek and French. In all other respects the curriculum remained unchanged, as originally revised in 1900.

The year 1913-1914 marks a significant change in the Latin School course of study in that the pupils were allowed the choice between Greek and German. [From 1896 to 1900 the choice between Greek and German had been offered but was then discontinued.]

Since 1920 the pupils in the First Class [Senior Class] have been allowed the choice of one of the following subjects: namely, Greek, German, French, or mathematics. As late as 1933 chemistry, which had been taught at various times since 1870, was introduced as a regular senior subject.

For three centuries the School has maintained a high standard of classical scholarship as a college-preparatory public school. The Boston Latin School now honors the memory of those educated Puritans who, with faith in higher education, established the School in 1635, inviting the sons of those less favored than themselves to share with their own sons the advantage of an education.

CHAPTER IX

OLD TEXTBOOKS USED AT THE BOSTON LATIN SCHOOL
FROM 1635 TO 1876

The school-books that were studied ten, twenty, thirty years ago have passed out of date; the scholars of to-day do not even know their names; but the purpose for which our school-books are studied, the things we are trying to get out of them, the things which, if they are properly taught and studied, the scholars of to-day do get out of them, are the same; and so across the years we clasp hands with our own school-boy days.

—Phillips Brooks (*Address,* February 22, 1881)

THE early writers of New England history paid very little attention to the textbooks used in the schools during the first century after their establishment. This silence in regard to books is further evidenced by an examination of the *Town Records* and *Selectmen's Minutes;* of the 1088 documents relating to Boston schools, compiled by the writer, only four give direct evidence concerning textbooks. These four documents, furthermore, refer to the catechism and psalter studied at the writing schools.

The sources of information concerning old textbooks used at the Boston Latin School the writer has classified into two groups, according to the type of evidence, namely, direct, based upon established facts, and indirect, based upon inference. Of the two types of evidence, direct and indirect, the former naturally carries more weight. In all historical research a conclusion drawn from indirect or circumstantial evidence is only highly probable at best; however, where the evidence is cumulative, converging, and corroborative, as in this case, the conclusions naturally carry some weight.

From 1635 to 1708, the year in which Ezekiel Cheever died, no definite list of books has been recorded. The first definite account of the textbooks used at the School is recorded by the Reverend Cotton Mather, in both his funeral sermon and poem on Ezekiel Cheever in 1708.[1] Perhaps the most interesting direct evidence about the books used at the School prior to this time is the textbooks themselves, identified by their inscriptions and dated autographs as belonging to boys known to have been students of the Boston Latin School. There is a large collection of these early Colonial textbooks in the Harvard College Library.[2] The inferences concerning the textbooks studied before 1708 are drawn from the following data, namely, the known books and exercises of English Latin grammar schools of the period,[3] the known schoolbooks of other New England Latin grammar schools of the period,[4] the entrance requirements of Harvard College in 1642,[5] textbooks imported by Boston booksellers before 1700,[6] textbooks written by men known to have been masters of the Boston Latin School, and textbooks printed in Boston.[7]

The earliest extant full record of the Latin School curriculum and textbooks is Nathaniel Williams's account in

---

[1] See page 256, for a full discussion.

[2] The writer acknowledges her indebtedness to Dr. E. R. Mosher, whose term thesis, entitled *Subjects Taught and Text-books Used in New England Grammar Schools from 1635 to 1789,* was written in 1921, under the guidance of Professor Arthur Orlo Norton, in the Harvard Graduate School of Education.

[3] See Foster Watson's *The English Grammar Schools to 1660: their Curriculum and Practice* and Charles Hoole's *A New Discovery of the old Art of Teaching Schoole,* edited by E. T. Campagnac in 1913.

[4] See George Emery Littlefield's *Early Schools and School-Books of New England.* Mr. Littlefield discusses the great similarity throughout New England in studies and textbooks used; it is natural to presume that such schoolbooks, known to have been in general use at this time, were used in Boston also.

[5] See page 255.

[6] See Worthington Chauncey Ford's *The Boston Book Market 1679-1700,* which contains lists of books ordered, inventories of books on hand, and inventories of estates. Among these we recognize some textbooks known to have been used in schools at this time, presumably in Boston also.

[7] If there are several editions of the same book, printed in Boston, it is reasonable to infer that the book had a market and would be used by private teachers, even though we may not find any direct evidence of its use at the Boston Latin School.

1712.[8] The next list of textbooks is that of Benjamin Dolbeare, Jr., who attended the Boston Latin School for seven years from 1752 to 1759, under Master John Lovell.[9] The next formal list of textbooks is that of 1789, under the "New System of Education." The next extant record of the curriculum and textbooks is that of 1808 (?), under the mastership of William Biglow. We note that Dalzel's *Collectanea Graeca Minora* and *Sallust* were added to the course of study to meet the new Harvard College entrance requirements of 1803. After 1814, under the mastership of Mr. Benjamin A. Gould, the curriculum was extended to a five-year course, and further changes were made in the textbooks. From 1826 to date the *Annual Catalogue of the Boston Latin School* gives not only the curriculum but the textbooks used; the Annual Catalogues were not published from 1835 through 1851.

Latin Grammars and Elementary Latin Readers

The manuals by which grammar was first taught in English were not English grammars but translations of the Latin accidence. Latin and English were combined in one book for the purpose of teaching both together and sometimes one through the medium of the other.[10]

The first Latin grammar printed in English was published in 1481, at Oxford, by Theodore Rood. Next in importance in the English incunabula grammar list is John Holt's *Lac Puerorum*, published about the year 1497.[11] John Wallis, D.D., published in London, in 1653, his *Grammar of the English Language in Latin*.

William Lily's *Latin Grammar* was authorized by King Henry VIII's proclamation of 1540 as the only grammar to be used in the schools. William Lily (c. 1468-1522) was a private teacher of grammar in London and was appointed the

---

[8] See page 261.

[9] See page 263.

[10] George Emery Littlefield, *Early Schools and School-Books of New England*, p. 219.

[11] Foster Watson, *The English Grammar Schools to 1660*, pp. 233, 234.

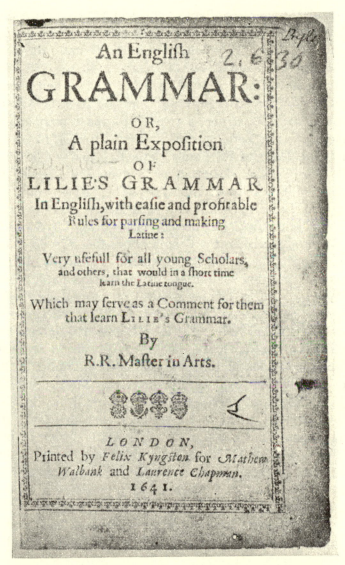

TITLE-PAGE OF *An English Grammar: or, A plain Exposition of Lilie's Grammar in English*

William Lily edited a Latin grammar in 1513.

By courtesy of the Harvard College Library.

first Head Master of St. Paul's School in 1510. Foster Watson[12] divides the history of Lily's grammar into three periods, namely, (1) from its publication in 1509 until the royal proclamation of about 1540, (2) from 1540 to 1758 when the grammar was appropriated by Eton College and became known as the Eton Latin grammar, and (3) from 1758 to the present. *Paul's Accidence,* a treatise of the construction of the eight parts of Latin speech, was written in 1513 by Dr. John Colet, Dean of St. Paul's Cathedral, and published in 1515. This treatise, dedicated to William Lily, formed the first part of Lily's *Latin Grammar.* The earliest edition of Lily's *Latin Grammar,* containing King Henry VIII's proclamation, was issued in 1542, twenty years after Lily's death.

We have record that a Boston bookseller, Mr. John Ive, in 1685, bought "30 Lillys Rules sticht. A Synopsis of Lilies Grammar," probably for the use of the Boston Latin School. The Harvard College Library possesses a copy of *An English Grammar: or, A plain Exposition of Lilie's Grammar in English, . . . Which may serve as a Comment for them that learn Lilie's Grammar,* written by "R. R. Master in Arts" and published in London in 1641.[13] The dated inscription in this book, "Joshua Gee Anno 1712," shows that it was owned by the Joshua Gee who entered the Boston Latin School in 1706, and was evidently used in his sixth or seventh year at the School. John Ward's edition of Lily's *Latin Grammar,* published in London in 1732, was introduced into the curriculum of the Latin School in 1789, under the "New System of Education." The Harvard College Library possesses a copy of Ward's 1784 edition of Lily's *Latin Grammar,* with the inscription "John Pippoon, Boston," identifying it as belonging to the John Pippoon who entered the Boston Latin School in 1787.

John Brinsley, the Elder, (fl. 1663) who was Master of the public school at Ashby-de-la-Zouch in Leicestershire and

---

[12] *Ibid,* p. 243.
[13] See page 309.

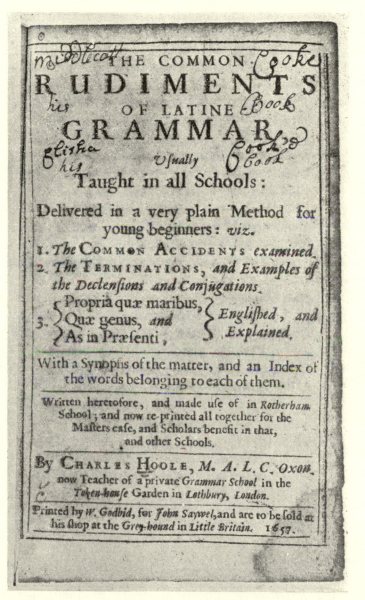

THE COMMON
RUDIMENTS
OF LATINE
GRAMMAR
Usually
Taught in all Schools:

Delivered in a very plain Method for
young beginners: *viz.*

1. *The* COMMON ACCIDENTS *examined*
2. *The* TERMINATIONS, *and Examples of*
the Declensions and Conjugations.
3. { Propriâ quæ maribus, } { *Englished, and*
  { Quæ genus, *and* } { *Explained.*
  { As in Præsenti, }

With a Synopsis of the matter, and an Index of
the words belonging to each of them.

Written heretofore, and made use of in *Rotherham*
School; and now re-printed all together for the
Masters ease, and Scholars benefit in that,
and other Schools.

By CHARLES HOOLE, M. A. L. C. *Oxon.*
now Teacher of a private *Grammar School* in the
Token-house Garden in *Lothbury, London.*

Printed by *W. Godbid*, for *John Saywel*, and are to be sold at
his shop at the *Grey-hound* in *Little Britain.* 1657.

TITLE-PAGE OF CHARLES HOOLE'S *The Common Rudiments of Latine Grammar*
By courtesy of the Harvard College Library.

afterwards a teacher in London, wrote several Latin textbooks which we know were used in New England, presumably in Boston also, although there is no direct evidence. In 1612 he published in London *Ludus Literarius: or, the Grammar Schoole; shewing how to proceede from the first entrance into learning to the highest perfection required in the Grammar Schooles.* In 1617 he published in London *Pueriles Confabulatiunculae: or Childrens Dialogues, little conferences, or talkings together, or Dialogues fit for children.* John Brinsley also published in London, in 1622, *A Consolation for our Grammar Schooles; or a faithfull encouragement for laying of a sure foundation of all good learninge in our Schooles.* In 1630 he published in London *The Posing of the Parts: or, a most plaine and easie way of examining the accidence and grammar by questions and answers.* In 1612 he translated grammatically *Sententiae Pueriles,* and in 1614 he edited *Corderius's Colloquies,* translated grammatically, a later edition of which appeared in London in 1653.

Charles Hoole (1610-1667), a famous private teacher in London, published there the following textbooks: *An Easy Entrance to the Latin Tongue, wherein are contained the Grounds of Grammar, a Vocabularie of Common Words, English and Latine,* in 1649; *Propria quae Maribus, Quae Genus and As in praesenti,* [i.e., Lily's *Latin Grammar*] *Englished and explayned,* in 1650; *Terminationes et Exempla Declinationum et Conjugationum . . . ,* in 1650; *Lily's Latine Grammar fitted for the use of Schools,* in 1651 and 1653; *Maturinus Corderius's School-Colloquies, English and Latine . . . ,* in 1657; *Vocabularium parvum Anglo-Latinum . . . ,* in 1657; *Leonhard Culmann's Sententiae Pueriles . . . translated into English,* in 1658; *J. A. Comenii Orbis Sensualium Pictus, translated into English,* in 1659; *Catonis Disticha de Moribus,* in 1659; *Pueriles Confabulatiunculae Anglo-Latinae,* in 1659; *Centuria Epistolarum Anglo-Latinarum,* in 1660; and *Examinatio grammaticae Latinae,* in 1660. Charles Hoole is also the author of *A New Discovery of the old Art of Teaching Schoole, in four small Treatises,* published in 1660.

The textbooks of Charles Hoole were studied at the Boston Latin School in the seventeenth century and the early part of the eighteenth century. The Harvard College Library owns a copy of the 1657 London edition of Charles Hoole's *The Common Rudiments of Latine Grammar* . . . , with the inscriptions "Elisha Cooke his book" and "Middlecott Cooke," both of whom were students of the Boston Latin School, entering in the years 1646 and 1712 respectively.[14] George Emery Littlefield describes his copy of the 1695 edition of Hoole's *The Common Accidence,* with the inscription "Joseph Taylor, 1761," evidently owned by the Joseph Taylor who entered the Boston Latin School in 1754 and used in his seventh and last year at the Latin School or in his freshman year at Harvard College. The Harvard College Library also owns a copy of the first American edition of Hoole's translation of Leonhard Culmann's *Sententiae Pueriles or Sentences for Children,* printed in Boston in 1702, bearing the inscription "William Williams His Book 1748," identifying the book as probably belonging to the William Williams who entered the Boston Latin School in 1747. The Boston bookseller, Mr. John Ive, on March 3, 1683/84, bought "100 Sententiae Pueriles" and the same bookseller, in 1685, bought "100 Hoolls Sententiae. By Leonhard Culmann, translated by Charles Hoole. London, 1658," probably for the use of the Boston Latin School and other New England Latin grammar schools.

William Walker (1623-1684), Head Master of Louth Grammar School and later of Grantham Grammar School, England, published in London the following textbooks: *A Treatise of English Particles, Shewing Much of the Variety of their Significations and Uses in English: And how to render them into Latine according to the Propriety and Elegancy of that Language. With a Praxis upon the same,* in 1655, the twelfth edition of which appeared in 1703; *A Dictionary of English and Latin Idioms,* in 1670; *Phraseologia Anglo-Latina*

[14]See page 311.

. . . , in 1672; *The Royal* [Lily's] *Grammar explained,* in 1674; and *English Examples of Latin Syntaxis,* in 1683. William Walker is also the author of a book of methods of teaching, entitled *Some Improvements to the Art of Teaching, especially in the First Grounding of a Young Scholar in Grammar Learning. Shewing a Short, Sure and Easie way to bring a Scholar to Variety and Elegancy in Writing Latin,* published in London in 1693, the seventh edition of which appeared in 1706.

The textbooks of William Walker were studied at the Boston Latin School. George Emery Littlefield, in his *Early Schools and School-Books of New England,* describes his copy of the 1703 edition of William Walker's *A Treatise of English Particles,* bearing the autographs of "John Taylor, 1716" and "Joseph Taylor, 1761." Joseph Taylor entered the Boston Latin School in 1754 and used the book either in his seventh year at the School or in his freshman year at Harvard College. The Harvard College Library owns a copy of William Walker's *Some improvements to the art of teaching Latin,* published in London in 1693, bearing the undated autographs of Richard Saltonstall and Samuel Danforth, who entered the Boston Latin School in 1740 and 1779 respectively.

The Latin Testament was studied at the Boston Latin School as early as the seventeenth century. The Boston bookseller, Mr. John Ive, on March 3, 1683/84, bought "10 Lattine Testaments," probably for the Latin School. The Reverend Cotton Mather recorded in his *Diary* on May 18, 1716: "To the Grammar-Schole in my neighborhood, I would send a Version of the Ten Commandments, in Latin Verse, to be recited by the Scholars."[15] The Harvard College Library owns the 1769 London edition of *Selecta e Veteri Testamento.* This was prescribed in the Boston Latin School curriculum of 1789.

Aesop's *Fables,* in English and Latin, were studied at the Boston Latin School in the seventeenth century and as late

---

[15]Cotton Mather lived in the old North End, near the North Grammar School.

as 1789, under the "New System of Education." The Reverend John Barnard, who entered the Latin School in 1689, has recorded in his Autobiography: "In the spring of my eighth year I was sent to the grammar-school under the tuition of the aged, venerable, and justly famous Mr. Ezekiel Cheever. . . . Master put our class upon turning Aesop's Fables into Latin verse." A Boston bookseller, Mr. John Foy, in 1682 listed "4 esops in english. . . . Printed, in 1670" and Mr. John Ive in 1685 listed a Latin edition of Aesop's *Fables,* entitled *Mythologia Aesopica,* printed in 1683. In the inventory of the estate of Michael Perry, a Boston bookseller in 1700, are listed "9 Aesops Fables" and "5 Aesops Fables Engl. and Lattin," probably for the use of the Boston Latin School. Charles Hoole's translation of Aesop's Fables was apparently not published until 1700. In the Harvard College Library there is a copy of Aesop's *Fables,* published in Eton in 1755, with the autograph of "Henry Jackson," a Boston Latin School boy who entered the School in 1756. Another Henry Jackson entered the School in 1784; since the autograph is not dated, the book may have belonged to either.

John Clarke,[16] a schoolmaster and pastor of the Church of Fiskerton, near Lincoln, England, wrote the following textbooks published in London: *Transitionum formulae in usum scholarum concinnatae quibus adiungitur Dux Poeticus,* in 1628 (?); *Formulae oratoriae in usum scholarum concinnatae una cum multis orationibus, declamationibus,* the fourth edition of which was published in 1632; *Dux grammaticus tyronem scholasticum ad rectam orthographiam, syntaxin, et prosodiam dirigens,* in 1633; *Dux oratorius,* in 1633; *Phraseologia puerilis Anglo-Latina,* in 1638; and *Paroemiologia Anglo-Latina in usum scholarum concinnata,* in 1639.

The Boston bookseller, Mr. John Foy, in 1682 received from abroad "12 Clarks formula," probably for the use of

---

[16] This John Clarke is not to be confused with another John Clarke (1687-1734) who wrote *An Essay Upon the Education of Youth in Grammar-Schools* in 1720, the second edition of which was published in London in 1730.

Harvard College or possibly for the use of the Boston Latin School. George Emery Littlefield, in his *Early Schools and School-Books of New England,* describes his copy of the eighth edition of John Clarke's *Formulae Oratoriae,* published in London in 1659, bearing the undated autographs of Jonathan Mitchell Sewall, who entered the Boston Latin School in 1755, and of John Higginson, who entered the School in 1821. Since neither is recorded as having attended college, the evidence is that either the textbook was used at the Latin School or was bought for a private library.

Ezekiel Cheever, the famous Master of the Boston Latin School from January 6, 1670/71, until his death in 1708, has been credited by some historians with the authorship of a Latin grammar, popularly known for over a century as Cheever's *Accidence.* As a matter of fact, the earliest edition, so far as known the first edition, was not published in Boston until 1709, one year after Ezekiel Cheever's death. The name of the author does not appear on the title-page, which reads as follows: *A Short Introduction to the Latin Tongue, For the Use of the Lower Forms in the Latin School. Being the Accidence Abbridg'd and Compiled in that most easy and accurate Method, wherein the Famous Mr. Ezekiel Cheever taught; and which he found the most advantageous by Seventy years experience.* This title suggests that the printed book was "Abbridg'd and Compiled" from Cheever's manuscript *Accidence.* The manuscript, however, is not extant. Evidence that Ezekiel Cheever was not the author of the published *Accidence* in its final form is the following statement on the title-page of the 1724 edition: "The Third Edition revised and corrected by the Author." Ezekiel Cheever had been dead for sixteen years! Mr. George Emery Littlefield, in his *Early Schools and School-Books of New England,* suggests that the printed *Accidence* may have been written by Cheever's son, the Reverend Thomas Cheever (Harvard, 1677), by his grandson, Mr. Ezekiel Lewis (Harvard, 1695), or by the Usher of the Boston Latin School, Mr. Nathaniel Williams (Harvard,

1693), who succeeded Ezekiel Cheever in 1708 as the Master of the School. All three of these men were living in 1724, the year in which the third edition appeared "revised and corrected by the Author." The last edition of the text was published in Boston as late as 1838. The Harvard College Library owns several editions and is the proud possessor of a copy of the first edition of 1709, purchased from the Essex Institute, Salem. A copy of the ninth edition, published in 1766, bears the inscriptions "Josh^a Green jun: Dec: 1774" and "Hic liber pertinet Josua Green Steal not this book for fear of shame For in it is the owner's name 1776," identifying the book as the property of Joshua Green who entered the Boston Latin School in 1773.

John Clarke (1687-1734),[17] the famous Master of the public grammar school at Hull, England, and later at Gloucester, published and edited the following books: *An Essay Upon The Education of Youth in Grammar-Schools: in which the Vulgar Method of Teaching is examined, and a New one proposed, for the more Easy and Speedy Training up of Youth to the Knowledge of the Learned Languages; together with History, Chronology, Geography, &c.*. in London in 1720, the second edition of which was published in London in 1730; *Formulae Oratoriae in usum Scholarum: una cum Orationibus; . . .*, in London in 1737; *An Introduction to the making of Latin, comprising the substance of Latin Syntax; &c.*, in London in 1733 (?); *Corderii Colloquiorum Centuria selecta, . . .*, in York in 1718; *Erasmi Colloquia selecta, or the select Colloquies of Erasmus, with an English translation as literal as possible*, in Nottingham in 1720; *Justinus*, in London in 1735; L. Florus's *A Compendious History of Rome. With an English Translation as Literal as possible*, the third edition of which appeared in London in 1739; and *Eutropii Historiae Romanae Breviarium*, the first American edition of which was printed in Boston by Peter Edes in 1793.

[17] This John Clarke is not to be confused with another John Clarke, of an earlier period, who was schoolmaster and pastor of the Church of Fiskerton, near Lincoln, England.

A Short

INTRODUCTION

TO THE

Latin Tongue,

For the Use of the Lower Forms in
the *Latin School*.

Being the Accidence Abbridg'd and
Compiled in that most easy and
accurate Method, wherein the
Famous Mr. *Ezekiel Cheever* taught ;
and which he found the most
advantageous by *Seventy* years
experience.

BOSTON in *N. E.*
Printed by *B. Green*, for *Benj. Eliot*, at
his Shop under the Town-house. 1709.

FIRST EDITION OF *A Short Introduction to the Latin Tongue,* POPULARLY
KNOWN AS CHEEVER'S *Accidence*
By courtesy of the Harvard College Library.

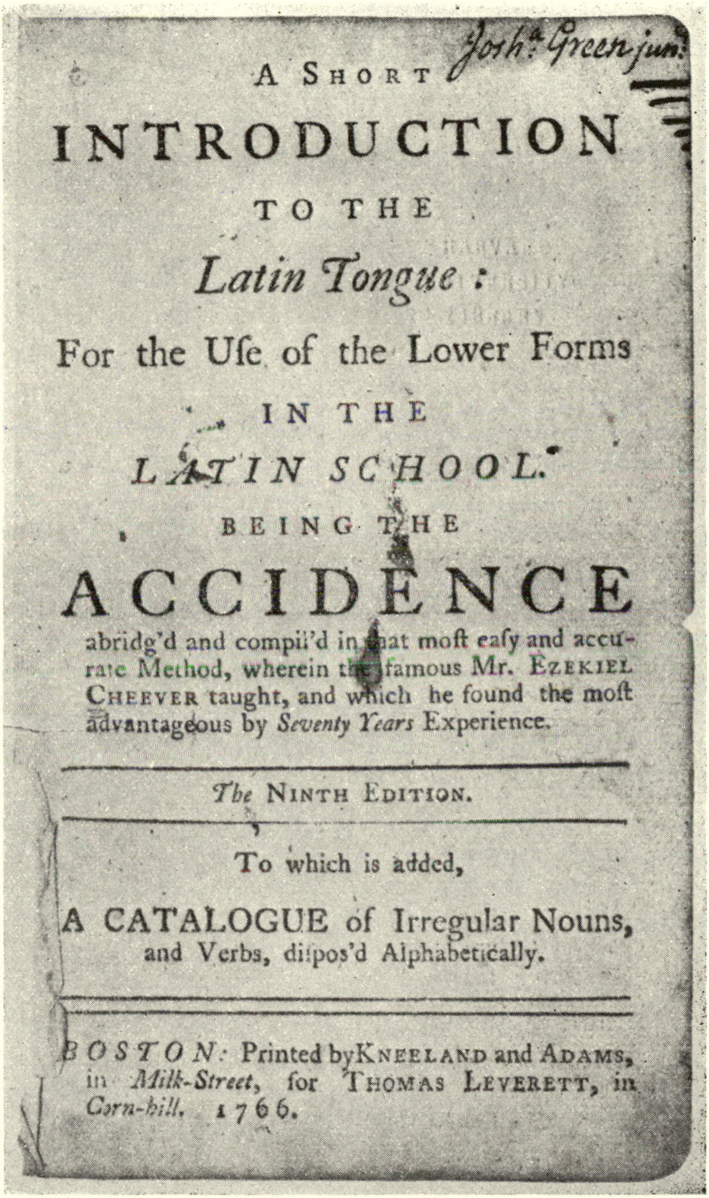

*Josh*ᵃ *Green jun:*

A SHORT

INTRODUCTION

TO THE

Latin Tongue :

For the Ufe of the Lower Forms

IN THE

LATIN SCHOOL.

BEING THE

ACCIDENCE

abridg'd and compil'd in that moft eafy and accurate Method, wherein the famous Mr. EZEKIEL
CHEEVER taught, and which he found the moft
advantageous by *Seventy Years* Experience.

The NINTH EDITION.

To which is added,

A CATALOGUE of Irregular Nouns,
and Verbs, difpos'd Alphabetically.

BOSTON: Printed by KNEELAND and ADAMS,
in *Milk-Street*, for THOMAS LEVERETT, in
Corn-hill, 1766.

NINTH EDITION OF CHEEVER'S *Accidence*
By courtesy of the Harvard College Library.

Several of these textbooks of John Clarke were studied at the Boston Latin School. Clark's *Introduction* [John Clarke's *An Introduction to the Making of Latin*] is among the books on the Benjamin Dolbeare, Jr., list from 1752 to 1759, and is also prescribed for the second year in the 1789 curriculum under the "New System of Education." The Harvard College Library owns a copy of the thirteenth London edition, published in 1742, with the autograph of Joseph Hooper, who entered the Boston Latin School in 1753.

J. Garretson's *English exercises for school-boys to translate into Latin* . . . , was published in London in 1683 and had many editions. Garretson's *Exercises* is listed in Nathaniel Williams's account of the curriculum in 1712, is on the Benjamin Dolbeare, Jr., list from 1752 to 1759, and is listed in the second year of the curriculum of 1789. The twenty-first edition was printed in London in 1755, with the following statement on the title-page: "The Author being deceased. . . . A Friend of his . . . hath made the following Alterations and Additions." The Harvard College Library owns a copy of this twenty-first edition of Garretson's *Exercises,* with the autograph of "Wm. Cheever," who entered the Boston Latin School in 1760 and was graduated from Harvard College in 1771. The Library also owns a copy of *Hermes Romanus, or A New Collection of Latin Words and Phrases, for the more Ready and Exact Translating of Garretson's English Exercises into Latin,*[18] written by "W. H. Teacher of a Private School" and published in London in 1717. The inscriptions "Benja Dolbeare Jr. Bot of Niffie Noyes for 1/6" and "Nathanael Noyes Wednesday September 19, 1754 he is eleven years old" positively identify the book as a Latin School text belonging to Benjamin Dolbeare, Jr., and Nathanael Noyes, both of whom entered in 1752. On page 131 of the text appears the inscription "A bad book for boys. I know by experience."

Other introductory Latin textbooks, which were published

---

[18] A facsimile of the title-page of *Hermes Romanus* appears on page 321.

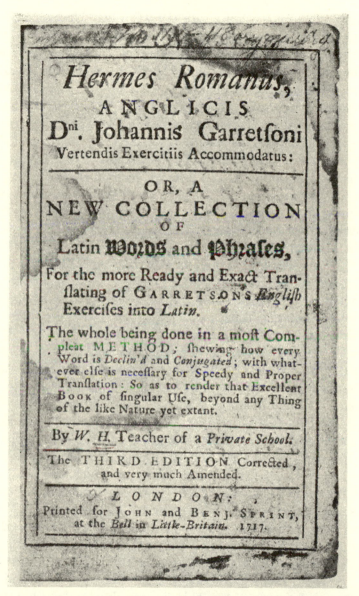

TITLE-PAGE OF *Hermes Romanus, ... or, A New Collection of Latin Words and Phrases, For the more Ready and Exact Translating of Garretson's English Exercises into Latin*
By courtesy of the Harvard College Library.

in the eighteenth century, are the following: Nathan Bailey's *English and Latin Exercises for School-Boys,* the ninth edition of which was published in London in 1734; the Reverend Thomas Dyche's *Vocabularium Latiale, or a Latin Vocabulary, in two parts,* in London in 1708 or 1709; James Otis's *Rudiments of Latin Prosody* in 1760; Thomas Ruddiman's *Rudiments of the Latin Tongue; or a Plain and Easy Introduction to Latin Grammar* in 1714, the first American edition of which was published in Philadelphia in 1786; Alexander Adam's *The rudiments of Latin and English grammar,* written in English in 1772, the first American edition of which was printed in Boston in 1799; and Caleb Alexander's *A New Introduction to the Latin Language . . . ,* in Worcester, Massachusetts, in 1795.

There is direct evidence that Alexander Adam's *Latin Rudiments and Grammar* was a Boston Latin School textbook. In the curriculum of 1808 Biglow's *Abridgment of Adam's Latin Grammar* is listed for the first year.   The records testify that Adam's *Latin Grammar* was studied in the first year, under the mastership of Benjamin A. Gould, from 1814 to 1828.   Mr. Gould also published an edition of Adam's *Latin Grammar,* in Boston in 1825, which was introduced into the course of study in 1825.   This had many editions.

William Biglow, who was the Master of the Boston Latin School from 1805 to 1814, published the following textbooks which were used at the School: *Elements of Latin grammar,* in Boston in 1801, the second edition of which was published in Boston in 1811; *New Latin primer,* in Boston in 1801, the second edition of which was published in Boston in 1809, and the third edition, in 1813; and *An introduction to the making of Latin,* in Salem in 1801, the second edition of which was published in Salem in 1809, and the third edition, in 1813.

Liber Primus is listed in the curriculum of 1823 and appears as late as 1834.   This is undoubtedly Joseph Dana's *Liber Primus, or a First Book of Latin Exercises: prepared for the use of Schools and Academies,* published in Newburyport in 1815. The second edition was published in Boston in 1818, the third edition, in Boston in 1821, and a stereotyped edition, in Boston in 1824.

Dana's *Latin Tutor* is listed in the curriculum from 1823 to 1826. This is Daniel Dana's *The Latin Tutor, or An Introduction to the Making of Latin* . . . [19] published in Newburyport in 1813. Mr. Benjamin A. Gould, the Master of the School from 1814 to 1828, has recorded: "The exercises in the Latin Tutor continue till the book is entirely written through once or twice. Much time and labor are saved in correcting these exercises."

Bradley's *Prosody* is listed in Benjamin A. Gould's account of the curriculum of 1823. This is undoubtedly Charles Bradley's (1789-1871) *Exercises in Latin Prosody and Versification,* the fourth edition of which was published in London in 1823. Charles Bradley was an English preacher and the editor of several school textbooks.

Edward Valpy's *Elegantiae Latinae; or Rules and Exercises illustrative of Elegant Latin Style,* published in 1803, is listed in the curriculum from 1823 to 1826. An edition was published in New Haven in 1819, from the fifth English edition. Edward Valpy (1764-1832) was Master of the Reading Grammar School, England, under his brother, Richard Valpy (1754-1836), who was Head Master of the School from 1781 to 1831. Richard Valpy was the author of Greek and Latin grammars which had a large circulation.

Viri Romae is listed in the 1823 curriculum and appears in the course of study as late as 1880. It reappears frequently in the curriculum after that date. This is Charles François L'Homond's *De viris illustribus urbis Romae a Romulo ad Augustum,* the first American edition of which was published in Philadelphia in 1810. The Harvard College Library owns a copy of the third edition, published in New York in 1821, bearing the autograph "Charles Sumner," identifying it as a Boston Latin School textbook owned by the famous Charles

---

[19] The Harvard College Library owns a copy.

Sumner who entered the School in 1821. In 1839 Frederic Percival Leverett and Thomas Gamaliel Bradford published in Boston *Viri Romae . . . introductory exercises,* later editions of which appeared in 1841 and 1845. Mr. F. P. Leverett was the Master of the Latin School from 1828 to 1831, and Mr. T. G. Bradford was the Usher of the School from 1823 to 1825 and again in 1828. In 1842 an edition of *Viri Romae, with notes by Ethan Allen Andrews* was published in Boston in 1842. The fourth edition of *Viri Romae; adapted to Andrews and Stoddard's Latin Grammar, and to Andrews' first Latin Book by E. A. Andrews* was published in Boston in 1850. In 1892 J. C. Rolfe published in Boston an annotated edition of *Selections from Viri Romae,* the sixth revised edition of which was published in Boston in 1897. In 1897 an edition of *Selections from Lhomond's Urbis Romae viri inlustres* [sic] was published in Boston, edited by G. M. Whicher. The Harvard College Library owns a copy of the 1905 edition.

Andrews and Stoddard's *A Grammar of the Latin Language; for the Use of Schools and Colleges,* published in Boston in 1836, was introduced into the curriculum in 1852, or possibly earlier. The tenth edition was published in Boston in 1844, and the sixty-fifth, in Boston in 1857. Ethan Allen Andrews (1787-1858), an American scholar and teacher, and Solomon Stoddard (1800-1847) were the authors. Ethan Allen Andrews is also the author of *Latin-English Lexicon,* published in 1850, based on Freund.

Arnold's *Latin Prose Composition,* published in 1839, was introduced into the curriculum of the Boston Latin School in 1852 or earlier. The Boston Public Library owns a copy of the 1846 New York edition, published from the sixth London edition. Thomas Kerchever Arnold (1800-1853), an English clergyman and scholar, published a number of popular textbooks for schools, among which are manuals for the Latin, Greek, French, and German languages.

Harkness's *A Latin grammar for schools and colleges,*

published in New York in 1864, was introduced into the curriculum in 1865. The revised standard edition was published in New York in 1881. Albert Harkness (1822-1907), an American classical scholar and educator, was the author of many well-known textbooks in Latin and Greek and school editions of various classical authors. In 1851 he published in New York his *First Latin Book* and in 1883 his *Complete Latin Course for the First Year.*

Allen and Greenough's *A Latin Grammar for Schools and Colleges, founded on Comparative Grammar,* written by Joseph Henry Allen and James Bradstreet Greenough, became a popular standard textbook and has been used for many years at the Boston Latin School. A revised edition was published in Boston in 1872. The book is not listed in the *Annual Catalogue of the Boston Latin School* until the year 1895-1896.

LATIN AUTHORS

Caesar's *Commentaries* was a textbook used at the Boston Latin School as early as 1752, if not earlier. The Harvard College Library owns a copy, published in London in 1706, with the inscription "Josha: Green junr 1780," which identifies it as a Latin School text, used in the seventh and last year by the Joshua Green who entered the School in 1773.

Dionysius Cato's *Disticha de Moribus ad Filium,* a small collection of moral precepts which for many centuries had been one of the most widely read and cited of all Latin works, was studied at the Latin School as early as the seventeenth century, when Ezekiel Cheever was Master. The Boston bookseller, Mr. John Ive, on March 3, 1683/84, bought "50 Latine Catos," probably for the use of the Latin School and other neighboring Latin grammar schools.

Marcus Tullius Cicero's *De Officiis,* his *Orations,* and his *Epistles* were studied at the Latin School as early as the seventeenth century, under the mastership of Ezekiel Cheever. Cicero was often called "Tully" by English writers. The

Boston bookseller, mentioned above, bought on March 3, 1683/84, "12 Sturmies Epistles," which were probably Cicero's *Epistles,* edited by John Sturm,[20] and in 1685 he bought "18 Tully's Offices." In the inventory of the estate of Michael Perry, a Boston bookseller in 1700, are listed "6 Tulleys Orations," "8 Tulleys Epistles," and "7 de officiis at 16 d.," probably for the Boston Latin School and other neighboring Latin grammar schools. Harvard College Library owns several old copies, a few of which have been identified as Latin School textbooks. One copy of Cicero's *Select Orations,* entitled *M. Tulli Ciceronis Orationum Selectarum Liber,* published in London in 1734, bears the autograph of "Stephen Minot," who entered the Latin School in 1747. Another copy of the same, published in Edinburgh in 1790, bears the dated autograph "H. Codman's 1802," identifying the book as a third-year text used by the Henry Codman who entered the School in 1799.

Castalio's [or Castellio's] *Dialogorum Sacrorum Libri IV,* a history of the Bible in the form of dialogues, was written by Sébastien Castalio and published at Geneva in 1543. This was for many years a well-known textbook.[21] It was studied at the Boston Latin School as early as 1752, if not earlier. Cotton Mather, the minister of the Second Church, recorded in his *Diary,* in March, 1710/11, the following "Good Devised":

5 G. D. I am concerned for the Welfare of the great Grammar School of the Town. I would unite Counsels with a learned, pious, honourable Visitor of the School, to introduce diverse good Intentions into it. This among the rest; that Castalio and Posselius, be brought into the School; and the lads for their Latin Exercises, turn into Latin such Things as may befriend the Interests of Christianity, in their Hearts and Lives;—particularly, the Quaestions and Answers, in our Supplies from the Tower of David.

[20] John Sturm (1507-1589), a famous teacher and editor of many classical textbooks, was Head Master of the Gymnasium at Strasburg from 1538 to 1581.

[21] Sébastien Castellion was born in Chatillon, a village of Savoy, in 1515. He was professor of Humanity at Geneva about 1540 and professor of Greek at Basle about 1544.

Corderius's[22] *Colloquia* was a Latin School textbook intro-
duced by Ezekiel Cheever, who was appointed the Master in
1670. Charles Hoole edited in 1657 Maturinus Corderius's
School Colloquies, English and Latin. . . . Mr. John Ive on
March 3, 1683/84, bought "30 Hoolls Corderius. M. Cor-
derius's school-colloquies. English and Latin, by Charles
Hoole, 1659," probably for the use of the Boston Latin School
and other neighboring Latin grammar schools. George Emery
Littlefield, in his *Early Schools and School-Books of New
England,* describes his copy of Hoole's edition of *Corderius's
Colloquies,* printed in London in 1719, with the inscription
"Johannis Taylor hunc Librum jure tenet. Anno 1748," which
identifies the book as belonging to John Taylor, who entered
the Boston Latin School in 1746. There is also direct evidence
that John Clarke's edition of *Corderius's Colloquia,* published
in London in 1759, was a Latin School textbook. The Harvard
College Library owns a copy of *Colloquiorum Centuriata
Selecta: or, a Select Century of the Colloquies of Corderius,*
published in Worcester, Massachusetts, in 1803, which has
been identified as a Latin School textbook.

Erasmus's *Colloquia,* written in 1524 by Desiderius
Erasmus, the famous Dutch scholar and philosopher, was
studied at the Boston Latin School as early as 1712, if not
earlier. The Boston Public Library owns a copy of Erasmus's
Colloquia,[23] published in London in 168-(?), on the back cover
of which is the inscription "Henry Messinger His Book 1709."
On page 98 is the statement, in manuscript, "The boys y^t
belonge to ye publick grammar school." On alternate pages,
beginning with page 99, are recorded the names of sixty-four
students, many of whom are known to have been Boston Latin

[22] Mathurinus Corderius is the Latinized form of the name used by
Mathurin Cordier (1479-1564), a schoolmaster in Paris and Geneva. He wrote
several textbooks for children, the most famous of which is his *Colloquia,* an
introductory Latin book of simple dialogues, which was studied in schools
for over three centuries.

[23] The writer is indebted to Professor Arthur Orlo Norton of Wellesley
College for the identification of this book as a Latin School textbook.

TITLE-PAGE OF SÉBASTIEN CASTELLION'S *Dialogorum Sacrorum Libri IV*
By courtesy of the Harvard College Library.

School boys. George Emery Littlefield describes his copy of John Clarke's edition of Erasmus's *Colloquia,* entitled *Colloquiorum Desiderii Erasmi Roterodami Familiarium Opus Aureum,* published in London in 1717, bearing the dated autograph of "Benjamin Dolbeare, Junr, 1757," who entered the Latin School in 1752. This is the very Benjamin Dolbeare, Jr., whose list of books used from 1752 to 1759 is in the possession of the Boston Latin School Association. The same book bears the autographs of "Ch. K. Dillaway, Dec. 20, 1872," who entered the School in 1818 and became the Master in 1831, and of "Francis Gardner, Jr.," who entered the School in 1822 and later became Head Master in 1851. An earlier edition of Erasmus's *Colloquia* appeared in London, edited by J. Clarke, in 1676. Mr. John Ive, on March 3, 1683/84, bought "12 Erasmus Colloquies Latin," probably for the Boston Latin School or some other Latin grammar school.

Sir Roger L'Estrange, an English journalist of the seventeenth century, published a translation of Erasmus's *Colloquies* in London in 1680. The Boston bookseller, mentioned above, on March 3, 1683/84, bought "6 Lestranges Erasmus in English. Made English by Roger L'Estrange. London, 1680" and the same bookseller, on April 13, 1685, bought "10 Erasmus Colloquies. English Lestrange." In 1712 Nathaniel Williams, the Master of the School, recorded in his account of the curriculum: "The 4th year, or sooner if their capacities allow it, they are entered upon *Erasmus,* to which they are allou'd no English, but are taught to translate it by the help of the Dictionary and Accidence. . . . "

The works of Horace were studied at the Boston Latin School as early as 1712, under Master Nathaniel Williams, if not earlier. The Boston bookseller, Mr. John Foy, in 1682 listed "38 Bonds horrace. Q. Horatius Flaccus, scholiis . . . illustrata a J. Bond. London, 1678," probably for the Boston Latin School or some neighboring Latin grammar school. The Harvard College Library owns a copy of the sixth edition of

Horace, published in London in 1717, bearing the dated auto-graph of "Joshua Green Liber 1744," used in the sixth year at the Boston Latin School by the Joshua Green who entered the School in 1738.

Ovid's *De Tristibus* and *Metamorphoses* were studied at the Latin School as early as the seventeenth century under Eze-kiel Cheever. Mr. John Foy in 1682 bought "4 ovid metamor-phosis," probably the edition of Thomas Farnaby, printed in London in 1650. Mr. John Ive, on March 3, 1683/84, bought "40 Ovid de Tristibus, Translated into English by Wye Saltonstall," a fifth edition of which appeared in 1681; he bought in 1685 "22 Farnabys Ovid," probably for the use of the Boston Latin School or some other Latin grammar school. The Harvard College Library owns a copy of the "Delphin" edition [edited for the French Dauphin] of Ovid's *Meta-morphoses,* published in London in 1737. This copy was owned by Francis Gardner, who was Master of the Latin School from 1851 to 1876. The Library also owns an edition of Ovid, published in London in 1765, bearing the inscription "Elias H. Derby's," evidently owned by Elias Hasket Derby, the founder of the Derby Medals, who entered the Boston Latin School in 1819.

The *Comedies* of Terence were studied at the Latin School, probably as early as the seventeenth century under Ezekiel Cheever, but definitely in 1745. Mr. John Foy in 1682 bought "12 Terrences"; Mr. John Ive in 1685 bought "12 Hoolls Terrence" and "12 Lattine Terrence. Printed in 1674. Terentius Christianus, sive Comoediae Duae Terentio Stylo conscriptae." The Harvard College Library owns a copy of Terence's *Comedies,* published in Amsterdam in 1691, with the inscription "Benjamin Gridley 1745," which identifies it as a textbook owned by the Benjamin Gridley who entered the Boston Latin School in 1740.

Virgil's *Aeneid* was a Latin School textbook studied as early as 1670, if not earlier. In the inventory of the estate of Michael Perry, a Boston bookseller in 1700, are listed "7

Virgill," probably for the Boston Latin School or other Latin grammar schools. Rufus Dawes, who entered the School in 1810, has recorded that Davidson's translation of Virgil "was always handed round for the use of the boys, who notwithstanding this indulgence, hardly ever took the trouble to study more than their respective sentences; for as the recitation invariably commenced with the head of the class, each one could calculate pretty nearly which passage would come to himself." Heyne's *Virgil*, published by Christian Gottlob Heyne,[24] is listed in the curriculum of 1808 (?) under the mastership of William Biglow. Gould's *Virgil*, published by Benjamin Apthorp Gould, the Master of the Latin School from 1814 to 1828, is listed in the curriculum of 1834. Mr. Gould also published editions of Ovid and Horace. The Harvard College Library owns a copy of the "Delphin" edition [edited for the French Dauphin], published in London in 1759, owned by Henry Williamson Haynes, who entered the Boston Latin School in 1842.

The works of Juvenal, the Roman satirist and poet, were studied at the Boston Latin School in 1712, in the seventh [the last] year of the course of study. Juvenal's sixteen satires, in heroic hexameter verse, are divided into five books. In the curriculum of 1823, under the mastership of Benjamin A. Gould, Juvenal's *Third Satire* and *Tenth Satire* were required to be committed to memory in the fifth year of the course.

The works of Persius, the Etruscan satirist, were studied in the seventh [the last] year at the Boston Latin School in 1712, under the mastership of Nathaniel Williams. His six satires, entitled *Satyrae,* comprising 650 hexameter lines, are extant, edited by Jahn in 1843 and by Heinrich in 1844. Persius is listed for the fifth year in the curriculum of 1823.

Florus's *Epitome Rerum Romanarum,* an account of the Roman people from King Romulus to Augustus Caesar, was

[24]Christian Gottlob Heyne (1729-1812), a professor at the University of Göttingen, was a celebrated classical philologian.

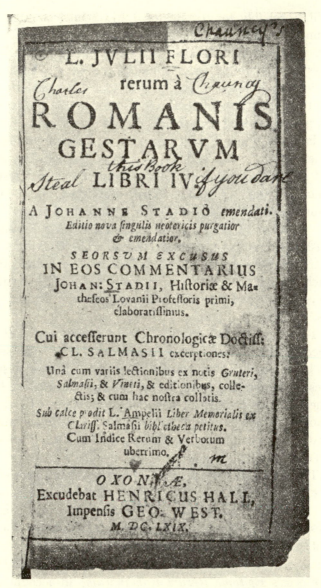

TITLE-PAGE OF LUCIUS FLORUS'S *History of Rome*
By courtesy of the Harvard College Library.

a Latin School textbook studied as early as 1712, if not earlier. In the inventory of the estate of Michael Perry, a Boston bookseller in 1700, is listed "1 Lucius Florus[25] Engl. The Roman History of Lucius Annaeus Florus made English. Printed in 1673." The Harvard College Library owns a copy of the third edition of John Clarke's English translation of L. Florus's *A Compendious History of Rome,* published in London in 1739, bearing the autograph of "Thomas Shirley," who entered the Boston Latin School in 1737, and the dated autograph of "Benjamin Gridley His Book 1742," who entered the School in 1740. The Harvard College Library also owns a copy of *L. Julii Flori rerum a Romanis Gestarum Libri IV.,*[26] published in Oxford in 1669, bearing the inscription "Charles Chauncy Steal this Book if you dare," which identifies it as belonging to the Charles Chauncy who entered the Latin School in 1712.

Justin's[27] [Justinus's] *Historia,* a compendium of Roman history in Latin, extracted from a vast work by Pompeius Trogus, was studied at the Boston Latin School definitely in 1712, and probably earlier. Mr. John Ive in 1685 bought "12 Lattine Justins, printed in 1677," probably for the Boston Latin School. The Harvard College Library owns a copy of John Clarke's edition of *Justinus,*[28] published in London in 1735, bearing the autographs of "Thomas Bulfinch," "Thomas Shirley," and "Benjamin Gridley his book," all three of whom were students of the Boston Latin School, entering in the years 1735, 1737, and 1740 respectively.

[25] The full name of Florus, the Roman historian, is a matter of dispute. In the earlier editions of his history he appears as L. Annaeus Florus. Titze maintained that he is the Lucius Julius Florus to whom two of Horace's epistles are addressed.

[26] See page 332 for a facsimile of the title-page.

[27] The first edition of *Justini Historiarum Philippicarum Libri XLIV.* was printed at Venice in 1470 by Jenson.

[28] This textbook, according to the librarian's note, was "found in Harvard Hall between the floor and plastering under the room where the library was kept before 1840."

Eutropius's *Breviarium ab Urbe Condita,* a compendium of Roman History from the foundation of Rome to the time of Valens, was studied at the Boston Latin School in 1752, if not earlier. An edition of John Clarke's *Eutropii Historiae Romanae Breviarium* was published in London in 1722 and an edition was published in Boston in 1793.

The works of Sallust, the historian, were required for admission to Harvard College in 1803. In the Latin School curriculum of 1808(?), which is the first extant curriculum after 1789, Sallust is listed for the third year. Of his *Historiarum Libri Quinque* only fragments are extant; his *Bellum Catilinarium* and *Bellum Jugurthinum* have been preserved and for many years have been much appreciated. In the Latin School curriculum of 1870 Sallust's *Catiline* is listed for the fourth year.

The works of Cornelius Nepos, the Roman historian, were introduced into the Latin School curriculum in 1823, or possibly earlier. Nepos wrote various works, all of which have been lost, with the exception of parts of his *De Viris Illustribus,* which originally contained at least sixteen books. The extant lives of Cato and Atticus were from the book *De latinis historicis.* The work *De excellentibus ducibus exterarum gentium,* which for many years has been used as a school textbook, has been identified as a part of the lost *De Viris Illustribus.*

Phaedrus's *Fabulae,* from Burman's text with English notes, was studied at the Latin School in 1823, if not earlier. Phaedrus wrote five books of fables, now extant but incomplete, containing ninety-three fables in all, many of which are only versifications of Aesop's *Fables.*

The works of Tacitus were studied at the Boston Latin School in 1826, or possibly earlier. His *Agricola,* a biography of his father-in-law, and his *Germania,* a description of early Germany, are listed in the the fifth year of the 1826 curriculum. In the curriculum of 1870 Tacitus's *Agricola* is listed for the fifth year and his *Annales* is listed for the sixth year.

The works of Livy, the historian, were introduced into the

Latin School curriculum in 1870. His *History of Rome,* from the foundation of the city to the death of Drusus in 9 B.C., was his greatest work, consisting originally of 142 books, only 35 of which are extant. The first printed edition appeared in Rome in 1469.

Quintilian's *Institutio Oratoria,* a work in twelve books on the art of oratory, was introduced into the curriculum in 1870. In the new and revised curriculum of 1876 Quintilian is omitted.

Quintus Curtius Rufus's *Historiae Alexandri Magni Macedonis,* an historical work on Alexander the Great, was also introduced into the curriculum in 1870, to be read in the third year. It is omitted in the curriculum of 1876.

The *Comedies of Plautus,* the Roman playwright, are listed in the curriculum of 1870. Plautus is omitted in the curriculum of 1876.

Extracts from Lucretius, the Roman poet, were studied at the Boston Latin School in 1870, in the sixth year. His poem *De Rerum Natura* contains six books, totaling more than seven thousand lines. Lucretius is not listed in the curriculum of 1876.

LATIN DICTIONARIES

One of the most popular of the sixteenth-century Latin dictionaries was Robert Estienne's[29] [Robertus Stephanus's] *Thesaurus Linguae Latinae,* printed in Paris in 1531 and 1532, the third edition of which appeared in 1543. The book was republished many times after that date. Although there is no direct evidence, this dictionary was probably used as a reference book at the Boston Latin School in the early part of the seventeenth century.

Another popular Latin dictionary was Thomas Cooper's[30] *Thesaurus linguae Romanae et Britannicae,* published in Lon-

---

[29] Robert Estienne, the Elder, (1503-1559) was born in Paris. He was printer to the King of Latin and Hebrew.

[30] Thomas Cooper (1517-1594) was Head Master of Magdalen College School. He was Bishop of Lincoln, in 1570, and of Winchester, in 1585.

don in 1565. The foundation of this work was Sir Thomas Elyot's *Dictionary* . . . , published in 1538, which Thomas Cooper edited in 1552, under the title of *Bibliotheca Eliotae.* This, too, was probably used as a reference book at the Boston Latin School in the early days after its establishment. The Massachusetts Historical Society owns a copy of Thomas Cooper's dictionary, with the undated autographs of "John Winthrop" and "Adam Winthrop," who entered the Boston Latin School in 1721 and 1756 respectively. Both are recorded as having been graduated from Harvard College. There is no proof that the book was definitely used at the Boston Latin School; it may have been used at the College.

In the seventeenth century several classical dictionaries were published, one of the best known of which was William Walker's[31] *Idiomatologia Anglo-Latina, or, A Dictionary of English and Latine Idiomes, wherein phrases of the English and Latine tongue answering in parallels each to the other are ranked under severall heads,* published in London in 1670. George Emery Littlefield, in his *Early Schools and School-Books of New England,* describes his copy of William Walker's *Idiomatologia Anglo-Latina,* bearing among others the autograph of Daniel Oliver, who entered the Boston Latin School in 1672. This book, according to Littlefield, was used in writing themes.

The fourth edition of Francis Gouldman's *A Copious Dictionary* was printed in Cambridge, England, in 1678. The Harvard College Library owns a copy of this edition, bearing the dated inscription, "Hic Liber pertinet mihi Jonathan Jackson Anno Domini 1757." This book belonged to the Jonathan Jackson who entered the Boston Latin School in 1750, and may have been used in his seventh and last year at the School or quite possibly in his freshman year at Harvard College. Mr. John Foy in 1682 received from abroad "4 Goulmans

[31]William Walker (1623-1684) was Head Master of Louth Grammar School and later of Grantham Grammar School. He later became Vicar of Colsterworth.

dictionarys," probably for the use of the Boston Latin School, some other Latin grammar school, or Harvard College.

Adam Littleton, D.D., a descendant of Sir Thomas Littleton, published in 1678 a dictionary of the Latin, Greek, Hebrew, and English languages, entitled *Linguae Latinae Liber Dictionarius Quadripartitus.* Although the study of Hebrew would identify it as a college text, the book may have been used at the Boston Latin School as a reference book in Latin and Greek. Mr. John Ive on March 3, 1683/84, bought "4 Littletons Dictionary."

The *Nomenclator* or *Nomenclatura,* a collection of words and terms, became very popular as an elementary-school lesson book and reference book. We have direct evidence from Nathaniel Williams's account of the curriculum of 1712 that the *Nomenclator* was used at the Boston Latin School in 1712. The *Nomenclatur* is on the Benjamin Dolbeare, Jr., list, from 1752 to 1759, and the *Nomenclator* is on the 1789 list of books. That the book was used at the Boston Latin School much earlier than 1712 is indirectly evidenced by the record that the Boston bookseller, Mr. John Ive, on March 3, 1683/84, bought "30 Nomen Claturas In usum Scholae Westmonasteriensis," probably for the use of the Boston Latin School and other Latin grammar schools. This was probably the *Nomenclatura brevis Anglo-Latino-Graeca,* written by Francis Gregory (1625-1707), the Usher of Westminster School, and published in London in 1675.

The most widely circulated dictionary for schools, according to Foster Watson,[32] and the one probably used at the Boston Latin School in 1635, the year of its establishment, was the following, an edition of which appeared in London in 1634: *A Dictionary in English and Latine; devised for the capacitie of Children and young Beginners. At first set forth by Withals, . . . And now at this last Impression enlarged with an encrease of Words, Sentences, Phrases, Epigrams, Histories, Poeticall fictions and Alphabeticall Proverbs. With a compendious*

---

[32] Foster Watson, *The English Grammar Schools to 1660,* p. 392.

Nomenclator newly added at the end. John Withals originally published the dictionary about 1554; Lewis Evans revised and enlarged it in 1574; Abraham Fleming added rhythmical verses in 1586; and William Clerk revised it in 1602.

One of the most popular of the eighteenth-century Latin-English dictionaries was that of Robert Ainsworth (1660-1743), entitled *Thesaurus linguae Latinae compendiarius,* published in London in 1736. Entick's and Ainsworth's Latin dictionaries are listed as reference books in the curriculum of 1823 and of 1826. John Entick (1703?-1773), an English schoolmaster and author, published *New Latin and English Dictionary* in 1771.

Elisha Coles (1640-1680) published in London in 1676 *An English Dictionary . . . ; together with the etymological derivations of them from their proper fountains, whether Hebrew, Greek, Latin, French, or any other Language.* A copy of the 1749 London edition of Elisha Coles's *English-Latin and Latin-English Dictionary,* now in the Harvard College Library, bears on the title-page the names of eleven Boston Latin School boys, all of whom entered the School in 1799. The names[33] are recorded in the same handwriting, apparently that of Master Samuel Hunt.

Alexander Adam (1741-1809), author of *The rudiments of Latin and English grammar,* published his *Compendious Dictionary of the Latin Tongue* in 1805. This dictionary is listed as a reference book in the curriculum of 1826.

Frederic Percival Leverett (1803-1836), who was the Master of the Boston Latin School from 1828 to 1831, edited a *Lexicon of the Latin Language,* which was published in Boston in 1837, one year after his death. This was a monumental piece of work, compiled from the *Lexicon* of Facciolati and others. Leverett's *Latin Lexicon* and Gardner's *Abridgment*

---

[33]The names are as follows: Wm. Smith 2; J. Jones 3; W. Andrews 4; D. Sears 6; J. Hall 5; E. Winslow 7; H. Colman 8; T. Dickason 9; J. H. Greene 10; J. M. Wright 11; and J. Foster 12. The numbers probably signify the order of admission to the Boston Latin School.

of Leverett's Latin Lexicon are listed in the curriculum of 1852 as books of reference.

Sir William Smith (1813-1893), the distinguished English editor and lexicographer, published in 1870 his *English-Latin Dictionary.* This dictionary was used at the Boston Latin School in the latter part of the nineteenth century as a book of reference.

LATIN PHRASE BOOKS

Thomas Drax, who was appointed Vicar of Dovercourt-cum-Harwich, Essex, in 1601, published in London in 1612 *Calliepeia: Or a rich store-house of proper, choyce, and elegant Latine words, and Phrases: collected (for the most part) out of Tullies Works; . . .* The second impression "reformed, refined and very much enlarged" appeared in 1613. The Harvard College Library owns a copy of the 1643 London edition,[34] bearing the inscription "Elisha Cooke, 1649," identifying it as belonging to the Elisha Cooke who probably entered the Boston Latin School in 1646.

One of the most popular of the elementary Latin phrase books was *Gradus Ad Parnassum,* a Thesaurus of synonyms, epithets, and poetical verses and phrases, written by Paul Aler, a member of the Society of Jesus, and published in London in 1694. A new edition was published in London in 1709. The book is on the Benjamin Dolbeare, Jr., list of textbooks studied at the Boston Latin School from 1752 to 1759. There is also direct evidence that the book was introduced into the curriculum as early as 1714. The curriculum of 1789 lists *Gradus Ad Parnassum* in the fourth year, and the curriculum of 1808(?) lists the book in the second year. The Harvard College Library owns a copy of *Gradus Ad Parnassum,*[35] published in London in 1709, with the autograph of "Benj. Gibson," who entered the Boston Latin School in 1714. The Harvard College Library also owns a copy of the 1794 London edition, with the autograph of "Abraham Wild," who entered the Bos-

[34] See page 341 for a facsimile of the title-page of *Calliepeia.*
[35] See page 342 for a facsimile of the title-page of *Gradus Ad Parnassum.*

ton Latin School in 1800. Rufus Dawes, who entered the Latin School in 1810, has recorded that Isaac Coffin, before he ran away to join the British Navy, gave his *Gradus Ad Parnassum,* ornamented with his pen drawings of ships, as a keepsake to Rufus Dawes's father. Sir Isaac Coffin, who became Admiral in the British Navy, and Colonel Thomas Dawes who became Judge of the Massachusetts Supreme Court and a member of the State Convention, were both classmates at the Boston Latin School, having entered the School in 1766.[36]

GREEK GRAMMARS AND ELEMENTARY GREEK READERS

William Camden (1551-1623), who was appointed Head Master of the Westminster School in 1593, published the standard school Greek Grammar, entitled *Institutio Graecae Grammatices Compendiaria,* in London in 1597. This was introduced at Eton and eventually became known as the *Eton Greek Grammar.* The Harvard College Library owns a copy of Camden's *Greek Grammar,*[37] published in London in 1734, with the inscription "Joseph Adams 1738," which identifies it as a book owned by Joseph Adams, who entered the Boston Latin School in 1737. The records also show that Camden's *Greek Grammar* was used at Harvard College until 1800, when the *Gloucester Grammar* was substituted.

Dr. Richard Busby (1606-169--), the famous English clergyman and Head Master of Westminster School from 1638 to 1695, published a Greek grammar, entitled *Busbaei Graecae Grammaticae Rudimenta in usum Scholae Westmonasteriensis,* written about 1647. In 1647 William Camden's *Greek Gram-*

---

[36]On January 25, 1933, the writer received the following communication from Charles Gates Dawes, former Vice-President of the United States: "I do not possess the book which you say Isaac Coffin gave to the Dawes family, and do not know where it could be located. Col. Thomas Dawes, who probably was the scholar of the Boston Latin School to enter in 1766, was a first cousin of my Great Great Grandfather, William Dawes, who rode with Paul Revere."

[37]See page 344 for a facsimile of the title-page of Camden's *Greek Grammar.*

CALLIEPEIA,

OR A

RICH STORE-HOUSE

OF

PROPER, CHOYCE, AND

elegant Latine words, and Phrases :

Collected (for the most part) out of TULLIES *Works ;*

And for the use and benefit of Scholars, di-
gested into an Alphabeticall order.

BY THOMAS DRAX.

CICERO *ad* BRUTUM.

Ipsum Latine loqui, est illud quidem in magna laude ponendum.
Verborum delectus origo eloquentiæ. Ibidem.
Fundamentum Oratoris est locutio emendata & Latina. Ibid.

LONDON,

Printed by M. F. for RICHARD WHITTAKER.
1 6 4 3.

TITLE-PAGE OF *Calliepeia, or a rich store-house of proper, choyce, and elegant Latine words, and Phrases*
By courtesy of the Harvard College Library.

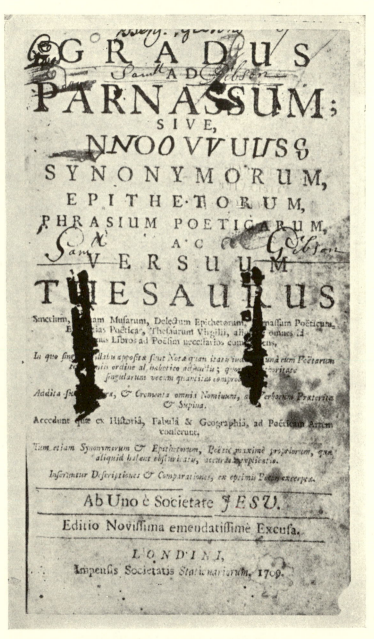

TITLE-PAGE OF *Gradus ad Parnassum*
By courtesy of the Harvard College Library.

mar was superseded by Dr. Richard Busby's *Greek Grammar* at the Westminster School. The Harvard College Library owns a copy of the 1663 London edition, bearing the inscription "Dr. Busby his Greek grammar used in Westminster school."[38] Later inscriptions in the book identify it as a textbook used at the Boston Latin School by Mather Byles, who entered the School in 1714.

Johannes Posselius, the Elder (1528-1591), professor of Greek in Rostock, published a Greek textbook, entitled *Familiarium colloquiorum libellus graece et latine,* in Wittenberg in 1586. In 1560 he published in Wittenberg *Syntaxis Graeca.* George Emery Littlefield, in his *Early Schools and School-Books of New England,* describes his copy of the 1710 London edition of Johannes Posselius's *Familiarium Colloquiorum Libellus,* with the inscription "Wm. Rand His Book. Began June Y^e 30, 1737," thus identifying it as a sixth-year Boston Latin School textbook, used by the William Rand who entered the School in 1731.

Eilhard Lubin (1565-1621), professor of literature and theology at Rostock, published in 1620 an elementary Greek textbook, entitled *Clavis Graecae linguae.* An edition of Eilhardus Lubinus's *Clavis Graecae linguae, sive vocabula latino-graeca* was published in Amsterdam in 1651. This book is written in Greek and Latin. The Harvard College Library owns the 1647 London edition, bearing the dated autograph "Elisha Cooke 1650," thus identifying it as a textbook used at the Boston Latin School by the Elisha Cooke who probably entered the School in 1646.

The Greek Testament, which was studied as an elementary reader to learn Greek construction, was read at the Boston Latin School definitely in 1712, and probably much earlier. Mr. John Ive, on March 3, 1683/84, bought "6 Greek Testaments, Edited by Charles Hoole, in 1674," probably for the Boston Latin School, or some other Latin grammar school.

[38]See page 346 for a facsimile of page of Dr. Busby's *Greek Grammar.*

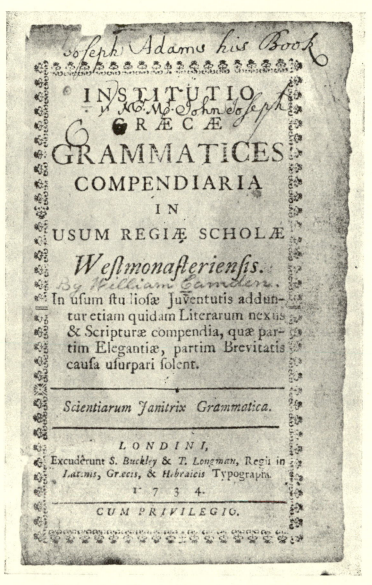

TITLE-PAGE OF WILLIAM CAMDEN'S *Greek Grammar*
By courtesy of the Harvard College Library.

John Holmes, Master of the Public Grammar School in Holt, wrote a Greek manual, entitled *Graecae Sententiae E variis Graecorum Libris hinc inde excerptae quibus insuper adduntur Aurea Carmina Pythagorae; cum Epitaphio Adonidis,* the seventh edition of which was published in London in 1775. This was a grammar-school textbook used in England and New England and might possibly have been used at the Boston Latin School, although there is no direct evidence.

Another well-known textbook was J. Milner's *Practical grammar of the Greek tongue,* an edition of which was published in London in 1739. The third enlarged edition was published in London in 1750. In the Harvard College Library there is a copy with the dated inscription "Stephen Hooper's 1752," evidently used by the Stephen Hooper who entered the Boston Latin School in 1750.

The Harvard College Library owns a copy of Nugent's *Greek Grammar,* published in London in 1797, with the undated autograph of "Francis Parkman," who entered the Boston Latin School in 1800 and was graduated from Harvard College in 1807. This was probably a college text or was bought for a private library, since there is no further evidence that Nugent's *Greek Grammar* was studied at the Boston Latin School.

One of the best known of the Greek grammars was the Gloucester Greek grammar, entitled *Grammar of the Greek Language: originally composed for the College-School, at Gloucester: in which it has been the editor's design to reject what, in the most improved editions of Cambden, is redundant: To supply what is deficient: To reduce to order what is intricate and confused:* . . . , the third improved edition of which was published in London in 1794. The name of the editor is not recorded in the book. In 1800 Isaiah Thomas and Ebenezer T. Andrews printed an edition in Boston. The Gloucester Greek grammar was introduced into the curriculum of Harvard College in 1800 and was studied at the Boston Latin School as early as 1808, if not earlier.

PAGE OF DR. RICHARD BUSBY'S *Graecae Grammaticae Rudimenta*
By courtesy of the Harvard College Library.

Neilson's *Greek Exercises for writing Greek* is listed as a book of reference in the 1823 curriculum of the Boston Latin School and is listed in the fourth year of the 1826 curriculum. This is undoubtedly William Neilson's (1760-1821) *Greek Exercises in Syntax, Ellipsis, Dialects, Prosody, and Metaphrasis,* published at Dundalk in 1804.

Jacob's *Greek Reader* is listed in the fourth year of the 1826 curriculum and in the fourth and fifth years of the 1834 curriculum. This is undoubtedly *The Greek Reader* by Friedrich C. W. Jacob, professor of the gymnasium at Gotha, which was edited by Edward Everett in Boston in 1823 from the seventh German edition.

The Greek textbooks of Richard Valpy (1754-1836), Head Master of the Grammar School in Reading, England, from 1781 to 1831, were studied at the Boston Latin School in the early part of the nineteenth century. Valpy's *Greek Delectus* is listed in the third year of the 1826 curriculum of the School, and reappears in the curriculum as late as 1834. This textbook is his *Delectus sententiarum Graecarum,* published in Cambridge in 1815, the third American edition of which was published in Boston in 1831. He is also the author of *Elements of Greek grammar,* the first American edition of which was published in Boston in 1814.

Sophocles's *Greek Grammar* and *Greek Lessons* are listed in the course of study of the Boston Latin School from 1852 to 1870. Evangelinus Apostolides Sophocles, professor of ancient, modern, and Byzantine Greek at Harvard College in 1860 and later, wrote the following Greek textbooks: *Greek Grammar* in 1838; *First Lessons in Greek* in 1839; *Greek Exercises* in 1841; *Greek Lessons for Beginners* in 1843; *Catalogue of Greek Verbs* in 1844; *History of the Greek Alphabet* in 1848; and *Glossary of Later and Byzantine Greek* in 1860, revised in 1870 as *Greek Lexicon of the Roman and Byzantine Periods.*

Dalzel's *Collectanea Graeca Minora,* published in England in 1789, was required for admission to Harvard College in 1803. The first American edition was published in Cambridge in 1804. The book is listed in the 1808 (?) course of study of the Boston Latin School, which is the first extant curriculum after 1789, but it was undoubtedly introduced in 1803. It is also listed in the curriculum from 1823 to 1826. Andrew Dalzel (1742-1806) was a distinguished English classical scholar.

Fisk's *Greek Grammar and Exercises* is listed in the curriculum of the Boston Latin School in 1834. There is no record of the number of years it continued in use, since the *Annual Catalogues of the Boston Public Latin School* were not published from 1835 through 1851. This is undoubtedly Benjamin Franklin Fisk's *Grammar of the Greek language,* published in Boston in 1830, the second edition of which was published in Boston in 1831. The twenty-sixth stereotyped edition was published in Boston in 1844.

Arnold's *Greek Prose Composition* is listed in the course of study of the Boston Latin School from 1852 to 1870. This is Thomas Kerchever Arnold's (1800-1853) *Practical Introduction to Greek Prose Composition,* the fourth edition of which was published in London in 1841, and the seventh edition, in 1849. The twelfth American edition was published in New York in 1854. Arnold is also the author of *Essentials of Greek Accidence,* published in 1838.

Felton's *Greek Reader,* published in Hartford in 1840, is listed in the curriculum of the Boston Latin School from 1852 to 1860. The second revised edition was published in Hartford in 1842. Cornelius Conway Felton (1807-1862), the author, was appointed Eliot professor of Greek literature at Harvard College in 1834; he was president of Harvard College from 1860 to 1862. Felton also published annotated editions of Homer, Aristophanes, Isocrates, and Aeschylus.

Goodwin and Allen's *Greek Reader* is listed in the curriculum of the Boston Latin School in 1876. The book was written by William Watson Goodwin, Eliot professor of Greek at Harvard College, and Joseph Henry Allen, D.D., a distinguished Unitarian preacher and scholar, and published in Boston in 1871. The second edition was published in 1877. Goodwin was also the author of a *Greek Grammar*, published in Boston in 1870, the second revised edition of which was published in Boston in 1877. Allen was the co-author of the famous Allen and Greenough *A Latin Grammar for Schools and Colleges*.

GREEK AUTHORS

Homer's *Iliad* was studied at the Boston Latin School, probably from the very beginning of the School. Cotton Mather, in his funeral sermon and poetical essay on Ezekiel Cheever in 1708, testifies that Homer was taught during the mastership of the famous Ezekiel Cheever from 1670/71 to 1708. Homer is on the Benjamin Dolbeare, Jr., list from 1752 to 1759 and also on the 1789 list of textbooks. Maittaire's *Homer* is listed in the curriculum from 1823 to 1826. The Harvard College Library owns a copy of Homer's *Iliad*,[39] published in London in 1736, with the dated inscription "Arnold Welles, 1740/1," which identifies the book as belonging to the Arnold Welles who entered the Boston Latin School in 1734. Homer's *Odyssey* is listed in the curriculum of 1876. An edition of *Clavis Homerica*,[40] published in Rotterdam in 1673, now in the possession of the Harvard College Library, bears the undated inscription "Peter Oliver's juner Clavis," probably owned by the Peter Oliver who entered the Boston Latin School in 1719. Facing the title-page is the following verse, written in Latin by Peter Oliver: "Here I place my name, since I do not wish to lose this book; If anyone steals it, he shall be hanged by the neck."

The works of Isocrates are listed in Nathaniel Williams's account of the curriculum of 1712. Isocrates's *Panegyric on Athens* is listed in the fourth year of the curriculum of 1870,

[39] See page 350 for a facsimile of title-page of Homer's *Iliad*, published in London in 1736.

[40] Antonius Roberti published *Clavis Homerica*, which was a Greek-Latin key to Homer, in Douai in 1636.

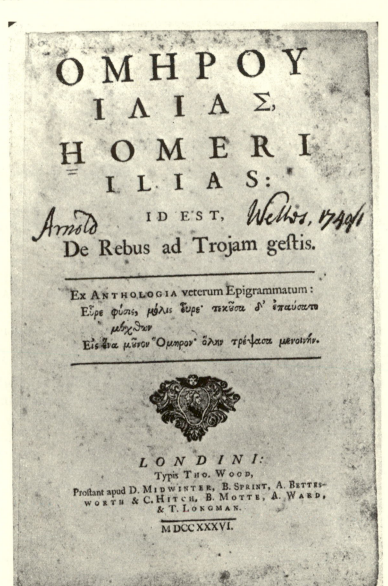

TITLE-PAGE OF HOMER'S *Iliad*
By courtesy of the Harvard College Library.

probably the American edition of Felton, the third edition of which appeared in 1866.

The writings of Hesiod are also listed in Nathaniel Williams's curriculum of 1712. Hesiod was claimed by the Greeks as the leading successor of Homer. The chief works attributed to him are the *Works and Days* and the *Theogony*.

The works of Xenophon were studied at the Boston Latin School as early as 1773, if not earlier. Xenophon's *Anabasis*, the story of the "Great March of the Ten Thousand Greeks," is listed for the fourth and fifth years in the 1823 curriculum and for the sixth year in the 1876 curriculum.

The works of Herodotus, who has been called "the father of history," were studied at the Boston Latin School as early as 1880. His history of the conflict between Persia and Hellas is the earliest surviving piece of Greek prose.

Aelian's *Extracts* is listed in the third year of the curriculum of 1870. Claudius Ælianus, who was born at Praeneste in the second century, wrote several works in Greek, of which his *Varia Historia, De Animalium Natura*, and some *Epistolae* are still extant.

Lucian's *Dialogues* is also listed in the third year of the curriculum of 1870. Lucian, the Greek satirist and essayist, was born at Samosata in Syria about 125 B.C. Of the works attributed to him, among the best known are *The Dialogues of the Dead, The Dialogues of the Gods, The Dream, The Cock*, and *How to Write History*. Lucian's *Art of Writing History* is listed in the fourth year of the curriculum of 1870.

Plutarch's *Parallel Lives* and his *Moralia* are listed in the curriculum of 1870. Of his historical works the most famous is the *Parallel Lives*, forty-six lives in twenty-three pairs, a Greek life being parallel to a Roman life. A revised English translation of Plutarch's *Morals* was published by William Watson Goodwin in Boston in 1870.

Of the three great Greek tragedians, Euripides, Sophocles, and Æschylus, the first two were studied at the Latin School.

Euripides's *Alcestis* is listed in the fifth year of the curriculum of 1870 and in the sixth year of the curriculum of 1876.

Sophocles's *Oedipus* is listed in the sixth year of the curriculum of 1870. Sophocles wrote 123 dramas, seven of which are extant, namely, *Ajax, Electra, Œdipus Tyrannus, Antigone, Trachiniae, Philoctetes,* and *Œdipus Coloneus.*

Demosthenes's *Olynthiacs* and *Philippics* are listed in the fifth year and his *De Corona,* in the sixth year, of the curriculum of 1870. Demosthenes has been called "the first of orators."

Plato's *Crito* and *Apologia* are listed in the fifth year of the curriculum of 1870, and in the sixth year of the curriculum of 1876. Plato is one of the most famous of the Greek philosophers.

Thucydides's *First Book* is listed in the sixth year of the curriculum of 1870. Thucydides wrote the history of the Peloponnesian war to 411 B.C. This history has come down to us in eight books.

Aristophanes's *Birds* and *Clouds* are listed in the sixth year of the curriculum of 1870. Aristophanes was the greatest of the Attic comic poets. Eleven, out of about forty, of his comedies are extant.

GREEK DICTIONARIES

There is no definite record of the Greek dictionaries used at the Boston Latin School before Benjamin A. Gould's account of the curriculum of 1823. Benjamin Dolbeare, Jr., lists a *Greek Lexicon,* bought for eleven shillings and four pence, in his list of textbooks studied at the Boston Latin School from 1752 to 1759. Mr. Gould, in his account of the reference books used in 1823, lists Schrevelius's *Greek Lexicon,* Hedericus's *Greek Lexicon,* Scapula's *Lexicon Graeco-Latinum,* and Morell's *Thesaurus.*

Henri Estienne's (Henricus Stephanus's)[41] *Thesaurus Graecae Linguae* was published in Paris in 1572. Although there is no direct evidence, his *Thesaurus* was probably used

---

[41] Henri Estienne (1528-1598), son of Robert Estienne, published an edition of *Plato* in 1578 and *La Précellence du Langage françois* in 1579.

as a book of reference in the early days after the establishment of the Boston Latin School in 1635. Abraham John Valpy (1787-1854), son of Richard Valpy, brought out Barker's edition of H. Stephen's *Thesaurus Graecae Linguae,* in eight volumes from 1815 to 1828.

Johann Scapula, who was born in Germany in the sixteenth century, published his *Lexicon Graeco-Latinum* in Basle in 1579. An edition of Scapula's *Lexicon Graeco-Latinum novum* . . . was published in Geneva in 1609. Benjamin A. Gould lists Scapula's *Lexicon* in his account of the curriculum of the Boston Latin School in 1823. The book was undoubtedly used at the School much earlier than 1823.

Cornelius Schrevelius (c. 1615-1664), who was born at Haarlem and became rector of the college at Leyden in 1662, published his *Lexicon manuale Graeco-latinum et Latinograecum* in Leyden in 1654. Benjamin A. Gould lists Schrevelius's *Greek Lexicon* in his account of the curriculum of the Boston Latin School in 1823. It was probably used at the School as early as the seventeenth century. In a list of bargains offered by Richard Chiswell to John Usher in 1680 appears "Schevelii Lex."

The *Greek Lexicon* of Benjamin Hedericus was published in Leipsic in 1722. This had a large sale in America and was probably used at the Boston Latin School in the eighteenth century, although it is not listed until 1823.

Thomas Morell (1703-1784) published in Eton in 1762 a Greek poetical dictionary, entitled *Lexicon Graeco-Prosodiacum.* He is also the author of *Thesaurus,* an edition of which was published in London as late as 1824. Morell's *Thesaurus* is listed as a book of reference in the curriculum of the Boston Latin School in 1823 and 1826.

John Pickering (1777-1846), an American philologist and archaeologist, published in 1826 his *Greek and English Lexicon,* the third revised and enlarged edition of which appeared in 1846. Pickering's *Greek Lexicon* is listed as a reference book in the curriculum of 1826 and Pickering's *Greek Lexicon, last edition* is listed in 1860.

Liddell and Scott's *Greek-English Lexicon,* begun in 1836 and published in 1843 by the Clarendon Press, is first listed in the Latin School curriculum in 1852. The eighth edition was published in 1897. Henry George Liddell (1811-1898) was Head Master of Westminster School from 1846 to 1855 and, in 1855, was appointed Dean of Christ Church. Robert Scott (1811-1887) was Master of Baliol in 1854 and, in 1870, was appointed Dean of Rochester.

History and Mythology

Thomas Godwin, Master of Abingdon School in 1609 and later rector of Brightwell, Berkshire, published *Romanae historiae anthologia: an English exposition of the Roman antiquities,* in Oxford in 1614. The sixteenth edition was published in London in 1696. The book was studied at the Boston Latin School definitely in 1712, and possibly earlier.

William King's (1663-1712) *Historical Account of the Heathen Gods and Heroes,* published in London in 1710, was studied at the Boston Latin School at least as early as 1752. We have record that in 1789, under the "New System of Education," the third class of the Boston Latin School studied "The making of Latin from King's History of the Heathen Gods."

Andrew Tooke's (1673-1732) *Pantheon, or History of the Heathen Gods,* an English translation of François Antoine Pomey's *Pantheum Mithicum,* was published in London in 1698. The book is first listed in the 1823 curriculum of the Boston Latin School. The thirty-fifth edition was published in London in 1824.

Alexander Adam (1741-1809), a Scottish scholar, published in Edinburgh in 1791 *Roman antiquities: or, an account of the manners and customs of the Romans,* the second enlarged edition of which was published in Edinburgh in 1792. The first American edition, from the fifth London edition, was published in Philadelphia in 1807. Adam's *Roman Antiquities* is listed as a book of reference in the Boston Latin

School curriculum in 1823 and 1826. Adam is also the author of *A summary of geography and history, both ancient and modern,* published in 1794, the fifth revised edition of which was published in London in 1816.

Basil Kennett, D.D., (1674-1714/15), an English scholar and educator, published in London in 1696 his *Romae Antiquae Notitia, or the Antiquities of Rome,* a work which for over a century was the standard textbook on the subject. Kennett's *Roman Antiquities* is listed in the 1826 curriculum of the Boston Latin School.

Wyttenbach's *Greek Historians* is listed in the 1823 curriculum of the Boston Latin School. This is undoubtedly Wyttenbach's *Selecta principum Graeciae Historicorum,* published in 1793. Daniel Albert Wyttenbach (1746-1820) was born in Berne, Switzerland, and was a distinguished scholar.

Valpy's *Chronology of Ancient and English History* is listed in the second year of the 1823 curriculum of the Boston Latin School. This is probably Richard Valpy's *Poetical Chronology of Ancient and English History,* an American edition of which was published in Boston in 1816. His *Greek Delectus* was also studied at the Latin School. He is also the author of *Elements of Mythology,* published in 1815.

Smith's *Dictionary of Antiquities* is first listed as a book of reference in the 1852 curriculum of the School. This is undoubtedly the *Dictionary of Greek and Roman Antiquities,* published in 1842 by Sir William Smith (1813-1893), the distinguished English lexicographer.

Potter's *Grecian Antiquities* is listed as a book of reference in the 1826 curriculum of the Boston Latin School. This is probably the *Archaeologia Graeca; or, the antiquities of Greece,* published in two volumes in 1697 and 1698 by John Potter, D.D., the fourth edition of which was published in London in 1722. A new edition was published in Edinburgh in 1818. John Potter, D.D., (1674-1747) was appointed Archbishop of Canterbury in 1737.

Robinson's *Grecian Antiquities* is listed as a book of reference in the 1826 curriculum of the Boston Latin School. This is undoubtedly the *Archaeologia Graeca, or the antiquities of Greece,* written by John Robinson, D.D., the second enlarged edition of which was published in London in 1827.

Thomas Wentworth Higginson's (1823-1911) *History of the United States* is listed in the first year of the curriculum of 1876. His *Young Folks' History of the United States* was published in 1875, and *A Larger History of the United States of America to the Close of President Jackson's Administration,* in 1885.

Jean Victor Duruy's (1811-1894) "Modern History in the French" is listed in the sixth year of the curriculum of 1876. Duruy's *Histoire des temps modernes* and his *Histoire du moyen age* appeared in his edition of *Histoire universelle* in 1846.

Edward Augustus Freeman's (1823-1892) *Outlines of General History* is also listed in the sixth year of the curriculum of 1876. This textbook was undoubtedly his *General Sketch of European History,* published in 1872.

Dillaway's *Roman Antiquities and Ancient Mythology,* published in Boston in 1831, is listed in the second year of the curriculum of 1834. The second edition was published in Boston in 1833. Charles Knapp Dillaway (1804-1889), the author, was Master of the Boston Latin School from 1831 to 1836.

Cleveland's *Grecian Antiquities* is listed in the fourth and fifth years of the curriculum of 1834. This is undoubtedly Charles Dexter Cleveland's (1802-1869) *Compendium of Grecian Antiquities,* the second edition of which was published in Boston in 1836. In 1832 he was appointed professor of Latin and Greek in Dickinson College and in 1834 he became professor of Latin in the University of the City of New York.

Stansbury's *Catechism on the Constitution of the United States* is listed in the fourth and fifth years of the 1834 curriculum. This is undoubtedly Arthur J. Stansbury's (1781-1845) *Elementary Catechism on the Constitution of the United States,* published in Boston in 1828.

Voltaire's *Histoire de Charles XII,* published in 1731, is first listed in the fourth year of the curriculum of 1852. A new edition was published in Geneva in 1788, and an American edition was published in New York in 1831 and 1842.

Bonnechose's *Histoire de France* is first listed in the sixth year of the curriculum of 1852. François Paul Emile B. de Bonnechose published his *Histoire de France* in Paris, the ninth edition of which was published in 1850.

CLASSICAL DICTIONARIES

Lemprière's *Classical Dictionary* is first listed as a book of reference in the 1823 curriculum of the Boston Latin School. John Lemprière, D.D., (1765-1824) published a small classical dictionary, entitled *Bibliotheca Classica,* in Reading, England, in 1788. The second enlarged edition was published in 1792 and has since been many times reprinted in Great Britain and the United States. It was based upon Sabbatier's *Dictionnaire des Auteurs classiques* and was in turn the basis of Charles Anthon's *Classical Dictionary.*

Charles Anthon (1797-1867), an American classical scholar and professor, published a new edition of Lemprière's *Classical Dictionary* in 1822. This is first listed as a book of reference in the 1852 curriculum of the Boston Latin School. Charles Anthon was appointed adjunct professor of ancient languages at Columbia College in 1820 and principal professor of the classics in 1835. He is also the author of *Dictionary of Greek and Roman Antiquities, A Grammar of the Greek language for the use of schools and colleges,* and *Introduction to Latin prose composition.*

Baird's *Classical Manual* is first listed as a book of reference in the 1852 curriculum of the Boston Latin School. This is undoubtedly *The Classical Manual: an epitome of geography, Greek and Roman mythology, antiquities, and chronology. Intended for the use of schools,* compiled by James Skerrett Shore Baird and published in Philadelphia in 1852.

ARITHMETIC

In 1803 a "knowledge of arithmetic to the rule of three" was required for admission to Harvard College. The study of arithmetic, however, is not listed in the 1808 (?) curriculum of the Boston Latin School, which is the earliest extant curriculum of the School following 1803. The Latin School boys, however, were dismissed an hour and a half each day, after 1789, to attend the South Writing School, for special instruction in "writing and cyphering."

In 1814 the sub-committee for the Latin School recommended that 'the two highest classes be taught arithmetic and geography as required for admission to Harvard College." In 1819 the school committee recorded: "In addition to the Latin & greek languages, the boys at the latin School are now taught such branches of the Mathematics & geography, with the Elements of Geometry & algebra, as are requisite for admission to Harvard College."

The records show that as early as 1645 the duty of the Usher of the Boston Latin School was to teach reading, writing, and "cyphering." There is no record of the textbooks used. In the early Colonial schools it was, in most cases, only the teacher who owned a textbook of arithmetic.

The first arithmetic printed in English was Record's *The Grounde of Artes, teachinge the Worke and Practise of Arithmeticke, both in whole Numbers and Fractions,*[42] written by Robert Record (1510-1558) and published in London in 1540. This was the textbook probably used by the Usher of the Latin School. A Boston bookseller, Mr. John Usher, in 1680 was offered as a bargain "Records arithmetick" and Mr. John Ive in 1685 lists "2 Records Arithmattick."

[42]A facsimile of the title-page of Record's *Arithmeticke* appears on page 359.

RECORDS
ARITHMETICKE:

Con'ayning the ground of
Arts: In which is taught the generall
parts, rules, and operations, of the fame
in wh.le Numbers and Fractions, after
a more eafie and exact methode then
euer heretofore : Firft written by
ROBERT RECORD, Do-
ктог in Phisicke.

Correcled and beautified by many Notes and augmented with moft briefe rules of
practice and others; neceffarie in the trade of Mer-
andife. Whereunto is added certaine Tables
of the valuation of all Coynes as they are currant
at this prefent time, with diuers other Tables and
their explication. Very profitable and delightfull vnto all Marchants, Gentlemen,
and others, as by the conte of
this booke doth appeare.
By *Iohn Mellis*.

Alfo the Art and application of Decimall Arithmeticke : A Table of Board and Timber
meafure, and the vfe thereof. The Extraction and De-
monftration of the Square and Cubicke roots.
with neceffary Queftions and Tables
for intereft after ten in the hundreth
is newly therevnto adioyned.
By R. N.

LONDON:
Printed by *T. S.* for *Roger Iackfon.* '51

TITLE-PAGE OF ROBERT RECORD'S *Arithmeticke*
By courtesy of the Harvard College Library.

Humphrey Baker, an English mathematician, wrote *The Well Spring of Sciences; which teacheth the perfect worke and practise of Arithmetic,* the first edition of which was published in 1562. It continued to be reprinted until 1687. Although there is no direct evidence, this textbook may have been used at the Boston Latin School and at the writing schools.

Edmund Wingate published in London in 1630 *Of Natural and Artificial Arithmetic, or Arithmetic made easy,* the edition of 1753, according to George Emery Littlefield, being considered the best. This was a popular elementary textbook and probably was used by the Usher of the Latin School and later by the Master of the South Writing School, although there is no direct evidence.

James Hodder, Master of the writing school in Lothbury in 1661, published his *Arithmetic* in London in 1661. This was a very popular textbook, the twentieth edition of which was published in London in 1697 and the twenty-fifth, in Boston, New England, in 1719. Mr. John Ive, on September 5, 1683, bought " 10 Hodder's Arithmetick" and in 1685 he bought "3 Hodders Arithmattick."

Edward Cocker's (1631-1675) *Arithmetick,* published in 1677 by John Hawkins, a writing master in Southwark, England, was probably used by the Usher of the Boston Latin School. Mr. John Ive in 1683 bought "12 Cockers Tutor to Writing and Arithmetick."

An edition of John Johnson's *Arithmetick; in Two Books. The First, of Vulgar Arithmetick. The Second, of Decimal Arithmetick; with Tables of Interest and Rebate* was published in 1671. Mr. John Foy in 1682 listed "4 Johnson arithmatick" and Mr. John Ive in 1685 bought "4 Johnsons Arithmattick."

Isaac Greenwood's *Arithmetick Vulgar and Decimal*[43] was published in Boston, New England, in 1729. This was the first arithmetic by an American author. Although there is no direct evidence, Greenwood's *Arithmetick* was probably

[43]A facsimile of the title-page of the 1729 edition appears on page 362.

used by the Usher of the Boston Latin School and by the Master of the South Writing School. After his dismissal from Harvard College, Mr. Isaac Greenwood was licensed by the Boston selectmen on September 20, 1738, to open a private school "for the Instructing of Youth and others in the Mathematicks, and other parts of Learning."

Thomas Dilworth published *The School-master's Assistant: Being a Compendium of Arithmetic, both Practical and Theoretical,* the nineteenth edition of which was published in London in 1776. He is also the author of a *Spelling Book*, *Bookkeeper's Assistant,* and *Miscellaneous Arithmetic.*

Nicholas Pike, who was graduated from Harvard College in 1766, published an edition of a *New and Complete System of Arithmetic*[44] in Newburyport, Massachusetts, in 1788. This was a popular textbook in New England and might possibly have been used by the Master of the South Writing School, although there is no direct evidence.

John Vinall, Master of the South Writing School in Boston from 1781 to 1795, published *The Preceptor's Assistant, or Student's Guide: being a Systematic Treatise of Arithmetic* in 1792. Although there is no direct evidence, this textbook of John Vinall was undoubtedly used at the South Writing School, which the Latin School boys attended an hour and a half each day after 1789, according to the "New System of Education." In the files of the Boston school committee is the following document:

The committee appointed, to examine, The Preceptor's Assistant, or Student's Guide: being a Systematic Treatise of Arithmetic, by John Vinall, Teacher of the Mathematics and Writing in Boston, have attended that Service, and are of opinion that the work is executed with judgment, and is as well calculated for the use of Schools, counting Houses & private Families, as any of the same compass, that has hitherto been offered to the public—

Mr Little pr order

[44] This book was recommended by President Washington and by the presidents of Harvard, Yale, Brown, and Dartmouth.

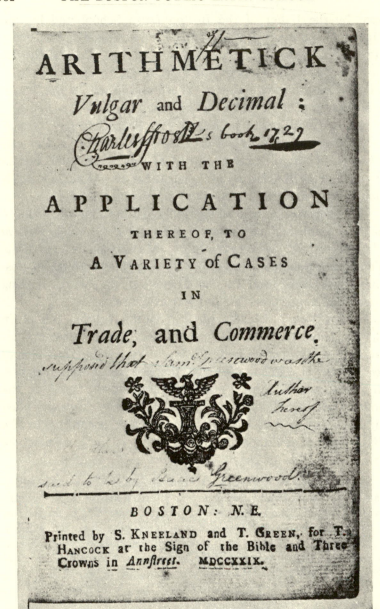

ARITHMETICK

Vulgar and *Decimal* :

WITH THE

APPLICATION

THEREOF, TO

A VARIETY of CASES

IN

Trade, and *Commerce.*

BOSTON: N. E.

Printed by S. KNEELAND and T. GREEN, for T. HANCOCK at the Sign of the Bible and Three Crowns in *Annstreet.* MDCCXXIX.

TITLE-PAGE OF ISAAC GREENWOOD'S *Arithmetick Vulgar and Decimal*
By courtesy of the Harvard College Library.

Warren Colburn, another Boston school teacher, published his *Mental Arithmetic* in 1821. This was one of the most famous and most widely translated and circulated textbooks ever published. Written on the plan of Pestalozzi, Warren Colburn's *First Lessons in Intellectual Arithmetic, upon the Inductive Method of Instruction,*[45] an edition of which appeared in Boston in 1827, radically changed not only the subject matter of arithmetic but also the method of teaching. Colburn's *First Lessons in Arithmetic* is listed in the third and fourth years of the 1823 curriculum of the Boston Latin School. Colburn's *Intellectual Arithmetic* is listed in the third year of the 1826 curriculum, and in the second and third years of the curriculum of 1828 and 1834. Colburn's *Sequel* is listed in the second year of the curriculum of 1852, 1860, and 1869.

Lacroix's *Arithmetic* is listed in the fifth year of the curriculum of 1823, under Master Benjamin A. Gould. Lacroix's *Written Arithmetic* is listed in the third year of the curriculum from 1826 to 1834. This textbook is probably that of Silvestre François Lacroix, the distinguished French mathematician, who was born in Paris in 1765.

Eaton's *Arithmetic* is listed in the first year of the curriculum of 1870. This is undoubtedly James S. Eaton's *The common school Arithmetic,* published in Boston in 1863.

Crittenden's *Calculations* is listed in the first year of the curriculum of 1870. This is probably the work of Samuel W. Crittenden, the author of *An inductive and practical treatise on book-keeping by single and double entry, . . . also, a set of steamboat books . . . a table of foreign coins and moneys of account,* a revised and enlarged edition of which was published in Philadelphia in 1859.

Algebra, Geometry, and Trigonometry

Algebra and geometry were introduced into the Latin School curriculum in 1819, or possibly earlier, as the follow-

[45]A facsimile of the title-page appears on page 365.

LETTER OF JOHN VINALL, DESCRIBING HIS *System of Arithmetic*
By courtesy of the Boston School Committee.

ing report of the school committee, dated June 21, 1819, testifies: "In addition to the Latin & greek languages, the boys at the Latin School are now taught such branches of the Mathematics & geography, with the Elements of Geometry &

COLBURN'S FIRST LESSONS.

INTELLECTUAL,

ARITHMETIC,

UPON THE

INDUCTIVE METHOD

OF

INSTRUCTION.

BY WARREN COLBURN, A. M.

STEREOTYPED AT THE BOSTON TYPE AND STEREOTYPE FOUNDRY

Boston:

HILLIARD, GRAY, LITTLE, AND WILKINS.

1827.

TITLE-PAGE OF WARREN COLBURN'S *Intellectual Arithmetic*
By courtesy of the Harvard College Library.

algebra, as are requisite for admission to Harvard College."
Trigonometry first appears in 1826.

Euclid's *Geometry,* by Euclid of Alexandria, the Greek
mathematician, and Euler's *Algebra,* by Leonard Euler (1707-
1783), the Swiss mathematician, are listed in the fifth year
of the curriculum of 1823, under the mastership of Benjamin
A. Gould.   Euler's *Algebra* and Colburn's *Algebra* are listed
in the fourth year of the curriculum from 1826 to 1828, and
in the fourth and fifth years of the curriculum of 1834.

Sherwin's *Algebra* is first listed in the fourth year of the
1852 curriculum. Thomas Sherwin's (1799-1869) *Elementary
Treatise on Algebra* was published in Boston in 1841. Thomas
Sherwin was a tutor in mathematics at Harvard College in
1826, Sub-Master of the English High School of Boston from
1828 and 1838, and Master of the School from 1838 to 1869.

Chauvenet's *Elementary Geometry* is first listed in the
third and fifth years of the 1870 curriculum of the Boston
Latin School.   Chauvenet's *Trigonometry* is listed in the
fourth and fifth years and Chauvenet's *Solid Geometry* is
listed in the fifth year of the 1870 curriculum.   William Chauvenet (1820-1870) was professor of mathematics and astronomy at the United States Naval Academy at Annapolis from
1845 to 1859.

Ray's *Elementary Algebra* is listed in the first and second
years of the 1870 curriculum.   A revised edition of Joseph
Ray's *Elementary Algebra. Part first* was published in Cincinnati in 1848.

Loomis's *Algebra* is listed in the fourth year of the 1870
curriculum.   Elias Loomis (1811-1889) published *The elements of algebra* in New York in 1851, the sixth edition of
which was published in New York in 1857.   His *Collection of
algebraic problems* was published in New York in 1878.

English Composition, English Literature, and American Literature

The study of English composition was not definitely introduced into the curriculum of the Boston Latin School until 1823, at which time "Themes in Latin and English" were required for the fifth year's course. "Declamation, Reading, and English Grammar" are first listed in the second and third years of the curriculum of 1826 and "English Composition and Forensic Discussions" are listed in the fifth year.

Blair's *Rhetoric* appears in the fifth year of the curriculum from 1828 to 1832. Hugh Blair, D.D., (1718-1800), who was appointed professor of rhetoric and belles-lettres in the University of Edinburgh in 1760, published his *Lectures on Rhetoric* in London in 1783. This became a popular textbook and was used in many schools and colleges.

Parker's *Aids to English Composition* is first listed in the third year of the curriculum of 1852. Richard Green Parker's *Aids to English Composition* was published in Boston in 1844, a new edition of which was published in New York in 1846.

Latham's *English Grammar* is first listed in the fifth year of the curriculum of 1852. This is undoubtedly the work of Robert Gordon Latham (1812-1888), the distinguished English philologian and ethnologist, who in 1841 was appointed professor of English literature in University College, London. He published a series of English grammars from 1843 to 1850.

English literature and American literature were not introduced into the Boston Latin School curriculum until 1870, when a "general culture course" was adopted. In the first year the boys read some of the writings of Scott, Goldsmith, Campbell, Wordsworth, Cowper, Tennyson, and Leigh Hunt; in the second year, Sterne, Mrs. Thrale, Beattie, Cowper, Hawthorne, Tennyson, Longfellow, Morris, and Hazlitt; in the third year, Gray, Addison, Moore, Burns, Irving, Bryant, Hood, Hawthorne, Shelley, and Rogers; in the fourth year, Milton, Pope, Irving, Thompson, Collins, Prescott, Coleridge,

Keats, Burke, Wordsworth, Holmes, and Tyndall; in the fifth year, Milton, Pope, Dryden, Spencer, Thackeray, Lamb, Tennyson, Lowell, Whittier, Ruskin, and Shakespeare; and, in the sixth year, Macaulay, Junius, Emerson, Marvell, George Herbert, Byron, Carlyle, Robert Hall, Channing, Ben Jonson, Bacon, and Shakespeare.

In the new and revised curriculum of 1876, founded largely on the advice of President Eliot of Harvard, added interest is given to the study of English. Scott and Goldsmith are listed in the first year of the 1876 curriculum; Hawthorne's *True Stories* and *Wonder Book,* Bulfinch's *Age of Fable,* and Macaulay's *Lays of Ancient Rome,* in the second year; Irving, Prescott, Burke, Gray, Longfellow, and Whittier, in the third year; reading in connection with the textbook in history, in the fourth year; three plays of Shakespeare and selections from Milton, in the fifth year; and "Compositions on subjects on which reading has been recommended," in the sixth year.

SCIENCES

In 1803 "a knowledge of geography" was required for admission to Harvard College. In the Boston Latin School curriculum of 1808 (?), however, no mention is made of the introduction of geography. The records show that Morse's *Geography, abridged,* based on the Reverend Jedidiah Morse's[46] *Geography made Easy,* published in New Haven in 1784, was introduced into the Boston reading schools as early as 1789. Since the Latin School boys received their required elementary preparation at the reading and writing schools, it is quite possible that this training in geography, received at the reading schools, would be accepted as a prerequisite for admission to Harvard College.

Geography was introduced into the curriculum of the Boston Latin School definitely in 1814 and possibly earlier. The textbook listed in the fifth year of the 1823 curriculum

---

[46] The Reverend Jedidiah Morse was the father of Samuel Finley Breese Morse, the inventor of the telegraph. See page 369.

GEOGRAPHY

MADE EASY.

BEING A SHORT, BUT COMPREHENSIVE

System

OF THAT VERY USEFUL AND AGREEABLE SCIENCE.

EXHIBITING

In an eafy and concife View, the Figures, Motions, Diftances, and Magnitudes of the heavenly Bodies :—A general defcription of the Earth confidered as a Planet; with its grand Divifions into Land and Water, Continonts, Oceans, Iflands, &c.—The Situation, Boundaries and Extent of the feveral Empires, Kingdoms, and States, together with an Account of their Climate, Soil, Productions and commerce :—The Number, Genius, and general Character of the Inhabitants.:—Their Religion, Government and Hiftory :—The Latitude, Longitude, Diftances, and Bearings of the principal Places from Philadelphia and London, and a Number of ufeful Geographical Tables.

Illuftrated with two correct and elegant MAPS, one of the World, and the other of the United States, together with a Number of newly conftructed Maps, adapted to the Capacities and Underftanding of Children.

Calculated particularly for the Ufe and Improvement of SCHOOLS in the United States.

By JEDIDIAH MORSE, A. B.

" There is not a SON or a DAUGHTER of Adam, but has
" fome concern in both GEOGRAPHY and ASTRONOMY."
                                           DR. WATTS.

" Among thofe Studies which are ufually recommended to
" young People, there can be few that might be improved to
" better Ufes than Geography."   *Effays on various Subjects.*

NEW-HAVEN:

Printed by MEIGS, BOWEN and DANA, in Chapel-Street.

TITLE-PAGE OF *Geography Made Easy*
By courtesy of the Harvard College Library.

is Worcester's *Elements of Geography, Ancient and Modern,* published in 1819 by Joseph Emerson Worcester, the distinguished American lexicographer. Worcester's *Geography, with the use of the globes,* appears in the curriculum as late at 1834.

Mitchell's *Geographical Questions* and *Geography,* undoubtedly the textbooks written by Samuel Augustus Mitchell, are first listed in the first and second years of the 1852 curriculum of the Boston Latin School. Mitchell's *Geographical Questions* appears in the curriculum of the School as late as 1869. Samuel Augustus Mitchell's *Primary Geography. An Easy Introduction to the Study of Geography: designed for the Instruction of Children* was published in Philadelphia in 1843. The second revised edition of his *School Geography* was published in Philadelphia in 1846 and the third revised edition, in 1852. An edition of his *Geographical Question Book; comprising Geographical Definitions, and containing Questions on all the Maps of Mitchell's School Atlas* was published in Philadelphia in 1868.

Somerville's *Physical Geography* is first listed in the fourth year of the curriculum of 1852. This is undoubtedly Mrs. Mary Fairfax Somerville's *Physical Geography,* an edition of which was published in Philadelphia in 1848. Mrs. Somerville was a distinguished English scientist and the wife of Dr. William Somerville.

It was not until 1870, under the new "general culture" course, that zoölogy, geology, botany, physics, astronomy, and chemistry were added to the curriculum. The only science books mentioned in the 1870 curriculum are the textbooks of Dana and Gray, and the only science textbooks mentioned in the 1876 curriculum are Morse's *Zoölogy* and Agassiz's *Seaside studies.*

James Dwight Dana, the distinguished American mineralogist, published several textbooks in geology and mineralogy. His *System of Mineralogy* was published in New Haven in 1837, the fifth revised edition of which came out in

New York in 1868. His *Manual of Mineralogy* was published in New Haven in 1848, a fourth revision of which appeared in New York in 1886. His *Manual of Geology* was published in Philadelphia in 1863, and a third edition was issued in New York in 1880. His *Text-Book of Geology* was published in 1864, a fourth revision of which was brought out in 1883.

Asa Gray, the distinguished American botanist and professor of natural history in Harvard University from 1842 to 1873, wrote several popular textbooks which were used extensively throughout the United States. His *Elements of Botany* first published in 1836, was republished as *Botanical Text-Book* in 1853, and later in 1858, as *Structural and Systematic Botany*. His *School and Field-Book of Botany* was published in 1875.

Edward Sylvester Morse, the American naturalist and biologist, published his *First Book in Zoölogy* in New York in 1875. He was professor of comparative anatomy and zoölogy in Bowdoin College, Maine, from 1871 to 1874. This textbook is listed in the 1876 curriculum of the Boston Latin School.

Alexander Agassiz published with his step-mother, Elizabeth Cary Agassiz, *Seaside Studies in Natural History* in Boston in 1865. This textbook is listed in the 1876 curriculum of the Boston Latin School. Alexander Agassiz was the only son of the famous Louis Agassiz.

FRENCH

French first appears in the Latin School course of study in 1852. In 1855 Marie Bernard Montellier De Montrachy was appointed special instructor in French.

Fasquelle's *French Grammar* is listed in the third year of the curriculum from 1852 to 1866. Jean Louis Fasquelle (1808-1862), professor of modern languages and literature in the University of Michigan from 1846 to 1862, published several textbooks in French. An edition of his *French Course, or a New Method for Learning to Read, Write, and Speak the French Language* was published in New York in 1854. He is also the author of *Telemaque, with Notes and Grammatical References, Colloquial French Reader,* and a *General and Idiomatical Dictionary of the French and English Languages.*

Magill's *French Grammar* and *French Reader* are first listed in the third and fourth years respectively of the curriculum of 1866. Edward Hicks Magill is the author of several French textbooks, namely, *French Grammar, Introductory French Reader, French Prose and Poetry, Key to French Grammar, Reading French Grammar,* and *Modern French Series.* His *French Grammar,* listed in the 1866 curriculum of the Boston Latin School, was published in Boston in 1865. Magill was principal of the classical department of the Providence High School from 1852 to 1859, Sub-Master of the Boston Latin School from 1859 to 1867, principal of the Swarthmore Preparatory School from 1869 to 1871, president of the Friends' College at Swarthmore, Pennsylvania, from 1871 to 1889, and afterwards professor of French language and literature in that college.

Otto's *French Grammar, first part, with exercises* is listed in the second year of the curriculum of 1870. This is undoubtedly Emil Otto's *French conversation grammar,* a revised edition of which was published in New York in 1864.

GERMAN

The study of German was first introduced into the Latin School curriculum in 1870, when the "general culture" course was adopted. Krauss's *German Grammar* is listed in the fourth year of the 1870 curriculum, Krauss's *Grammar, with German Reader,* in the fifth year, and *German prose writers and poetry,* in the sixth year. Ernst Carl Friedrich Krauss published his *Elements of German grammar* in Boston in 1867, the second revised edition of which was published in Boston in 1872. His *First Book in German* was published in Boston in 1869, the second revised edition of which was published in Boston in 1872. His *German Manual, or First instruction in the German language* was published in Boston in 1864, the third edition of which was published in Boston in 1866.

CHAPTER X

METHODS OF TEACHING SPECIAL SUBJECTS

THE early writers of New England history did not record the details of methods of teaching. This silence is further evidenced by an examination of over one thousand documents, compiled by the writer from the *Town Records*, the *Selectmen's Minutes*, and the *School Committee Records*, only two of which discuss methods of teaching, namely, (1) a "Memorial" presented to the town by the selectmen on March 13, 1710/11, concerning a "Regulation of ye methodes of Teaching Lattin", and (2) "The System of Mutual Instruction" in 1821, based on the monitorial system of Joseph Lancaster.

Records testify that new methods of teaching were introduced into the schools in England in the last part of the seventeenth and the beginning of the eighteenth century. The Colonial schools in New England were patterned after the English precedent, adopting not only the curricula but also the methods of teaching.

John Brinsley, the Elder, a distinguished English schoolmaster, published in London in 1612 *Ludus Literarius: or, The Grammar School*, which gives detailed information concerning the teaching methods in the early seventeenth-century grammar [Latin grammar] school. Another advocate of new methods was Charles Hoole, a prominent English schoolmaster and textbook writer, who published in London in 1660 *A New Discovery of the old Art of Teaching Schoole, in four small Treatises, . . . Shewing how Children in their playing years may Grammatically attain to a firm groundedness in and exercise of the Latine, Greek and Hebrew Tongues.* New interest in educational methods was awakened by John Locke, the distinguished English philosopher, who in 1693 published *Thoughts Concerning Education.* John Clarke, another well-known textbook writer, published in London in 1720 *An Essay upon the Education of Youth in Grammar-Schools.*

LATIN

The earliest record of a proposal to improve the methods of teaching Latin at the Boston Latin School is dated March 13, 1709/10, when a committee reported to the town the following recommendations:

We further propose and recommend, as of Great Service and Advantage for the promoting of Diligence and good literature, That the Town Agreeably to the Usage in England, and (as we understand) in Some time past practiced here, Do Nominate and Appoint a Certain Number of Gentlemen, of Liberal Education, Together with Some of ye Revd Ministers of the Town to be Inspectors of the Sd Schoole under that name Title or denomination, To Visit ye School from time to time, when and as Oft, as they shall thinck fit to Enform themselves of the methodes used in teaching of ye Schollars. . . .

On March 10, 1710/11, the selectmen voted to present a "Memorial," concerning the methods of teaching Latin at the Boston Latin School, at the next town meeting to be held on March 13. An extract of this "Memorial" follows:

Whereas according to the Information of Some of the Learned, who have made Observation of the easie & pleasant Rules and Methodes used in Some Schools in Europe, where Scollars p'haps within the compass of one year, have attained to a Competent Proficency So as to be able to read, and discourse in Lattin and of themselves capable to make Considerable progress therein: And that according to the methodes used here Very many hundreds of boyes in this Town, who by their Parents were never designed for a more Liberal Education have Spent two, three, four years or more of their more Early dayes at the Lattin School, which hath proved of very Little, or no benefit as to their after Accomplishmt.

It is therefore proposed to the Town that they would Recõmend it to those Gentlem whom they shall chuse as Inspectors of the Schools, Together with ye ministers of the Town, To Consider whether in this Town (where the Free School is maintained cheifly by a Town Rate on the Inhabitants) That Supposeing the former more Tedious and burthensome methode may be thought the best for such as are designed for Schollars (which is by Some questioned). Yet for the Sake & benefitt of others who usually are the greater number by far in Such Schools, Whether it might not be adviseable that Some more easie and delightfull methodes be there attended and put in practice, And to Signifie to yᵉ Town their thoughts therein, in order to the Encouragement of the Same.

The earliest extant description of the methods of teaching Latin at the Boston Latin School is that of Master Nathaniel Williams, who in 1712 sent to Nehemiah Hobart, then senior fellow of Harvard College, an account of the curriculum and methods of instruction.[1] He states that the first three years are spent "first in Learning by heart & then acc. to their capacities understanding the Accidence and Nomenclator, in construing & parsing acc. to the English rules of Syntax Sententiae Pueriles Cato & Corderius & Aesops Fables." Besides translating the Latin authors, the boys were required "to recite by heart" long passages of the text, and to write themes, letters, and verses in Latin. Mr. Williams's plan of teaching does not show much use of the "new methods."

John Locke, as early as 1693, had disapproved the English method of learning by heart the "Latin Grammar," and severely criticized the system of "Repetition," or "learning by heart great parcels of the authors which are taught." Locke also condemned the practice of taking so much time with making Latin themes and verses. The following extract from his *Thoughts on Education* testifies how bitterly opposed Locke was to the current methods of teaching Latin:

For do but consider what it is in making a Theme that a young lad is employed about; it is to make a speech on some Latin saying, as *"Omnia vincit amor"*; or *"Non licet in bello bis peccare, &c."* And here the poor lad, who wants knowledge of those things he is to speak of, which is to be had only from time and observation, must set his invention on the rack to say something where he knows nothing; which is a sort of Egyptian tyranny to bid them make

---

[1] The original manuscript document is in the possession of Professor Kenneth B. Murdock of Harvard University and, with his kind permission, a facsimile is here reproduced. See page 261.

bricks who have not yet any of the materials. . . . In the next place consider the Language foreign to their country, and long since dead everywhere: a language which your son, 'tis a thousand to one, shall never have an occasion once to make a speech in as long as he lives after he comes to be a man; . . .

The records show that in the seventeenth and eighteenth centuries the parallel-translation method, containing both the Latin text and the English translation, was used in teaching Latin at the Boston Latin School. Dr. James Jackson, who entered the School in 1784, has recorded that this parallel-translation method was used in studying Corderius's *Dialogues*. Dr. Jackson writes: "This book was made easy by the English translation of its short sentences, in columns opposite the Latin; and I am satisfied that this easy introduction to the reading of a foreign language is the most eligible mode, at least for little boys."

The Reverend James Freeman Clarke, in his *Autobiography,* criticizes the methods of teaching Latin grammar at the Boston Public Latin School as late as 1821, the year in which he entered the School. He states that the first year was wholly occupied in committing to memory the most abstract formulas of Adam's *Latin Grammar*. Furthermore, he asserts that this method of "cramming the memory with indigestible facts had a benumbing effect on the mind."[2] This method naturally inspired a distaste for study and strong dislike for the subjects taught.

Charles William Eliot, who was president of Harvard University from 1869 to 1909, has recorded the methods of teaching Latin at the Boston Latin School when he was a student there [1844]. Dr. Eliot writes:

At ten years of age I committed to memory many rules of syntax, the meaning of which I had no notion of, although I could apply them in a mechanical way. The rule for the ablative absolute, for

[2] From James Freeman Clarke's *Autobiography, Diary and Correspondence,* edited by Edward Everett Hale, by permission of Houghton Mifflin Company, publishers.

instance—"A noun and a participle are put in the ablative, called absolute, to denote the time, cause, or concomitant of an action, or the condition on which it depends"—I could rattle off whenever I encountered a sample of that construction, but it was several years after I learnt the rule that I arrived at even the faintest conception of what it meant. The learning by heart of the grammar then preceded rather than accompanied as now exercises in translation and composition.[3]

History

The records show that ancient history was studied at the Boston Latin School as early as 1712, if not earlier. Lucius Florus's *History of Rome,* written in Latin, and Justin's *Roman History,* also written in Latin, were studied at the Latin School in the eighteenth century. The emphasis, however, was on the Latin translation and not on the subject matter of the history. In 1789, under the "New System of Education," the third class of the Latin School studied "The making of Latin from King's *History of the Heathen Gods.*"

In the early part of the nineteenth century, under the mastership of Mr. Benjamin A. Gould, more emphasis was placed on the subject matter itself and ancient and English history were added to the curriculum. The textbooks used were *Graeciae Historiae Epitome, Viri Romae,* Valpy's *Chronology of Ancient and English History,* Wyttenbach's *Greek Historians,* and Adam's *Roman Antiquities.*

Geography

Geography had an insignificant place in the curriculum of the Boston Latin School. The knowledge incidentally obtained in this subject was derived from the reading lessons and from translations of descriptions of Athens and Rome. It was not until 1789 that geography was introduced into the Boston reading schools. The records show that passages in the Reverend Jedidiah Morse's *Geography, abridged* were committed to memory.

[3] Address by Charles William Eliot, delivered at the 275th anniversary of the Boston Latin School, printed for the Boston Latin School Association in 1910.

It was not until the early part of the nineteenth century that geography was added to the curriculum of the Latin School, to meet the 1803 entrance requirements of Harvard College. Mr. Benjamin A. Gould, who was appointed the Master of the Latin School in 1814, has recorded the following description of the method of teaching geography:

Worcester's Geography is the text book in that branch; and here constant and particular use is made of the maps. The boys are required to find upon them the rise and course of every river, the situation of each town, etc., in their lesson; and beside getting the text of the book, to answer any question which may arise upon the map of the country whose geography they are studying.

Arithmetic

The records testify that the Usher of the Latin School taught "writing and cyphering" until the establishment of the South Writing School in the Common in 1717, after which the Latin School boys were dismissed an hour a day to attend the Writing School for instruction in penmanship and arithmetic.

The method of teaching arithmetic was similar to that used in teaching writing. The early Colonial schools had but few arithmetic textbooks; it was usually only the teacher who owned a copy. The Master of the Writing School made "cyphering books," for the use of the pupils, into which the problems were neatly copied after they had been correctly solved on a separate sheet of paper. The arithmetic which was taught in the writing schools was very elementary, including only the four fundamental operations, fractions, simple interest, and "the single Rule of Three." It is interesting to note, in this connection, that arithmetic was not taught to children before they were about ten years of age.

The "Cyphering" method of teaching arithmetic was used until the first part of the nineteenth century. Warren Colburn's *First Lessons in Arithmetic,* written on the plan of Pestalozzi, the Swiss educational reformer, was published in

Boston in 1821; this textbook radically changed the methods of teaching arithmetic.

It was not until the early part of the nineteenth century, under the mastership of Mr. Benjamin A. Gould, that arithmetic, beyond simple "cyphering," was added to the curriculum of the Latin School, to meet the 1803 entrance requirements of Harvard College. Mr. Gould, in his article in the *Prize Book* written in 1823, has recorded the following account of the method of teaching arithmetic:

> The study of arithmetic is commenced the latter part of the third year, or the beginning of the fourth, with Colburn's "First Lessons." Recitations in this are made two or three times each half day by those who are studying it. The boys are not expected to commit to memory the answers to the several questions, but to find them repeatedly before the recitation that their answers may then be given with more facility; and, in order that the operations, by which they solve the questions, may be strictly intellectual, numbers are often announced by the instructor different from those in the book, and only the form of the questions is adhered to. . . . After all the questions in a section have been understood, and solved, each boy is called upon to state the general method of their solution, or the rule for working them. This rule, thus made by the boys, not given them, when corrected as to phraseology by the teacher is written in a manuscript book, and committed to memory. The same system of advancing from particular examples to the general rule is observed in teaching Lacroix's Arithmetic and Euler's Algebra; Synthesis being considered preferable to Analysis, in these studies.

ALGEBRA AND GEOMETRY

Algebra and geometry were not taught at the Boston Latin School until the first part of the nineteenth century. In the files of the school committee is a document, dated June 21, 1819, that states that "In addition to the Latin & greek languages, the boys at the latin School are now taught such branches of the Mathematics & geography, with the Elements of Geometry & algebra, as are requisite for admission to Harvard College."

Mr. Benjamin A. Gould, the Master of the Boston Latin School from 1814 to 1828, has given us the following account of the methods of teaching algebra and geometry at his School:

In Geometry the diagrams of Euclid are taken off, first on paper, with figures instead of letters, that nothing may be committed to memory without being understood. When they have been demonstrated from the paper, they are afterwards drawn by the pupil on the blackboard, with figures; when the proposition is demonstrated without a book, or any aid to the memory whatever.

In teaching Geometry, very little classification was practicable. As the lessons were generally learnt in the presence of the instructor, and all had consequently the same length of time to study, it was rarely found that more than two or three learnt equally fast, even when, in all other things, they were of nearly equal capacities.

A similar method is employed in teaching Algebra. Very simple questions leading to an equation are proposed, to be solved on the slate; such verbal explanations are given as may be necessary, and the pupil is thus led on from the more simple operations to the more difficult, without the use of a book. Text-books, however, both in Arithmetic and Algebra are employed, and those hitherto used, are Lacroix's Arithmetic, and Euler's Algebra. These have been used rather to accustom the boys to understand the abstract reasonings employed on those subjects in books, and necessarily much more difficult than verbal explanations, than because they were thought essential to the perfect teaching of Arithmetic or Algebra.

WRITING

The records show that at the Boston Latin School much emphasis was placed on penmanship. After the opening of the South Writing School in the Common in 1719/20 the Latin School boys were dismissed an hour a day to attend this writing school for instruction in "writing and cyphering." Perhaps the most famous writing master of this School was Abiah Holbrook, who bequeathed to Harvard College his *Demonstration of Penmanship*,[4] a book of more than twenty-

---

[4] Abiah Holbrook's will, now in the possession of the Suffolk County Court House, is dated May 14, 1768, and was presented for probate on February 24, 1769. He willed this *Demonstration of Penmanship* to his wife, requesting

TITLE-PAGE OF ABIAH HOLBROOK'S *Demonstration of Penmanship*
By courtesy of the Harvard College Library.

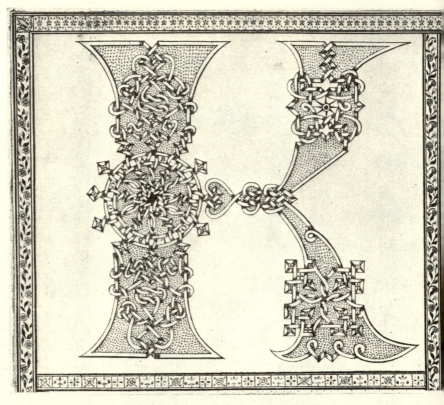

DETAIL OF PAGE OF ABIAH HOLBROOK'S *Demonstration of Penmanship*
By courtesy of the Harvard College Library.

six pages, written with a quill pen, which required seven years
to finish.   The original title-page, a diminished copy of which
is here reproduced,[5] contains different styles of writing and
printing; each page of the book, written in several colors of
ink, has a border embellished with elaborate and intricate
"filagree."   John Hancock, who entered the Boston Latin

---

her to sell the same at "one hundred pounds lawful Money" and to allow
John Hancock the "first offer of them."   In case the work was not sold within
two years after Holbrook's death his widow was to "bequeath them unto
Harvard Colledge to be reposited in the Library."

[5]See page 381 for a facsimile of this title-page.

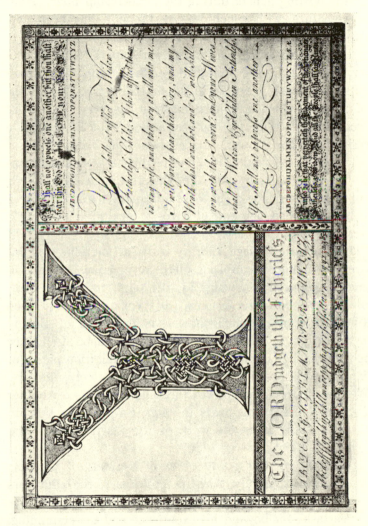

Page from Abiah Holbrook's *Demonstration of Penmanship*
By courtesy of the Harvard College Library.

School in 1745, was a pupil of the famous Abiah Holbrook at the South Writing School during the penmanship hour. Hancock's signature, with which we are familiar, has been perpetuated by the John Hancock Life Insurance Company.

Other famous writing masters were John Tileston, James Carter, John Vinall, and Jonathan Snelling, samples of whose beautiful penmanship are included in this work. The penmanship of the Boston writing masters has very deservedly won recognition; in fact, it has been called "The Boston Style of Writing." The masters made their own "copy books"[6] and the scholars attempted to imitate their master's penmanship. The records show that the masters taught their pupils how to make and repair their goose-quill pens. Ink wells were made by sawing off one end of a cow's horn and inserting a wooden base.

The Harvard College Library owns a portfolio containing over two hundred exhibition pieces of penmanship done in the middle eighteenth century by the pupils of Abiah Holbrook. Several of these specimens of penmanship have been identified by their dated signatures as the work of Boston Latin School boys, done before and during their attendance at the School. For example, there are two exhibition pieces of William Palfrey, dated 1748 and 1754, respectively, done by the William Palfrey who entered the School in 1749. Another specimen of handwriting bears the signature "Lewis Vassall, 1751," identifying it as the work of the Lewis Vassall who entered the Latin School in 1750.

In conclusion, this study of early methods of teaching reveals quite conclusively that, in most cases, the educators did not consider the psychology of the individual child. He was given tasks far beyond his experience and understanding. The modern methods of teaching, expounded by the twentieth-century educational psychologists, have completely revolutionized these long-established methods of teaching.

---

[6] Caleb Bingham, the celebrated Master of the Centre Reading School in Boston from 1789 to 1796, published a series of copy slips in 1796.

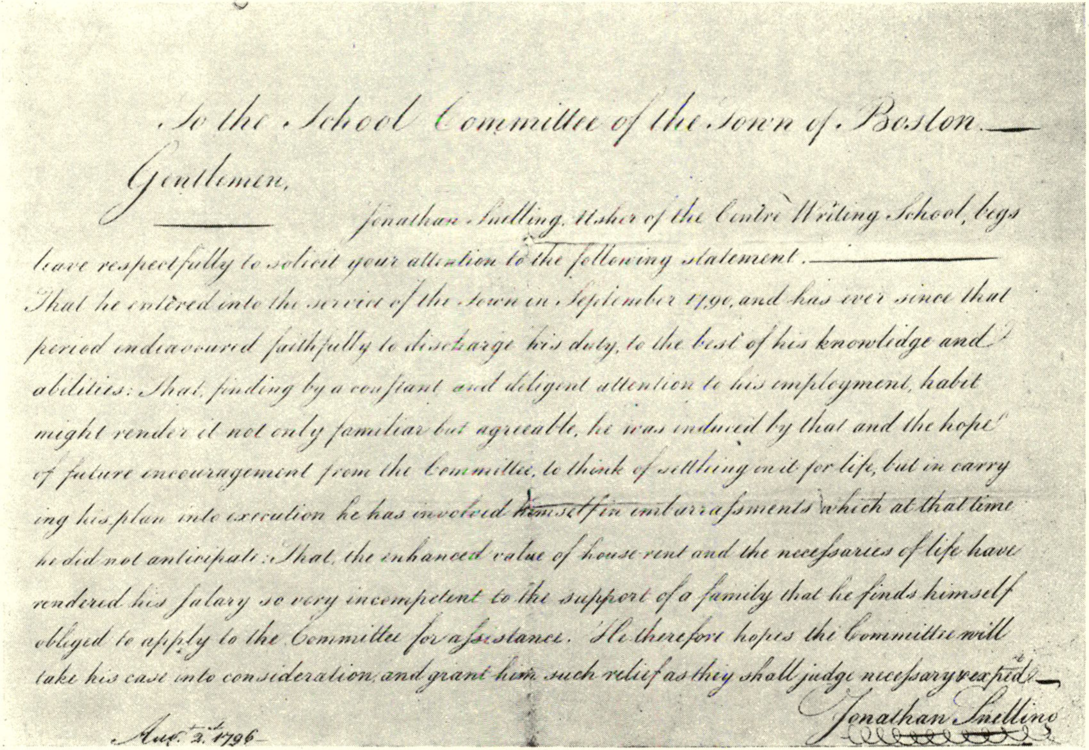

To the School Committee of the Town of Boston.—

Gentlemen,

Jonathan Snelling, Usher of the Centre Writing School, begs leave respectfully to solicit your attention to the following statement.—
That he entered into the service of the Town in September 1790, and has ever since that period endeavoured faithfully to discharge his duty, to the best of his knowledge and abilities: That, finding by a constant and diligent attention to his employment, habit might render it not only familiar but agreeable, he was induced by that and the hope of future encouragement from the Committee, to think of settling in it for life; but in carrying his plan into execution he has involved himself in embarrassments which at that time he did not anticipate: That, the enhanced value of house-rent and the necessaries of life have rendered his salary so very incompetent to the support of a family that he finds himself obliged to apply to the Committee for assistance. He therefore hopes the Committee will take his case into consideration, and grant him such relief as they shall judge necessary resp.ted—

Jonathan Snelling

Aug. 2. 1796—

Letter of Jonathan Snelling
By courtesy of the Boston School Committee.

CHAPTER XI

CONCLUSION

In reviewing the history of the Colonial beginnings of the Boston Public Latin School, the oldest public secondary school, with continuous existence, in the United States, several significant facts are worthy of emphasis.

When, three hundred years ago, the citizens of Boston "Att a Generall meeting upon publique notice" agreed y^t o^r brother Mr Philemon Pormort shalbe intreated to become scholemaster for the teaching & nourtering of children wth us," they not only established the free Latin Grammar School for boys but they founded the public-school system of America.

We note the English influences in American Colonial education not only in the development of the curriculum of the School but also in the methods of teaching and the choice of textbooks. The early settlers of Boston, which was founded in 1630, were the Puritans. Their leaders were well-educated English country squires and yeomen. They came of thrifty and well-to-do stock; all had had educational advantages and many had been students or graduates of Cambridge and Oxford Universities. Boston, as the chief settlement, became the center of the intellectual life of the Massachusetts Bay Colony.

Religious freedom for themselves was the dominant motive of the Puritans, and religion was the rock on which the State was founded. Their philosophy of education was fashioned not only by their conviction that learning was the foundation of Church and State but also by their experience in the schools and universities of the England of their times. Since substantially every voter belonged to the established Congregational Church, the question of sectarian instruction did not arise.

A new and epoch-making policy was pursued in the Colony

of Massachusetts, namely, the policy of the State enacting a law for a scheme of universal education. The significance of the laws of 1642, 1647, and 1648, enacted by the General Court of the Massachusetts Bay Company, is that they laid the foundation of the whole system of public education in the United States and established the principles upon which that system was later developed. It is worthy of note that the town of Boston had as early as 1635 established the Latin School, more than a decade before the law requirement of 1647. Later school legislation, moreover, had little to do with the Boston Latin School, since its policies and practices were usually ahead of the law.

Another unprecedented policy was the support of schools by general taxation. With faith in education, such men as John Winthrop, Henry Vane, and the Reverend John Cotton attempted to do what the older countries had not accomplished, for this School, as contrasted with the English private, endowed schools, represented the fundamental policy of public support for education. The Boston Latin School, in successive stages of its development, was supported from the following sources: voluntary contributions of the "richer inhabitants"; income from town property, including income from the rental of islands in Boston Harbor granted to Boston by the General Court, income from the rental of a tract of land in Braintree owned by the town of Boston, and income from town lands, docks, ferries, and house rents; and finally by general town taxation. Additional income was provided from one or a combination of two or more of the following sources: personal gifts and legacies of land and money; fines from Colonial lawbreakers; tuition fees of non-residents; and "entrance" and "fire" money. In 1751 entrance charges for children of the town were forbidden, but money "for defreying the Expence of Firing" was permitted. It was not until 1784 that the town voted to abolish the system of "Entrance and Fire Money."

It appears from the early records that the schools of Boston, the Public Latin School and the other schools, were under the supervision and control of the town or the selectmen appointed by the town until 1789, when, according to the "New System of Education," drawn up by Samuel Adams and other influential citizens, the regular school committee of twelve members, one from each ward, was first established. This reform of 1789, furthermore, is significant because it made the first provision for the education of girls in the public writing and reading schools, during the summer months.

The steadfast principles of the early Puritan settlers and their unswerving loyalty to duty and ideals were reflected in the administration and supervision of the Boston schools from their first inception. These founders of the Boston Latin School with their faith in the future of this great country "builded better than they knew," and Colonial school days in Ye Olde Boston Publick Latin Schoole became the basis of future school days for the boys and girls of the American nation.

APPENDICES

APPENDIX I

HISTORY OF THE QUEEN STREET WRITING SCHOOL, THE CENTRE SCHOOL, AND THE ADAMS SCHOOL

It was on a part of the original Bendall lot, near the present Scollay Square, that the free writing school, later known as the Queen Street Writing School, was built in 1683/84. A tablet has been erected, at the south subway entrance of Scollay Square, to mark the site of this old school.[1] On March 8, 1696/97, the town voted "that there be a hous built for the Writing School adjoyning to the old school hous."

In the *Town Records,* dated December 20, 1698, we find the first definite mention of the location of this new writing school: "The Distance from the Southerly Corner of the New School house at Cotton Hill to the North^{ly} Corner of Capt Leggs Land is 55 foot, from s^d N^{ly}. corner of s^d school house to the South^{ly} post of Capt Sewells gate. . . ." In the *Selectmen's Minutes,* dated January 30, 1698/99, the same location is described "in the Prison lane on the side of the hill Over against the Land of Capt. Sam^{ll}. Sewell." Prison Lane, so called because of the location of the old Boston Jail, was later named Queen Street and in 1784, after the Revolutionary War, Court Street.

The first Master of the Queen Street Writing School was John Cole, who was appointed by the selectmen on November 24, 1684, "to Keepe a Free schoole to teach ye Children of the Towne to read & write for one yeare from the 1st of this instant Nov^r." He was reappointed the Master on March 10, 1689/90. On March 16, 1713/14, he "signified his desire to be dismist from that Service." He continued in office until April 12, 1714, when he was succeeded by Jacob Sheafe.

In 1750 the inhabitants of the centre of the town petitioned for further provision for the writing school. The town, accordingly, voted "to Enlarge said School in Queen Street." Three years later, on March 23, 1753, the town again voted "to Enlarge the Writing School in Queen Street." After the Revolutionary War[2] the school was often referred to as "Master Carter's School," as is evidenced by the following unique vote of the selectmen, dated June 28, 1786: "Voted to procure flaps for covering the Necessary at Master Carters School, to allay in some measure the disagreable effluvia arising therefrom."

---

[1] The schoolhouse lot was at the southern end of the triangular plot within Prison Lane. See Samuel C. Clough's *Map of the Book of Possessions,* reproduced on page 236.

[2] The Queen Street Writing School was reopened on November 8, 1776.

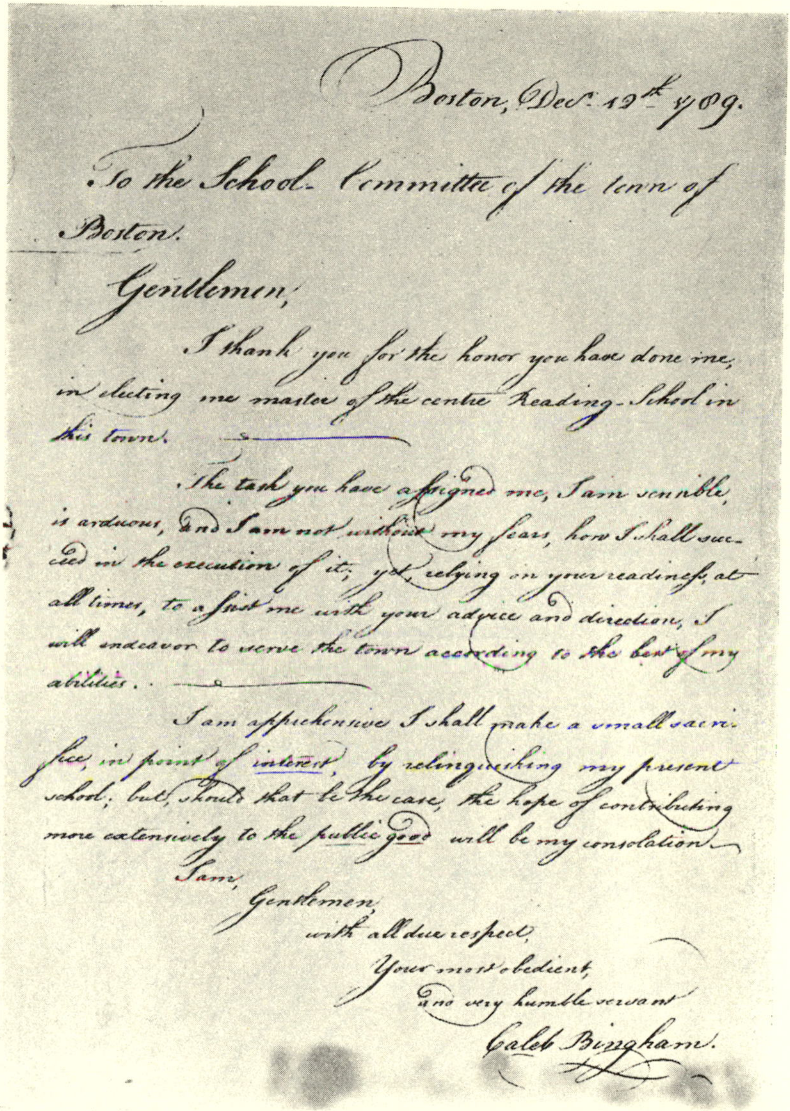

Boston, Dec: 19th 1789.

To the School-Committee of the town of
Boston.

Gentlemen,

I thank you for the honor you have done me,
in electing me master of the centre Reading-School in
this town.

The task you have assigned me, I am sensible,
is arduous, and I am not without my fears, how I shall succeed in the execution of it; yet, relying on your readiness, at
all times, to assist me with your advice and direction, I
will endeavor to serve the town according to the best of my
abilities.

I am apprehensive I shall make a small sacri-
fice, in point of interest, by relinquishing my present
school; but, should that be the case, the hope of contributing
more extensively to the public good will be my consolation.

I am,
Gentlemen,
with all due respect,
Your most obedient,
and very humble servant,
Caleb Bingham.

CALEB BINGHAM'S ACCEPTANCE OF APPOINTMENT AS MASTER OF CENTRE READING
SCHOOL
By courtesy of the Boston School Committee.

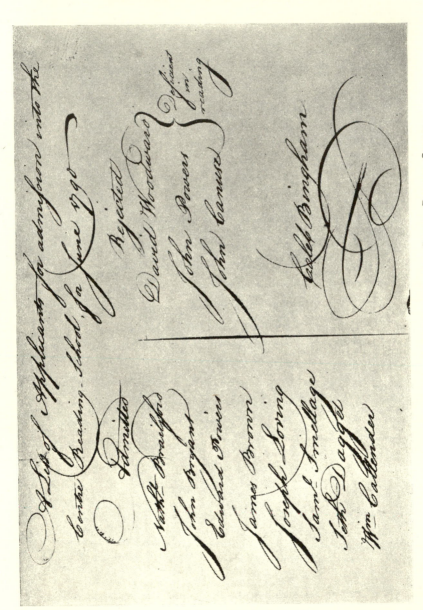

A LIST OF APPLICANTS FOR ADMISSION INTO THE CENTRE READING SCHOOL,
JUNE, 1790

By courtesy of the Boston School Committee.

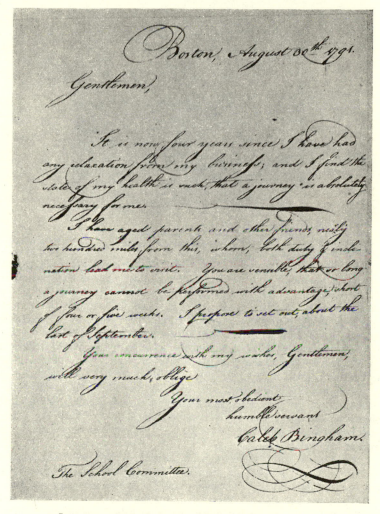

LETTER OF CALEB BINGHAM, REQUESTING A VACATION
By courtesy of the Boston School Committee.

In 1789 Master Carter is recorded as keeping the Centre Writing School on Tremont Street, in a wooden continuation on the east end of Scollay's Buildings. Under the "New System of Education," adopted in 1789, it was voted "That the School House in Tremont Street now occupied by M^r. Carter, be the Central Writing School." The town also voted to rent "a Building for a Reading School in the Centre of the Town."

THE ADAMS SCHOOLHOUSE ERECTED IN 1848
From the *Boston Almanac of 1849*

On May 11, 1790, the school committee reported "that the School houses in the Centre of the Town are insufficient for the accomodation of the Children." The town, accordingly, voted to authorize the selectmen "to make sale of the House And Land in Tremont Street Now occupied by Mr. Carter . . ." and "to Pull down the Dwelling House in School Street Now Occupied by Master Hunt, and erect on the Lot where the Same Now Stands A School house with two Stories Sufficient to Accomodate the Children of the Centre of the Town, with a reading & Writing School."

The new Centre School was built on the North Side of School Street, where the City Hall now stands, the exact location of which is shown on Carleton's map of Boston printed in 1797. While the school was being constructed the Centre Reading School was temporarily held at Faneuil Hall.

On May 20, 1812, the town voted to remove the Centre Reading and Writing School "in front of the new Court House" and to rebuild or enlarge the Latin School to accommodate the two Centre Schools. Later records show that the old Boston Latin schoolhouse, on the south side of School Street, was pulled down, and a new building of three stories was built on the same site to accommodate the Latin School and also the Centre Schools.

In 1817 the Centre Reading School was removed to the new Mason Street School,[3] and in 1819 the Centre Writing School was also removed

---

[3] The new Mason Street School was built in 1816. At first the building accommodated both the South Writing School and the Centre Reading School. In 1819, after the South Writing School was removed to Franklin Hall, the Centre Writing School was also removed to this Mason Street School.

to the Mason Street School. The two schools were united as two departments of the same school, and in 1821 the school was named the Adams School, in honor of Samuel Adams. In 1848 a new schoolhouse was erected on this same site, a copy of which, originally published in the *Boston Almanac of 1849,* is herewith reproduced.

The Masters of the Queen Street Writing School, under town government, were the following: John Cole, 1684-1714; Jacob Sheafe, 1714-1722; Edward Mills, 1722-1732(?); Samuel Holyoke, 1732/33-1768; Samuel Holbrook, 1753-1754; John Proctor, Jr., 1754-1773; James Carter, 1773-1775, and 1776-1797; and Jonathan Snelling, 1798-1822(?). It is to be noted that from 1753 to 1768 there were two Masters, the enrollment of the school at one time being over 250. The Masters of the writing department of the Adams School, succeeding Jonathan Snelling, were D. B. Tower, Josiah Fairbank, Robert W. Wright, and Samuel W. Bates, the last of whom was in office as late as 1849, according to the *Boston Almanac of 1849.*

The Ushers of the Queen Street Writing School, under town government, were the following: James Carter, 1768-1773; Abiah Holbrook,[4] 1773-1775; John Fox, 1784-1789; Robert Fox, 1789-1794(?); and Jonathan Snelling, 1794-1797(?).

The Masters of the Centre Reading School were the following: Caleb Bingham, 1789-1796; Samuel Brown, 1796-1800; John Haskell, 1800-1818(?); B. Dudley Emerson, 1818-1828(?); and Samuel Barret, 1828-1849(?). It is beyond the scope of this present study to present the subsequent history of the reading and writing departments of the Adams School.

[4] This Abiah Holbrook was the nephew of the famous Abiah Holbrook.

APPENDIX II

HISTORY OF THE NORTH WRITING SCHOOL
AND THE ELIOT SCHOOL

On April 30, 1683, the selectmen voted to establish two schools "for teachinge of children to write and cipher." The Queen Street Writing School was definitely opened in 1684. It appears from manuscript records that another writing school was established in the North End of Boston, but the school is not definitely recorded in the town records until March 11, 1699/1700.

The first Master of the writing school in the North End, of which there is any record, was Joshua Natstock,[1] who was appointed by Sir Edmund Andros, Governor of New England, on May 24, 1687. The order of Governor Andros, dated Boston, May 24, 1687, is as follows:

Upon the Petition of Joshua Natstock and Recommendation of many of the Inhabitants of the North part of the Towne of Boston I doe hereby approue of the Said Joshua Natstock to be Master of the Publick Schoole there and to haue and Injoy Such proffits Beneffitts and advantages as haue been heretofore payed and allowed to his predecessors. . . .[2]

There is no extant record of the number of "predecessors" and the exact date of the opening of the school, but, according to the following report of June, 1686, the school was in operation in 1686: "The standinge charge of this town at this time is about 400^{ld}. p. ann-aboue 200^{ld}. of which is in maintaineinge three Free Schools, mending the high wayes in Boston, Rumny Marsh & Muddie riuer."[3]

The school was discontinued after a few years and on March 11, 1699/1700, the town voted "That the Selectmen should agree wth a Schoolmaster for the North end of the Town . . . for the Teaching to Write and Cypher," after some of the "Inhabitants of the North end of the Town" had requested such a free school. Mr. Richard Henchman was appointed the Master on November 1, 1700, according to the record in the *Selectmen's Minutes,* dated April 28, 1701, that "M^{r}. Richard Henchman be paid his half years salery wch begun the first of Novemb^{r} last at Forty pounds p Annum, and four pounds p Annum for the rent of his School House." When he became old he retired from teaching and applied for a license to sell liquor. In the *Boston News-Letter* for the week of February 11-18, 1725, is the following obituary

---

[1] See page 397 for facsimile of Natstock's petition.

[2] *Massachusetts Archives,* Vol. 242, Number 342.

[3] The three free schools were the Latin School, the Queen Street Writing School, and this North End Writing School.

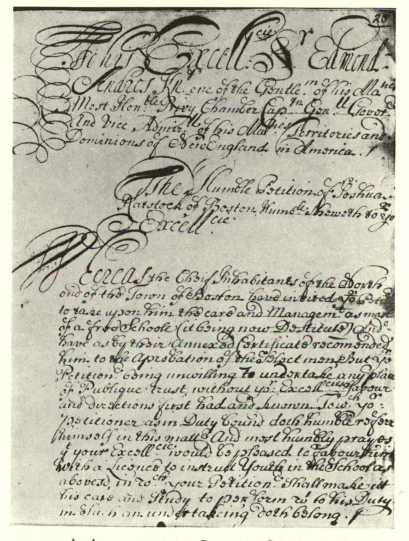

AN APPLICATION FOR THE POSITION OF SCHOOLMASTER

The petition of Joshua Natstock, addressed to Governor Edmond Andros, requesting to be appointed Master of a free writing school in the North End, Boston, "it being now Destitute."

From the original in the Massachusetts State Archives Division, State House, by courtesy of Mr. Frederic W. Cook, Secretary of The Commonwealth.

THE ELIOT SCHOOLHOUSE ERECTED IN 1838
From the *Boston Almanac of 1849.*

notice: "On Monday last the 15th Instant about 3 o Clock afternoon, Dyed here Mr. Richard Henchman, A School-Master for many Years at the North End, Aged about 70."

At the town meeting on March 13, 1715/16, a committee was appointed "to Consider of a Sutable place at the Norterly part of this Town, whereon to Erect a Writeing School . . . pursuant to a proposal formerly made by Thoˢ and Edwᵈ Hutchinson Esqʳˢ." These brothers had proposed to finance the building of a "House Convenient for a Free writing School at the Northerly part of Boston." On March 11, 1717/18, the town voted "That a Convenient part of that peice of Land wᶜʰ the Town Formerly purchased of Mʳˢ Susanna Love be aplyed to that use." Mrs. Love was the only daughter of Richard Bennet, and the streets, Love Lane and Bennet Street, were named in honor of the family. This land on which the school was erected is described in the *Town Records* as "abutting one end thereof On Bennet Street, and the other end on Love Street." In 1718 this new building for the North Writing School was erected, with the entrance on Love Lane. The street was later named Tileston Street, in honor of the famous writing master, John Tileston, who for sixty years was the Master of this school.

Under the "New System of Education," adopted in 1789, it was voted:

That the School House in Love Street in which Mʳ. Tileston now teaches, be continued for the North Writing School, and that the North Latin School House [The North Latin School was abolished in 1789.] nearly contiguous be annexed to it in order to accommodate Writing

John Tileston

JOHN TILESTON
Master of the North Writing School, 1761-1821. Edward Everett was one of
his pupils.
From Edward G. Porter's *Rambles in Old Boston New England.*

Scholars, should their number be greater than the former House will
conveniently contain.

In 1792 a new schoolhouse was built on North Bennet Street, to
accommodate both the North Writing and the North Reading Schools,
on the land where the North Grammar School, established in 1713,
formerly stood. This school was named the Eliot School[4] in 1821, in
honor of the Reverend John Eliot, the Apostle to the Indians. In 1838,

[4] Previous historians have incorrectly stated that the Eliot School was
founded in 1713 by John Eliot, the Apostle to the Indians. It is a matter
of record that the Reverend John Eliot died in Roxbury in 1690. It was the
North Grammar School that was established in 1713.

on the same lot on North Bennet Street, a new building was erected for the Eliot School, a copy of which, originally published in the *Boston Almanac of 1849,* is here reproduced.

The Masters of the North Writing School, under town government, were the following: the "predecessors" of Joshua Natstock, 1683(?)-1687; Joshua Natstock, 1687-(?); Richard Henchman, 1700-1719; Jeremiah Condy, 1719-1730/31; John Proctor, 1730/31-1742/43; Zachariah Hicks, 1742/43-1761; and the famous John Tileston, 1761-1775 and 1776-1819(?). The Writing Masters who followed Tileston in succession were Elisha Webb and Levi Conant, the latter of whom was in office as late as 1849, according to the *Boston Almanac of 1849.* It is beyond the scope of this present study to list the Masters of the Eliot School to date.

The Ushers of the North Writing School, under town government, were the following: Zachariah Hicks, 1732-1742; Abiah Holbrook, 1742-1742/43; John Proctor, Jr., 1743-1754; John Tileston, 1754-1761; James Carter, 1761-1768; William Dall,[5] 1768-1775 and 1776-1777; Joseph Carrol, 1778-1779; Nathan Webb, 1783-1789; and Rufus Webb, 1792-1795.

[5] On October 15, 1777, Mr. Doll [*sic*] acquainted the Selectmen "that he had resigned his Office as Usher of the said School" [the North Writing School].

APPENDIX III

HISTORY OF THE NORTH GRAMMAR SCHOOL

The following document, with no signatures attached, entitled "Proposition for a Free Gramer School at the North End of Boston. Reced Mar. 10th 1711.12" is the earliest proposal presented to the town for the establishment of a Latin grammar school in the North End.

CONSIDERATIONS RELATING TO A FREE GRAMER SCHOOL IN THE NORTH PART OF BOSTON.

It Cannot but be Thot Strange that One Grammer School Should be Thot sufficient for a Town of above Two Thousand Families when the Law of the Province Imposes one upon Every Town that hath above One Hundred.

Education is as great and Good an Intrest as can be prossecuted by any People, and the more Liberally it is Prosecuted the more is done for the honour and Welfare of such a People.

The Gramer School in this Town is as full of Scholars as can well Consist with a faithfull Discharge of Duty to them.

The North Part of this town bares no Inconsiderable Share in the Publick Expences and we hope are not altogether unworthy of the Publick benefitts.

It is known that when an hundred and odd Children have been found in the Publick Gramer School not one of that Hundred nor any but the few odd Ones have been Sent from that Part of the Town.

The Distance hath hindred many Parents from Exposing their Tender Children to the Travells of the Winter and the Sumer thither.

Some that Can't be satisfy'd without bestowing a good Cultivation on their Children are at the Charge of a Private Gramer School in the Neighbourhood. Others do Send their Children abroad in the Country.

When the People of that Neighbourhood were Prevail'd withall to Come into the Vote for Additional Incouragements unto the Present Gramer School, they were made to hope that they should ere long be favoured with another Nearer unto themselves.

If the Town will Smile on this Just and fair Proposal, it is Probable their will Appear some perticuler Gentlemen whose desire to Serve the Publick will Exert it self on this Occasion and make liberal advances towards the Providing of such Necessary Preliminaries.

These Considerations are humbly offer'd to the Inhabitants of Boston to be Laid in the Ballances of Equity in the Next General Meeting.[1]

[1] *New England Historical Genealogical Register,* Vol. 13, pp. 260-261.

LIST OF THE MASTERS FROM 1713 TO 1789

RECOMPENSE WADSWORTH, MARCH, 1713-JUNE, 1713

Recompense Wadsworth, who was graduated from Harvard College in 1708, was appointed the first Master on March 30, 1713, to begin his services on April 20 of that year. The town had previously voted on March 9, 1712/13, "to allow him Sixty pounds for one year." In the files of the city clerk is an interesting testimonial to his fidelity signed by Increase Mather and other ministers of the town. He died on June 9, 1713, soon after his appointment. As late as December 22, 1878, the superintendent of Copp's Hill Burying Ground discovered an old gravestone, with the following inscription: "Recompense Wadsworth, A.M. First Master of ye Grammar Free School at ye North End of Boston. Aged about 25 years; Died June ye 9th, 1713."

JOHN BARNARD, 1713-1718/19

John Barnard of Salem, who was graduated from Harvard College in 1709, was appointed the Master of the North Grammar School on August 18, 1713, to begin his services on August 27 of that year. On January 13, 1718/19, the selectmen accepted his resignation and voted to "return him thanks for his past care and Conduct." The Harvard College Library owns a letter of Peter Clarke, the minister of Salem, dated January 14, 1718/19, in which he recommends that Mr. Ames Angier be engaged "to Supply the vacancy in the North Grammar School."

JOSHUA GEE, JR., JANUARY, 1718/19-APRIL, 1719

Joshua Gee, Jr., was appointed by the selectmen on January 13, 1718/19, to be temporary Master of the North Grammar School "until that vacancy be Supplyed."

THOMAS ROBIE (Appointed but did not accept)

On February 3, 1718/19, the selectmen appointed Thomas Robie the Master of the school, and this appointment was approved by the town on March 10, 1718/19. Mr. Robie evidently wished to wait until after the commencement at Harvard College before accepting the position, for the selectmen on April 16, 1719, ordered the town clerk to notify Mr. Robie that they could not wait until commencement and desired "his Imediate complyance wth the Invitation formerly given him."

Mr. Thomas Robie was born in Boston in 1689 and was graduated from Harvard College in 1708. He was tutor, librarian, and fellow of Harvard College. He published an account of a remarkable eclipse of the sun, occurring on November 27, 1722.

PELEG WISWALL, 1719-1767

Peleg Wiswall,[2] who was graduated from Harvard College in 1702, was appointed Master by the town on April 29, 1719, after it was voted

---

[2] See page 403 for facsimile of letter of Peleg Wiswall, dated May 1, 1729, asking the selectmen for relief.

LETTER OF PELEG WISWALL, DATED MAY 1, 1729, ADDRESSED TO THE SELECTMEN
By courtesy of the Harvard College Library.

not to wait any longer for Mr. Robie. He was the Master for forty-eight years and on February 5, 1767, he presented his resignation to the selectmen, because of his age and "infirmities." The town afterwards granted him a pension. He died the next fall in September, 1767, at the age of eighty-four.

JAMES LOVELL, FEBRUARY, 1767-APRIL, 1767

James Lovell, son of John Lovell, who was the Master of the South Latin School on School Street, was appointed by the selectmen on

February 5, 1767, as acting Master of the North Latin School until the next general town meeting. At the town meeting on March 9, 1767, it was voted to refer the choice of a schoolmaster to the selectmen. At the next town meeting on March 23, 1767, it was voted to refer the appointment to the May meeting and in the meantime to allow the North Latin School boys to attend the South Latin School under John Lovell. Several gentlemen requested the appointment of Mr. Nathaniel Oliver, but he was not elected.

SAMUEL HUNT, 1767-1775

Samuel Hunt of Watertown, a Harvard graduate of the class of 1765, was unanimously appointed by the selectmen on April 8, 1767, as Master of the North Grammar School, and on April 20 of that year the selectmen introduced him to the scholars. He continued as Master until August 6, 1775, at which time the school was closed because of the Revolutionary War. He was transferred to the South Latin Grammar School on School Street on June 5, 1776, when the selectmen voted that it was "expedient" to open some of the schools again. The North [Latin] Grammar School was not reopened until 1779, after some of the inhabitants of the North End had sent a petition to the town for a schoolmaster.

WILLIAM BENTLEY, 1779-1780

William Bentley, who had been Usher of the South Latin School [the original Boston Latin School] since July 30, 1777, was appointed Master of the North Latin School on March 17, 1779, "he to enter upon that charge in one month from this day, or sooner if an Usher can be provided for the South Grammar School." He resigned at the end of the first year, and on February 23, 1780, the selectmen recorded that he intended to leave the school "next Satturday."

AARON SMITH, 1780-1781

Aaron Smith, who had been Usher of the South Latin School since January 19, 1780, was appointed Master of the North Grammar School on March 8, 1780, after having applied for the appointment, and the selectmen voted to "induct" him into the school on "Satturday next." He resigned on April 25, 1781, after one year of service. The selectmen voted to advertise for a Master in the Thursday newspaper. Several candidates applied, but the appointment was not made until June of that year, when Nathan Davies was chosen.

NATHAN DAVIES, 1781-1789

Nathan Davies, a graduate of Harvard College in 1759, was appointed Master on June 13, 1781, and was introduced to the scholars on August 13, 1781. He continued to be the Master for eight years until 1789, when under the "New System of Education" the North Latin Grammar School was discontinued.

REVISED LIST OF THE USHERS FROM 1738 TO 1767[3]

From 1738, when sixty boys attended the North Grammar School, until 1767, when only thirty boys attended, Peleg Wiswall was assisted by an Usher. The Ushers were the following: Jonathan Helyer, September, 1738-January, 1741/42 [resigned]; Samuel White, January, 1741/42-May, 1745 ["to be discharged at end of next quarter because school is so small"]; Ephraim Langdon, December, 1758-December, 1764 [died in 1765]; Andrew Eliot, Jr., January 11, 1765 [substitute for one month]; Jeremy Belknap, Jr., November 27, 1765 [appointed but no record of acceptance]; and Josiah Langdon, December, 1765-February, 1767.

[3] The only names listed in Henry F. Jenks's *Catalogue of the Boston Public Latin School*, published in 1886, are Ephraim Langdon and Josiah Langdon.

APPENDIX IV

HISTORY OF THE MUDDY RIVER WRITING SCHOOL

On March 8, 1685/86, the inhabitants of Muddy River, now a part of Brookline, petitioned the town of Boston for a writing school, and on March 29, 1686, the question was again referred to the selectmen. On February 25, 1686/87, the selectmen ordered that "henceforth the said Hamlet of Muddie River, be free from Towne rates to y° Towne of Bostone, they maintaineinge theire owne high wayes and poore, and other publique charges. . . And that within one yeare next comeinge they raise a schoole-house . . . as alsoe maintaine an able readinge and Writinge Master there. . . ."

At the town meeting on March 10, 1689/90, it was voted that "Muddy riuer Inhabitants are not discharged from Bostone to be a hamlett by them selues, but stand related to Bostone as they were before the yeare 1686."

The inhabitants of Muddy River on March 11, 1700/1, petitioned to be a "hamlet" separate from the town of Boston. This petition was "voted in the negative" but for their encouragement it was voted "that the Selectmen should provide a School-master for them, To teach their children to read, Write & Cypher, & order him his pay out of the Town Treasury."

On June 17, 1704, the inhabitants of Muddy River petitioned to be a separate village, and on November 13, 1705, Muddy River was established as Brookline.

APPENDIX V

HISTORY OF THE RUMNEY MARSH WRITING SCHOOL

The town of Boston supported a writing school at Rumney Marsh until January 8, 1738/39, when the district of Rumney Marsh was incorporated as the town of Chelsea.

At the Boston town meeting on March 11, 1700/01, the inhabitants of Rumney Marsh, "seeing the Town in so good a frame," requested that "a free school might be granted them to Teach to Read, Write & Cypher." It is interesting to note that they made this request when the town was in a good frame of mind! The town voted that if the number of children at Rumney Marsh warranted a school the selectmen of Boston should agree with a schoolmaster, whose service "should be payd out of the Town Treasury."

The inhabitants of Rumney Marsh waited patiently for eight years and then, on February 7, 1708/9, reminded the selectmen of Boston of their former vote to provide a school. The selectmen then agreed "that in case Mr. Thomas Cheever do undertake and Attend the Keeping Such School at his House . . . he Shall be allowed & paid out of the Town Treasury after the Rate of Twenty pounds p Annum for his Service." On February 7, 1709, the selectmen voted to continue Mr. Thomas Cheever "for yᵉ year ensueing on yᵉ Same terms as was for yᵉ Last year," and again, on February 19 of the next year, he was reappointed "as School Master at R. Marsh as formerly."

The Reverend Thomas Cheever, the son of the famous Ezekiel Cheever, was ordained at Malden in 1681 and was chosen the pastor of the First Church of Rumney Marsh in 1715. He was well qualified for both preaching and teaching, having been graduated from Harvard College in 1677.

The New England Historic and Genealogical Society has in its possession "An account of yᵉ schollars attending yᵉ School in Rumnymarish for reading, writing and cyphering, in the last quarter: ending February: 8th 1709/10." This list of thirty-three names is signed by Thomas Cheever. On August 8, 1711, he sent to the selectmen of Boston a list of eleven scholars "Entred in yᵉ School at Rumney Marish For Reading, Writing & Cyphering yᵉ 2ᵈ Quarter, Ending August 8ᵗʰ: 1711" and on February 19, 1713/14, he sent to the selectmen a list of twenty-five scholars.

At the Boston town meeting on March 10, 1728, the inhabitants of Rumney Marsh petitioned for allowance for a schoolmaster, and Boston voted to add twenty pounds to the amount formerly allowed

407

An account of ye Schollars entred
at ye School in Rumny marish for reading
writing & cyphering for the two last
quarters, ending ffebuary: w: 17 13/14

3	Of Mr Hugh ffloyds.
1	Joseph Belcher
1	Thomas Waitt
7	Nathaniel Richerdson
1	Edward Tuttle jun^r
2	John Chamberlane sen^r
1	Elisha Tuttle.
2	Daniel ffloyd.
1	John ffloyd jun^r
2	William Hafy
3	John Chamberlane jun^r
1	Jacob Hafy
3	Isaac Lewis.
1	Widdow Cole

ffebruary 19 · 17 13/14

¶ Thomas Cheever.

THOMAS CHEEVER'S ACCOUNT OF SCHOLARS AT RUMNEY MARSH WRITING SCHOOL
From Justin Winsor's *The Memorial History of Boston.*

to Mr. Thomas Cheever, "provided that the inhabitants there procure A sutable Person to the Satisfaction of the Selectmen." On March 10, 1729, the town voted to allow forty pounds for the schoolmaster at Rumney Marsh "for the year Ensueing." On March 13, 1731, the town voted an additional twenty pounds, "which Makes Sixty pounds," and again, on March 12, 1732/33, the town voted sixty pounds "for a School master at Rumny Marsh." On May 28, 1733, several inhabitants of Rumney Marsh requested an addition to their schoolmaster's salary, the consideration of which was referred to the next meeting, on March 12, 1733/34, when the town voted an increase of ten pounds. It appears from the *Town Records* that the successor of Thomas Cheever was Belcher Hancock.

On April 4, 1739, three of the selectmen of the town of Chelsea, "late the District of Rumney Marsh," requested that the town of Boston pay the salary of their schoolmaster "to the 21st of March last past." On April 11 of that year the selectmen of Boston voted "That the Sum of Twenty Pounds be drawn payable to m^r. Belcher Hancock in full for his Service as School master at Rumney Marsh from the 21st. of December to the 21st. of March last past." After January 8, 1738/39, when Rumney Marsh was incorporated as the town of Chelsea, Boston ceased to support a schoolmaster there.

APPENDIX VI

HISTORY OF THE SOUTH WRITING SCHOOL AND THE FRANKLIN SCHOOL

The South Writing School "in the Common" was established as the result of the town vote of March 13, 1715/16, "That a writeing School be Erected at the Southerly Part of this Town." On May 15, 1717, the town voted to have the selectmen "Sett out a convenient Peice of Land accordingly, viz' upon ye Comon adjoyning to Cowells Lott over ag' m' Wainrights." The houses, including the gun house and the schoolhouse, near the present Tremont Street, between School Street and Boylston Street, were considered as "in the Common."

The first Master of the school was Mr. Ames Angier, who on March 15, 1719/20, was appointed "School master at y° new writing School at y° South." On May 15, 1722, the town voted not to continue Mr. Angier and, accordingly, appointed a committee "to provide an able & Sutable master for Said School."

During the early years of the Revolutionary War, the school was closed. On July 17, 1776, the selectmen directed the town clerk "to give the Cryer a Notification, that the Writing School in the Common will be opened . . . on Monday next. . . ."

It appears from the *Town Records* that in 1780 the schoolhouse was "consumed by Fire." On February 23 of that year the selectmen applied to the overseers of the poor "for the use of the Workhouse Hall" to accommodate the South Writing School, until a new building could be erected. In the next month a special committee reported to the selectmen that "the Labratory will answer for a School tho not without a very great expense to the Town in fitting it up."

The question of "accomodating the youth of the South part of the Town with a School House" was discussed at five different town meetings, and finally on December 18, 1780, the town voted to hire the large room "in the Manufactory House." It was not until the following March that the town voted to direct the selectmen "to apply to the General Assembly of this Commonwealth at their next Sessions for the use of a Room in the Manufactory House so called." Their request was granted and the room was accordingly fitted up for the school.

On March 15, 1782, the town appropriated three hundred pounds "for the building a School House for the accomodation of the Youth of the Southerly part of the town." It appears from the *Selectmen's Minutes* that a new schoolhouse was built on West Street, a picture of which is here reproduced.[1]

[1] See page 412.

THE FRANKLIN SCHOOLHOUSE ERECTED IN 1845
From the *Boston Almanac of 1849*

Under the "New System of Education," adopted in 1789, it was voted "That the School House in West Street now occupied by Mr. Vinal, be the South Writing School."

On January 31, 1816, the selectmen agreed to the proposal of Mr. David Greenough to exchange the West Street lot "for land immediately north of the new Medical College in Mason street . . . he contracting to build a two story brick school house thereon on or before the 15th of August next."

In 1819 the South Writing School and the South Reading School[2] were united as two departments of the same school and occupied the schoolhouse on Nassau Street [In 1824 the name was changed to Common Street.], on the site later occupied by the old Brimmer School. The school was named the Franklin School in 1819, in honor of Benjamin Franklin.

In 1826 a new schoolhouse was built for the Franklin School on Washington Street. This was totally destroyed by the fire of 1844, and in 1845 a new building was erected on the same site, a picture of which, originally published in the *Boston Almanac of 1849*, is herewith reproduced.

The Masters of the South Writing School, under town government, were the following: Ames Angier, 1719/20-1722 (dismissed); Jacob Sheafe, 1722-1727(?); Peter Blin, 1727-1730/31(?); Samuel Allen, 1730/31-1742(?); Zachariah Hicks, May, 1742-March, 1742/43; Abiah Holbrook, 1742/43-1769 (died); Joseph Ward, January, 1768/69-April, 1769; Samuel Holbrook (brother of Abiah Holbrook), 1769-1775; James Carter (pro tem.), 1776; Samuel Holbrook, 1776-1780; John

[2] See page 418 for the history of the South Reading School.

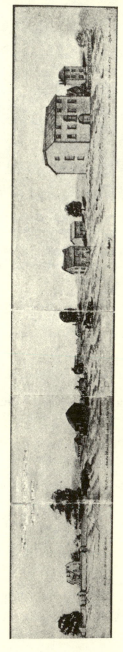

Tremont Street in 1800, Showing Master Webb's South Writing School-house on West Street

Vinall, 1781-1795; Rufus Webb, 1795-1820(?); and Otis Pierce, 1820(?)-1822(?). Nathan Merrill succeeded Otis Pierce and resigned in 1848, when the school was reorganized under the single-headed plan.

The Ushers of the South Writing School, under town government, were the following: Samuel Holbrook, 1745-1753; John Vinall, 1753(?)-1764(?); Assistant (name not recorded), 1764(?)-1773; John Fenno, 1773-1774; Andrew Cunningham, 1774-1775; Abiah Holbrook (nephew of the famous Abiah Holbrook), 1778(?)-1779; John Vinall, Jr., 1783-1788; Dudley Walker, May, 1788-December, 1788; and Robert Hinckley, 1788-1789.

In 1789 the Southermost Writing School became the South Reading School. The Masters of the South Reading School were the following: Elisha Ticknor, 1789-1794 (resigned); Samuel Payson (appointed but declined); Foster Waterman, 1795-1797 (dismissed); Asa Bullard, 1797-1808(?); Rev. Mr. Mc Kean, 1808-1815(?); and Thomas Payson, 1815-1822(?). The Masters of the reading department of the Franklin School, succeeding Thomas Payson, were Ebenezer Bailey, William J. Adams, William Clough, Mr. R. G. Parker, and Barnum Field, the last of whom was in office as late as 1849, according to the *Boston Almanac of 1849*. It is beyond the scope of this present study to present the subsequent history of the old Franklin School.

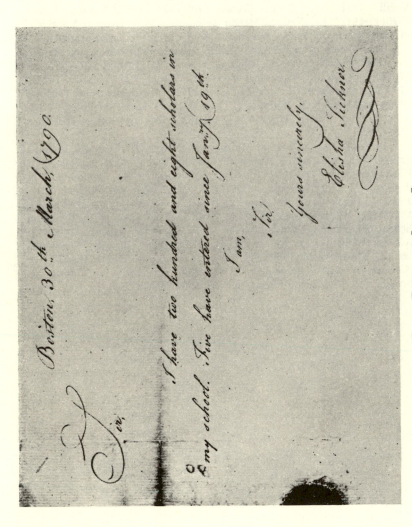

Boston, 30th March, 1790.

Sir,

I have two hundred and eight scholars in my school. Five have entered since January 19th.

I am, Sir,

Yours sincerely,

Elisha Ticknor

LETTER OF ELISHA TICKNOR TO SCHOOL COMMITTEE
By courtesy of the Boston School Committee.

JOHN VINALL
From the collection of Mr. Frank Bulkeley Smith.

APPENDIX VII

HISTORY OF THE SPINNING SCHOOLS

About 1718 a company of Scotch-Irish from Londonderry, Ireland, arrived in Massachusetts, bringing with them implements for manufacturing linen. The inhabitants of Boston became interested and, at the town meeting on September 28, 1720, a committee of seven was chosen "to Consider ab^t promoting of a Spinning School or Schools for the Instruction of the children of this Town, in Spinning." The committee reported at the town meeting on December 27, 1720, as follows:

That if the Town do not See cause either to build or Hire a house, they may yet give encourragement to Such as Will Sett up Such a School by allowing them two or three hundred pounds on good Security without Intrest, that they may be enabled to promote So good an Undertakeing, which wee conceive will be a very great advantage to us.

Little seems to have been done towards establishing spinning schools until June 2, 1753, when the town petitioned the legislature for a building. In 1754 a law was passed granting a duty to be levied upon carriages of all kinds for the benefit of the proprietors or managers of the linen manufacture in Boston, to aid them in the purchasing a piece of land and erecting or purchasing a suitable house within the town for carrying on the business of spinning, weaving, and other necessary parts of the linen manufacture. Under this law the building called the "Manufactory House" was erected on Longacre Street. The manufacture of linen was begun here with a spirit too enthusiastic to secure permanent success. The women of the town, rich and poor, appeared on the Common with their wheels and competed with each other in their skill in spinning. The enterprise lasted only three or four years.

A few years later, on April 4, 1769, a committee previously appointed to consider the employment for the poor reported "that it would answer a very valuable purpose if a number of Schools were set up . . . to learn such Children to Spin (free of Charge)." There is no further record concerning spinning schools, in the *Town Records* and the *Selectmen's Minutes,* other than the fact that the town accepted the above report.

SIGNERS OF A PETITION TO GOVERNOR
SPENCER PHIPS

SIGNERS OF A PETITION IN 1753 ASKING THE GOVERNMENT TO ENCOURAGE THE
MANUFACTURE OF LINEN
From Justin Winsor's *The Memorial History of Boston.*

APPENDIX VIII

HISTORY OF THE SOUTHERMOST WRITING SCHOOL AND THE SOUTH READING SCHOOL

A petition was presented to the town on March 13, 1769, "that another Writing School may be Erected in some convenient place at the South End." It was not until 1780 that a lot of land on the south side of Pleasant Street was purchased "by certain proprietors" upon which to erect a schoolhouse. The town hired this school building and on September 1, 1784, appointed Mr. Samuel Cheney the Master "for three months."

It appears that Mr. Cheney had antagonized some of the inhabitants, because on December 8 of that year several of the citizens requested the selectmen to appoint Mr. Richards the Master. The several "gentlemen" for and against Mr. Cheney interviewed the selectmen, and on April 20 of that same year Mr. Samuel Cheney was again appointed "for four months." In August the "proprietors of the schoolhouse" informed the selectmen "that they were ready to let said School to the Town for another year, provided a Master might be appointed in the room of Mr. Cheney."

On October 19, 1785, the proprietors consented that the town retain the schoolhouse, provided that the selectmen dismiss Mr. Cheney and appoint Mr. Elisha Ticknor as Master. The selectmen informed the proprietors that they had provided another schoolhouse for Mr. Cheney near the center of the town and that "within a Fortnight, . . . their School House will be delivered up to them."

After this no school was provided in the "southermost" part of the town until February 29, 1788, when another petition for a school was presented to the selectmen. On March 10, 1788, the town voted to "hire the School of the present Proprietors," and on March 12, 1788, the selectmen appointed Mr. Elisha Ticknor the Master. Mr. William Bosson was appointed his assistant in July.

Under the "New System of Education," adopted in 1789, it was recommended "That the School House in Pleasant Street now occupied by Mr. Ticknor, be the South Reading School untill a further provision be made by a new Building."

On March 5, 1790, the selectmen ordered the town treasurer to pay Deacon Richard Gridley sixty pounds for land in Nassau Street [now Common Street], "for the purpose of Erecting a School thereon for Reading for the convenience of the So. part of the Town."

Later records show that certain "gentlemen" were permitted to build a story over the South Reading School on Nassau Street. This "chamber" was named Franklin Hall. On April 4, 1792, the selectmen requested the "Proprietors of the Chamber of the South Reading School" not to let the chamber without their consent, and in 1794 the selectmen voted that "The Gentlemen who were permitted to build a Story over the South Reading School, have leave to let said Room as a Dancing School."

Later Franklin Hall was occupied by the Hollis Street Society until April 28, 1819, when the selectmen voted "to purchase all rights of the same," by paying $600 to the Society. The South Writing School was then transferred from Mason Street to Franklin Hall, over the South Reading School, and the two schools, then named the Franklin School, were united as two departments of the same school.

APPENDIX IX

HISTORY OF THE NEW NORTH WRITING SCHOOL AND THE NORTH READING SCHOOL

In the fall of 1785 the selectmen established another writing school, in a remodeled church in the North End, "in the House formerly called Sandermans Meeting," and appointed Mr. Samuel Cheney the Master. This church, founded by Robert Sandeman, a Scotchman, was located on the west side of Middle Street [now Hanover Street], between Cross and Parmenter Streets. Two years later the selectmen agreed with the proprietors of this building to lower the rent to fifteen pounds per year. The school was named the New North Writing School, to distinguish it from the original North Writing School.

In 1786 Mr. Edward Holden was appointed the assistant to Samuel Cheney, after a committee reported that the school had 110 scholars. The next year the selectmen permitted Master Cheney to employ his son as an assistant.

Under the "New System of Education," adopted in 1789, it was agreed "That the Building in Middle Street now occupied by Mr. Cheney, be retained for the North Reading School."

On April 21, 1790, the selectmen recorded that the school committee had provided a new schoolhouse for Master Cheney, Master of the North Reading School. The location of the school is not recorded in the *Town Records,* but it was undoubtedly in the North End. In 1791 the inhabitants of the North End petitioned for a new schoolhouse, and in 1792 a new building, later named the Eliot School, was erected on North Bennet Street, to accommodate both the North Writing School and the North Reading School.

Samuel Cheney was retained as Master for only a short time, and on August 10, 1792, the school committee requested his resignation, having received a petition for his removal. His friends, one of whom was Samuel Adams, rallied to his support by sending to the school committee a petition in his favor, a facsimile of which is herewith reproduced. He was dismissed, nevertheless, and Amos Crosby was appointed his successor on October 27, 1792. He, too, had his difficulties and resigned on April 25, 1795, because "some parents at the North End of Boston were against him because of his punishments."

The Masters of the North Reading School who succeeded Amos Crosby, under town government, were the following: Jonathan F. Sleeper, 1795-1801; Ezekiel Little, 1801-1819; and Nathaniel Storr, 1819-1822(?). Boston became a city in 1822. In 1821 the North

420

Boston Sept. 17th 1792

To the Gentlemen constituting the School-Committee of the Town of Boston

The subscribers beg leave to represent, that by a Vote of the Committee published in the Papers it appears, that Mr. Samuel Cheney is to be superseded in the care of the North Reading-School on the first of November next; — That they are informed by Certificates, signed by a great number of the Parents of the Children under his care, that they are fully satisfied with his Ability, Integrity and Application, — A copy of which Certificates has been laid before your respectable Body. The subscribers, concerned for the situation of a worthy Man, and desirous to save an helpless and amiable Family from ruin, with the Committee to inform Mr. Cheney whether these Testimonials have had any effect to alter the determination of the Committee, — And they request, as Inhabitants of the Town of Boston, that a Meeting of the Committee may be held, and an answer returned to this Application, as soon as may be

Richard Green
Stephen Cleverly
Henry Bass,
Wm. Marshall,
Nathl. Curtis
Ephraim May
Willm. Lowder

S Adams
Peter Thacher
Samuel Ruggles
John Sweetser Jr.
Samuel Wells
John Avery junr.
John Deming
Mr. B. Bass.

PETITION IN FAVOR OF SAMUEL CHENEY, SIGNED BY SAMUEL ADAMS AND OTHERS
By courtesy of the Boston School Committee.

Writing School and the North Reading School were named the Eliot School. The Masters of the reading department of the Eliot School, succeeding Nathaniel Storrs, were Cornelius Walker, David B. Tower, Charles B. Sherman, Edwin Wright, and William O. Ayres, the last of whom was in office in 1849, according to the *Boston Almanac of 1849*. It is beyond the scope of this study to give the subsequent history of the Eliot School.

THE SYSTEM OF PUBLIC EDUCATION OF 1789

THE

SYSTEM

OF

Public Education,

Adopted by the Town of BOSTON, 15th Octob. 1789.

I. THAT there be one School in which the rudiments of the Latin and Greek languages shall be taught, and scholars fully qualified for the Universities. That all candidates for admission into this School shall be at least ten years of age, having been previously well instructed in English Grammar; that they shall continue in it not longer than four years, and that they have liberty to attend the public writing Schools at such hours as the visiting Committee shall direct.

II. That there be one writing School at the South part of the town; one at the Centre, and one at the North part; that, in these Schools, the children of both sexes be taught writing, and also arithmetic in the various branches usually taught in the Town-Schools, including Vulgar and Decimal Fractions.

III. That there be one reading School at the South part of the Town, one at the Centre, and one at the North part; that,

in

(2)

in thefe Schools, the children of both fexes be taught to fpell, accent, and read both profe and verfe, and alfo be inftructed in Englifh Grammar and Compofition.

IV. That the children of both fexes be admitted into the reading and writing Schools at the age of feven years, having previoufly received the inftruction ufual at Women's Schools ; that they be allowed to continue in the reading and writing Schools till the age of fourteen, the boys attending the year round, the girls from the 20th of April to the 20th of October following; that they attend thefe Schools alternately, at fuch times, and fubject to fuch changes, as the vifiting Committee in confultation with the Mafters fhall approve.

V. That a Committee be annually chofen by ballot, to confift of twelve, in addition to the Selectmen, whofe bufinefs it fhall be to vifit the Schools once in every quarter, and as much oftener as they fhall judge proper, with three of their number at leaft, to confult together in order to devife the beft methods for the inftruction and government of the Schools ; and to communicate the refult of their deliberations to the Mafters ; to determine at what hours the Schools fhall begin, and to appoint play-days ; in their vifitations to enquire into the particular regulations of the Schools, both in regard to inftruction and difcipline, and give fuch advice to the Mafters as they fhall think proper ; to examine the Scholars in the particular branches which they are taught ; and, by all proper methods, to excite in them a laudable ambition to excel in a virtuous, amiable deportment, and in every branch of ufeful knowledge.

VOTES

(3)

VOTES of the Committee appointed to carry into Execution the Syftem of public Education adopted by the Town of Bofton, 15th October 1789.

AT a Meeting of the faid Committee, held Decemb. 1, 1789.

VOTED, I. That the Latin Grammar School be divided into four Claffes, and that the following Books be ufed in the refpeftive Claffes.

    1ft Clafs—Cheever's Accidence.
           Corderius's Colloquies—Latin and Englifh.
           Nomenclator.
           Æfop's Fables—Latin and Englifh.
           Ward's Latin Grammar, or Eutropius.

    2d Clafs—Clarke's Introduftion—Latin and Englifh.
           Ward's Latin Grammar.
           Eutropius, continued.
           Selectæ è Veteri Teftamento Hiftoriæ, or,
           Caftalio's Dialogues.
      The making of Latin, from Garretfon's Exercifes.

    3d Clafs—Cæfar's Commentaries.
           Tully's Epiftles, or Offices.
           Ovid's Metamorphofes.
           Virgil.
           Greek Grammar.
  The making of Latin from King's Hiftory of the Heathen Gods.

    4th Clafs—Virgil, continued.—Tully's Orations.
           Greek Teftament.—Horace.
           Homer.—Gradus ad Parnaffum.
           The making of Latin continued.
                      That

(4)

That thofe Boys who attend the Latin School, be allowed to attend the Writing Schools in the following Hours, viz. The 1ft Clafs from half paft Nine o'clock, A. M. 'till Eleven, or from half paft Three P. M. as fhall be found moft convenient, and the 2d Clafs in the fame manner for the firft half of that year.

II. That the following Books be ufed in the Reading Schools. viz.—The Holy Bible.
        Webfter's Spelling Book, or 1ft part of his Inftitute.
        The young Ladies Accidence——And
        Webfter's American Selection of Leffons in Reading and
          Speaking; or 3d part of his Grammatical Inftitute.
That the Mafters introduce the following Books when found expedient, viz.—The Children's Friend.
        Morfe's Geography, abridged.
That the News Papers be introduced occafionally, at the difcretion of the Mafters.
That the upper Clafs in the Reading Schools be inftructed in Epiftolary Writing and other Compofition.

III. That an uniform method of teaching Arithmetic be ufed in the feveral Writing Schools, viz.
        Numeration.
        Simple Addition.
        —— Subtraction.
        —— Multiplication.
        —— Divifion.
        Compound Addition.
        —— Subtraction.
        —— Multiplication.
        —— Divifion.
        Reduction.

The

(5)

The fingle Rule of Three, direct.
Practice.

Tare and Tretr, Interest, Fellowfhip, Exchange, &c. are confidered as
included in the above Rules.

Vulgar and Decimal Fractions.

That the Children begin to learn Arithmetic at 11 Years
of Age.

That at 12 Years of Age, the Children be taught to make Pens.

IV. That the Reading Schools be divided into four Claffes.
—That from the third Monday in October to the third Monday
in April, for one Month, viz. from the first Monday in the
Month, the first and second Claffes attend the Reading, and the
third and fourth, the Writing Schools in the Morning.—
The first and second, attend the Writing Schools, the third and
fourth the Reading Schools in the Afternoon.—The Month
following, the order be reverfed, and fo alternately during the
above time.—And that from the third Monday in April to the
third Monday in October, for one Month, viz. from the first
Monday in the Month, all the Boys attend the Reading Schools,
and all the Girls the Writing Schools in the Morning; that all
the Boys attend the Writing Schools, and all the Girls the
Reading Schools in the Afternoon; the Month following the
order to be reverfed, and thus alternately during thofe fix Months.
—That it be underftood that from the third Monday in April
to the first Monday in June, be confidered as the first Month of
the Summer Term. That from the third Monday in October
to the first Monday in December, be confidered as the first
Month of the Winter Term.

V. That

(6)

V. That the following Hours be punctually observed in all
the Schools, viz. From the third Monday in April to the third
Monday in October, the Schools begin at half past 7 o'Clock,
A. M. and continue 'till eleven, and begin at half past 1 o'Clock,
P. M. and continue 'till five.—That from the third Monday in
October to the third Monday in April, the Schools begin at
half past 8 o'Clock, A. M. and continue 'till eleven, and begin
at half past 1 o'Clock, P. M. and continue 'till half past four.

That in future the Schools keep 'till 11 o'Clock in the Forenoon on Thursdays, as well as other Days.

VI. That the Masters be excused from keeping School on
the following Days and Times, viz.

The Afternoon of every Thursday and Saturday throughout
the year.

The Afternoon preceding Fasts and Thanksgivings.

Four half days of Artillery Training, in the Afternoon.

First Monday in April.

Six days in Election Week.

First Monday in June.

Fourth Day of July, or Anniversary of Independence.

The four last Days in Commencement Week.

Christmas Day, and

On the general Training Days.

December 7, 1789.

Voted, That the Committee be divided into seven equal parts,
as Sub-Committees for the purpose of inspecting the respective
Schools, and examining the scholars ; so that one Committee
be assigned to each School. And the Committee was
divided accordingly.

Voted,

(7) .

Voted, That the infpecting Committees be enjoined to vifit their refpective Schools at leaft once every month, and as much oftener as they may think proper.

Voted, That the infpecting Committees make the laws of the State refpecting Schools, the votes of the Town, and of this Committee, the rule of their conduct in vifiting the Schools.

Voted, That the firft Monday in January 1790 be the time affigned for putting into operation the new Syftem of Education, as adopted by the Town, and regulated by this Committee.

December 14, 1789.

Voted, That it be the indifpenfable duty of the feveral School-Mafters, daily to commence the duties of their office by prayer and reading a portion of the facred Scriptures, at the hour affigned for opening the School in the morning; and clofe the fame in the evening with prayer.

December 21, 1789.

Voted, That the Mafters never expel any boy from School, but with the confent, and in the prefence of the infpecting Committee.

Voted, That the Inftructor of the Latin School be entitled *The Latin Grammar Mafter* ; the Inftructors of the Reading Schools be entitled *Englifh Grammar Mafters*; the Inftructors of the Writing Schools be entitled *Writing Mafters*.

APPENDIX XI

MEMBERS OF THE BOSTON SCHOOL COMMITTEE FROM 1789 THROUGH 1822

COMPILED FROM THE *TOWN RECORDS*

At the town meeting in Boston on October 20, 1789, the first regular school committee of twelve members was chosen, one from each ward, "who in addition to the Selectmen are to carry the new System of Education which has been adopted by the Town into operation."

Members of the committee from 1789 through 1822 are as follows:

Appleton, Nathan W., Dr.	1789-1794	
Dawes, Thomas	1789-1807	Resigned
Dexter, Aaron, Dr.	1789-1821	Resigned
Freeman, James, Rev.	1789-1792	Resigned
Gore, Christopher	1789-1792	
Jones, John Coffin	1789-1794	Resigned
Lathrop, John, Rev.	1789-1796	Resigned
Mason, Jonathan, Jr.	1789-1792	
Minot, George Richards	1789-1797	Resigned
Tudor, William	1789-1796	Resigned
Welsh, Thomas, Dr.	1789-1821	
West, Samuel, Rev.	1789-1802	Resigned
Clark, John, Rev.	1792-1795	
Austin, Jonathan Loring	1793-1796	Resigned
Smith, William	1793-1816	
Townsend, David	1794-1797	Resigned
Stillman, Samuel, Rev.	1795-1800	Resigned
Crocker, Joseph	1796-1797	
Eustis, William	1796	
Spooner, William, Dr.	1796-1800	Resigned
Wells, Arnold, Jr.	1796-1813	Resigned
Gray, Edward	1797-1806	Resigned
Green, David	1797-1812	
Kirkland, John T., Rev.	1797-1811	Resigned
Amory, Rufus G.	1798-1800	Resigned
Eckley, Joseph, Rev.	1800-1809	Resigned
Emerson, William, Rev.	1800-1811	
Quincy, Josiah,	1800-1806	Resigned
Popkin, John S., Rev.	1802	
Phillips, John	1803-1812	
Davis, Charles	1806-1819	

Heard, John	1806-1817	Resigned
Davis, John	1807-1810	Resigned
Channing, William Ellery, Rev.	1808; 1810-1813	Resigned
Prescott, William	1810-1812	
Buckminster, Joseph S., Rev.	1811-1812	
Lowell, Charles, Rev.	1811-1822	
Holley, Horace, Rev.	1813-1819	Resigned
Oliver, Francis J.	1813-1821	
Thacher, Peter Oxenbridge	1813-1819	
Warren, John Collins, Dr.	1813-1818	
Welles, William	1813-1822	
Cary, Samuel, Rev.	1814-1815	
Thacher, Samuel Cooper, Rev.	1816	
Wigglesworth, Thomas	1816-1818	Resigned
Huntington, Joshua, Rev.	1817-1819	
Russell, Benjamin	1817-1821	
Oliver, Henry J.	1818-1821	
Frothingham, Nathaniel L., Rev.	1819-1821	
Pierpont, John, Rev.	1819-1821	
West, Benjamin	1819	Resigned
Coffin, John G.	1820-1821	
Sharp, Daniel, Rev.	1820-1821	
Shaw, Lemuel	1820-1821	
Dean, Paul, Rev.	1821	
Bassett, Francis	1822	
Bean, Horace, Dr.	1822	
Clap, Elisha	1822	
Dall, William	1822	
Dutton, Warren	1822	
Eaton, Asa, Rev.	1822	
Jenks, William, Rev.	1822	
Little, William	1822	
Parmenter, William	1822	

It is to be noted that, of the total of sixty-four names, twenty-two were leading ministers of Boston.

APPENDIX XII

BOSTON SCHOOL COMMITTEE MANUSCRIPT DOCUMENTS
FROM 1789 THROUGH 1822

The following is a list of manuscript documents relating to the Boston Latin School from 1789 to 1822, now in the possession of the Boston School Committee at 15 Beacon Street. These Professor Arthur Orlo Norton and the writer have rearranged chronologically through 1822, giving a descriptive title to each. Since some bear no date, it has been necessary to study the documents very carefully in order to arrange them according to the chronological sequence of events. The doubtful ones are dated with a question mark. All of these documents are the original manuscripts and for this reason are extremely valuable. In addition to the information they contain, they furnish direct evidence as to the style of penmanship of the various writing masters.

April 5, 1784. [In file, 1796-1809.]
> Report of a special committee on a further arrangement of the free schools. [Samuel Adams was a member of this committee.]

May ?, 1789.
> Schedule of salaries of Masters, 1770-1775, 1782-1784, 1786-1787, and 1789.

June 25, 1789.
> Statute respecting schools, passed June 25, 1789.

October 15, 1789.
> Propositions for reforming present system of public education.

October 20, 1789.
> Vote of town for school committee. Twelve chosen. [Copy by town clerk.]

November 1, 1789.
> Nathan Davies, Master of the North Latin Grammar School, reports names of scholars.

November ?, 1789.
> Master Carter's return of boys in Court Street School. [143 constant and 28 from the Boston Latin School.]

December 17, 1789.
> Copy of letter from Noah Webster offering two copies of *Grammatical Institute*, Part 3, as prizes for each school.

December 18, 1789.
> Questions and answers at conference between school committee and Masters respecting discipline.

December 21, 1789.
> Recommendation of school committee to Masters on discipline.

December 21, 1789.
> Report of committee respecting books, hours, and play days. [Includes votes of committee on Dec. 1, 7, 14, 21, 1789.]

January 19, 1789.
> Abstract of votes of school committee from Nov. 3, 1789, to Jan. 19, 1790.

March 8, 1790.
> Shippie Townsend, to school committee, urging against gambling by children.

March 18, 1790.
> Ebenezer Burditt's agreement for repairs of North Latin School. [This encloses list of repairs of North schools as agreed to by sub-committee.]

April 1, 1790.
> Report of Committee on Latin School. [John Scollay, chairman.] This encloses Master Hunt's return of 64 boys at the Boston Latin School, July, 1790.

April 1, 1790.
> Mr. Carter's return of 225 boys at Centre Writing School. Latin School boys included.

April 29, 1790.
> Testimonials for Joseph Dana, Jr., from Joseph Dana and from Levi Frisbie. [Joseph Dana, Jr., was appointed Usher of the Boston Latin School, resigning Oct. 2, 1791.]

June 29, 1790.
> Letter from Nathan Davies applying for position as assistant to Master Samuel Hunt.

August 2, 1790.
> Report of sub-committee on Latin School.

September 21, 1790.
> John Barrett applies for position as Usher of Latin School.

January 7, 1791.
> Anonymous writer warns committee against allowing Masters to keep private schools. [Dated on back Jan. 7, 1791. Letter itself dated Nov., 1790.]

April ?, 1791.
> Samuel Hunt's return of 62 boys at Latin School.

July 1, 1791.
> Plan for visiting the schools and plan for luncheon.

October 2, 1791.
> Joseph Dana resigns as Usher of Latin School.

October 31, 1791.
> Samuel Hunt's report on adjustment of Latin School to "New System of Education."

November 8, 1791.
> Minutes of conference between school committee and Masters on keeping private schools.

January 26, 1792.
> Petition of Boston schoolmasters to be permitted to keep private schools. [Dated on back, Feb. 7, 1792.]

March ?, 1792.
> Petition of Ushers of schools for increase in salary. [Signed by William White, Stephen Patten, Rufus Webb, and Samuel Cheney, Jr.]

April 3, 1792.
> Separate petition from William White.

April 1, 1793.
> Charles Bulfinch, treasurer of school committee, gives account for 1791, 1792, and 1793.

May 17, 1793.
> Samuel Hunt's return of 48 boys at Latin School.

August 1, 1793.
> Joseph Callender's receipt for making 21 Franklin medals.

July ?, 1794.
> Samuel Hunt's return of 12 boys who are sent to Latin School.

May ?, 1795.
> Charles Cutler, Usher of Latin School, applies for mastership of the North Reading School, Boston.

June 18, 1795.
> Joseph Callender's receipt for payment for 21 Franklin medals.

September ?, 1795.
> Petition of Ushers of schools for increase in salary. [Signed by Charles Cutler, Samuel Brown, Asa Bullard, Benjamin Holt, and John N. Parsons.]

January 28, 1796.
> Rev. Joseph Eckley's complaint against Master Hunt and Usher Cutler for maltreatment of son.

March 4, 1796.
> Joseph Eckley, in reply to school committee, gives details regarding punishment of son.

April 29, 1796.
> Ushers of public schools request increase in salary.

June 3, 1796.
> Joseph Callender's receipt for payment for 21 Franklin medals.

April 26, 1797.
> Samuel Hunt, Master of the Latin School, requests increase in salary.

July 7, 1797.
> Joseph Callender's receipt for payment for 14 Franklin medals.

August 1, 1797.
> Charles Cutler, Usher of Latin School, requests appointment to South Reading School, Boston.

August 11, 1797.
> Petition of Ushers of schools for increase in salary. [Signed by Charles Cutler, Benjamin Holt, John W. Gurley, Jacob Gates, Ashur Adams and Asa Bullard.]

June 28, 1798.
> Joseph Callender's receipt for payment for 7 Franklin medals.

August 22, 1798.
 Petition of Masters of schools for increase in salary. [Signed by
 Samuel Hunt, Jonathan F. Sleeper, Asa Bullard, John Tileston,
 Samuel Brown, Jonathan Snelling and Rufus Webb.]
July 15, 1799.
 Joseph Callender's receipt for payment for 14 silver Franklin
 medals.
June 27, 1800.
 Joseph Callender's receipt for payment for 2 Franklin medals.
February 6, 1801.
 Votes of school committee on Masters and Ushers. They must be
 University graduates. School committee must approve all appoint-
 ments. No students of law or medicine shall be appointed without
 special permission of school committee.
April 2, 1801.
 Adverse report of sub-committee on condition of Latin School.
May 1, 1801.
 Report of sub-committee on powers of Master and Assistant Master
 of Latin School. Committee recommends that no translation of
 higher classics be allowed.
July 12, 1801.
 Receipt for payment for 12 Franklin medals. [Signed by Jacob
 Perkins of Newburyport.]
July 17, 1801.
 Joseph Callender's receipt for payment for 2 Franklin medals.
March 19, 1802.
 Josiah Quincy's account as treasurer of school committee from
 Mar. 31, 1801, to Mar. 19, 1802.
October 18, 1802.
 Jacob Perkins's receipt for payment for 18 Franklin medals.
March 17, 1803.
 William Emerson's account as treasurer of school committee from
 Mar. 19, 1802, to Mar. 17, 1803.
July 13, 1803.
 Jacob Perkins's receipt for payment for 18 Franklin medals at $.92
 each.
August 25, 1803.
 Receipted bill for engraving on 30 silver medals. [Signed by
 Thomas Callender, Jr.]
March 13, 1804.
 William Emerson's account as treasurer of school committee from
 Mar. 20, 1803, to Mar. 13, 1804.
August 8, 1804.
 Jacob Perkins's receipt for payment for 24 silver medals.
October 17, 1804.
 Samuel Hunt, to Charles Bulfinch, Chairman, requests information
 as to who called together the school committee, to discuss the sub-
 ject of their last meeting.
October 26, 1804.
 Samuel Hunt, to Charles Bulfinch, appeals for consideration by the
 school committee.

1804.
> Petition of Masters of the schools for increase of salary, owing to high cost of living. [Signed by Samuel Hunt, John Tileston, Rufus Webb, Jonathan Snelling, Asa Bullard, John Haskell, Ezekiel Little, Cyrus Perkins, and Benjamin Holt.]

January 16, 1805.
> Samuel Hunt's refusal to resign, because he has family of 5 children under 14 years of age.

February 15, 1805.
> Thomas Cole, to Thomas Dawes, Jr., applies for mastership of Latin School.

February 15, 1805.
> Stephen Farley applies for mastership of Latin School. [Addressed Pembroke, Mass.]

February 20, 1805.
> William Keegan applies for mastership of Latin School.

February 27, 1805.
> Ebenezer Pemberton, of Billerica, applies for mastership of Latin School. [Encloses letter, dated April 2, 1805, to Rev. Dr. Kirkland on same subject.]

March 25, 1805.
> Nathanael Howe, to John T. Kirkland, recommends Jeremy Stimpson for mastership of Latin School.

August 17, 1805.
> Jacob Perkins's receipt for payment for 24 Franklin medals. [$24.]

May 2, 1806.
> Caleb Loring complains against Master Biglow and Usher Ripley, of Boston Latin School, for severe flogging of son. [Encloses certificates of son's good conduct and scholarship, signed by William Biglow, in Biglow's private school, from Nov. 9, 1805, to April 12, 1806.]

July 21, 1806.
> Nathanael Briggs, to school committee, applies for increase of salaries of assistants.

February 22, 1808.
> Thomas Cole, of Marblehead, applies for recommendations forwarded when he was applicant for Latin School. Receipt of Henry Rice for these papers on same sheet, dated Feb. 25, 1808.

March 21, 1812.
> Jonathan Wainwright applies for ushership of Latin School. [Encloses testimonial from President Kirkland of Harvard College, dated Mar. 10, 1812.]

May 20, 1812.
> Town vote to remove the Centre Reading and Writing schoolhouse from front of new Court House on School Street and to rebuild or enlarge the Latin School to accommodate the Reading and Writing School.

May 22, 1812.
> Minutes of school committee meeting. Bids called for enlargement of Latin School.

August 28, 1812.

Jonathan Wainwright is elected Usher of Latin School. [This is a minute of school committee meeting, of this date.]

March ?, 1813.

Minutes of school committee meeting. Arrangement of sub-committee for visiting schools. Voted grant of $100.00 to each Master and $50.00 to each Usher.

March 18, 1814.

Report of sub-committee on Latin School, proposing certain measures to improve Latin School, especially by increasing the Master's salary. Five recommendations for improving School.

April 15, 1814.

Report of sub-committee on Latin School, recommending appointment of Benjamin A. Gould as Master. [Signed by Peter Thacher.]

June 28, 1814.

Sub-committee for Latin School reports recommending: (1) Five-year course; (2) three lowest classes to be dismissed at 11 o'clock to attend writing schools at private hours; (3) two highest classes to be taught arithmetic and geography as required for admission to Harvard College; and (4) lads required to write in fair hand.

August 15, 1814.

Thomas B. Wait offers to the school committee Rev. Mr. Mc Kean's *Sacred Extracts from the Scriptures of the Old and New Testaments* for the use of schools.

September 1, 1815.

Benjamin A. Gould, Headmaster of Latin School, accepts reappointment on condition of vacations in spring and autumn.

September 19, 1817.

Report of sub-committee on Latin School recommending an additional permanent Master.

September 16, 1818.

Benjamin A. Gould's letter to sub-committee for Latin School. Requests an additional room for the Latin School. The lower floor of the school house to be used. Also requests increase of salaries of his assistants.

September 29, 1818.

Sub-committee for the Latin School approves Gould's petition for more room and more assistance.

1819.

Report of sub-committee on Latin School praising work of Mr. Gould. [No date on document. Date given is entered in pencil on back by a late hand.]

May 7, 1821.

Benjamin Whitwell, to school committee, requests special vote, if necessary, for admission of his ward to Latin School in May, instead of waiting until August.

APPENDIX XIII

HISTORY OF THE MAYHEW SCHOOL

THE MAYHEW SCHOOLHOUSE ERECTED IN 1847
From the *Boston Almanac of 1849.*

The Mayhew School, named for the Rev. Jonathan Mayhew in 1821, was first established in 1803 on Hawkins Street in the West End. At the town meeting on March 14, 1803, a number of the inhabitants of West Boston petitioned the town for a school, and the town, at this same meeting, voted to refer the case to the school committee. On March 23 of that year the school committee reported that they unanimously recommended the establishment of a reading and writing school at West Boston, "so situated however as that it shall likewise accommodate those who live near the centre of the town." The town accepted the report and empowered the school committee to procure "a suitable piece of land whereon to erect a School house as proposed by the Inhabitants of Ward No. 7 and that they proceed to build said school house and to establish a writing and English grammar school with all convenient speed."

A piece of land was bought of Mr. Lyman, at the corner of Chardon Street and Hawkins Street, and the schoolhouse was built in the spring of 1803. At the town meeting on May 29, 1820, a petition "that a new School House may be erected at the Westerly part of the Town" was referred to the school committee, but it was not until 1847 that a new school was built on Hawkins Street. A water color sketch of this building is in the possession of the Boston Public Library; a copy of this sketch, originally published in the *Boston Almanac of 1849,* is herewith reproduced.

The Masters of the grammar department from 1803 to 1849, in chronological order of their service, were Cyrus Perkins, Hall J. Kelley, John Frost, R. G. Parker, William Clough, Moses W. Walker, and William D. Swan. The Masters of the writing department were Benjamin Holt, Benjamin Callender, Aaron Davis Capen, and John D. Philbrick.

THE HAWES SCHOOLHOUSE ERECTED IN 1823
From the *Boston Almanac of 1849*

APPENDIX XIV

HISTORY OF THE HAWES SCHOOL IN SOUTH BOSTON

A part of Dorchester, now South Boston, was annexed to Boston in 1804 by an act of legislature, with the agreement that the proprietor of the tract should "assign and set apart three lots of land on the same for public use, viz, one lot for the purpose of a market place, one lot for a schoolhouse, and one lot for a burial-ground."

Previous to May, 1807, no school existed in this locality other than private schools. In that year the first schoolhouse was built, by the subscription of the people, on the south side of G and Dorchester Streets.

On March 14, 1811, the inhabitants of South Boston sent a petition to Boston, stating that they had paid $1000 in taxes and yet had no public school. This petition was approved by the town of Boston on May 27, 1811, at which time $300 was appropriated for the support of a school for one year. No immediate action seems to have taken place, for two more petitions were sent to the town, one on June 12, 1811, and the other on August 17 of that year.

Boston, accordingly, appointed Mr. Zephaniah Wood the Master of the school in South Boston. Five years later, on June 28, 1816, the citizens of South Boston petitioned for a further grant. The school committee then appropriated an increase of $100 and also a grant of five cords of wood.

A new building was erected in 1823 on Broadway, South Boston. The school was named the Hawes School in 1827, in honor of John Hawes, the donor of the land. A picture of this school, originally published in the *Boston Almanac of 1849*, is herewith reproduced.

440

APPENDIX XV

HISTORY OF THE SMITH SCHOOL FOR COLORED CHILDREN

The first reference to education for colored children, found in the *Town Records* and the *Selectmen's Minutes,* is dated May 15, 1798, when the selectmen gave Mr. Elisha Sylvester a permit "to open a School . . . for the Instruction of Youth more especially the African Youth, in Reading Writing & Arithmetic." The next year the selectmen, having previously received a petition from Prince Hall and others, gave a license to Mr. Nester Pendleton, a colored man, "as a Schoolmaster to Instruct their black Children . . . & to be at their expence."

The school was kept in the house of Prince Hall until it was forced to close because of yellow fever. Three years afterwards it was revived by the Rev. Mr. Morse of Charlestown, the Rev. Mr. Kirkland of Harvard College, the Rev. Mr. Channing, the Rev. Mr. Lowell, and the Rev. Mr. Emerson, who supported it for two years. It was then proposed to have the colored people hire a building; a carpenter's shop was accordingly selected where the school continued for three years. The African Baptist Church later erected a meetinghouse, the basement of which the school occupied in 1808. The ministers mentioned above supported the school, with aid from subscriptions, until 1812, when the town of Boston on May 20, 1812, voted "That the sum of Two hundred Dollars be appropriated towards maintaining a School for African children, under the direction of the School Committee." The next year, on May 24, 1813, the town again voted an appropriation of two hundred dollars, and the same vote was passed the next year at the town meeting held on May 24, 1814.

At a meeting of the selectmen on January 24, 1816, a letter from Barney Smith, brother of the late Abiel Smith, was read, containing the following extract of the will of the said Abiel Smith [Died in 1815]:

. . . that they shall collect & receive the net income thereon . . . to the maintenance & support of a school or schools under their direction for the instruction of people of color meaning Africans & their descendants, either clear or mixed, in reading writing and arithmetic . . . & if said Selectmen shall & do accept this donation within one year from the time of my decease . . . I then order my executor to transfer to them all my title to said property for the purposes aforesaid.

It is interesting to note that the selectmen waited over a year and finally on February 5, 1817, voted to appoint a treasurer to manage the fund left by Mr. Smith for the support of an African school. After this the town then took the school under its entire charge. On February 25,

1818, at a meeting of the selectmen, the chairman reported that he had "viewed the school for people of colour in Belknap street" and that he had agreed with Mr. James Walter to take the school on trial," the Board to allow him (out of the donation of Abiel Smith Esq. deceased) such sum as they shall think he deserves in addition to the $200 allowed by the School Committee." On May 20, 1818, the selectmen voted a salary to James Walter "instructor of the school for people of colour in Belknap street" and they also voted that Mrs. Walter assist her husband "to teach the children the first rudiments of education, sewing &c."

In 1834 a new schoolhouse was erected on Belknap Street [now Joy Street], which in 1835 was named the Smith School in honor of its benefactor. The picture of this new schoolhouse, originally published in the *Boston Almanac of 1849*, is herewith reproduced.

THE SMITH SCHOOLHOUSE ERECTED IN 1834
From the *Boston Almanac of 1849*

APPENDIX XVI

HISTORY OF THE BOYLSTON SCHOOL

THE BOYLSTON SCHOOLHOUSE ERECTED IN 1819
From the *Boston Almanac of 1849*

The Boylston School, named for Thomas Boylston, was established on May 25, 1818, when the town voted:

That the Town Treasurer be authorized to borrow . . . a sum not exceeding twenty thousand Dollars for the express purpose of erecting two additional School houses in the Town for the use of the Town; which schools shall be called the Boylston town Schools and that the like sum of twenty thousand Dollars from the money secured to be paid to the Town by Ward N. Boylston Esqr. arising out of the will of the late Thomas Boylston of London Esqr. deceased . . . be appropriated to the discharge of this debt.

A committee was appointed, consisting of Peter O. Thacher, Benjamin Russell, and Samuel Dorr, to redistrict the town and further systematize the schools. This committee reported that "it would improve the order of the schools if each should be considered as consisting of two divisions, one for writing and arithmetic, and the other for reading and the other branches of an English education; . . . both divisions being accommodated with separate rooms in the same building."

According to this recommendation, the Boylston School was built in 1819 in Washington Place, Fort Hill, to accommodate both the Reading School, under the mastership of Mr. John J. Stickney, and the Writing School, under the mastership of Mr. Ebenezer E. Finch. A picture of this Boylston School, originally published in the *Boston Almanac of 1849*, is herewith reproduced.

APPENDIX XVII

HISTORY OF THE PRIMARY SCHOOLS

On May 1, 1817, a number of the inhabitants petitioned the select-men for the instruction of children between four and seven years of age, requesting a town meeting on the subject. There was considerable agitation for and against the suggested establishment of primary schools.

In a report of the sub-committee against the establishment of primary schools, dated November 3, 1817, is recorded the following:

In the public Schools in this town, the children are taught the principles of the English language, and likewise the elements of Writing, Arithmetic and Geography. . . . The only qualification for admission to the public Schools is, that the child should know his letters and be able to combine syllables, and the instances are rare indeed where children have been refused admission from the want of this qualification.

At the town meeting on May 25, 1818, the application of the inhabitants for the establishment of schools for the instruction of children under seven years of age was read. A committee of nine was appointed to report at the adjournment of the town meeting. The report of this committee was accepted by the town on June 11, 1818, and $5000 was appropriated towards the establishment of primary schools.

The Primary School Board was organized on June 23, 1818, with Thomas L. Winthrop, Esq., the chairman and James Savage, Esq., the secretary. At a town meeting on May 31, 1819, the first report of the Primary School Board was read. This report was so encouraging that the appropriation for 1819 was increased to $8000 to support the twenty-eight primary schools then in operation. In 1822, the year in which Boston became a city, there were forty-two primary schools, including two for the colored population, with a total enrollment of 2205 pupils.

APPENDIX XVIII

HISTORY OF PRIVATE SCHOOLS

The study of private schools in Boston has revealed two striking facts. In the first place, the amount of private teaching is much greater than previous writers have indicated; the private teachers actually listed in any one year considerably outnumber the public teachers. In the second place, the types of schools and subjects taught show a greater diversity than previous writers have realized. There were not only dame schools and elementary schools of reading, writing, and artithmetic, but also advanced schools, vocational schools, and schools for special accomplishments. The study of private schools gives a picture of the social and literary interests of the Colonial and post-Revolutionary days in Boston.

Private schools and private instruction were carried on from at least as early as 1666. This is the earliest reference in the records. The selectmen on June 26, 1666, recorded the following: "Mr Jones one the 28:3mo :1666 being sent for by the Select men for keep^g a schoole and being required to performe his promise to the Towne in the Winter to remoue himselfe and famyly in the springe: And forbideng to Keep schools any longer."

There may have been earlier private schools of which no records exist. Edward Howes wrote a letter to John Winthrop, Jr., on February 25, 1644, from the Ratcliffe Free School, England, saying that he desired to purchase land in Boston on which to build a "Mathematicall Schoole." There is no further evidence, however, that the school was established.

Public primary schools for children between four and seven years of age were not established until 1818. Since reading ability was a requirement for admission to the public writing schools, it follows that private elementary instruction was a necessity until 1818. As late as 1817 there were 164 private schools, 135 of which were taught by women. Thus we see that the school system in Boston was not, strictly speaking, all public until the establishment of these public primary schools in 1818.

These private schools were entirely informal as to their curricula. The list of subjects, given below, represents the entire range of studies and not the curriculum of any one school.

Dame Schools
    Children were taught, by means of the hornbook, the alphabet and simple rudiments of reading.

Schools For Teaching Elementary Subjects
  Reading, writing, and arithmetic
  English grammar and composition
  Literature
Schools For Teaching Advanced Subjects
  Classical languages
  Modern languages
  Pure mathematics and applied mathematics
  Navigation
  Sciences
  History
  Natural philosophy
  Law
  Medicine
Schools For Teaching Vocational Subjects
  Bookkeeping and accounting
  Shorthand
Schools For Teaching Special Accomplishments
  Dancing
  Manners
  Fencing
  Music
  Singing
  Drawing, engraving, and printing
  Sewing, embroidery, knitting, and trimmings
  Riding

APPENDIX XIX

LIST OF PRIVATE TEACHERS IN BOSTON FROM 1630-1822
COMPILED FROM THE *TOWN RECORDS* AND
SELECTMEN'S MINUTES

Jones, M[r].
> On June 26, 1666, license not granted to continue to teach "a schoole."

Howard, Mr. Will
> On April 29, 1667, license granted to teach "childeren to writte and to keep accounts."

Canon, Mr. Robt
> On August 31, 1668, license granted to "keepe schoole."

Cleate, Charles
> On July 29, 1678, listed as a "Dancing Mast[r]."

Haynes, Wm.
> On July 29, 1680, listed as a "writinge Master."

Haynes, William
> On April 25, 1681, listed as a "schoolmaster."

Tippinge, Henery
> On October 30, 1682, listed as a "school master."

Stepny, Francis
> On September 24, 1685, listed as a "Dancinge Master."

Sheafe, Jacob
> On June 9, 1712, license granted to teach youth "to write &c."

Goddard, Edw[d]
> On June 9, 1712, license granted to teach youth "to write &c."

Mills, Edw[d]
> On September 8, 1712, license granted "to Exercise the Keeping of School."

Harrise, Owen
> On September 8, 1712, license granted "to Exercise the Keeping of School."

Taper, Hannah
> On September 8, 1712, license granted "to Exercise the Keeping of School."

Stanhope, Mr. R.
> On January 31, 1714/15, license not granted to continue to keep a "Publick Danceing School."

Sanderline, John
> On March 20, 1715/16, license granted to teach "Navigation, writing and Arithmatick."

Stanhope, Rivers
>   On April 3, 1716, license not granted to keep a "School of manners or Danceing School."

Enstone, Edwd
>   On April 3, 1716, license not granted to keep a "School of manners or Danceing School."

Foster, W^m
>   On July 12, 1716, listed as a "School Master."

Granger, Sam^ll
>   On January 27, 1719/20, license granted to teach "writeing, Logick & Merchants Acco^ts."

Procter, John
>   On November 26, 1722, license granted to teach "Writing, Cyfering &c."

Swinerton, John
>   On July 26, 1725, license granted to teach "Reading wrighting."

Phillips, Caleb
>   On December 6, 1727, license granted as a "Teacher of Short Hand."

Langlaserie, Lovis
>   On October 21, 1730, license granted "to keep a School for Teaching and Instructing in the french Tongue."

Champion, Richard
>   On January 12, 1730/31, license granted to teach "writing, Arechmetick . . . Navigation . . . Mathamaticks."

Phipps, Mr. C.
>   On June 20, 1733, license granted to teach "Writing and Cyphering."

Grainger, Thomas
>   On January 16, 1733/34, license granted to carry on his father's school, "under the Inspection of Mr. Andrew Le Mercier."

Brownell, George
>   On August 14, 1734, license granted to teach youth "Reading, Writing, Cyphering, Dancing, and the use of the Needle."

Oliver, Capt. Nathanael
>   On March 4, 1734/35, license granted to teach "Children Or youth in Reading, Writing, Or any Other Science."

Brownell, m^r.
>   On July 28, 1735, license granted to teach youth "Reading, Writing, Cyphering, Dancing and the use of the needle."

Williams, Rev. m^r. Nathanael
>   On December 10, 1735, license granted to teach "Children or youth in Reading, Writing or any other Science."

Kent, Mr. Joseph
>   On October 6, 1736, license granted to teach "Youth &c. in Mathematical Arts and Sciences."

Hincke, Mrs. Elizabeth
> On March 30, 1737, license granted to teach children "Sewing, in Philligree and Writing."

North, m^{rs}. Rebekah
> On April 13, 1737, license granted to teach children "Reading, and the Use of the Needle."

Scammel, m^r.
> On December 7, 1737, license not granted to continue to teach "a Mathematical School."

Pelham, Mr. Peter
> On December 28, 1737, license granted to teach children "Reading, Writing, Needle work, Dancing . . . Painting upon Glass &c."

Baker, Mr. Thomas
> On April 5, 1738, license granted to teach "Reading, Writing and Arithmetick."

Swan, Mr. Ebenezer
> On August 16, 1738, license granted to teach "Writing, Arithmetick and Merchants Accounts."

Greenwood, m^r. Isaac
> On September 20, 1738, license granted to teach youth and others "Mathematicks, and other parts of Learning."

Turner, m^r. Ephraim
> On February 14, 1738/39, license granted to teach children and others "Dancing, in the House where m^r Brownell lately kept his School."

Leddel, Mr. John
> On April 11, 1739, license granted to teach children and others "Writing, arithmetick, Geometry, Algebra &c."

Linch, m^r Cornelius
> On November 19, 1740, license granted to teach "Reading Writing Arithmetick Navigation &c."

Holbrook, m^r. Abia, Junr.
> On May 6, 1741, license granted to teach "Writing and Arithmetick"

Hovey, mr. James
> On September 1, 1742, made application to teach "Grammar Arithmetick & divers Sorts of Writing." On September 22, 1742, license granted to keep "a School."

Prince, mr. Nathan
> On February 28, 1742/43, license granted to teach "any Persons . . . In Arithmetick, The Elements of Geometry & Algebra, in Trigonometry & Navigation, In the Arts of Dialling, Surveying, Gauging & other kinds of mensuration; In Astronomy & Geography with the Use of the Globes & in Several Kinds of the Projection of the Sphere As also in the General Principles & Rules of Fortification & Gunnery together with Lectures on History & Natural Philosophy."

Dukes, m^r. James
> On October 5, 1743, license granted "to Open a School . . . for teaching Children to Dance & for his Wifes teaching needle Work."

Swinnerton, John
> On May 9, 1744, license not granted to keep a "Free School for the learning of Children to Spell & Read."

Holbrook, m^r. Abia
> On August 1, 1744, license granted to teach youth "Rules of Psalmody."

Gebande, m^r. Peter
> On August 15, 1744, license not granted to teach "Latin & French Languages."

Trevett, M^r. John
> On September 12, 1744, license not granted to teach "Writing & Arithmetick."

Cheever, Mr. Edward (from Lynn)
> On April 19, 1749, made application to teach youth "the Latin Tongue to Read, Write and Cyper." On May 24, 1749, license granted "to keep a School to Teach Children to Read in the English Tongue."

Leach, Mr. John
> On May 24, 1749, license granted to teach the "Art of Navigation and other Branches of the Mathematicks."

Green, M^r. Richard
> On July 30, 1753, license granted to teach "Writing Arithmetick &c."

Holbrook, M^r. Samuel
> On August 1, 1753, license granted to "improve the School (Queen Street Writing School) out of School hours." On August 15, 1754, license granted "to open a private School for the instruction of Children in Writing and Arithmetick."

Procter, M^r. John, jun^r.
> On August 9, 1754, license granted "to have the improvement of the School (Queen Street Writing School) out of School-hours."

Brett, M^r.
> On October 20, 1756, made application "to Open a School for Teaching the French Tongue."

Vinal, M^r. John
> On April 15, 1761, license granted "to open a private School . . . for the teaching of Writing & Arithmetick, out of School Hours."

Ross, M^r. Vere
> On April 20, 1762, made application "to open a School under M^r. Turners Dancing Masters House, for the Instruction of Youth in the Mathematicks."

Oliver, Nathaniel, Esq.
On June 1, 1764, license granted "to open a private School . . . for the Education of Youth, in such Arts and Sciences as are within his Capasity."
Shannon, James (from Annapolis)
On June 23, 1764, listed as "a Schoolmaster."
Venables, Richard
On August 21, 1765, license not granted to keep "a Dancing School at the Green Dragon Tavern."
Connell, James (from Greenock)
On April 16, 1766, listed as "a School master."
Pope, M^r. William (from Burmuda)
On September 17, 1766, made application to teach youth "Dancing and Fencing" and, on September 24, 1766, license granted.
Barry, M^r. (from Ireland)
On September 29, 1766, listed as a "School Master."
Dorson, Tim^y (from Ireland)
On September 29, 1766, listed as a "Schoolmaster."
Scott, Willm (from Ireland)
On September 29, 1766, listed as a "School Master."
Osborne, M^r. Patrick Mathew (from Quebec)
On September 14, 1767, listed as a "School Master."
Mitchell, M^r. (from Connecticut)
On May 23, 1768, listed as a "Schoolmaster."
Elott, M^r. John (from N. Carolina)
On June 9, 1768, listed as a "School-master."
Pope, M^r. William
On January 3, 1770, made application to keep a "Dancing & Fencing School."
Curtis, M^r.
On May 2, 1771, license granted to keep a "dancing School."
Delile, Louis
On June 24, 1772, made application to teach "y^e. French Language."
Ward, M^r.
On September 23, 1772, license granted to teach children "to Read &c."
Vaidale, Francis (from Tours)
On March 16, 1774, made application "to teach French."
Payne, M^r. William
On August 10, 1774, made application to teach "English Grammar Writing & Arithmetick."
Shimmin, M^r. Charles
On April 28, 1779, license granted to teach "Writing &c. at the House lately improved by M^r. Payne."

Pond, M^r. Enoch

On July 7, 1780, recorded as teaching "a School" without a license. On July 12, 1780, made application and license granted "to open an English Grammar School."

Dennie, M^r.

On December 20, 1780, the selectmen appointed a committee to confer with him "relative to the hire of a Chamber . . . he has lately purchased, for a School."

Leach, John

On May 23, 1781, listed as a "Schoolmaster." On October 31, 1781, on January 21, 1784, and on April 17, 1786, also listed as a "Schoolmaster."

Lemonier, Phineas Solomon

On October 31, 1781, was forbidden "to keep School" without a license.

Pullaen, M^r.

On October 31, 1781, was forbidden "keeping School" without a license.

Byles, M^r. Elisha

On November 14, 1781, license granted "for his Wife to open a School for teaching Children Reading &c."

Bingham, M^r. Caleb

On May 12, 1784, license granted to teach "young Ladys in the useful branches of Reading writing &c."

Mary, M^r. John

On May 14, 1784, license not granted to keep "a french School."

Shermin, Mr.

On May 27, 1784, listed as a "School Master."

China, M^r.

On June 2, 1784, made application "to open a School."

Brightmann, M^r. Joseph

On July 26, 1784, license granted to teach youth "to write Cypher, English Grammar &c."

Richards, M^r. George

On August 18, 1784, made application to teach "reading writing, Arithmetic & English Grammar." On August 25, 1784, license granted.

Sutherland, Charlotte and Jane Caroline

On September 1, 1784, license granted "to keep a School for teaching Young Ladys to embroidering work &c."

Jastram, M^r.

On February 9, 1785, license granted to teach "the French language."

Pope, M^r. John

On September 14, 1785, license granted to teach "Reading, Writing, Arithmetic & Branches of the practical Mathematicks."

Ticknor, Elisha

On October 5, 1785, made application to keep "a private School." On October 12, 1785, license granted to teach youth "Grammar & Arithmetick."

Simpson, M^r. Matthew

On June 21, 1786, license granted "to keep a School . . . for the Instruction of Youth of both Sexes in Writing Arithmetic & Mathmatticks."

Leach, M^r. James

On August 28, 1786, made application to teach "Arithmetick on Evenings." On September 13, 1786, license granted to teach youth "Arithmetick & other branches of Mathematicks." On October 4, 1786, not allowed "to improve the North Grammar School for Evening Instruction."

Campbell, M^r. Andrew

On November 7, 1786, license granted to teach "Writing Reading &c."

Montague, M^r.

On November 15, 1786, license granted to teach "a singing Company."

Hawkes, M^r. Elkanah

On March 21, 1787, license not granted to keep a "private School." On March 26, 1787, license granted to be "an Assistant to M^r. Shimmins." On August 29, 1787, license granted "to open an Evening School for the Instruction of Youth in Writing &c." In May, 1788, license granted to teach youth "Writing &c."

Carleton, M^r. Osgood

On August 1, 1787, license granted to teach "the Mathematicks— and that only."

Nutting, M^r. John

On August 1, 1787, not allowed to continue to teach "reading & writing" without a license.

Revaut, Monsieur

On August 1, 1787, not allowed to continue to teach "the French Language" without a license. On August 8, 1787, license granted.

De Nancrede, M^r.

On September 24, 1787, license granted to teach the "French Language."

Griffith, M^r. John

On November 19, 1788, license granted to teach "Dancing."

Davis, Nathan
>On April 7, 1790, license granted to open "a private School for teaching Grammar &ᶜ. &ᶜ."

Raymer, Betsy and Ammy
>On May 19, 1790, license granted to teach "reading & sewing."

Bishop, Mʳ. Abraham
>On March 30, 1791, license granted to keep a "private School."

White, Mʳ. William
>On August 31, 1791, license granted to open "a private School in State Street, lately improved by Mʳ. Bishop, for the instruction of Youth in Writing Arithmatick & English Grammar."

Dearborn, Mʳ. Benjamin
>On September 7, 1791, license granted to teach "Youth of both Sexes in the variuos branches of a polite & useful education."

Dana, Mʳ. Joseph
>On October 5, 1791, license granted "to open a School . . . for the Instruction of Youth in the branches taught in the public Schools."

Nancrede, Mʳ. Joseph
>On December 21, 1791, made application "for the use of Mʳ. Binghams School Room four Evenings in a Week, for teaching the French Tongue." On December 28, 1791, license granted.

Carter, Mʳ. James
>On March 12, 1792, made application to keep a private school. On May 10, 1792, the town voted "That the several School masters cannot, . . . be permitted to keep a private school, until after the hours of the public school. . . ."

Goodhue, Mʳ. Samuel Bartlet
>On March 20, 1793, license granted to teach "Writing &c."

Goyneau, Mʳ. Bᵈ.
>On September 24, 1794, license granted to teach "the French Language."

Nadan, Mʳ.
>On September 10, 1794, license granted to let "a Story over the South Reading School . . . as a Dancing School . . . provided it is not improved in School hours."

Nichols, Mʳ. Francis
>On March 25, 1795, license granted "to open a private School . . . for the Instruction of Young Persons in English Latin Mathematics & Natural Philosophy & in such other parts of Learning as he may think fit."

Everit, Mʳ. David
>On September 16, 1795, license granted to teach youth "English & Latin Grammar, Writing & Arithmetic."

Duport, M[r].
>On December 30, 1795, license granted to keep a "School for dancing."

Ruddock, M[r]. Samuel A.
>On August 24, 1796, license not granted to keep an "Accounting School."

Sales, M[r]. (Professor of Languages)
>On September 7, 1796, license not granted to keep "a French Evening School in the Center Reading School."

Sylvester, M[r]. Elisha
>On May 15, 1798, license granted "to open a School . . . for the Instruction of Youth more especially the Affrican Youth, in Reading Writing & Arithmetic."

Pendleton, M[r]. Nester ("a black man")
>On May 1, 1799, license granted "as a Schoolmaster to Instruct their black Children."

Ring, M[r].
>On June 11, 1799, license granted to teach "reading, writing, & Arithmetik."

Thatcher, M[r]. Stephen
>On May 7, 1800, license granted "as a keeper of a private School."

Clark, M[r]. Josiah
>On May 7, 1800, license granted "as a keeper of a private School."

Aikin, M[r]. Joseph
>On May 7, 1800, license granted "as a Keeper of a private School."

Wyman, M[r].
>On April 30, 1800, listed as keeping a "private School" without a license. On June 11, 1800, ordered "to desist from keeping a School . . . not having produced recommendations."

Whitney, M[r]. John
>On August 26, 1801, license granted to keep "a private School."

Perkins, M[r]. Cyrus (from Bridgewater)
>On October 6, 1802, license granted to keep "a private School."

Hewes, M[r]. Robert
>On September 7, 1803, license not granted "for the use of Faneuil-hall as a School to teach the exercise of the broad Sword."

Hull, M[r]. Nathan
>On April 30, 1810, license granted to teach "the mathematics."

Oliver, M[r]. Daniel Greenleaf
>On September 30, 1811, license granted to teach "the English, Latin & Greek languages."

Rand, M[r]. Benjamin
>On October 9, 1811, license granted to teach "Latin, Greek and English languages."

APPENDIX XX

LIST OF PRIVATE TEACHERS IN BOSTON FROM 1630-1822 COMPILED FROM OLD NEWSPAPERS, MANUSCRIPTS, AND SUFFOLK COUNTY PROBATE RECORDS

Name	Dates
Appleton, Samuel	1786
Beek, John	1762
Burr, Peter	1693-1694
Chamberlain, Theophilus	1768
Corlett, William	1767
Dassett, Joseph	1692-1693
Druitt, John	1773-1789
Elphinstone, William	1755
Felton, Nicholas	1749
Fisher, Dr. John Carlton	1820
Green, John	1706-1709
Green, Deacon Samuel	1819-1821
Griffith, John	1764-1774
Hodgson, John	1774
Hogan, Cornelius	1763
Joan, James	1768-1770
Lewis, Charles	1730
Mackay, George	1754
Mc Alpine, Donald	1769-1774
Parker, Caleb	1820
Pateshall, Richard	1754-1767
Pigott, Nathaniel	1728
Rawlins, John	1715
Regnier, ———	1773-1775
Rogers, Peter	1767
Royse, ———	1762
Sanford, John	1674
Suckling, George	1751
Tymms, Browne	1718
Ward, Joseph	1769-1772
Warren, Abraham	1775
Webster, Ezekiel	1800
Williams, ———	1762
Williams, Mrs. Nathaniel	1711

APPENDIX XXI

LIST OF PUBLIC AND PRIVATE TEACHERS IN BOSTON COMPILED FROM THE *TOWN DIRECTORIES,* 1789-1822

Name	*Occupation*	*Dates*
Adams, Lydia K.	Schoolmistress	1818-1821
Adams, Penelope	Schoolmistress	1796-1803
Aeortez, G. M.	Teacher of Spanish, French, Latin, and Greek	1821
Aiken, Joseph	Schoolmaster	1803
Alden, Timothy	Ladies academy	1809
Algers, Israel	Academy	1820
Algier, Israel	Schoolmaster	1822
Allen, Thaddeus	Schoolmaster	1821-1822
Allen, Thomas	Schoolmaster	1820
Andrews, Mary C.	Schoolmistress	1816
Appleton, Hannah	Schoolmistress	1820
Artiguenave, Joseph	Professor of French	1820-1822
Asylum for indigent boys		1822
Asylum for female orphans		1822
Aves, Meribeth	Schoolmistress	1810-1816
Babb, Lois	Schoolmistress	1810-1822
Bacon, Patty	Schoolmistress	1798
Bacon, Susan	Governess of female asylum	1810-1822
Badger, Mary	Schoolmistress	1800
Badger, Rebecca	Schoolmistress	1813-1822
Badger, Willard	Schoolmaster	1813-1822
Badger, William	Schoolmaster	1818-1821
Bagnell, Sarah	Schoolmistress	1810-1820
Baily, Eliza	School for young ladies	1821
Baker, Ann	Schoolmistress to female asylum	1803
Baker, Anna	Schoolmistress	1800
Baker, Elisha	Schoolmaster	1813
Baker, Henrietta M.	Schoolmistress	1813
Bale, Catharine	Schoolmistress	1798
Ball, Maria V.	Schoolmistress	1800-1813
Ballard, Mary	Schoolmistress	1822
Bancroft, Mary	Schoolmistress	1818
Barber, Susan F.	Schoolmistress	1818
Barber, Susannah	Schoolmistress	1822
Bark, Lavinia P.	Schoolmistress	1822

Name	Occupation	Dates
Barker, George	Schoolmaster	1805
Barrell, Anna	Instructress	1798
Bass, Abiel	Schoolmaster	1821
Batchelor, Ann	Schoolmistress	1798
Battelle, Anna	Instructress	1798-1803
Beck, Frederick	Schoolmaster and accountant	1818-1822
Belcher, John H.	Schoolmaster	1818-1822
Bell, Mary Ann	Schoolmistress	1821-1822
Bell, Sarah	Schoolmistress	1810
Bent, Mary Ann	Schoolmistress	1813
Biglow, William	Schoolmaster	1805-1813
Billings, William	Singingmaster	1796-1798
Bingham, Caleb	Schoolmaster	1789
Blaney, Elizabeth	Schoolmistress	1820-1822
Boardman, Lydia	Schoolmistress	1820
Bonner, Mary	Schoolmistress	1807
Bonner, Ruth	Schoolmistress	1809-1810
Bonner, Sarah	Schoolmistress	1813-1816
Bonynge, Elizabeth	Schoolmistress	1796
Bothaw, Mary	Schoolmistress	1809-1813
Boucher, Sally	Schoolmistress	1807
Boucher, Sarah	Schoolmistress	1798-1800; 1810-1813; 1818-1820
Bourgoin, Joseph	Teacher of languages	1816-1818
Bouve, Elizabeth	Schoolmistress	1800
Bowen, John B.	Schoolmaster	1822
Bowles, Samuel	Usher of Hawkins Street School	1821
Bradford, Mary	Schoolmistress	1796
Bridge, Nathaniel	Schoolmaster	1810-1820
Bridge, Rachel	Schoolmistress	1816-1818
Brightman, Joseph	Schoolmaster	1789
Brown, Betsey	Schoolmistress	1821
Brown, David L.	Drawing academy	1818-1822
Brown, E. & H.	Academy	1813-1821
Brown, Eliza	Schoolmistress	1813-1821
Brown, Hannah	Schoolmistress	1813-1821
Brown, Tryphena	Schoolmistress	1818-1822
Buck, Mary Ann	Schoolmistress	1807-1813
Buckingham, Joseph T.	Schoolmaster	1816
Burr, Rev. Jonathan	Academy	1818
Burrill, Lemuel	Schoolmaster	1820
Burroughs, Rebecca	Schoolmistress	1810;1816
Burton, Mrs.	Schoolmistress	1796

Name	*Occupation*	*Dates*
Burton, Rebecca	Schoolmistress	1798;1807
Burton, Alice	Schoolmistress	1798;1807
Butterfield, Susanna	Schoolmistress	1813
Callahan, Lucretia	Schoolmistress	1816
Callender, Benjamin	Writing academy	1821
Calvary, Mary A.	Schoolmistress	1820
Campbell, Andrew	Schoolmaster and teacher of bookkeeping	1789-1821
Campbell, Hannah	Matron of asylum for indigent boys	1816-1822
Cannata, A.	Fencing master	1818-1820
Cannell, Rebecca	Schoolmistress	1803
Capt, John S.	Teacher of French	1796-1798
Carey, Sarah L.	Schoolmistress	1822
Carleton, Osgood	Teacher of mathematics	1789-1813
Carlisle, Eliza	Schoolmistress	1816
Carter, James	Schoolmaster	1789-1796
Carter, Joseph	Dancing master	1809-1822
Cazneau, Margaret	Schoolmistress	1796-1803
Cazneau, Susannah	Teacher of primary school	1821
Chamberlain, Benjamin	Schoolmaster	1816-1818
Chandler, Abigail	Schoolmistress	1803-1805
Chandler, Joanna	Schoolmistress	1818-1820
Chaplin, Elizabeth	Schoolmistress	1820-1821
Chapman, Eliza	Schoolmistress	1821
Cheney, Samuel	Schoolmaster	1789-1800
Chessman, Mary	Schoolmistress	1813
Chessman, Sarah	Schoolmistress	1813
Child, Isabella	Schoolmistress	1813
Child, Simeon	Schoolmaster	1822
Child, Susan	Schoolmistress of charity school	1820-1822
Clapp, Elisha	Schoolmaster under First Church	1810-1818
Clark, Amos	Schoolmaster	1816-1818
Clark, Josiah	Schoolmaster	1800
Clark, Lydia	Schoolmistress	1798
Clark, Susannah	Schoolmistress	1796
Cleall, Rebecca	Schoolmistress	1820
Clough, Nancy	Schoolmistress	1816
Cobb, Enos	Writing master	1821
Cobb, Gershom	Writing master	1821
Colburn, Edmund	Schoolmaster	1818
Colburn, Warren	Writing master	1821-1822

Name	*Occupation*	*Dates*
Conant, Peter	Schoolmaster	1820-1822
Cook, Susan F.	Schoolmistress	1821-1822
Cordwell, Elizabeth	Schoolmistress	1810-1820
Cotting, Rev. John R.	Preceptor of the academy on Salem Street	1816-1820
Crocker, Mary	Schoolmistress	1809
Cross, Sarah	Schoolmistress	1818
Croswell, William	Teacher of navigation	1798-1807
Cummings, Jacob A.	Schoolmaster	1810
Cushing, Mary	Schoolmistress	1809-1813
Dam, Leader	Writing instructor	1816-1822
Davidson, Andrew C.	Schoolmaster	1822
Davis, Eleanor	Treasurer of female asylum	1822
Davis, Elizabeth [Eliza]	Boarding school 1809-1813;	1816-1822
Davis, Nathan	Grammar schoolmaster, Bennet Street	1789
Davison, Andrew G.	Schoolmaster	1820-1821
Dawes, Mrs. ———	Ladies academy	1809
Dearborn, Benjamin	Schoolmaster and auctioneer	1796-1798
Degrass, Monsieur	Fencing master	1821
Delarue, Sarah	Schoolmistress	1798-1803
Deon, Frederick	Fencing master	1822
Dickinson, William	Schoolmaster	1816
Dix, Sarah	Schoolmistress	1822
Doane, Eliza	Young ladies academy	1821
Doble, Mary	Schoolmistress	1796,1822
Doggett, ———	Schoolmistress	1821
Dorothy, Mary	Schoolmistress	1818
Doubleday, Mary	Schoolmistress	1796-1820
Douglass, Elizabeth	Schoolmistress 1803-1805;	1810-1813
Dunn, Mary	Schoolmistress	1813-1818
Dupee, Elias	Schoolmaster	1789
Dupee, Grace	Schoolmistress	1798
Duplessis, Mrs. Emilia	Teacher of French	1810-1820
Duport, Landrin Peter	Dancing master	1796-1798
Durang, Jacob	Dancing master at Boylston Hall	1813
Durivage, Francis S.	Ladies academy on Franklin Street	1822
Draper, Susanna	Schoolmistress	1789-1810
Druit, Eleanor	Boarding school	1798
Druitt, John	Ladies boarding school	1789
Dyer, Jane	Schoolmistress and tailoress	1813-1818

Name	Occupation	Dates
Eastman, Luke	Schoolmaster	1821
Eaton, Elizabeth	Schoolmistress	1813-1818
Eaton, Mary	Schoolmistress	1818-1822
Eayrs, Sarah	Schoolmistress	1813-1818
Edes, Eliza	Schoolmistress	1818
Edes, Sarah	Schoolmistress	1798-1803
Edwards, Mary	Schoolmistress	1803
Eleck, Sarah	Schoolmistress	1813
Ellenwood, Henry S.	Academy	1820-1821
Elmer, Vallentine	Writing school	1821
Emerson, Benjamin D.	Schoolmaster	1822
Emerson, Charlotte	Schoolmistress	1821-1822
Emerson, William	Schoolmaster	1822
Emmons, Mary	Schoolmistress	1800
Emmons, Ruth	Schoolmistress	1796-1798
English, Elizabeth	Schoolmistress	1796-1822
Everett, James	Schoolmaster	1816
Falconi, John	Dancing master	1813
Farnum, Louisa	Schoolmistress	1820
Farnum, Charlotte	Schoolmistress	1820
Farrar, Ephraim H.	Schoolmaster	1822
Farrington, Eliza	Schoolmistress	1813-1816
Fauchier, John B.	Teacher of French	1810
Faucon, Nicholas	Teacher of French	1806-1813
Fessenden, John	Schoolmaster	1805-1813
Field, Mary	Schoolmistress	1805-1821
Fisk, Mary	Schoolmistress	1821
Flagg, Hannah	Schoolmistress	1810-1821
Flinn, Mrs.	Schoolmistress	1789
Floyd, Rachel	Schoolmistress	1818-1822
Foot, Sarah	Schoolmistress	1800
Fox, Margaret	Schoolmistress	1820
Fox, Mercy	Schoolmistress	1810-1816
Fracker, Charlotte	Schoolmistress	1820
Frazer, Ignatius C.	Dancing master	1800
French, Elizabeth	Schoolmistress	1813
French, Nancy	Schoolmistress	1821
Frye, Enoch	Schoolmaster	1822
Geyer, Mary	Schoolmistress	1816
Gill, Moses	Schoolmaster	1813-1822
Goddard, Rebecca	Schoolmistress	1820
Goodenough, Julia	Schoolmistress	1816-1818
Gordon, Mary	Schoolmistress	1822

Name	*Occupation*	*Dates*
Gould, Benjamin A.	Principal of Public Latin School	1822
Gowen, Mary	Schoolmistress	1818
Gragg, William	Schoolmaster	1822
Groupner, Gottlieb	Teacher of music at Mrs. Rowson's academy	1809-1818
Gray, Hannah	Schoolmistress	1803-1822
Greeley, Samuel	Schoolmaster	1816-1822
Green, Amey	Schoolmistress	1796
Green, Elizabeth	Schoolmistress	1803; 1813-1816
Green, Lucy H.	Schoolmistress	1818
Green, Mr. ————	Schoolmaster	1822
Griffith, Mary	Teacher of primary school	1822
Griffiths, Mr. ————	Dancing master	1789
Guliker, Elizabeth	Schoolmistress	1821-1822
Hager, Maria	Schoolmistress	1822
Hale, David	Academy	1821
Hall, George	Schoolmaster	1813
Hall, Mary	Schoolmistress	1816-1822
Hall, Mehitable	Schoolmistress	1813
Hammand, Jane	Schoolmistress	1813
Hansell, Hannah H.	Teacher of primary school	1821-1822
Harlow, Elizabeth	Schoolmistress	1820-1821
Harriot, Mary	Schoolmistress	1796-1803; 1807; 1810-1816
Harris, Hannah	Schoolmistress	1800
Harris, Sarah	Schoolmistress	1813-1816
Harris, Susan	Charity school of Mr. Lowell's Society	1821
Haskell, Ezra	Schoolmaster	1822
Haskell, John	Schoolmaster	1806-1818
Haslett, Elizabeth	Schoolmistress	1796-1798; 1809-1822
Haslett, Martha	Schoolmistress	1800-1803
Haswell, Mary	Academy	1813
Hathorne, Elizabeth	Schoolmistress	1810
Hawkes, Elkanah	Private schoolmaster	1789
Hayden, Priscilla	Schoolmistress	1818-1822
Hayward, Eunice	Schoolmistress	1813-1818
Hayward, Martha	Schoolmistress	1813-1820
Heany, Miss ————	Schoolmistress	1818-1820
Heath, Elizabeth	Schoolmistress	1800-1807
Hentz, N. M.	Teacher of languages	1822
Hewes, Hannah	Schoolmistress	1796-1803

Name	Occupation	Dates
Hewes, Robert	Fencing master	1803-1818
Hewett, Eliza	Teacher of music	1822
Hewitt, James P.	Teacher of music	1813-1816
Heywood, Martha	Schoolmistress	1816
Hichborn, Eliza	Schoolmistress	1810-1818
Hill, Jonathan C.	Schoolmaster	1809;1820
Hill, Uri K.	Teacher of music	1806-1809
Hogins, Asa B.	Schoolmaster	1821
Holbrook, Elizabeth	Schoolmistress	1810-1813
Holland, Elizabeth	Schoolmistress	1805; 1810-1813
Holland, Ralph B.	Music master	1820-1821
Holt, Benjamin	Schoolmaster	1803-1822
Homans, Mary (Mary Ann)	Schoolmistress	1805; 1809-1810; 1821-1822
Homes, Ebenezer	Dancing master	1805
Holmes, Mary	Schoolmistress	1818-1822
Hooton, Mary	Schoolmistress	1805
Hope, Ann	Schoolmistress	1820-1822
Horton, Elizabeth M.	Schoolmistress	1813-1818
Howard, Dorcas	Schoolmistress	1813
Howard, Eleanor	Schoolmistress	1805-1806
Howard, Submit	Schoolmistress	1816-1820
Howe, James B.	Schoolmaster	1810-1813
Huggerford, Priscilla	Academy	1810-1822
Hunt, Mary	Schoolmistress	1800-1803
Hunt, Samuel	Master of Grammar School [Latin]	1789-1805
Huntington, Jonathan	Schoolmaster	1816-1822
Hurley, Elizabeth	Schoolmistress	1893; 1809-1810
Hyde, Hepzibah	Schoolmistress	1810-1813
Hyde, Mary	Schoolmistress	1809-1822
Ingraham, Daniel G.	Schoolmaster	1818-1822
Ingraham, Mary	Schoolmistress	1813
Jackson, George	Doctor of music	1816-1822
Jackson, P. W.	Schoolmistress	1816
Jackson, Samuel	Drawing master	1821-1822
Jackson, Thomas	Schoolmaster	1820
James, John	Schoolmaster	1816
Jenks, Elizabeth	Schoolmistress	1800-1813
Jenks, Rev. William	Schoolmaster	1818
Jennison, John T.	Schoolmaster	1800
Jennison, William	Schoolmaster	1809;1816
Jewett, Edward	Academy	1821-1822

Name	Occupation	Dates
Jewett, Sally	Teacher of primary school	1822
Jordy, Frederick	Teacher of languages	1805-1807
Keith, George	Schoolmaster	1813
Kendrick, John	Teacher of navigation	1821-1822
Kendrick, William	Teacher of navigation	1820
Kerr, Dorcas M.	Schoolmistress	1813
Kilborn, Clarissa H.	Schoolmistress	1809
Kimball, John	Singing master	1789
Kimball, Lydia	Schoolmistress	1820
Kimball, Ruth	Schoolmistress	1818-1821
Kuhn, George	Schoolmaster	1796-1816
Labottier, George	Dancing master	1806-1810
Lamb, Mary	Schoolmistress	1813
Lane, Oliver Willington	Schoolmaster	1789
Lathrop, John, Jr.	Academy	1810
Lathrop, Lucius E.	Schoolmaster	1816
Leach, John	Schoolmaster	1789
Leeds, Mary	Schoolmistress	1810-1820
Lemon, Eliza	Teacher of dancing	1820
Little, Ezekiel	Schoolmaster	1803-1820
Locke, Susan	Schoolmistress	1822
Lopaus, Hannah	Schoolmistress	1816-1818
Lord, Sarah	Schoolmistress	1796
Loring, Mary	Schoolmistress	1821
Loring, Sarah P.	Schoolmistress	1809
Low, Harriet	Academy	1821
Luce, Harriet	Schoolmistress	1822
Lynch, Elizabeth	Schoolmistress	1810
Lyon, Abner	Schoolmaster	1820
Lyon, Gardner P.	Schoolmaster	1822
Lyon, Lawson	Schoolmaster	1809-1821
Lyon, Olive	Schoolmistress	1809-1810
MacKay, Samuel	Teacher of French	1806-1818
Mallett, Francis	Teacher of music	1807-1813
Mallet, Francis D.	Dancing master	1818-1822
Mangan, Cornelius	Schoolmaster	1810
Marden, Enoch	Schoolmaster	1820
Marichaux, Monsieur	Teacher of French	1805
Martin, Enoch	Schoolmaster	1818-1820
Masi, Vincent	Dancing master	1816-1818
Mayo, Eliza	Schoolmistress	1818
McBride, Patrick	Schoolmaster	1798-1822
M'Clench, Nancy	Schoolmistress	1810-1813

Name	*Occupation*	*Dates*
M'Clure, Anna	Schoolmistress	1796
M'George, Sarah	Schoolmistress	1806-1810
Miller, Deborah	Schoolmistress	1818-1820
Mitchell, Rhoda	Schoolmistress	1813
M'Neir, Sarah	Schoolmistress	1798
Montgomery, Jane	Schoolmistress	1816
Moody, Elizabeth	Schoolmistress	1803-1816
Moody, Henrietta	Schoolmistress	1818-1821
Morey, Lucretia	Schoolmistress	1810
Morrill, Susannah	Schoolmistress	1818
Morrison, Franklin D.	Schoolmaster	1813
Morton, Eunice B.	Schoolmistress	1813
Mullikin, Joseph	Schoolmaster	1810-1818
Murch, Sarah	Schoolmistress	1813-1818
Murray, Mary	Schoolmistress	1796
Nancrede, de P. I. G.	Teacher of French	1789
Nash, Hannah	Schoolmistress	1803;1807
Newell, Andrew	Teacher of navigation	1818-1820
Newman, Mary	Schoolmistress	1822
Newmarch, Laura R.	Teacher of primary school	1821
Newton, Ann	Boarding school	1807-1810
Newton, Sarah	Schoolmistress	1806
Nichols, Francis	Schoolmaster	1798-1800
Nichols, Francis D.	Teacher of dancing	1810
Nicholson, Elizabeth	Schoolmistress	1810
Nickson, Elizabeth	Schoolmistress	1806
Orrok, Hannah	Schoolmistress	1796
Orrok, Ann	Schoolmistress	1796
Paine, William	Schoolmaster	1798-1807
Park, John, Dr.	Academy for ladies	1813-1821
Parker, Susanna	Schoolmistress	1803-1807
Parks, Dana	Teacher of dancing	1821
Parks, Mary	Schoolmistress	1810
Passage, Augustine	Fencing master	1822
Payson, Thomas	Schoolmaster	1810-1822
Pearse, Richard	Academy	1816
Peirce, Otis	Schoolmaster	1818
Peirce, Warren	Schoolmaster	1818-1821
Pemberton, Ebenezer	Schoolmaster	1810-1822
Pepper, Sarah	Schoolmistress	1796
Perkins, Cyrus	Schoolmaster	1803
Perry, Elizabeth	Schoolmistress	1798
Perry, Mary	Schoolmistress	1809-1822

Name	Occupation	Dates
Peterson, Sarah L.	Schoolmistress	1813
Phillips, Betsy	Schoolmistress	1822
Pierce, Mrs. ———	Boarding school for young ladies	1789
Plimpton, Job	Teacher of music	1821-1822
Pollard, Alice	Schoolmistress	1813-1816;1822
Pollock, George	Teacher of German flute	1822
Pope, John	Schoolmaster	1789
Prescott, Ruth	Schoolmistress	1813
Rainsford, Mary L.	Academy	1822
Raybould, Henry	Academy	1805-1809
Raymar, Anne	Schoolmistress	1810
Read, Mrs. Mary	Schoolmistress	1789-1798
Reed, Clarissa	Schoolmistress	1820
Reed, Jacob	Schoolmaster	1813
Reed, Rachel	Schoolmistress	1813-1820
Rhodes, Zachariah	Teacher of mathematics and navigation	1810-1822
Rice, Mary	Schoolmistress	1813
Rice, Sarah	Schoolmistress	1818-1820
Richards, George	Schoolmaster	1789
Rider, Margaret	Schoolmistress	1816-1822
Ridgeway, Mehitable	Schoolmistress	1800-1803
Ridgeway, Sarah	Schoolmistress	1809-1813
Ripley, Daniel B.	Schoolmaster	1806
Ripley, Maria	Schoolmistress	1821
Robb, Anna	Schoolmistress	1796-1800
Robbins, James	Schoolmaster	1818-1820
Robinson, James	Schoolmaster	1813-1822
Robinson, Mary	Schoolmistress	1813-1822
Rockwell, Rebecca	Governess of asylum	1807
Rogers, Amelia	Schoolmistress	1813-1816
Roulstone, John	Riding master	1813-1822
Rowson, Mrs. Susanna	Academy	1807-1822
Ruggles, Richard	Dancing master	1810
Sales, Francis	Teacher of French, Spanish, Italian, and Portuguese	1796-1822
Sargent, Sarah	Schoolmistress	1810-1820
Savage, Miss ———	Schoolmistress	1820
Schaeffer, George, Jr.	Teacher of music	1810
Schaffer, George	Dancing master	1809-1818
Schaffer, William	Dancing master	1807
Scholfield, Anastasia	Schoolmistress	1810

Name	*Occupation*	*Dates*
Scollay, Catherine	Academy	1810-1813
Scott, Elizabeth	Academy	1810-1822
Scott, Eunice M.	Schoolmistress	1816-1822
Seavey, Joseph	Schoolmaster	1813
Shaw, Ralph	Teacher of music	1807
Shimmin, Charles	Schoolmaster	1789
Siders, Susannah	Schoolmistress	1822
Slade, John (colored)	Singing master	1822
Slade, Lucy	Schoolmistress	1810
Sleeper, Jonathan F.	Schoolmaster	1796-1798
Small, Lydia	Schoolmistress	1806
Smith, John R.	Teacher of drawing	1809-1816
Smith, Mary	Schoolmistress	1798
Smith, Sophia	Schoolmistress	1810-1813
Snelling, Jonathan	Schoolmaster	1796-1822
Snelling, William	Schoolmaster	1816
Snow, Mrs. Deborah	Boarding school	1796-1803
Souther, Mary	Schoolmistress	1816
Spalding, Amos	Schoolmaster	1821-1822
Speed, Sarah	Schoolmistress	1810-1816
Spoffard, Hannah	Schoolmistress	1813-1816
Sprague, Abigail	Schoolmistress	1813-1818
Sprague, Phoebe	Schoolmistress	1818
S——, Georges Peter B. (*sic*)	Teacher of French	1813
Staniford, Daniel	Schoolmaster	1798-1820
Stanney, Catherine	Schoolmistress	1796-1800
Steele, Mary	Schoolmistress	1810-1816
Stetson, Miss ——	Schoolmistress	1818
Stimson, Abigail	Schoolmistress	1816-1822
Stimson, Lovet	Dancing master	1813-1822
Stockwell, Sam'l	Teacher of music	1813
Stone, Mary	Schoolmistress	1810-1820
Stone, Sarah	Schoolmistress	1821
Storrs, Nathaniel	Schoolmaster	1820-1821
Sumner, Ruth	Schoolmistress	1818
Taylor, Samuel P.	Teacher of music	1820-1822
Thatcher, Samuel C.	Schoolmaster	1805-1806
Thaxter, Mary Ann	Schoolmistress	1816-1822
Thayer, Gideon F.	Schoolmaster	1822
Thompson, Gabriel	Schoolmaster	1822
Thompson, George H.	Mathematical school	1821
Thompson, Isabella	Schoolmistress	1813-1816
Thompson, Mary	Schoolmistress	1813-1816

Name	Occupation	Dates
Thoreau, John	Schoolmaster	1822
Thorp, Sarah	Schoolmistress	1820
Thresher, George	Schoolmaster	1820
Thwing, James	Schoolmaster	1820-1822
Ticknor, Elisha	Schoolmaster	1789
Tidmarsh, Mary	Schoolmistress	1800-1805
Tileston, John	Schoolmaster	1789-1822
Tileston, Mehitable	Schoolmistress	1796-1810
Todd, Joshua	Schoolmaster	1810-1816
Topliff, Anne	Schoolmistress	1818
Townsend, Louisa	Schoolmistress	1803-1805
Tracey, Peter (colored)	Schoolmaster	1818
Trench, Nancy	Schoolmistress	1810-1822
Tringue, Peter	Teacher of fencing	1810-1822
Tromelle, William	Teacher of fencing	1810-1822
Tufts, Fanny	Schoolmistress	1816-1822
Turner, William	Teacher of dancing	1796-1822
Turrell, Sarah	Schoolmistress	1805; 1810-1818
Valentine, Elliot	Teacher of writing	1821-1822
Valentine, Elmer	Teacher of writing	1821-1822
Vallett, Mary	Schoolmistress	1813-1822
Vernon, Elizabeth	Schoolmistress	1813-1822
Vinall, John	Schoolmaster	1789
Vinton, Sarah	Schoolmistress	1818-1822
Von Hagen, Lucy	Schoolmistress	1816
Von Hagen, Peter A.	Teacher of music	1809-1810
Walcutt, Elizabeth	Schoolmistress	1803
Walcutt, Widow	Schoolmistress	1789
Waldeck, James	Schoolmaster	1818-1821
Wallis, Rachel	Schoolmistress	1809
Walsh, Michael	Schoolmaster	1818-1821
Ware, Jonathan	Teacher of Russian, Greek and French	1820
Warner, Ann B.	Schoolmistress	1813
Waterman, Thomas	Academy	1810
Waters, Sally	Schoolmistress	1810
Webb, Elisha	Schoolmaster	1810; 1820-1822
Webb, Margaret	Schoolmistress	1800-1806
Webb, Rufus	Master of the South Writing School	1798-1810;1822
Welch, Sarah	Schoolmistress	1809-1810
Wells, Prudence	Schoolmistress	1813
Wells, Ruth	Schoolmistress	1818

Name	*Occupation*		*Dates*
Whale, Thomas	Teacher of dancing		1821-1822
Whitcome, Elizabeth	Schoolmistress		1813
Whitcome, Sarah	Schoolmistress		1809
White, Margaret	Schoolmistress		1810-1816
Whiting, Abel	Schoolmaster		1822
Whiting, Elizabeth	Schoolmistress		1816
Whiting, Persis	Schoolmistress		1809-1813
Whitman, Miss ———	Schoolmistress		1813
Whitney, Abel	Schoolmaster		1816-1822
Whitney, Barnabas	Teacher of writing		1822
Whitwell, Susanna	Schoolmistress	1805-1809;	1813-1818
Wigglesworth, Charlotte	Schoolmistress		1818
Wilder, Mary	Schoolmistress		1813-1822
Williams, Hannah	Schoolmistress		1822
Williams, Jane	Schoolmistress		1818
Williams, Sarah	Schoolmistress		1816-1822
Williams, Tryphena	Governess of female asylum		1809
Wilson, Abigail	Schoolmistress		1822
Wilson, George E.	Schoolmaster		1807-1810
Wilson, Hannah	Schoolmistress		1798
Windsor, Lucv	Schoolmistress		1820-1821
Winslow, Abigail	Schoolmistress		1813
Withington, Ebenezer	Schoolmaster		1813-1822
Wolfe, Louisa	Schoolmistress		1820-1822
Wood, Zephaniah	Schoolmaster		1816
Woodman, Olivia	Schoolmistress		1818
Woods, Harriet	Schoolmistress		1821
Woodward, Susanna	Schoolmistress		1796
Wrifford, Abel	Teacher of writing		1816
Yarnald, Benjamin	Teacher of music		1809-1813

APPENDIX XXII

HISTORY OF THE SCHOOL OF MUTUAL INSTRUCTION

On July 2, 1821, the town voted to appropriate $1000 for the establishment of a "School on the System of mutual instruction," based on the Lancasterian System. In September of that year a small room was fitted up for the school in the basement of the Boylston School at Fort Hill. The school committee engaged Mr. Dale, "principal teacher of the Lancastrian schools in Albany," to organize and establish the school.

About 150 boys and girls were admitted, who with few exceptions were too old for the primary schools and unqualified to enter the grammar schools. This large class was instructed by one master, with the aid of his student monitors, in the same branches as were taught in the other elementary schools, with much less expense. With few exceptions the monitors were girls and "it is an interesting circumstance that so many boys should for so long a time have quickly received instruction from their equals of the other sex."

Here Mr. Dale continued to teach for five or six weeks, leaving it in the care of a gentleman "who appears to be well qualified to conduct it." Later records testify that his successor was Mr. William B. Fowle, who continued to conduct the school until 1822, when it was discontinued.

APPENDIX XXIII

HISTORY OF THE ENGLISH CLASSICAL SCHOOL
[ENGLISH HIGH SCHOOL]

On June 17, 1820, Mr. Samuel A. Wells offered "Resolutions" to the school committee, relative to the establishment of an English Classical School. After due consideration it was voted to refer the matter to a sub-committee of five. On November 9 of that year the school committee accepted their report and voted to establish the school. It was not until January 15, 1821, however, that the town agreed to authorize them to carry this project into effect and to revise the course of study from year to year, as they deemed expedient.

The school actually went into operation in 1821, with an enrollment of 102 boys, under the mastership of Mr. George Barrell Emerson. Soon afterwards Mr. Joshua Flint was appointed his assistant. The school occupied the upper floor of the new Derne Street Grammar School until 1824, when a new building was erected for it on Pinckney Street. In 1844 a new schoolhouse was erected on Bedford Street, to accommodate both the Boston Latin School and the English High School. In 1881 the schools were removed to Warren Avenue, the English High School occupying the Montgomery Street side of the building. It is beyond the scope of this present study to trace the subsequent history of the English High School.

APPENDIX XXIV

LIST OF THE SUBSCRIBERS TO THE SUPPORT OF THE BOSTON LATIN SCHOOLS IN 1636

On August 12, 1636, the "richer inhabitants" of the town of Boston made voluntary contributions, totaling nearly fifty pounds, for the support of "a free school master." The list of the subscribers, as recorded in the *Town Records*,[1] follows.

At a general meeting of the richer inhabitants there was given towards the maintenance of a free school master for the youth with us, Mr. Danyel Maud being now also chosen thereunto:—

The Governor, Mr. Henry Vane, Esq.,	x	1.		
The Deputy Governor, Mr. John Winthrop, Esq.,	x	1.		
Mr. Richard Bellingham,	x	l s.		
Mr. Wm. Coddington,	xxx	s.		
Mr. Winthrop, Jr.,	xx	s.		
Mr. Wm. Hutchinson,	xx	s.		
Mr. Robte. Keayne,	xx	s.		
Mr. Thomas Olyvar,	x	s.		
Thomas Leveritt,	x	s.		
William Coulbourn,	viii	s.		
John Coggeshall,	xiii	s.	iiii	d.
John Coggan,	xx	s.		
Robte. Harding,	xiii	s.	iiii	d.
John Newgate,	x	s.		
Richard Tuttell	x	s.		
Wm. Aspenall,	viii	s.		
John Sampford,	viii	s.		
Samuel Cole,	x	s.		
William Balstone,	vi	s.	8	d.
William Brenton,	——			
James Penne,	vi	s.	8	d.
Jacob Ellyott,	vi	s.	8	d.
Nicholis Willys,	——			
Raphe Hudson,	x	s.		
William Hudson,	——			
William Peirce,	xx	s.		
John Audley,	iiii	s.		
John Button,	vi	s.		

[1] This record was copied into the *Town Records* at the back of the book.

Edward Bendall,	v	s.
Isaac Grosse,	v	s.
Zakye Bosworth,	iiii	s.
William Salter,	iiii	s.
James Pennyman,	v	s.
John Pemberton,	iii	s.
John Bigges,	iiii	s.
Samuell Wilkes,	x	s.
Mr. Cotton,	——	
Mr. Wilson,	xx	s.
Richard Wright,	vi	s. viii d
Thomas Marshall,	vi	s. 8 d.
William Talmage,	iiii	s.
Richard Gridley,	iiii	s.
Thomas Savidge,	v	s.
Edward Ransforde,	v	s.
Edward Hutchinson,	iiii	s.

APPENDIX XXV

SALARIES OF MASTERS AND USHERS OF THE BOSTON LATIN
SCHOOL FROM 1635 TO 1796 COMPILED FROM THE
RECORDS OF THE TOWN, SELECTMEN,
AND SCHOOL COMMITTEE

Date	Master's Salary	House Rent	Usher's Salary
———— 1635	No record		
August 12, 1636	Nearly 50 £		
March 11, 1649/50	50 £		
June 27, 1653		Repairs 40s.	
March 26, 1666			40 £
March 14, 1669/70		8 £	
January 30, 1670/71	Grant of 10 £		
November 27, 1671			Grant of 10 £
May 29, 1693	60 £		
August 28, 1699			40 £
May 12, 1701			45 £
August 25, 1701		9 £ for rent	
		Repairs 56s.	
March 2, 1701/02			£ 11.5.0 (¼ Yr.)
May 12, 1702		£ 4.10 (½ Yr.)	
August 31, 1702			£ 22.10.0 (½ Yr.)
April 26, 1703	60 £		
April 27, 1703			45 £
June 25, 1703			80 £
March 12, 1704/05			80 £
March 11, 1705/06			80 £
March 13, 1709/10	100 £		40 £
March 12, 1710/11		House	
March 30, 1713			Increase of 10 £
June 23, 1718	Grant of 50 £		
March 14, 1720/21			50 £
March 12, 1722/23	150 £		
March 11, 1728/29			80 £
July 28, 1732			Increase of 20 £
January 9, 1733/34			80 £
March 11, 1734/35			100 £
April 28, 1736	Increase of 60 £		
March 14, 1737/38	Increase of 40 £		

Date	Master's Salary	House Rent	Usher's Salary
May 11, 1742	Increase of 50 £ Old Tenor		
May 4, 1743	Increase of 50 £ Old Tenor		Increase of 25 £ Old Tenor
May 14, 1746	Increase of 50 £ Old Tenor		
March 15, 1747	Increase of 200 £ Old Tenor		
May 9, 1749	600 £ Old Tenor		
May 15, 1750	120 £ "Lawful Money"		50 £ "Lawful Money"
May 14, 1751	120 £		50 £
March 10, 1752	120 £		50 £
May 28, 1753	120 £		50 £
May 15, 1754	120 £		50 £
May 16, 1755	120 £		60 £
May 11, 1756	120 £		60 £
May 10, 1757	120 £		60 £
May 16, 1758	120 £		60 £
May 15, 1759	120 £		60 £
May 16, 1760	120 £		60 £
May 12, 1761	120 £		60 £
May 11, 1762	100 £		60 £
May 10, 1763	120 £ & grant of 20 £		60 £
May 15, 1764	120 £		60 £
May 14, 1765	120 £		60 £ & grant of 40 £
May 26, 1766	120 £		60 £ & grant of 40 £
May 8, 1767	120 £ & grant of £13.6.8.		60 £ & grant of 40 £
May 4, 1768	120 £		60 £ & grant of 40 £
May 5, 1769	120 £		60 £ & grant of 40 £
May 8, 1770	120 £		60 £ & grant of 40 £
May 27, 1771	120 £		60 £ & grant of 40 £
May 20, 1772	120 £		60 £ & grant of 40 £
May 14, 1773	120 £		60 £ & grant of 40 £
July 19, 1774	120 £		60 £ & grant of 40 £
November 8, 1776	120 £ & grant of 80 £		
May 26, 1777	120 £ & grant of 80 £		
November 26, 1777			60 £ & grant of 40 £
December 15, 1777	Grant of 100 £		Grant of 50 £
June 3, 1778	120 £ & grant of 180 £		60 £ & grant of 80 £
November 17, 1778	Grant of 250 £		Grant of 135 £
November 23, 1778	Grant of 350 £		Grant of 175 £
July 9, 1779	1000 £ (½ Yr.)		

Date	Master's Salary	House Rent	Usher's Salary
November 30, 1779	1800 £ (½ Yr.)		
June 23, 1780	Grant of 90 £ (½ Yr.)		
May 16, 1781	90 £ (½ Yr.)		45 £ (½ Yr.)
January 7, 1782	100 £ (½ Yr.) and 735 £ credit		50 £ (½ Yr.)
March 12, 1782	100 £ (½ Yr.)		50 £ (½ Yr.)
January 2, 1783	100 £ (½ Yr.)		50 £ (½ Yr.)
July 3, 1783	200 £		100 £
April 12, 1784	230 £		
June 9, 1785	230 £		
March 22, 1786	195 £		£ 97.10.0.
May 16, 1787	195 £		£ 97.10.0.
May 21, 1788	185 £		£ 92.10.0.
May 22, 1789	35 £ (¼ Yr.)		20 £ (¼ Yr.)
December 2, 1789	35 £ (¼ Yr.)		20 £ (¼ Yr.)
1794	120 £	30 £ for rent	
1796	200 £		

APPENDIX XXVI

SALARIES OF MASTERS AND USHERS OF THE NORTH [LATIN] GRAMMAR SCHOOL FROM 1713 TO 1789 COMPILED FROM THE RECORDS OF THE TOWN AND SELECTMEN

Date	Master's Salary	House Rent	Usher's Salary
March 30, 1713	60 £		
August 18, 1713	60 £		
March 16, 1713/14	80 £		
March 14, 1714/15	80 £		
March 13, 1715/16	Increase of 20 £	15 £	
May 15, 1717		20 £	
March 10, 1718/19	100 £		
March 9, 1723/24	Increase of 30 £		
March 15, 1725/26	Increase of 30 £		
May 6, 1729	Increase of 40 £		
May 3, 1737	Increase of 80 £		
September 7, 1738			90 £
March 16, 1742/43	Grant of 100 £		Increase of 40 £
May 4, 1743	Increase of 50 £ Old Tenor		
May 3, 1745			Grant of 30 £ Old Tenor
March 15, 1747	Increase of 200 £ Old Tenor	70 £ Old Tenor	
May 15, 1750	100 £ "Lawful Money"		
May 14, 1751	120 £ "Lawful Money"		
March 10, 1752	120 £ "Lawful Money"		
May 28, 1753	120 £ "Lawful Money"		
May 15, 1754	120 £ "Lawful Money"		
May 16, 1755	120 £ "Lawful Money"		
May 11, 1756	120 £ "Lawful Money"		
May 10, 1757	120 £		
May 16, 1758	80 £		
December 13, 1758			60 £ "Lawful Money"
May 15, 1759	60 £		60 £
May 16, 1760	60 £ & grant of 20 £		60 £
May 12, 1761	80 £		60 £
May 11, 1762	80 £		60 £

Date	Master's Salary	House Rent	Usher's Salary
May 10, 1763	100 £		60 £
May 15, 1764	100 £		60 £
May 14, 1765	100 £		60 £
May 26, 1766	100 £		60 £
March 9, 1767	Grant of 100 £		
May 8, 1767	100 £		
May 4, 1768	100 £		
May 5, 1769	100 £		
May 8, 1770	100 £		
May 27, 1771	120 £		
May 20, 1772	100 £		
May 14, 1773	120 £		
March 5, 1774		30 £	
July 19, 1774	120 £		
July 9, 1779	650 £ (½ Yr.)		
November 30, 1779	1500 £ (½ Yr.)		
May 16, 1781	90 £ (½ Yr.)		
January 7, 1782	100 £ (½ Yr.)	40 £	
March 12, 1782	100 £ (½ Yr.)	20 £ (½ Yr.)	
January 2, 1783	100 £ (½ Yr.)	20 £ (½ Yr.)	
July 3, 1783	200 £	40 £	
April 12, 1784	230 £	40 £	
June 9, 1785	230 £	40 £	
March 22, 1786	195 £	40 £	
May 16, 1787	195 £	40 £	
May 21, 1788	185 £	30 £	
May 22, 1789	£ 32.10.0 (¼ Yr.)	5 £ (¼ Yr.)	

APPENDIX XXVII

APPROPRIATION FOR SALARIES FROM 1789 THROUGH 1821
COMPILED FROM TOWN RECORDS

1789-1803 Seven Schools
(Seven Masters and Six Ushers)

Date	Total
1789	£ 1288.0.0
1792	£ 1960.0.0
1794	£ 1960.0.0
1795	£ 2227.0.0
1796	$ 9400.00
1797	$ 10,000.00
1798	$ 10,000.00
1800	$ 11,100.85
*1801	$ 10,000.00 (Approximately)

1803-1818 Eight Schools
(Eight Masters and Eight Ushers)

Date	Total
1806	$ 13,000.00
1807	$ 13,300.00
1808	$ 13,300.00
1809	$ 13,300.00 and $ 1,100. (Fire wood and repairs)
1810	$ 13,800.00

1818 Primary Schools established
1821 English Classical School established

1821   Total $ 25,430.55

* In the fall of 1933, the Roving Reporter of the *Boston Herald* reported the finding, in an ancient trunk in an attic on Beacon Hill, of Charles Bulfinch's "Expense Account of the Town of Boston for the year May, 1801, to May, 1802." From this parchment document we learn the following:

"In 1801, Boston had seven schoolmasters and six ushers or undermasters. The former were paid $666.64 each with a grant of $200. The ushers received half of this total. In addition to this, $400. was appropriated for wood for the schools and $63.33 for ink and glasses."

APPENDIX XXVIII

NUMBER OF PUPILS IN THE TWO LATIN GRAMMAR SCHOOLS FROM 1738 TO 1789

COMPILED FROM THE RECORDS OF THE TOWN AND SELECTMEN

Date of Visitation	Boston Latin School Established in 1635	North Latin Grammar School Established in 1713
June 26, 1738	120 (approximate)	60 (approximate)
June 25, 1739	110	66
June 23, 1740	85	60
June 17, 1741	87	65
June 23, 1742	94	65
June 22, 1743	90 (approximate)	65
June 22, 1744	107	—
June 25, 1745	124	40
June 25, 1746	109	35
June 19, 1747	110	40
June 28, 1748	120	38
June 23, 1749	120	45
June 22, 1750	117	43
June 19, 1751	120	49
June 29, 1753	120	43
July 5, 1754	120	40
June 27, 1755	125	28
June 25, 1756	128	32
June 24, 1757	115	36
June 28, 1758	107	35
July 4, 1759	117	33
July 1, 1761	117	57
June 29, 1762	119	68
June 29, 1763	135	53
July 10, 1764	120	47
June 26, 1765	119	47
June 25, 1766	145	34
July 1, 1767	147	35
July 6, 1768	141	55
July 5, 1769	142	60
July 4, 1770	137	56

Date of Visitation	Boston Latin School Established in 1635	North Latin Grammar School Established in 1713
July 10, 1771	138	61
July 1, 1772	130	59
July 7, 1773	139	60
July 11, 1781	91	39
May ?, 1785	52	12
June ?, 1789	No record	School discontinued

APPENDIX XXIX

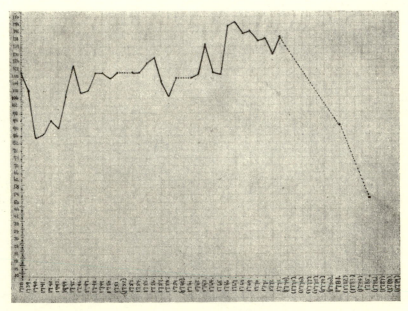

GRAPH SHOWING NUMBER OF PUPILS IN THE BOSTON LATIN SCHOOL FROM
1738 TO 1789

APPENDIX XXX

CHART SHOWING THE GROWTH OF THE BOSTON LATIN SCHOOL FROM 1789 TO 1935 COMPILED FROM THE RECORDS OF THE SCHOOL COMMITTEE, FROM THE BROADSIDE CATALOGUES, AND FROM THE ANNUAL CATALOGUES* OF THE SCHOOL

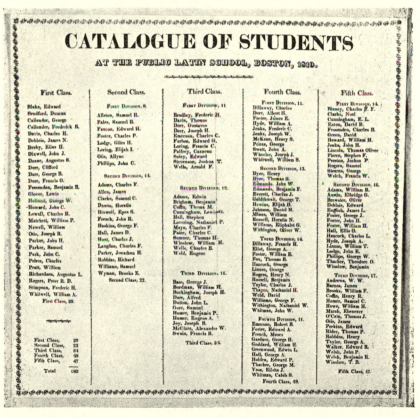

BROADSIDE CATALOGUE OF STUDENTS AT THE BOSTON LATIN SCHOOL IN 1819
Reduced from the original in the possession of the Boston Latin School, by courtesy of the Boston Latin School Association.

* The annual catalogues were not published from 1835 through 1851.

Year	Number of students	Year	Number of students
1789	No record	1831	151
1790	64	1832	170
1791	62	1833	158
1792	—	1834	160
1793	48	1835	—
1794	48	1836	—
1795	—	1837	—
1796	—	1838	—
1797	—	1839	—
1798	—	1840	—
1799	—	1841	—
1800	—	1842	—
1801	—	1843	—
1802	—	1844	—
1803	—	1845	—
1804	—	1846	—
1805	—	1847	—
1806	—	1848	—
1807	—	1849	—
1808	—	1850	—
1809	—	1851	—
1810	—	1852-1853	195
1811	—	1853-1854	204
1812	—	1854-1855	203
1813	—	1855-1856	215
1814	—	1856-1857	206
1815	—	1857-1858	194
1816	—	1858-1859	246
1817	—	1859-1860	244
1818	—	1860-1861	238
1819	180	1861-1862	267
1820	207	1862-1863	269
1821	206	1863-1864	267
1822	225	1864-1865	252
1823	237	1865-1866	283
1824	214	1866-1867	315
1825	180	1867-1868	304
1826	167	1868-1869	271
1827	170	1869-1870	250
1828	148	1870-1871	244
1829	—	1871-1872	225
1830	—	1872-1873	213

Year	Number of students	Year	Number of students
1873-1874	194	1904-1905	590
1874-1875	327	1905-1906	651
1875-1876	373	1906-1907	655
1876-1877	420	1907-1908	654
1877-1878	431	1908-1909	736
1878-1879	428	1909-1910	838
1879-1880	393	1910-1911	817
1880-1881	341	1911-1912	831
1881-1882	375	1912-1913	830
1882-1883	381	1913-1914	831
1883-1884	376	1914-1915	906
1884-1885	367	1915-1916	1040
1885-1886	383	1916-1917	988
1886-1887	434	1917-1918	961
1887-1888	467	1918-1919	1017
1888-1889	484	1919-1920	1005
1889-1890	488	1920-1921	1088
1890-1891	486	1921-1922	1259
1891-1892	470	1922-1923	1415
1892-1893	507	1923-1924	1350
1893-1894	590	1924-1925	1398
1894-1895	605	1925-1926	1469
1895-1896	648	1926-1927	1544
1896-1897	685	1927-1928	1805
1897-1898	648	1928-1929	2004
1898-1899	679	1929-1930	2170
1899-1900	666	1930-1931	2372
1900-1901	599	1931-1932	2307
1901-1902	612	1932-1933	2338
1902-1903	601	1933-1934	2238
1903-1904	597	1934-1935	2324

APPENDIX XXXI

THE TEACHING STAFF OF THE BOSTON PUBLIC LATIN SCHOOL FROM 1635 TO 1935[1]

N.B. In 1867 the Master was raised to the grade of Head Master, and the teachers were raised to the grade of Masters, Sub-Masters, or Ushers.

Name	*Position*	*Years of Service*
Appleton, Benjamin Barnard	Usher	1837
Appleton, Edward	Usher	1837-1838
Arnold, Louis Wales[2]	Junior Master	1905-1916
	Master	1916-1929
	Senior Master	1929-
Atkins, Charles Howard	Junior Master	1894-1898
Baker, Arthur Eaton	Instructor	1909-1911
	Junior Master	1911-1914
Baker, Lucas	Supervisor of Drawing	1878-1880
Barrett, Samuel	Usher	1833 [pro tem.]
Barry, Charles Alfred	Drawing Instructor	
		1870-1873; 1876-1878
Bartholomew, William Nelson	Drawing Instructor	1858-1859
Bartlett, Boyd	Instructor	1909-1911
Bateman, Frank Eliot	Junior Master	1893-1894
Beatley, James Augustus	Usher	1877-1878
	Junior Master	1881-1882
Bell, James Carleton	Master	1904-1905 [pro tem.]
Benjamin, James	Usher	1830-1832
Benson, Edwin Francis Aloysius	Master [Head of English Department]	1925-

[1] The list of Masters and Ushers from 1635 to 1822, the year in which Boston became a city, was prepared by the writer from the *Town Records* and the *Selectmen's Minutes*. The list of Head Masters, Masters, and Instructors from 1635 to 1917 was prepared by Mr. Horace Henry Morse for *Catalogue of Graduates of the Public Latin School in Boston, 1816-1917, with a List of Teachers from the Foundation of the School in 1635*, edited by Thomas Franklin Currier in 1918. The list of Head Masters, Masters, Junior Masters, and Instructors from 1917 to date was prepared by Mr. Lee Joseph Dunn, the librarian of the Boston Public Latin School.

[2] The name of Louis Wales Arnold is third in the list of twenty-three Senior Masters for the year 1934-1935.

Name	Position	Years of Service
Bentley, William[3]	Usher	1777-1779
Benyon, Lt. Col. George Henry	Instructor in Military Drill	1894; 1899-1920
Bergen, Joseph Young, Jr.	Instructor in Physics	1888-1889
Berry, George Stillman, Jr.	Junior Master 1896-1897 [pro tem.]	
Bigelow, Jacob	Usher	1808-1809
Biglow, William	Master [Head of School]	1805-1814
Bôcher, Ferdinand	French Instructor	1862-1864
Bourgeois, William Louis	Junior Master	1931-1934
Bowker, Elmer Roy	Junior Master	1917-1929
	Master [Head of Mathematics Department]	1929-
Bradford, Duncan	Usher	1826-1827
Bradford, Gamaliel	Usher	1816
Bradford, George Partridge	Usher	1828-1829
Bradford, Thomas Gamaliel	Usher	1823-1825; 1828
Brewer, George Maltby	Usher	1817-1821
Brickley, Edward Francis	Junior Master	1927-
Brooks, Phillips	Usher	1855
Buck, Augustus Howe	Master [See N.B. above]	1870-1873
Bulfinch, George Storer	Usher	1817-1818
Bulfinch, Thomas	Usher	1814-1815
Bumstead, Nathaniel Willis	Usher	1856
Burgess, Helen M.	Librarian	1926-1927
Burgess, Isaac Bronson	Junior Master	1889-1892
Burton, Richard Emerson	Teacher	1934-
Butler, Matthew Patrick	Teacher	1925-1927
Cadigan, John Joseph	Master [Head of Latin Department]	1926-
Callanan, James Aloysius Stanislaus	Teacher	1926-1927
	Junior Master	1927-
Campbell, Patrick Thomas	Junior Master	1897-1908
	Master [Head of History Department]	1908-1920
	Head Master	1920-1929
Campbell, Thomas	Junior Master	1927-1929
Campbell, William Taylor	Junior Master	1892-1903
	Master	1903-1911
Cannell, Winburn Scott	Junior Master	1921-1929
	Senior Master	1929-

[3] The dates of William Bentley's years of service, compiled by the writer from the *Town Records* and the *Selectmen's Minutes,* do not agree with Jenks's *Catalogue of the Boston Public Latin School,* published in 1886.

Name	Position	Years of Service
Capen, Charles James	Usher	1852-1867
	Sub-Master	1867-1870
	Master [See N.B. above]	1870-1909
	Leave of absence	1909-1910
Carroll, Francis Patrick	Teacher	1927-1928
	Junior Master	1928-
Carter, Frank	Teacher	Sept.-Dec., 1875
Chadwick, Joseph Webber	Usher	1866-1867
	Sub-Master	1867-1871
	Master [See N.B. above]	1871-1874
	Sub-Master	1874-1877
	Master [See N.B. above]	1877-1906
Chamberlain, Timothy Dutton	Usher	1845-1848
Chandler, Thomas Henderson	Usher	1853-1856
Cheetham, Charles Lee	Junior Master	1928-1933
	Senior Master	1933-1935
Cheever, Ezekiel[4]	Master [Head of School]	1670/71-1708
Chesley, Egbert Morse	Usher	1877-1878
	Junior Master	1878-1880
Child, David Lee	Sub-Master	1817-1821
Clapp, Henry Austin	Usher	1860-1861
Clark, Justin Wright	Usher	1818-1819
Cleary, Francis Charles	Teacher	1925-1927
	Junior Master	1927-
Cleary, Gerard Bartholomew	Teacher	1922-1924
	Junior Master	1924-
Collins, John Edward	Teacher	1926-1927
	Junior Master	1927-
Cooke, John Winthrop	Junior Master	1895-1896
Coquard, Edouard	French Instructor	1864-1866
Corson, Ralph Maurice	Junior Master	1915-1918
	Government Service	1918-1919
	Junior Master	1919-1929
	Master Ornatus	1929-
Cray, John Francis	Teacher	1926-1927
	Junior Master	1927-
Cross, Robert	Usher	1819-1820
Croswell, William[5]	Usher	1780-1782

[4] Ezekiel Cheever was appointed Master on December 29, 1670, and was installed on January 6, 1670/71.

[5] The date of William Croswell's appointment is not recorded in Jenks's *Catalogue of the Boston Public Latin School,* published in 1886.

Name	Position	Years of Service
Curry, John Joseph	Junior Master	1930-1931
	Master Ornatus	1931-
Curtin, Laurence James	Teacher	1926-1927
Cutler, Charles[6]	Usher	1794-1800(?)
Dana, Joseph, Jr.[7]	Usher	1790-1791
Danahy, John Joseph	Teacher	1925-1926
Davenport, Edwin	Usher	1848-1850
	Sub-Master	1874
Davis, Abner Harrison	Usher	1862-1863
Davis, Edward Gardiner	Usher	1820-1823
Davis, John Brazer	Usher	1815-1816
Davis, William Franklin	Sub-Master	1867-1869
Dearborn, Josiah Greene	Master [See N.B. above]	1870-1874
Denvir, Robert Francis	Teacher	1926-1927
Devotion, John	Usher	1790
Dike, James	Usher	1874-1877
Dillaway, Charles Knapp	Usher	1827-1830
	Sub-Master	1830-1831
	Master [Head of School]	1831-1836
Dimmock, William Reynolds	Usher	1855-1859
	Sub-Master	1863-1867
	Master [See N.B. above]	1867-1868
Dingley, Amasa[8]	Usher	1786-1790
Dixwell, Epes Sargent	Sub-Master	1828-1830
	Master [Head of School]	1836-1851
Dixwell, John (Née Samuel Hunt)	Usher	1801-1802
Dobbyn, John Francis	Junior Master	1927-
Doherty, Francis Raphael	Teacher	1930-1932
Dole, Frederick Howard	Instructor	1911-1912
	Junior Master	1912-1928
	Master Ornatus	1928-
Downey, James Edward	Junior Master	1905-1907
Doyle, John Joseph	Junior Master	1929-1932
	Senior Master	1932-
Dracopolis, Nicolas F.	French Instructor	1875-1876

[6] The dates of Charles Cutler's years of service, compiled by the writer from the manuscript school committee documents, do not agree with Jenks's *Catalogue.*

[7] Joseph Dana, according to Jenks's *Catalogue,* was in office between 1790 and 1795.

[8] The first name of Amasa Dingley is not definitely recorded in Jenks's *Catalogue.*

Name	Position	Years of Service
Drummey, Robert Bulman	Junior Master	1924-1932
	Senior Master	1932-
Dunbar, Samuel[9]	Usher	1724-?
Dunn, Francis DeMaurice	Junior Master	1887-1901
	Master [See N.B. above]	1901-1916
Dunn, Lee Joseph	Librarian	1928-
Eaton, Frank Herbert	Master	1891-1892 [pro tem.]
Eaton, George	Sub-Master	1857-1858
Eayrs, William Newhall	Usher	1858-1860
Eichberg, Julius	Music Instructor	1872-1880
Emery, Caleb	Sub-Master	1850-1855
Emery, Grenville Cyrus	Junior Master	1882-1888
	Master [See N.B. above]	1888-1891
	Leave of absence	1891-1892
	Master	1892-1898
Fairfield, Josiah Milton	Usher	1861-1862
Fales, Stephen	Usher	1810-1811
Falvey, John Michael	Junior Master	1929-
Farr, Theodore Parker	Junior Master Sept., 1888-Mar., 1889	
Faxon, Archer Linwood	Instructor	1909-1911
	Junior Master	1911-1929
	Senior Master	1929-
Fearing, Clarence White	Junior Master	1892-1893
Finn, Julius Gerstein	Junior Master	1929-
Fiske, Arthur Irving	Master [See N.B. above]	1873-1901
	Acting Head Master	1901-1902
	Head Master	1902-1909
	Leave of absence	1909-1910
Fitzgerald, Charles Stanislaus	Teacher	1922-1924
	Junior Master	1924-
Fitzgerald, John Bernard	Teacher	1919-1920
	Junior Master	1920-1930
	Senior Master	1930-
Fitzpatrick, Thomas Edward	Junior Master	1927-
Ford, Henry Leo	Teacher	1925-1926
Fraser, Henry Edward	Junior Master	1894-1900
Freeborn, Frank Wilton	Usher	1875-1877
	Sub-Master	1877-1878
	Junior Master	1878-1884
	Master [See N.B. above]	1884-1897

[9] The name of Samuel Dunbar is not recorded in Jenks's *Catalogue*.

Name	Position	Years of Service
French, Charles Ward	Instructor	1910-1911
	Junior Master	1911-1929
	Senior Master	1929-
Frothingham, Nathaniel Langdon	Usher	1811-1812
Gallagher, William, Jr.	Sub-Master	1877-1878
	Junior Master	1878-1884
	Master [See N.B. above]	1884-1885
Galline, Francis Edmund	Junior Master	1931-
Gamwell, Franklin Bert	Usher	1861-1862
Gardner, Francis	Usher	1831-1836
	Sub-Master	1836-1850
	Leave of absence	1850-1851
	Master [Head of School]	1851-1867
	Head Master	1867-1876
Gardner, Henry Rozalvin	Assistant Instructor	1908-1909
	Instructor	1909-1910
	Junior Master	1910-1926
	Master [Head of Latin and Greek Department]	1926-
Gardner, Nathaniel, Jr.[10]	Usher	1750-1760
Gartner, John Albert	Teacher	1922-1923
Gay, Augustine Milton	Usher	1865-1867
	Master [See N.B. above]	1867-1876
	Head Master	1876
Getchell, Frederick Gardner	Master [Head of German Department]	1928-
Gibbens, Edwin Augustus	Usher	1856-1859
Gibson, Benjamin[11]	Usher	1721/21-?
Gibson, Samuel[12]	Usher	1734-1750
Gilbert, Frank Asaph	Teacher	1923-1927
	Junior Master	1927-
Gilman, Samuel[13]	Usher	1812
Gleason, Benjamin	Usher	1806 or 1807

[10] The dates of Nathaniel Gardner, Jr.'s years of service, compiled by the writer from the *Town Records* and the *Selectmen's Minutes*, do not agree with Jenks's *Catalogue*. The records testify that he was appointed Usher on August 27, 1750, and was reappointed annually until 1760, when he was succeeded by James Lovell.

[11] The name of Benjamin Gibson is not recorded in Jenks's *Catalogue*.

[12] The dates of Samuel Gibson's years of service, compiled by the writer, do not agree with Jenks's *Catalogue*.

[13] Samuel Gilman was the author of *Fair Harvard*.

Name	Position	Years of Service
Gleason, Charles William	Teacher	1928-1929
Glover, Leon Otis	Assistant Instructor	1908-1909
	Instructor	1909-1911
	Junior Master	1911-1929
	Senior Master	1929-
Godfrey, Roland James	Junior Master	1930-1933
	Senior Master	1933-
Goodale, William Franklin	Teacher	1925-1926
	Junior Master	1926-1932
Gordon, Aaron	Junior Master	1929-
Gould, Benjamin Apthorp	Head Master	1814-1828
Grandgent, Charles Hall	Director of Modern Languages	1889-1896
Green, Joseph[14]	Usher	1722-1724
Gridley, Jeremiah[15]	Usher	1727-1733/34
Gretsch, Abraham Hosea	Junior Master	1928-1929
	Senior Master	1929-
Griffin, La Roy Freese	Sub-Master	1876-1877
Groce, Byron	Junior Master	1878-1882
	Master [See N. B. above]	1882-1907
	Head of English Department	1907-1915
Guiney, Cornelius Anthony	Teacher	1914-1915
	Junior Master	1915-1918
Hale, Charles	Usher	1851-1852
Hale, Edward Everett	Usher	1839-1841
Hale, Joseph Augustine	Usher	1859-1866
Hamer, Myron Clifton	Junior Master	1931-1933
Hamlin, Charles Joseph	Teacher	1923-1924
Harris, Francis Augustine	Sub-Master	1867-1870
Hartigan, William Albert	Teacher	1926-1929
	Junior Master	1929-1932
Hartwell, Edward Mussey	Usher	1874-1877
Haskell, John	Usher	1799(?)
	Master of Centre Reading School	1800-1818
Haynes, John	Junior Master	1898-1901
Henchman, Daniel[16]	Usher	1665/66-1670/71

[14] The name of Joseph Green is not recorded in Jenks's *Catalogue.*

[15] The dates of Jeremiah Gridley's years of service, compiled by the writer, do not agree with Jenks's *Catalogue.*

[16] The dates of Daniel Henchman's years of service, compiled by the writer from the *Town Records* and the *Selectmen's Minutes,* do not agree with Jenks's *Catalogue.*

Name	Position	Years of Service
Henderson, William Pride	Junior Master	1897-1907
	Master [Head of French Department]	1907-
Hennessey, Francis Patrick	Junior Master	1929-
Hitchings, Henry	Drawing Instructor	1873-1876
Hobbs, Joseph Wilson	Junior Master	1913-1929
	Senior Master	1929-
Hodge, James Albert	Master [See N.B. above]	1875
Hopkinson, Joseph William	Teacher	1929-1930
	Junior Master	1930-
Howe, William Woods	Junior Master 1896-1897 [pro tem.]	
Howell, Selah	Junior Master	1893-1903
	Master	1903-1910
Howes, George Edwin	Junior Master	1887-1891; 1894
Hunt, Samuel	Master [Head of School]	1776-1805
Hunt, Samuel (See John Dixwell)		
Jackson, Edward Payson	Sub-Master	1877-1878
	Junior Master	1878-1884
	Master [See N.B. above]	1884-1904
Jenks, Francis	Usher	1817-1818
Jones, Henry Champion	Instructor	1883-1884
	Junior Master	1884-1897
	Master	1897-1906
	Master [Latin Department]	1906-1913
	Head of Latin Department	1913-1926
	Master Emeritus	1926-
Kane, Martin Francis	Teacher	1925-1929
	Junior Master	1929-1933
Keetels, Jean Gustave	French Instructor	1876-1877
Kelley, Wilfred Frederick	Teacher	1916-1918
	Junior Master	1918-1925
	Master Ornatus	1925-
Kendall, Henry Payson	Usher	1825-1827
Kennedy, William Henry Joseph[17]	Junior Master	1914-1920
	Master [Head of History Department]	1920-1922
	Master Ornatus	1922-
Kew, Arthur John	Instructor	1910-1911
Kiggins, Peter (Née Higgins)	Usher	1806(?)

[17] Mr. Kennedy is now President of the Teachers College of the City of Boston.

Name	Position	Years of Service
Kinne, William	Usher	1856-1857
Kirwen, Joseph	Instructor	1909-1910
Knapp, Arthur Mason	Usher	1865-1866
Le Breton, Edmund Louis	Usher	1824-1825
Leverett, Frederic Percival	Usher	1821-1824
	Sub-Master	1824-1828
	Master [Head of School]	1828-1831; 1836
Levine, Max	Junior Master	1915-1923
	Leave of absence	1923-1924
	Junior Master	1924-1929
	Senior Master	1929-
Lewis, Ezekiel[18]	Usher	1699-1703
Liberfarb, Benjamin	Teacher	1934-
Long, John Davis[19]	Usher	1860 [pro tem.]
Looney, William Francis	Teacher	1920-1921
	Junior Master	1921-1933
	Senior Master	1933-1934
	Master Ornatus	1934-
Lord, Eugene Hodgdon	Junior Master	1929-
Lovell, James[20]	Usher	1760-1775
Lovell, John	Usher	1729-1734
	Master [Head of School]	1734-1775
Lucey, Henry	Teacher	1927-1928
	Junior Master	1928-
Magill, Edward Hicks[21]	Sub-Master	1859-1867
Mahan, Thomas Fallon	Junior Master	1927-
Marnell, William Henry	Teacher	1928-1929
	Junior Master	1929-
Marsh, George Edward, Jr.	Junior Master	1896-1898
Marson, Philip	Junior Master	1926-1929
	Senior Master	1929-
Maude, Daniel	Master [Head of School]	1636-1643
McCarthy, Leo Joseph	Teacher	1928-1929

[18] Ezekiel Lewis was the grandson of Ezekiel Cheever.

[19] John Davis Long was governor of Massachusetts from 1880 to 1882.

[20] The dates of James Lovell's years of service, compiled by the writer from the *Town Records* and the *Selectmen's Minutes,* do not agree with Jenks's *Catalogue.*

[21] Edward Hicks Magill was president of the Friends' College at Swarthmore, Pennsylvania, from 1871 to 1889. His daughter, Helen Magill, has the distinction of being the only girl who attended the Boston Latin School.

Name	Position	Years of Service
McGuffin, Richard Laurence Edgar	Junior Master	1929-
McKay, Edward Francis	Teacher	1918-1919
	Junior Master	1919-1925
McKim, George Leonard	Teacher	1924-1925
Mendum, Samuel Warren	Junior Master	1893-1894
Merrill, James Cushing	Usher	1842-1843
Merrill, Moses	Usher	1858-1867
	Sub-Master	1867-1869
	Master [See N.B. above]	1869-1876
	Acting Head Master	1876
	Head Master	1877-1901
	Leave of absence	1901-1902
Minns, George Washington	Special Master	1870-1872
	Master [See N.B. above]	1872-1874
Montrachy, Marie B. Montellier de	French Instructor	1855-1862
Moore, Gen. Hobart	Instructor in Military Drill	1862-1894
Morand, Prospère	French Instructor	1866-1875; 1877-78
Morse, William Russell	Junior Master	1893-1899
	Master	1899-1924
Motley, Leo Vincent	Teacher	1928-1929
Mullen, Thomas Aloysius	Junior Master	1886-1893
Murphy, Charles Faustinus	Junior Master	1921-1925
Murphy, Cornelius John	Teacher	1927-1928
	Junior Master	1928-
Murphy, John Patrick	Teacher	1933-1934
Murray, Joseph Girard	Teacher	1931-1932
Nash, Louis Edward	Junior Master	1928
Nelson, Brown	Usher	1793(?)
Nemzoff, Alexander Samuel	Junior Master	1929-
Neville, Cyrus Alison	Sub-Master	1874-1878
	Junior Master	1878-1880
Newell, William	Usher	1824-1826
Noble, George Washington Copp	Usher	1858-1860
Noble, John	Usher	1851-1855
	Sub-Master	1855-1856
Norton, William Kimball[22]	Junior Master	1900-1908
	Master	1908-1929
	Senior Master	1929-
Oakman, Otis Briggs	Teacher	1922-1923

[22] The name of William Kimball Norton is first in the list of twenty-three Senior Masters for the year 1934-1935.

Name	Position	Years of Service
O'Brien, Frederick James	Junior Master	1912-1923
O'Brien, John Alphonse	Junior Master	1931-
O'Callahan, Edward Patrick	Junior Master	1928-
O'Donnell, John Albert	Teacher	1928-1930
	Junior Master	1930-
O'Donnell, Thomas Aloysius	Junior Assistant	1922-1923
	Junior Master	1923-
O'Hayre, John Bernard	Teacher	1922-1926
O'Keefe, John Aloysius	Junior Master	1930-
O'Leary, Wilfred Leo	Teacher	1932-1933
	Junior Master	1934-
Oliver, Nathaniel, Jr.[23]	Usher	1733/34-Aug., 1734
Oliver, Nathaniel Kemble Greenwood	Usher	1809-1814
	Acting Master [Head of School]	1814
Otis, George Alexander	Usher	1821-1824
Paget, Capt. Joseph T.	Instructor in Military Drill	1894-1897
Paine, Charles Goodell Goddard	Usher	1866-1867
Paine, Robert Treat[24]	Usher	Apr.-Aug., 1750
Palmer, Albert	Usher	1860-1865
Palmer, Joseph	Usher	1821-1825
Parker, Francis Edward	Usher	1841-1842
Parker, George Stanley	Usher	1840-1846
Parker, Samuel Parker	Usher	1824-1828
	Sub-Master	May-Oct., 1828
Parkhurst, Louis Henry	Junior Master	1878-1881
Patten, John Stephen	Teacher	1933-
Patten, Merrill Campbell	Teacher	1922-1923
Payson, Samuel	Usher	1782-1786
Peirce, Benjamin Osgood	Junior Master	1880-1881
Peirce, William Henry Hathaway	Master [Head of History Department]	1923-
Penney, Col. George Samuel	Instructor in Military Drill	1921-1924
	Junior Master	1924-1930
	Senior Master	1930-

[23] The dates of Nathaniel Oliver, Jr.'s years of service, compiled by the writer, do not agree with Jenks's *Catalogue*.

[24] Robert Treat Paine was appointed Usher on April 4, 1750, "to Enter on that Service on Monday next the ninth instant."

Name	Position	Years of Service
Pennypacker, Henry	Junior Master	1891-1905
	Master	1905-1909
	Acting Head Master	1909-1910
	Head Master	1910-1920
Pennypacker, Thomas Ruston	Teacher	1922-1923
	Junior Master	1923-
Perrin, Willard Taylor	Sub-Master	1870-1871
Phelps, Francis	Usher	1838-1839
Pierce, George Winslow	Special Master	1871-1872
	Master [See N.B. above]	1872-1873
Pike, Fred Parker Hamilton	Instructor	1909-1911
	Junior Master	1911-1929
	Senior Master	1929-
Pollen, Israel	Teacher	1929-1930
Pormort, Philemon[25]	Master [Head of School]	
		1635-1638(?)
Powers, Joseph Lawrence	Junior Master	1906-1914
	Master [Head of Mathematics Department]	1914-1929
	Head Master	1929-
Quinn, John Joseph	Teacher	1922-1923
	Junior Master	1923-1929
	Master Ornatus	1929-
Quinn, Ralph Francis Visnet	Teacher	1918-1921
	Junior Master	1921-1928
	Leave of absence	1928-1929
	Junior Master	1929-1932
	Senior Master	1932-
Randall, Frank Eldridge	Usher	1874-1877
Reardon, George Andrew	Teacher	1922-1923; 1926-1927
Reed, Albert Franklin	Instructor	1911-1912
	Junior Master	1912-1925
	Master Ornatus	1925-
Reed, Frederick Silas Gregory	Junior Master	1898-1905
Reed, James	Usher	1855-1856
Reid, William Thomas	Master [See N.B. above]	1870-1872
Repetto, Frank Albert	Teacher	1928-1929
Reycroft, William Joseph	Teacher	1925-1927
	Junior Master	1927-
Reynolds, William Albert	Sub-Master	1877-1878

[25] The name is often spelled Pormont in the *Town Records*.

Name	Position	Years of Service
Rice, William Foster	Junior Master	1904-1915
	Master	1915-1927
	Leave of absence	1927-1928
	Master	1928-1929
	Master Ornatus	1929-
Rich, Herbert Thomas[26]	Junior Master	1898-1909
	Master	1909-1910
	Master [Head of Greek Department]	1910-1916
	Master [Head of Greek and German Department]	1916-1928
	Master Ornatus	1928-
Richardson, John Kendall	Sub-Master	1877-1878
	Junior Master	1878-1885
	Master	1885-1913
Ripley, Daniel Bliss	Usher	1806-1807
Robbins, Chandler	Usher	1830-1831
Robinson, Walter Augustine	Junior Master	1894-1902
	Master	1902-1925
Robinson, Warren Eastman[27]	Junior Master	1914-1916
	Military service	1916-1918
Roche, William Joseph	Teacher	1930-1931
	Junior Master	1931-
Rogers, Samuel	Usher	1831
Roland, Francis James	Junior Assistant	1922-1923
	Junior Master	1923-1933
	Master Ornatus	1933-
Rollins, George William	Junior Master	1881-1888
	Master	1888-1905
Ropes, William Ladd	Usher	1846-1848
Russell, Walter Herbert	Junior Master 1899-1900 [pro tem.]	
Russo, Mark Francis	Teacher	1923-1927
	Junior Master	1927-
Ryan, James Denvir	Teacher	1915-1917
	Leave of absence	1917-1919
	Junior Master	1919-1928
	Master Ornatus	1928-
Sands, William Jacob	Senior Master	1930-
Savage, Thomas	Usher	1813-1814

[26] Mr. Rich is now Head Master of the Brighton High School.
[27] Mr. Robinson was killed in action near Verdun, on November 6, 1918.

Name	Position	Years of Service
Schmidt, George Adam	German Instructor	1874-1878
Scully, Benjamin Charles	Junior Master	1927-
Seager, Edward	Drawing Instructor	1843-1850
Sénancour, M. Phillippe de	French Instructor	1877-1886
Shaw, Moses	Usher	1815-1816
Shaw, Zebulon Leonard	Usher	1816
Shea, Daniel Joseph	Junior Master	1929-
Sheehan, John Francis	Teacher	1932-1933
Sheehan, Thomas William	Junior Master	1923-1929
	Senior Master	1929-
Shepard, George Clarence	Usher	1876-1877
Simmons, William Cowper	Sub-Master	1868-1870
Smith, Aaron[28]	Usher	Jan.-Mar., 1780
Smith, William	Usher	1807-1808
Snelling, Jonathan	Writing Instructor	1830-1847
Snow, Freeman	Master [See N.B. above]	1875-1876
Southworth, Stacy Baxter[29]	English Instructor	1907-1910
	Junior Master	1910-1920
	Master Ornatus	1920-
Sprague, Rufus William	Junior Master	1897-1898
Stearns, Edward Josiah	Sub-Master	1856-1857
Stevenson, Jonathan Greely	Usher	1819-1821
	Sub-Master	1821-1824
Stoddard, John Lawson[30]	Master [See N.B. above]	1873-1874
Stone, Alaric	Junior Master	1896-1902
	Master	1902-1925
	Master Emeritus	1925-1934 (Died)
Streeter, Sebastian Ferris	Sub-Master	1831-1836
Strong, William Thaddeus	Usher	1877-1878
	Junior Master	1878-1884
Sullivan, George Henry	Junior Master	1930-
Taylor, Charles Ralph	Junior Master	1925-1929
	Senior Master	1929-

[28] The name of Aaron Smith is not recorded in Jenks's *Catalogue*.

[29] Stacy Baxter Southworth is now Head Master of Thayer Academy, Braintree.

[30] John Lawson Stoddard later became universally known as a lecturer. Dr. Edward Southworth Hawes, who entered the School as a pupil in 1870, has recorded in his article on "The Boston Latin School, 1870-1876," published in the *Latin School Register* of April, 1926, the following: "Another interesting person was John L. Stoddard, . . . He was a young exquisite, very popular, and taught us French."

Name	Position	Years of Service
Thacher, Samuel Cooper	Usher	1804-1805
	Acting Master [Head of School]	1805
Thayer, Ebenezer[31]	Usher	1708(?)-1709/10
Thayer, Herbert Milton	Instructor	1910-1911
Thayer, Joseph Henry	Usher	1850-1851
Thayer, Norton	Usher	1832-1833
Thompson, Albert Alexander	Junior Master	1930-
Tompson, Benjamin[32]	Master [Head of School]	1667-1670/71
Torrey, Henry Warren	Usher	1833-1835
Townsend, William Edward	Usher	1839-1840
Tuson, Richard Hayes	Junior Master	1927-1929
Van Daell, Alphonse Naus	Director of Modern Languages	1886-1889
Van Steenbergen, Albert Joseph	Teacher	1928-1931
	Junior Master	1931-
Wainwright, Jonathan Mayhew	Usher	1812-1813
Wales, Robert Webster	Junior Master	1929-
Walker, Leonard	Usher	1857-1858
Wallace, Cranmore	Usher	1829-1830
Ware, George Frederick	Usher	1838-1839
Weaver, Lt.-Col. Erasmus Morgan	Instructor in Military Drill	1897-1899
Webster, William	Usher	1862
Weinert, Joseph	Junior Master	1929-
Wells, William	Usher	1802-1804
Wenners, Paul Joseph	Junior Master	1929-
Wheelwright, Henry Blatchford	Usher	1844-1845
White, John Stuart (Née John Silas White)	Master [See N.B. above]	1870-1873
White, William[33]	Usher	1792-(?)
White, William Henry	Usher	1875-1877
Wigglesworth, Edward[34]	Usher	1714-1720/21
Wilbur, Clinton Burnett	Junior Master	1920-1929
	Senior Master	1929-

[31] The dates of Ebenezer Thayer's years of service, compiled by the writer, do not agree with Jenks's *Catalogue*.

[32] Benjamin Tompson resigned on January 6, 1670/71, having accepted "a call to Charlestowne."

[33] The first name of William White is not recorded in Jenks's *Catalogue*.

[34] The dates of Edward Wigglesworth's years of service, compiled by the writer, do not agree with Jenks's *Catalogue*.

Name	*Position*	*Years of Service*
Wilder, James Humphrey	Usher	Apr.-Sept., 1835
Williams, Frederic Dickinson	Drawing Instructor	1851-1857
Williams, Nathaniel[35]	Usher	1703-1708
	Master [Head of School]	1708-1734
Winslow, Charles Fenno[36]	Junior Master	1905-1915
	Master	1915-1929
	Senior Master	1929-
Woodbridge, John	Master [Head of School]	1643-(?)
Woodmansey, Robert	Master [Head of School]	1650-1667
Yeames, Herbert Hilarion	Instructor	1906-1907
Young, Alexander	Usher	1820-1821
Young, Edward James	Usher	1848-1850
Young, Ernest	Master [See N.B. above]	1873-1874

[35] On November 29, 1703, the selectmen recorded: "Ordered that M^r. Nathan^ll. Williams be paid his Sallery as the Same doth become due he haveing entered upon the Service of the Free School the 12th day of July Last."

[36] The name of Charles Fenno Winslow is second in the list of twenty-three Senior Masters for the year 1934-1935.

APPENDIX XXXII

THE POSITION OF THE SCHOOLS IN THE LIFE OF THE COMMUNITY

Today when we hear so much about the position of the schools in the social life of the community it is interesting to inquire what views our forefathers held on this subject. Could the school buildings be used for other than strictly academic purposes? Did they believe in social activities connected with the schools? What organizations could hold meetings in the school buildings? This study aims to answer these questions.

The writer found no reference to social activities connected with the schools themselves, such as school clubs, musical clubs, and entertainments. The introduction of these social activities into our schools has been quite recent, due to the greater appreciation of the value of the social interests, as expounded by educational psychologists. Many references were found, however, showing that the school buildings were used for various community purposes, such as church meetings, choir rehearsals, private teaching after school hours, court-martials, ward elections, and even the renting of the cellars for retailing liquor. The documents, compiled from the *Town Records* and the *Selectmen's Minutes*, are as follows:

CHURCH MEETINGS AND BENEVOLENT SOCIETY MEETINGS

On January 29, 1704/5, the selectmen voted that the Congregation of French Protestants "have the liberty to meet in S^d new Schol-House [Boston Latin School] for the Worship of God."

On November 18, 1741, the selectmen granted permission to Mr. Samuel Mather "to Preach on the Lords Days" at the North Writing School.

On June 16, 1742, Samuel Mather and a committee of the new North Church, lately erected, thanked the selectmen for the past use of the North Writing School.

On March 15, 1748, the Rev. Andrew Le Mercier of the French Congregation requested the selectmen to allow them to meet in the South Grammar School [Boston Latin School], "in Order for carrying on the Publick Worship on the Lords Days."

On April 7, 1773, the sect called Sandemanians, founded by Robert Sandeman, were permitted by the selectmen to use the North Latin School on Sabbaths, their "House of Worship" having been lately destroyed by fire.

On February 23, 1785, the selectmen granted Mr. William Black liberty to preach in the North Grammar School "on condition that all damages that may be sustained shall be made good."

On July 14, 1789, the selectmen permitted "the Blacks to have the use of Mr. Vinals School for public worship, on the Afternoons of the Lords Day." On September 2, 1789, the selectmen wrote the minister of "the Blacks" and again gave them permission to use Master Vinal's School.

On September 8, 1790, Mr. Lee, a Methodist Preacher from Virginia, applied to the selectmen "for liberty to preach in Faneuil Hall on Evenings until next Monday." The request was not granted because Faneuil Hall was then occupied "for a Reading School."

On December 17, 1800, the selectmen allowed the Society of the First Church "to make use of the Latin School House two Evenings in the Week."

On March 18, 1818, the selectmen allowed the Rev. Mr. Huntington and Mr. Thurston "to occupy the North School house and the school house in Mason street for Sunday school."

On March 29, 1820, the selectmen allowed the "Society for Moral & Religious Instruction of the Poor" to use the Boylston School-house on Fort Hill for a Sabbath school.

On October 25, 1820, the Howard Benevolent Society requested the use of the Boston Latin School for their annual meeting.

On January 10, 1821, the Third Baptist Society in Charles Street requested the use of the school house in Temple Street for a Sunday School.

On December 7, 1821, the school committee voted not to permit Sunday Schools the use of school buildings. On December 26, 1821, the Society of Moral and Religious Instruction of the Poor protested against the vote of the school committee excluding the Society from school buildings.

CHOIR REHEARSALS AND SINGING SCHOOLS

On May 8, 1782, the selectmen granted permission to Mr. Billings and a committee from a singing company to use the Boston Latin School on Monday evenings "for the purpose of improving in Psalmody."

On November 15, 1786, the selectmen granted permission to Mr. Montague, a preacher at the North Church, to use the North Latin School "For the purpose of teaching a singing Company."

On October 15, 1801, the selectmen permitted the Society in Brattle Street to use the Centre Reading School "for the purpose of instruction in singing to their choir of singers." The Society of the Old Brick Church was allowed to use the Boston Latin School.

On November 10, 1802, the selectmen permitted Dr. Lothrop and

Dr. Eliot to use one of the North Schools "for the purpose of a singing School."

On May 14, 1804, the selectmen permitted the new North Society to use the North Reading School in the evening "for the Instruction of their singers in psalmody." On July 18, 1804, the selectmen again permitted the North Society to use the Centre Reading School "for the instruction of the members of their Society in Psalmody."

On December 10, 1806, the West Boston Meeting House requested the school committee to permit them to continue to use the Hawkins Street School for their singers.

On October 14, 1807, the selectmen requested Mr. Biglow, Master of the Latin School, not to allow anyone the use of the schoolhouse in the evening, "information having been given that the Latin School continued to be occasionally used of evenings as a singing school contrary to the vote of the School Committee."

On January 6, 1819, the selectmen considered making remuneration to the Hollis Street Society for the upper story of the South Reading School, which the Society had been using for a singing school before the town took possession of it for a writing school. On April 7, 1819, a committee was appointed, which reported on April 28, 1819, that $600 was an adequate compensation.

Private Teaching After School Hours

On August 1, 1753, Mr. Samuel Holbrook was appointed Master of the Queen Street Writing School by the selectmen, who allowed him "to improve the School for his own advantage out of school hours."

On August 9, 1754, Mr. John Proctor, Jr., was appointed Master of the Queen Street Writing School by the selectmen, who allowed him "to have the improvement of the School out of school hours."

On August 28, 1786, Mr. James Leach applied to the selectmen for a license to teach "arithmetick in evenings" at Mr. Davis's [North Latin Grammar] School. On October 4, 1786, the selectmen voted not to grant a license to Mr. Leach "as it would be entirely out of Rules to grant the Prayer of the Petition."

On December 28, 1791, the selectmen permitted Mr. Joseph Nancrede to occupy Mr. Bingham's school "four evenings in a week for teaching the French Language, Mr. Bingham having no objection."

On December 10, 1794, the selectmen permitted Mr. Nadan to rent the upper story over the South Reading School for a dancing school, "provided it is not improved in school hours."

On September 7, 1796, the selectmen refused to permit Mr. Sales, professor of languages, "to keep a French Evening School in the Centre Reading School . . . , apprehending that they cannot be justified in granting the use of a publick school house to any private school master whatsoever."

Court-Martial

On October 27, 1806, the selectmen permitted the Judge Advocate of Militia to hold a court-martial the next day at the Centre Reading School, because they could not meet at the County Courthouse. The schoolmasters of the School were requested to keep the children in order, so that "they should not suffer by this arrangement."

Ward Elections

On March 18, 1807, the selectmen permitted the Board of Health to hold ward elections at the West School and at the South Writing School.

Cellar of Schools Rented for Retailing Liquor

On September 2, 1776, the selectmen gave a license to Sarah Low "to retail" at the North Writing School.

On March 25, 1795, the selectmen rented the cellar of the North School to Mr. James, "a Brewer at the North end."

On October 23, 1797, the selectmen appointed a committee to rent the cellar of the North School "for the most they can obtain."

On September 29, 1802, the selectmen determined that the cellar under the Centre School "shall no longer be kept as a place to Retail Liquors . . . complaint having been received against Persons frequenting the cellar."

Lectures and Orations Not Permitted

On June 12, 1805, the selectmen unanimously voted not to allow the use of the Centre Reading School for a political oration on the Fourth of July.

On November 12, 1806, the selectmen refused the use of the North Reading School "for the purpose of delivering an Address before the Library Association."

Picture-Frame Making in Cellar Not Permitted

On November 25, 1805, the selectmen refused to allow Andrew Parker to use the cellar of the Centre School for picture-frame making, because "the building would be endangered by such use."

APPENDIX XXXIII

A PARODY ON VIRGIL'S *ÆNEID*, WRITTEN BY
GEORGE SANTAYANA IN 1881

THE ÆNEID
BOOK FIRST

Æneas comes to land
On Afric's torrid strand.

I sing of arms and of the man and boy
Who first went West after the fire in Troy;
While travelling by land they suffered much,
But while on board their sufferings were such
As, though so oft, Alas! imposed by fate,
It is not fit in Epics to relate.
In love and war, for so it was decreed,
This harmless man fared very ill indeed
(A single combat or a lady's whim,
To say the truth, oft proved too much for him),
Until they built a city,—whence it is
Spring Latin grammars, dates, and histories.

O muse, recite to me the cause or reason,
The purpose and result of Juno's treason
'Gainst pious Æneas, who, the whole world knows,
At church was never seen to sneeze or doze,
And never would consent to go to bed
Before to her his prayers were duly said,
But who to ruin by her wrath was driven:—
Do ladies with sour tempers go to heaven?

For Carthage, great affections Juno bore,
Nor liked she Mt. Desert or Newport more,
And there she kept her carriages and horses;
But she had heard that by the Trojan forces
That very place would one day be destroyed,
And by this rumor she was much annoyed.
Of Trojan, Paris' choice, she also thought,
When Venus, Pallas, and herselfe each sought
To be declared the handsomest, and tried
To bribe him in her favor to decide.
Juno herself proposed unseemly cash,

506

And Pallas, glory, fame, and all such trash,
But Venus promised him the blameless joys
Of home—a wife and little girls and boys.
Some have maintained that, like the modern school,
This Trojan lady-killer was a fool;
I hardly dare to favor either side:—
Pray let the *Female* Latin School decide!
And lastly, when the Olympians dined in state,
Queen Juno's daughter, Hebe, used to wait
Upon the table, till, with one accord,
The gods inquired if she could not afford
A trained male waiter,—such alone were fit
To serve a banquet at which gods should sit;
So Ganymede, a Trojan, was engaged,
And thrifty Juno justly was enraged.

Thus Carthage, Paris, and this Ganymede,—
Not I,—must answer for the things you read.

Æneas, with full sail and bending oar,
Was gladly leaving the Sicilian shore,
When Juno thus soliloquized: "Forsooth,
I cannot kill this good-for-nothing youth!
The fates forbid!—And yet Minerva could—
Although her reasons were not half so good—
Sink Ajax' fleet, and Ajax, person knock
And split in pieces on a pointed rock;
Whilst I, who strut a queen, Jove's sister-wife,
Am ever with a conquered race at strife!
If I don't show I am as good as she,
Who henceforth will be found to worship me?"

The goddess, by her meditations flurried,
To Æolus, the king of tempests, hurried,
Who keeps the winds locked up within a cave,
And, sitting on them, makes them all behave.
To him Queen Juno told her purpose thus:
"That Trojan race I hate, good Æolus,
Is cruising now not very far from here;
Let loose the winds at once, and never fear;
Drive them about and sink them on their way:
These kind attentions I shall soon repay.
With fourteen charming girls my home is blessed,
All most accomplished and divinely dressed;
Lest such abundance should confuse your heart,
The most deserving I shall set apart,

And you may marry her without delay.
I shall arrange it in the smoothest way,
For if you're shy or can't afford the ring
To pop the question is a trying thing."
Thus spoke this honest goddess; he replied:
"Two things my heart delights in you provide;
I need a wife,—'tis yours, O queen, to win her,—
And mine to eat what you have cooked for dinner."
This said, he bids the stormy winds arise
And toss the mountain billows to the skies.
At once Æneas' limbs are chilled; he grasps
The mast with both his hands, and gasps,
"O thrice and four times happy those who died
Tucked in their beds, a doctor by their side,
Or who at least were killed on solid ground,
But I—help, Mother, help!—I shall be drowned!
Oh, if I must be drowned, could it not be
In Simois Brook, not in this raging sea?"

Already Neptune felt in every bone
That Juno's tactics quite outdid his own;
And so he raised on high his dripping head,
And spat and blinked, as to the winds he said:
"How now! how dare you, scoundrels you! whom I . . .
But first 'tis well the storm to pacify,
Away! and tell your king that 'tis for me
And not for him to rule the boundless sea;
It is my privilege to murder there;
Great Jove can do so in the fields of air;
He rules the clouds and thunderbolts and rain;
The earth alone is everyone's domain,
There all the gods their kindly feelings vent
And torture mortals to their hearts' content;
While Pluto, in whose realm the dead are found
Forever keeps them busy underground,"
Thus Neptune spoke; and, sooner done than said,
A glassy calm upon the waters spread.

As when among a crowd of idle boys
At times arises playfulness and noise,
And spit-balls fly around and beans and chalk,—
For mischief lends them weapons,—if in walk
By chance a teacher, each his glee restrains
The noise is hushed and guilty silence reigns,—
So, at the sight of Neptune's awful form,
Did sudden calm succeed the sudden storm.

Disgusted with the sea, Æneas' band
Pull for the shore and make the nearest land;
And when they reach the beach for which they long
They feel another longing quite as strong.
One, hard-worked heroes naturally feel,—
So they prepare a good substantial meal.
At sight of which Æneas dries his tears
And with these words his valiant comrades cheers:
"You've gone through much, but don't cry any more;
It's dinner time, and you've fared worse before.
We shall see better times, and we may find
It pleasant then to call these things to mind."
So, while their strength by eating they revive
And wonder when their lost friends will arrive,
Of their forlorn condition they complain
And fill themselves with cake and old champagne.

At dawn Æneas, as explorer, meant
To make his way "through the dark continent,"
When (wonderful to tell!) before him stood,
Just in the very middle of a wood,
A strange, heterogeneous sort of creature,
Male in attire but feminine in feature.
She wore a picturesque and flowing dress—
A Highlander's costume, nor more nor less,
At once she cried, "Hallo, young man, I say
Has any of my sisters passed this way
Chasing a foaming wild-boar with a shout?"
Æneas said—though he could not make out
What such strange sights and sounds as these could mean—
"None of your sisters have I heard or seen.—
What shall I call you? Girl, I scarcely can,
And yet your voice is not that of a man,
O surely you are the embodied form
Of woman's rights or ladies' dress reform!
Whate'er you be, be of some use to me,
And tell me where I am." "Dear me!" said she,
"You do me too much honor; sporting suits
Are stylish now, with quivers and top-boots.
That town is Carthage, African these bounds,
Although we stand in widow Dido's grounds.
A husband and a brother Dido had,
One very rich, the other very bad.
The husband, named Sychæus, and the brother
Began, of course, to quarrel with each other;
And, when in church, they came to blows one day,

The whole thing ending in a tragic way,
Sychæus died intestate; but his shade
His business-like propensities displayed.
In life Sychæus may have been a miser
But then his ghost determined to be wiser:
It came to widow Dido in a dream—
So Dido says but no one heard her scream—
Bade her depart, and showed her sums untold
Of hidden silver and of buried gold.
Induced by this, she quickly went on board,
Loading the ship with the discovered hoard,
And came to settle on this Hybian shore
And built the mansion we are now before.
Go in to see her now and you will find,
I dare be sworn, this widow Dido kind,"
She ended: as to go she turns around
Her lengthened dress begins to sweep the ground,
Her face to shine, her ringlets to dispell
Of gods' pomatum a decided smell,
And by her gait, while climbing to the skies,
She shows that she was Venus in disguise.

Before his mother left Æneas there,
She wrapped him close in a thick cloud of air,
To shield his modest form from curious eyes,
Just as glass cases keep away the flies.
Thus sheltered, he walked up the avenue
Till near to widow Dido's house he drew.

"O happy one," he said, "who dost not roam
A wanderer still! there is no place like home."
He goes right in, nor stops to ring the bell;
And all the time, oh wonderful to tell!
He, hidden quite by the convenient cloud,
Is seen by none, though passing through a crowd.
Here, as at the upholstery he stared,
Æneas first to hope for comfort dared;
These new surroundings somewhat calmed his fear
And made him hope that better times were near.
For, as he looked around him in the hall,
He saw, hung in a row along the wall,
The Trojan battles in which came to grief
Many an Argive and Dardanian chief.
He stood amazed, ànd floods of tears he shed
And groaned and moaned, and finally he said:
"What country is there now beneath the sun

That is not full of the great deeds we've done?
See, here the Greeks fight with the Trojan forces;
There noble Diomed is stealing horses;
Achilles here, thrice round the city walls
Is chasing Hector, there brave Hector falls;
His naked corpse, suspended by the heels,
Is dragged at great Achilles' chariot wheels;
Who by all this surpassing glory gains,
And profits, too, by selling the remains."
While pious Æneas, spell-bound still, admired
The paintings that these envious thoughts inspired;
The pleasing Mrs. Dido came down stairs
To attend as usual to her household cares,
Just as an officer of recent date,
Who with his new position is elate,
Carries his sword with pleasure in his hand
And feels it quite his province to command,
And lifts his head far higher than the rest
While secret joys are thrilling through his breast,
So did this widow Dido feel and look
The dinner order and reprove the cook.

    But suddenly Æneas was astounded
To see that Mrs. Dido was surrounded
By Trojans whom the storm the previous day
Had driven off from where the others lay.
The oldest of them spoke for all the rest
And, coming nearer Dido, thus addressed:
"Over the land and sea we Trojans roam;
You, Mrs. Dido, have a pleasant home.
Under these circumstances 'twere a sin
For you not to be glad to take us in.
We do not come to plunder or to steal,
No such brave promptings do the conquered feel.
There is a place that people call the West,
A modern land, with splendid harvests blessed,
And this we hope some happy day to reach.
A storm has cast us up on this, your beach.
Your servants drive us from the kitchen fire
And money for our lodging would require!
What does this mean? If you don't think us strong,
The gods, at least, remember right and wrong."
Then widow Dido blushed, and shook her head,
And looking at the carpet, briefly said:
"Don't be afraid; I'll make this matter right,
Who has not heard about the Trojan fight?

My house is large, my family is small;
I can most easily make room for all.
Would that your king, Æneas, too, were here!
I'll send to see if he has landed near."
She had not finished when the vanished cloud
Unveiled Æneas to the astonished crowd.
In the bright light more brightly did he shine;
His features and his figure were divine.
For (though her operations were unseen,
Being hidden by the wonderful air screen)
His mother had, with her accustomed care,
Just washed his face and combed and brushed his hair.

Æneas' unexpected introduction
By so obscure a process of induction
Perplexed poor Dido, quite untaught to fix
Her thoughts on Bacon's or on Venus' tricks.
But soon she said: "Well, now that you are here
You and your friends have nothing more to fear.
I hope you'll stay some little time with me
Before you sail away again to sea,
A prey to tempests and Olympian scamps:
A wanderer too, I learn to succor tramps."
Æneas (for all summer he might stay
And no hotel bills would he have to pay)
Exclaimed: "What fitting language can I find
To thank a friend so beautiful and kind?
Ye gods! how noble her reward would be,
If to reward her you deputed me!"
And then he sent Achates on the run
For young Iulus, his much petted son;
And presents, too, he ordered him to bring,
For Mrs. Dido they were just the thing:
A yellow shawl embroidered all in gold,
Which Spartan Helen, so the story's told,
Got from her mother many years ago
And brought to Troy as part of her *trousseau,*
And which Æneas purchased second-hand;
A golden necklace, which, I understand,
Had been his wife's, (why should Æneas buy it,
Not knowing to what use he should apply it?)
And his wife's jewels he had kept in mind
Although herself he chanced to leave behind;
And then a jeweled, golden crown to match,
Which from the fire he'd had the luck to snatch.
Meantime fair Venus, with consummate art,

Thus lays a plot against poor Dido's heart:
She summons Cupid and her plan discloses:
"You know my son Æneas now proposes
To take at Carthage a few weeks' vacation;
He's in sad need of some such relaxation.
To make it pleasant for him, it is best
Some lady's heart in him to interest.
I'll show you how the business may be done.
You are a boy, so is Æneas' son;
Well, then, exchange for more essential things—
His shirt and trousers—these angelic wings,
And go to Dido in Iulus' stead.
I'll see that he is safely put to bed.
When she begins to kiss you and caress,
For she is sure to do so more or less,
Just breathe upon her love's insidious breath;
'Twill comfort her for good Sychæus' death."
That day the Trojans and the Tyrians shared
A splendid banquet Dido had prepared.
At the close of such, as history can show,
Up stairs the ladies never used to go;
Men didn't smoke, so 'twas but right, I think,
The ladies should remain with them and drink.
So Dido did; she sipped the foaming bowl
Which others drenched themselves by drinking whole.
Fair reader, be not shocked; the classic mind
Loved also pleasures of another kind.
Long-haired Iopas read them a discourse
Upon the nature of the planets' course,
Declaring, too, the scientific reason
Why nights are longer in the winter season.
The origin of species he expounded
And the Darwinian theory propounded.
Nothing could please the learned Trojans more;
The Tyrians loudly called for an *encore*.
But Dido, clinging to that cruel boy,
Asked many things about the siege of Troy,
Said she delighted in those deeds of glory,
And begged her guest to tell the famous story.

THE ÆNEID
Book Second

> Which shows what latent forces
> May be in wooden horses.

All shut their mouths and opened wide their ears.
Blowing his nose and brushing off his tears

And feeling he was an important man,
Æneas cleared his throat, and thus began:

"Ah! Mrs. Dido, you can hardly know
How oft my tears like mountain torrents flow,
How oft I wail and shriek in piercing tones,
How oft cold chills run up and down my bones,
How oft in fear of what the skies portend,
My bristling locks in terror stand on end,
For, if you knew all this, you would not fail
To spare me the recital of this tale.
Besides, the stars are shining overhead,
And it is time the pious went to bed.
But if you want so very much to know
How came to Troy its final overthrow,
Although to think what trouble I was in
Still moves and frightens me,—I will begin.

"The Greeks despaired, and well I think they might,
Of taking Troy in fair and open fight;
And so they had recourse to stratagem,
For which the wise Ulysses, one of them,
Was eminent, as well as for deceit,
Wit, eloquence, adventures, and conceit.
They built a horse, a mountain in its size;
If any modern sceptic this denies,
There is a proof which men but seldom see:
Just here all the authorities agree.
Within the horse's body laid away,
A chosen band of Argive heroes lay,
And filled completely, crowded side by side,
The caves and caverns hollowed out inside.
Their situation could not have been pleasant,
For, although men were tougher than at present,
The question had not yet been agitated,
How dwellings should be drained and ventilated.
Then all the other Greeks, to our delight,
Retired from Troy and soon were out of sight.
We liked to go where they had been before,
And view their camp on the deserted shore.
Some crowd around the horse, and with surprise
Behold its quite unprecedented size:
And one—whether for gain I cannot tell,
Or loving art not wisely but too well—
Proposed to move the horse from its position
And place it in the town on exhibition.
But, on the contrary, the good and wise

That we destroy the monster all advise,
But as to methods they do not agree;
Some wish to cast the horse into the sea;
Some, to explore each hollow and recess;
And while the zealous and devout express
For an *auto de fe* their predilection,
The scientific favor vivisection.

"Since parties were so evenly divided,
The horse's fate remained long undecided.
At last Laocoon with earnest words addressed
The meeting, and his anxious fears expressed:
'What, fellow citizens! how can you be so green?
There may be something bad in this machine;
It may be infernal and contain a lot
Of dynamite, torpedoes, and what not.
Think you the Greeks, with no ends of their own,
Would give us gifts? Thus is Ulysses known?
There's something wrong; men seldom prove so kind
When they have nothing practical in mind.'
Laocoon had ceased and soon withdrew.
We all were still uncertain what to do;
But all our doubts at last were dissipated
By an event that none anticipated.
Laocoon had gone in bathing; —well,
What do you think I am about to tell?
That he was drowned?—I should not shudder so,
If that were all. He had the cramp? Oh no!
Two—think of it, now—(for they were twins)
Two horrid monster lobsters clutched his shins!
As clings the miser to his hoarded gold,
As clings self-love to boastful lies once told,
As clings the ship-wrecked to a floating plank,
So clung each lobster to a helpless shank.
He screams; we run—not to his aid—but all
To take the horse within the city wall;
For who can be so stupid, not to see
What must the meaning of this portent be?
Two lobsters by some god, 'twas clear, were sent
To inflict on him a cruel punishment,
Which proves he must have been a wicked man;
And so, it follows, we must take to Troy
The horse he madly urged us to destroy.
A string around the horse's neck we tie;
Each leg with wheels we thoughtfully supply;
To let it pass, our gates and turrets fall;

The fatal engine scales the battered wall;
All help; 'the boys, too, sing a sacred song
Around the unmarried girls'; it moves along.
Oh Ilium, dwelling of the gods! Oh Fate!
Four times it stuck in passing through the gate;
Four times the whole was on the point of breaking;
Four times those heroes got a thorough shaking.
But all in vain it was, and all in vain
Cassandra sang her melancholy strain.
Of seers and prophets she has proved the best,
The striking opposite of all the rest,
For, strange to tell, she never was deceived,
And, stranger still, she never was believed.

"There was a sound of revelry by night—
In fact, you'll find what now I have to write
All written in Childe Harold, canto third,
To which the curious reader is referred.
But one important thing is there omitted
Which to insert I beg to be permitted.
Though witty, Byron's muse is sentimental,
Unsteady in the moral and the mental;
But mine is modelled, for the greater part,
On wholesome principles of classic art,
And does not try to make out heroes frantic
With patent griefs, despairs, and loves romantic.
Or show, in sonnets of the impassioned school,
That pretty girls have flirted with a fool.
But being sensible, my lady muse,
To notice well known facts will not refuse;
For instance, she'll not say that this digression
Is the effect of sudden inspiration,
But honestly and simply will confess
It was suggested by the painful stress
Of having nothing ready for the press.
I was about to tell, when I digressed,
Of something that Lord Byron has suppressed,
The revelry was more than just a ball;
That hardly had been revelry at all.
Our noble Trojans, hearty and robust,
Were very fond of going 'on a bust';
That day some slight excess might be forgiven
Since from our town we thought the foe was driven.
Full many times we fill both plate and glass
And many times around the bottles pass,
Until, stretched here and there upon the floor,

By ten o'clock we all begin to snore.
The Greeks could have it all in their own way
For buried deep in wine and sleep we lay.
And I, as the most pious and robust,
Had had the largest share, it was but just;
But then, alas! old nature is so blind
To my prerogatives, and so unkind,
Nay, so unjust!—for which is justice true,
To give the same to all, or each his due?
But nature's undiscriminating laws
Hardheartedly unite effect and cause;
Lest ample cause its due effect should lack,
The nightmare came my reeling brain to rack.
I see dead Hector's ghost, unearthly sight,
Rise up before me to a towering height:
His feet are swollen; in his matted hair
The blood is clotted; all his wounds are bare;
Unwonted tears his bloodshot eye-balls dim;
'Tis Hector still, but oh! how changed from him
Who to the hostile galleys pushed the fight,
With Vulcan's flames and Vulcan's armor bright.
Upon this sight, in wonder and amaze
(As Mrs. Hemans would have said) I gaze;
At last I say, 'O Hector, are you dumb?
Tell me at least from which place you have come.
You don't look happy; tell me what you seek;
Or have you come for nothing? speak, speak, speak.'
The vision grew more hideous as I spoke;
I could not bear it now, I screamed, I woke;
But scarcely was that apparition gone
When one, more horrible, I looked upon:
Men see in dreams the sweetest things they see,
Would that the saddest but a dream might be!

"I was awakened by a dreadful noise;
Down every street there ran a stream of boys;
Teams rattled by, the air with yells resounded;
In fact 'twas clear the fire alarm had sounded.
I learned then that the Greeks of Troy were masters,
And I expected nothing but disasters
But e'en that knowledge could not make me stay;
I wished to join the crowd without delay;
For there are some that sooner would expire
Than not be in the way at every fire.
So furiously I rushed to meet my death
That I was very soon quite out of breath.

I had to stop: to me it then occurred
That fearful, needless dangers I incurred.
The brazen-coated Greeks were in the town,
And I had only on my dressing gown.
This midnight summons rang the war's alarms,
And it behooves the brave to die in arms.
Then happily I saw just at my feet
A murdered Greek outstretched there in the street.
I put his armor on, that this disguise
Might blunt the sharpness of Greek spears and eyes.
In war 'tis as in politics, you know,
Honor and fraud are all one in a foe.
Ashes of Troy and of my home! be ye
My witnesses: I swear, I did not flee
From any battle or from any strife
Except when there was danger of my life,
And, but for fate, I might have chanced to die.
Yes, none had e'er as large a share as I
Of that consummate valor in his heart
Of which discretion is the better part.

"On every side the Greeks and fate prevailed;
To fight with them would little have availed.
But I encountered one on whom to wreak
The vengeance that my baffled rage did seek,
For I met Helen; was she not a Greek?
I had not had good luck when fighting men;
Here was a woman; I might try again.
Her murder would have been a culmination
Suiting the hero and the situation,
But suiting neither, may be, quite as well
As what instead now actually befell.
I know not how, the nightmare came once more,
No doubt for the same reason as before;
But this was less surprising than the other:
It was not Hector now, it was my mother.
'If Priam could be saved or Priam's land
They had been saved,' said she, 'by your right hand.
Enough of them.   But look out now, my son,
For your own father, wife, and little one.
To blame my lovely Helen were a shame;
It is the gods, the gods, you ought to blame.
Do what your mother bids, that all may say
I've brought you up in a right pious way.'
Thus spoke my goddess mother: as I heard
I hastened to obey her timely word.

And, under cover of the friendly night,
To save myself and family by flight.

"Now suddenly there went forth a report
Throughout the world of a most painful sort.
There is a kind of being whom in speed
No other form of evil can exceed;
He waxes strong through change and agitation,
And gets his living by exaggeration;
At first all smiles, politeness, deference,
Soon queries endless, boundless impudence.
He has wide-open ears and watchful eyes
As many as his quills, and garbles lies
As many as the questions that he plies.
As much the publisher he is, in sooth,
Of falsehood, as the herald of the truth.
This race men name the newspaper reporters,
But all immortals call them the distorters.
Hear how into their hands we heroes fall,
And from one slander learn to know them all,
The manner of my famous flight from Troy
With my dear father and my little boy,
Was not that which some laughter-loving scribe
Has taken cruel pleasure to describe.
I did not sling Anchises on my back
As if the old gentleman had been a pack;
I took my father with me in a hack,
Of which in Troy, of course, there was no lack.
Besides, who could have told that mean reporter
I ever was a packman or a porter?
Or who can say, if their lives are surveyed,
That heroes ever had an honest trade?
My little son Iulus was conveyed
In his own baby carriage by the maid.
How cruel to have made him run a race
With one who flees from foes at such a pace!
For, though my arms in battle are not strong,
For flight my legs are fortunately long.

"My dear papa Anchises, I must own,
Was far too helpless to be left alone;
My piety and filial love prescribed
That with him in the carriage I should ride.
My wife would have to walk,—but never mind.
I told her she might keep some yards behind
But never let the hack get out of sight,
Else she would lose her way in such a night.

Indeed the terror of it was excessive;
The darkness and the silence were oppressive.
Darkness, I think, and silence too, is hateful:
They seem to me more ominous and fateful
Than even hostile armies in array
From which it's possible to run away,
You've chanced to hear that soldierly remark,
That every man's a coward in the dark;
Now of the brave this may or may not be,
But it is eminently true of me.
And here I wish to call the quick attention
Of the Society for the Prevention
Of Cruelty to Children to a fact
On which immediately it ought to act.
Some children have a native hate and dread
Of being sent up in the dark to bed;
They fear the silence and the darkness; why,
They nightly feel as on that night did I;
Yet no one thinks of what they have to bear,
While I am called a hero everywhere.
Our trip was almost done, when down the street
Was heard the distant sound of tramping feet.
Out of the window then I put my head,
And, peering out into the darkness, said:

    " 'On, driver, faster! they are drawing near;
I see their flashing arms, their measured tread I hear.
They come! the Greek! the Greek!' I cannot say
What happened next; I fainted dead away;
Nor did full consciousness return to me
Till we had reached the margin of the sea.
But, Oh! when all were ready to set sail,
Escape the Greeks, and catch the favoring gale,
I missed my wife Creusa; everywhere
I looked for her, but no, she was not there.
Some accident had carried her away;
Or she got tired, or wandered from the way;
Or of our hack she may have lost the trace
When danger counselled us to mend our pace;
For the result, which still remains the same,
The hostile gods are very much to blame,
Some madness took possession of my brain
And I resolved to enter Troy again,
To run new dangers and to risk my life;
And all for what? why, just to find my wife!
I need not say such mental aberration

In one like me must be of brief duration;
And, when I found my former home on fire,
I saw the wisest plan was to retire:
My lost Creusa never would be found;
Ghosts and armed Greeks were stalking all around;
I dread the sight of one of either kind,
But then, on seeing hosts of both combined,
My voice stuck in my throat, I could not speak,
My hair stood upright, color left my cheek.
It had been suicide to stay; then, too,
What would my poor abandoned father do
Without my words to quiet his alarm
Or the protection of my valiant arm?
I hurried back as quickly as I could
To where my father and Iulus stood;
We all embarked, and bade our home farewell.

"This is the story you would have me tell:
But in narrating it I must not fail
To point a moral and adorn the tale.
Had not my piety been quite so great,
On that dread night I should have met my fate;
If I had left my aged father's side
And in that hack refused with him to ride,—
If I had failed to see that my own life
Was far more needful to him than my wife,—
My warm blood would have dyed a Grecian sword.
Thus did my virtue prove its own reward."

APPENDIX XXXIV

THE TERCENTENARY CELEBRATION OF THE BOSTON LATIN SCHOOL ON APRIL 22 AND 23, 1935

The tercentenary exercises of the Boston Latin School began on Monday afternoon, April 22, 1935, with the unveiling of the tercentenary tablet, the work of John F. Paramino, a Boston sculptor. This exercise was followed by a gymnastic exhibition and the review of School regiments.

A tercentenary pageant in three acts with a prologue and epilogue, written by the Masters of the School, was played by the students in the School Hall, on Monday afternoon, at 2:00 P.M. This performance, which was repeated on April 24, 25, and 26, was received with great enthusiasm by the School and by the public.

The Founders Day exercises were held in Symphony Hall on Tuesday afternoon, April 23, at 2:00 P.M. A tercentenary letter, written by George Santayana (1882), was printed on the program of order of exercises reproduced below.

In the evening the alumni banquet was held at the Copley-Plaza Hotel.

ORDER OF EXERCISES

ORGAN PRELUDE: EDWARD PRESCOTT ILLINGWORTH, '06

PRESENTATION OF THE CHAIRMAN, PATRICK THOMAS CAMPBELL, '89
President of the Alumni Association
By Head Master JOSEPH LAWRENCE POWERS, '96

ORCHESTRA: Introduction to Act III, "Lohengrin"   *Wagner*
ARTHUR FIEDLER, '14, conducting

INVOCATION: RABBI JOSEPH SOLOMON SHUBOW, '16

CHORUS: "Prayer of Thanksgiving"   *Kremser*
ARCHIBALD THOMPSON DAVISON, '02, conducting

ADDRESS: HIS HONOR FREDERICK WILLIAM MANSFIELD
Mayor of Boston

522

ENGLISH POEM: "Enter to Grow in Wisdom"
   ROBERT MONTRAVILLE GREEN, '98

ORCHESTRA: "Academic Overture"   *Brahms*

ADDRESS: HIS EXCELLENCY JAMES MICHAEL CURLEY
   Governor of the Commonwealth

CHORUS: "Ad Scholam Matrem"   *Green, '98*

ADDRESS: PAYSON SMITH
   Commissioner of Education

ADDRESS: CHARLES EDWARD MACKEY
   Chairman of Boston School Committee

CHORUS: "Let Their Celestial Concerts All Unite"   *Händel*

ADDRESS: A. LAWRENCE LOWELL
   President Emeritus of Harvard University

CHORUS: "Jesu Dulcis"   *Vittoria*

BENEDICTION: THE REVEREND MICHAEL JAMES CUDDIHY, '91

THE STAR SPANGLED BANNER

The music is by the Harvard University Glee Club and by Members of
the Boston Symphony Orchestra

Tercentenary Program of Exercises held at Symphony Hall on April 23, 1935.

BIBLIOGRAPHY

ORIGINAL SOURCES

Autobiographies

Clarke, James Freeman, *Autobiography, Diary and Correspondence.* Edited by Edward Everett Hale. Boston: Houghton Mifflin Co., 1891.

Franklin, Benjamin, *The Life of Benjamin Franklin, Written by Himself.* Edited by John Bigelow. Philadelphia: J. B. Lippincott & Co., 1881.

Diaries and Letter-Books

Mather, Cotton, "Diary, 1681-1724." Boston: *Collections of the Massachusetts Historical Society,* Seventh Series, Vols. VII and VIII.

Sewall, Samuel, "Diary." Boston: *Collections of the Massachusetts Historical Society,* Fifth Series, Vols. V, VI, and VII.

Sewall, Samuel, "Letter-Book." Boston: *Collections of the Massachusetts Historical Society,* Sixth Series, Vols. I and II.

Tileston, John, *Diary from 1761 to 1766.* Edited by Daniel C. Colesworthy. Boston: Antiquarian Book Store, 1887.

Wadsworth, Benjamin, *Account Book, Jan. 1692/93.* In possession of Massachusetts Historical Society.

Manuscript Documents

In possession of Boston Public Latin School; Boston School Committee; Boston Public Library; Massachusetts Historical Society; Massachusetts State Archives Division; Harvard College Library; Boston Athenæum; Suffolk County Probate Court; and in the private collection of Professor Kenneth B. Murdock of Harvard University.

Maps of Boston

In possession of Boston Public Library; Bostonian Society; Massachusetts Historical Society; Boston Athenæum; Massachusetts State Library and State Archives Division; and in the private collection of Mr. Samuel C. Clough.

Massachusetts Legislation

Records of the Governor and Company of the Massachusetts Bay in New England, Vols. I-V. Edited by Nathaniel B. Shurtleff. Boston: Printed in 1853 and 1854.

Massachusetts Acts and Laws, Passed by the Great and General Court or Assembly of the Massachusetts-Bay, in New-England, from 1692 to 1719. London: Printed by John Baskett, 1724.

Province Laws: Acts and Resolves of the Province of the Massachusetts Bay. Boston: 1869.

NEWSPAPERS

The *Boston Evening Post;* the *Boston Gazette;* the *Boston Weekly News-Letter;* the *Boston Post Boy and Advertiser;* the *Independent Chronicle and the Universal Advertiser;* the *Massachusetts Gazette;* the *Massachusetts Spy;* the *New England Weekly Journal;* the *Weekly Post Boy;* and the *Weekly Rehearsal.*

PAMPHLETS IN THE POSSESSION OF THE HARVARD COLLEGE LIBRARY

Education in Boston, 1635-1839.

The Seasons: an Interlocutory Exercise at the South Grammar School, June 26, 1765. Being the Day of the annual Visitation of the Schools in Boston. Boston: T. & J. Fleet, 1765.

The System of Public Education, Adopted by the Town of Boston, 15th Octob. 1789.

The System of Public Education Adopted by the Town of Boston. Printed for the School Committee of Boston in 1808(?).

PICTURES AND PORTRAITS

Collections in Boston Athenæum; Boston Public Latin School; Boston Public Library; Bostonian Society; Goodspeed's Book Shop; and State Street Trust Company.

REWARDS OF MERIT

Rewards of merit of Boston Schools, 1807-1824. In possession of Boston Public Library.

Approbation cards in possession of the Boston Latin School.

TEXTBOOKS USED AT THE BOSTON LATIN SCHOOL

In possession of Boston Public Latin School; Boston Public Library; Massachusetts Historical Society; and Harvard College Library.

TOMBSTONES

Copp's Hill Burying Ground, Boston.

TOWN DIRECTORIES, 1789-1822

1789. Boston: Printed and sold by John Norman, at Oliver's Dock.

1796. Boston: Printed by Manning and Loring, For John West, No. 75, Cornhill.

1798. Boston: Printed by Rhoades and Laughton, For John West, No. 75, Cornhill.

1800. Boston: Printed by John Russell, For John West, No. 75, Cornhill.

1803. Boston: Published by Edward Cotton, No. 47, Marlborough Street. Printed by David Carlisle, Cambridge Street.

1806. Boston: Published by Edward Cotton, No. 47, Marlborough Street. Printed by E. Lincoln.
1807. Boston: Published by Edward Cotton, No. 47, Marlborough Street. Printed by Munroe and Francis.
1809. Boston: Published by Edward Cotton, No. 47, Marlborough Street. Printed by Munroe, Francis, and Parker.
1810. Boston: Published by Edward Cotton, No. 47, Marlboro' Street. Printed by Munroe and Francis.
1813. Boston: Published by E. Cotton, No. 47, Marlboro' Street. Printed by E. G. House.
1816. Boston: Published by E. Cotton, No. 47, Marlboro' Street. Printed by James Loring.
1818. Boston: Published by E. Cotton, No. 47, Marlboro' Street. Printed by J. H. A. Frost.
1820: Boston: Published by John H. A. Frost and Charles Stimpson, Jr., and for sale by them at No. 3 Spear's Buildings, Congress Street, and 12 & 13 Exchange Street. Printed by J. H. A. Frost.
1821. Boston: Published by John H. A. Frost and Charles Stimpson, Jr. Printed by John H. A. Frost.
1822. Boston: Published by John H. A. Frost and Charles Stimpson, Jr., and for sale by them at No. 3 Spear's Buildings, Congress Street and 80 State Street. Printed by John H. A. Frost.

TOWN RECORDS AND SELECTMEN'S MINUTES

Reports of the Record Commissioners. Printed by Rockwell and Churchill.

Vol. 1. *Boston tax lists &c., 1674-1695.* Printed in 1876.
Vol. 2. *Boston town records, 1634-1661. The book of possessions of Suffolk County, Mass.* Printed in 1877.
Vol. 3. *Charlestown land records, 1638-1802.* Printed in 1878.
Vol. 4. *Dorchester town records, 1632-1687.* Printed in 1880.
Vol. 5. *Gleaner articles.* Printed in 1880.
Vol. 6. *Roxbury land and church records.* Printed in 1881.
Vol. 7. *Boston records, 1660-1701.* Printed in 1881.
Vol. 8. *Boston records, 1700-1728.* Printed in 1883.
Vol. 9. *Boston births, baptisms, marriages and deaths, 1630-1699.* Printed in 1883.
Vol. 10. *Miscellaneous papers.* Printed in 1886.
Vol. 11. *Records of Boston selectmen, 1701-1715.* Printed in 1884.
Vol. 12. *Boston records, 1729-1742.* Printed in 1885.
Vol. 13. *Records of Boston selectmen, 1716-1736.* Printed in 1885.
Vol. 14. *Boston town records, 1742-1757.* Printed in 1885.
Vol. 15. *Records of Boston selectmen, 1736-1742.* Printed in 1886.
Vol. 16. *Boston town records, 1758-1769.* Printed in 1886.

Vol. 17. *Selectmen's minutes, 1742/3-1753.* Printed in 1887.
Vol. 18. *Boston town records, 1770-1777.* Printed in 1887.
Vol. 19. *Selectmen's minutes, 1754-1763.* Printed in 1887.
Vol. 20. *Selectmen's minutes, 1764-1768.* Printed in 1889.
Vol. 21. *Dorchester births, marriages, and deaths to the end of 1825.* Printed in 1890.
Vol. 22. *The statistics of the United States direct tax of 1798, as assessed on Boston. The names of the inhabitants of Boston in 1790, as collected for the first national census.* Printed in 1890.
Vol. 23. *Selectmen's minutes, 1769-1775.* Printed in 1893.
Vol. 24. *Boston births, 1700-1800.* Printed in 1894.
Vol. 25. *Selectmen's minutes, 1776-1786.* Printed in 1894.
Vol. 26. *Boston town records, 1778-1783.* Printed in 1895.
Vol. 27. *Selectmen's minutes, 1787-1798.* Printed in 1896.
Vol. 28. *Boston marriages, 1700-1751.* Printed in 1898.
Vol. 29. *Miscellaneous Papers.* Printed in 1900.
Vol. 30. *Boston marriages, 1752-1809.* Printed in 1903.
Vol. 31. *Boston town records, 1784-1796.* Printed in 1903.
Vol. 32. *Aspinwall notarial records, 1644-1651.* Printed in 1903.
Vol. 33. *Selectmen's minutes, 1799-1810.* Printed in 1904.
Vol. 34. Drake, F. S., *The town of Roxbury.* Printed in 1905.
Vol. 35. *Dorchester vital records, 1826-1849.* Printed in 1905.
Vol. 36. *Boston town records, 1796-1813.* Printed in 1905.
Vol. 37. *Boston town records, 1814-1822.* Printed in 1906.
Vol. 38. *Selectmen's minutes, 1811-1818.* Printed in 1908.
Vol. 39. *Selectmen's minutes, 1818-1822.* Printed in 1909.

SECONDARY WORKS

PROCEEDINGS OF THE AMERICAN ANTIQUARIAN SOCIETY

New Series, Vol. XII, Part I, pp. 76-182. Article by Eames, W., *Early New England Catechisms.*

PROCEEDINGS OF THE BOSTONIAN SOCIETY

Vol. II. Proceedings for 1891, *The Petitions of Barnard and Lovell.*

PUBLICATIONS OF THE BOSTONIAN SOCIETY

Vol. III. Prince, John Tucker, *Reminiscences of an Old School-Boy.*
Vol. V. *Petition of Barnard for Increase in Salary, 1715/16.*
Vol. IX. *Taking Book, 1780.* [Antedates Town Directory of 1789.]
Vol. X. *List of Inhabitants of Boston, 1695.*

PUBLICATIONS OF THE COLONIAL SOCIETY OF MASSACHUSETTS

Vol. XXVII, pp. 21-29. Article by Murdock, Kenneth B., *The Teaching of Latin and Greek at the Boston Latin School in 1712.*

Vol. XXVII, pp. 130-156.   Article by Seybolt, Robert F., *Schoolmasters of Colonial Boston.*

COLLECTIONS OF THE MASSACHUSETTS HISTORICAL SOCIETY

Second Series, Vol. XIX, pp. 204-220.   *Location of Town Schools in 1789.*
Fourth Series, Vol. VIII, p. 635.   *Letter of Benjamin Tompson to Increase Mather.*
Fifth Series, Vol. VI, pp. 230-231.   *Death of Ezekiel Cheever,* described by Judge Sewall.

NEW ENGLAND HISTORICAL AND GENEALOGICAL REGISTER

Vol. VIII, p. 368.   *Funeral sermon for Nathaniel Williams,* by Thomas Prince.
Vol. X, p. 362.   *Will of Thomas Scottow.*

HISTORIES OF THE BOSTON LATIN SCHOOL

Catalogue of Graduates of the Public Latin School in Boston, 1816-1917. Edited by Thomas Franklin Currier.   Boston: 1918.
Gould, Benjamin A., *The Prize Book of the Publick Latin School in Boston.* Vols. I-VI.   Published by Cumming and Hilliard.   Printed by Hilliard and Metcalf, 1820-1826.
Gould, Elizabeth Porter, *Ezekiel Cheever, Schoolmaster.*   Boston: The Palmer Co., 1904.
Jenks, Henry F., *Catalogue of the Boston Public Latin School, with an Historical Sketch.*   Boston: Boston Latin School Association, 1886.
Mosher, E. R., *Subjects Taught and Textbooks Used in New England Grammar Schools from 1635 to 1789.*   Unpublished term thesis written under the guidance of Professor Arthur Orlo Norton of the Harvard Graduate School of Education, February, 1921.
Powers, Joseph L., and Dunn, Lee J., *Boston Public Latin School, with an Historical Sketch and List of Eminent Latin School Men.*   Pamphlet published by the Boston Latin School, 1934.

GENERAL HISTORIES OF BOSTON SCHOOLS

Boston Almanac for the year 1849.   Article by Shepard, Isaac F., "The Public Schools of Boston."   Boston: B. B. Mussey and Co., 1849.
Brayley, Arthur Wellington, *Schools and Schoolboys of Old Boston, An Historical Chronicle of the Public Schools of Boston from 1635 to 1844, to which is added a Series of Biographical Sketches, with Portraits of Some of the Old Schoolboys of Boston.*   Boston: Louis P. Hager, 1894.
City Document, No. 26, 1845.   *Reports of the Annual Visiting Committees of the Public Schools of the City of Boston, 1845.*   Boston: J. H. Eastburn, 1845.

Finance Commission of Boston, *A Chronology of the Boston Public Schools.* Boston: 1912.

Homans, Isaac Smith, *Sketches of Boston Past and Present.* Boston: Phillips, Sampson, and Co., 1851.

Seybolt, Robert Francis, *The Public Schools of Colonial Boston, 1635-1775.* Cambridge: Harvard University Press, 1935.

GENERAL HISTORIES OF MASSACHUSETTS AND BOSTON

Butterworth, Hezekiah, *Young Folks' History of Boston.* Boston: Estes and Lauriat, 1881.

Crawford, Mary Caroline, *Famous Families of Massachusetts.* Vols. I and II. Boston: Little, Brown, and Co., 1930.

Crawford, Mary Caroline, *Old Boston Days and Ways.* Boston: Little, Brown, and Co., 1909.

Crawford, Mary Caroline, *Romantic Days in Old Boston.* Boston: Little, Brown, and Co., 1910.

Crawford, Mary Caroline, *Social Life in Old New England.* Boston: Little, Brown, and Co., 1914.

Dearborn, Nathaniel, *Boston Notions; being an Authentic and Concise Account of "That Village" from 1630 to 1847.* Boston: Nathaniel Dearborn, 1848.

Drake, Samuel G., *The History and Antiquities of Boston, 1630-1770.* Boston: Luther Stevens, 1856.

Fifty Years of Boston, A Memorial Volume Issued in Commemoration of The Tercentenary of 1930. Compiled by the Subcommittee on Memorial History of the Boston Tercentenary Committee, 1932.

Hart, Albert Bushnell, *Commonwealth History of Massachusetts.* Edited by Albert Bushnell Hart. Vols. I-V. New York: The States History Company, 1928.

Loring, James Spear, *The Hundred Boston Orators Appointed By The Municipal Authorities and Other Public Bodies from 1770 to 1852.* Boston: John P. Jewett Co., 1854.

Mann, Albert W., *Walks and Talks About Historic Boston.* Boston: Mann Publishing Co., 1916.

Massachusetts of To-day, A Memorial of the State Historical and Biographical issued for the World's Columbian Exposition at Chicago. Edited by Thomas C. Quinn. Boston: Columbia Publishing Co., 1892.

Orcutt, William Dana, *Good Old Dorchester.* Cambridge: Published by the Author, 1893.

Porter, Rev. Edward Griffin, *Rambles in Old Boston New England.* Boston: Cupples, Upham, and Co., 1886.

Rossiter, William S., *Days and Ways in Old Boston.* Boston: R. H. Stearns Co., 1915.

Shaw, Charles, *A Topographical and Historical Description of Boston.* Boston: Printed by Oliver Spear, 1817.

Shurtleff, Nathaniel Bradstreet, *A Topographical and Historical Description of Boston*. Boston: Printed by Request of the City Council, 1871.

State Street Trust Company, *Boston's Story in Inscriptions, Being Reproductions of the Markings that are or have been on historic sites*. Boston: 1908.

State Street Trust Company, *A Bird's-Eye View of Boston's Increase in Territory and Population From Its Beginning to the Present*. Boston: 1910.

Street Laying-Out Department, *Annual Report for 1896*. Boston: Municipal Printing Office, 1897.

Street Laying-Out Department, *Record of Streets, City of Boston*. Boston: 1910.

Thwing, Annie Haven, *The Crooked and Narrow Streets of Boston 1630-1822*. Boston: Marshall Jones Co., 1920.

Winsor, Justin, *The Memorial History of Boston, 1630-1880*. Edited by Justin Winsor. Vols. I-IV. Boston: James R. Osgood Co., 1881.

Winthrop, Governor John, *Journal*. In the possession of the Massachusetts Historical Society.

GENERAL WORKS ON EDUCATION

Barnard, Henry, *American Journal of Education*, Vols. 5, 27, and 28.

Cubberley, Ellwood P., *Public Education in the United States*. Boston: Houghton Mifflin Co., 1920.

Earle, Alice Morse, *Child Life in Colonial Days*. New York: The Macmillan Co., 1899.

Educational Review. Vols. 2 and 25.

Ford, Worthington Chauncey, *The Boston Book Market 1679-1700*. Boston: The Club of Odd Volumes, 1917.

Fowler, Thomas, *John Locke*. Edited by John Morley. New York: Harper and Bros., 1880.

Hoole, Charles, *A New Discovery of the old Art of Teaching Schoole, in four small Treatises*. Edited with Bibliographical Index by E. T. Campagnac. London: Constable & Co., Ltd., 1913.

Jackson, George Leroy, *The Development of School Support in Colonial Massachusetts*. New York: Published by Teachers College, Columbia University, 1909.

Jernegan, Marcus Wilson, *Laboring and Dependent Classes in Colonial America, 1607-1783*. Chicago: The University of Chicago Press, 1931.

Johnson, Clifton, *Old-time Schools and School-books, with many illustrations collected by the Author*. New York: The Macmillan Co., 1904.

Knight, Edgar W., *Education in the United States*. Boston: Ginn and Co., 1934.

Littlefield, George Emery, *Early Schools and School-Books of New England*. Boston: The Club of Odd Volumes, 1904.

Martin, George H., *Evolution of the Massachusetts Public School System*. New York: D. Appleton and Co., 1902.

Morison, Samuel Eliot (editor), *The Development of Harvard University Since the Inauguration of President Eliot 1869-1929*. Cambridge: Harvard University Press, 1930.

Morison, Samuel Eliot, *The Founding of Harvard College*. Cambridge: Harvard University Press, 1935.

Norton, Arthur Orlo, *Educational Legislation in Massachusetts from 1642 to 1837*. Unpublished chronology, containing the text of the laws with comments, mimeographed in 1920. In the possession of the Department of Education of Wellesley College.

Quincy, Josiah, *The History of Harvard University*. Vols. I and II. Cambridge: published by John Owen, 1840.

Small, Walter Herbert, *Early New England Schools*. Boston: Ginn and Co., 1914.

The Centennial History of the Harvard Law School, 1817-1917. Published by the Harvard Law School Association, 1918.

Watson, Foster, *The English Grammar Schools to 1660: their Curriculum and Practice*. Cambridge, England: University Press, 1908.

ENCYCLOPAEDIAS AND DICTIONARIES OF BIOGRAPHY

Allen, William, *American Biographical Dictionary*. Cleveland: John P. Jewett and Co., 1857.

Appletons' Cyclopaedia of American Biography. Edited by James Grant Wilson and John Fiske. New York: D. Appleton and Co., 1888.

Dictionary of American Biography. Edited by Dumas Malone. New York: Charles Scribner's Sons, 1932-1934. Incomplete.

Dictionary of National Biography. Edited by Leslie Stephen. London: Smith, Elder, and Co., 1887.

Drake, Francis S., *Dictionary of American Biography*. Boston: James R. Osgood and Co., 1872.

Hyamson, Albert M., *A Dictionary of Universal Biography*. New York: E. P. Dutton and Co., 1916.

Johnson's Universal Cyclopaedia. Edited by Charles Kendall Adams. New York: A. J. Johnson Co., 1895.

Sprague, William B., *Annals of the American Pulpit; or Commemorative Notices of Distinguished American Clergymen of Various Denominations, ...* Vols. I-V. New York: Robert Carter and Bros., 1857.

The Encyclopaedia Britannica. Cambridge, England: University Press, 1911.

The National Encyclopedia. New York: P. F. Collier and Son Co., 1932.

The Twentieth Century Biographical Dictionary of Notable Americans. Edited by Rossiter Johnson. Boston: The Biographical Society, 1904.

Wright, Carroll D., *The New Century Book of Facts*. Springfield: The King-Richardson Co., 1909.

INDEX